SELECT TREATISES

OF

S. ATHANASIUS,

ARCHBISHOP OF ALEXANDRIA,

IN CONTROVERSY WITH THE ARIANS,

TRANSLATED,

WITH NOTES AND INDICES.

WIPF & STOCK · Eugene, Oregon

Wipf and Stock Publishers
199 W 8th Ave, Suite 3
Eugene, OR 97401

Select Treatises, Part 1
In Controversy with the Arians
By S. Athanasius, Archbishop of Alexandria and Newman, John Henry
Softcover ISBN-13: 978-1-6667-3430-0
Hardcover ISBN-13: 978-1-6667-9001-6
eBook ISBN-13: 978-1-6667-9002-3
Publication date 8/20/2021
Previously published by John Henry Parker, 1842

This edition is a scanned facsimile of the original edition published in 1842.

EPISTLE

OF

S. ATHANASIUS,

ARCHBISHOP OF ALEXANDRIA,

IN DEFENCE OF THE NICENE DEFINITION.

CHAP. I.

INTRODUCTION.

The complaint of the Arians against the Nicene Council; their fickleness, they are like Jews; their employment of force instead of reason.

1. THOU hast done well, in signifying to me the discussion thou hast had with the advocates of Arianism, among whom were certain of the friends of Eusebius, as well as very many of the brethren who hold the doctrine of the Church. I hailed thy vigilance for the love of Christ, which excellently exposed the irreligion[a] of their heresy; while I marvelled at the effrontery which led the Arians, after all the past detection of unsoundness and futility in their arguments, nay, after the general conviction of their extreme perverseness, still to complain like the Jews, " Why did the Fathers at Nicæa use terms not in Scripture[b], ' Of the substance' and

---

[a] εὐσέβεια, ἀσέβεια, &c. here translated " religion, irreligion, religious, &c. &c." are technical words throughout, being taken from St. Paul's text, "Great is the mystery of *godliness*," εὐσεβείας, i. e. orthodoxy. Such too seems to be the meaning of " godly admonitions," and " godly judgments," and " this godly and well-learned man," in our Ordination Services. The Latin translation is " pius," " pietas." It might be in some respects suitably rendered by " devout" and its derivatives. On its familiar use in the controversy depends the blasphemous jest of Eudoxius, Arian Bishop of Constantinople, which was received with loud laughter in the Cathedral, and remained in esteem down to Socrates's day, " The Father is

ἀσεβὴς, as being without devotion, the Son εὐσεβὴς devout, as paying devotion to the Father." Socr. Hist ii. 43. Hence Arius ends his Letter to Eusebius with ἀληθῶς εὐσεβὶς Theod. Hist 1. 4.

[b] It appears that the Arians did not venture to speak disrespectfully of the definition of the Council till the date (A.D. 350) of this work; when Acacius headed them Yet the plea here used, the unscriptural character of its symbol, had been suggested to Constantius on his accession, A.D. 337, by the Arian priest, the favourite of Constantia, to whom Constantine had entrusted his will, Theod. Hist. ii. 3, and Eusebius of Cæsarea glances at it, at the time of the Council, in the letter to his Church, which is subjoined to this Treatise.

2   *The Arians, like the Jews, unwilling to believe,*

NICEN. 'One in substance?'" Thou then, as a man of learning,
DEF. in spite of their subterfuges, didst convict them of talking
ὁμοούσιον to no purpose; and they in devising them were but acting
suitably to their own evil disposition. For they are as
variable and fickle in their sentiments, as chameleons in
their colours ᶜ; and when exposed they look confused; and
when questioned they hesitate, and then they lose shame,
and betake themselves to evasions. And then, when detected
in these, they do not rest till they invent fresh matters which
Ps. 2, 1. are not, and, according to the Scripture, *imagine a vain
thing,* all that they may be constant to their irreligion.

2. Now such endeavours ᵈ are nothing else than an obvious
token of their defect of reason ᵉ, and a copying, as I have said,
of Jewish malignity. For the Jews too, when convicted by the
John 6, Truth, and unable to confront it, used evasions, such as *What
30. sign doest Thou, that we may see and believe Thee? What dost
Thou work?* though so many signs were given, that they said
John 11, themselves, *What do we? for this man doeth many miracles?*
47. In truth, dead men were raised, lame walked, blind saw afresh,
lepers were cleansed, and the water became wine, and five
loaves satisfied five thousand, and all wondered and worshipped the Lord, confessing that in Him were fulfilled the
prophecies, and that He was God the Son of God; all but
the Pharisees, who, though the signs shone brighter than the
John 10, sun, yet complained still, as ignorant men, *Why dost Thou,
33. being a man, make Thyself God?* Insensate, and verily
blind in understanding! they ought contrariwise to have
said, "Why hast Thou, being God, become man?" for His
works proved Him God, that they might both worship the

ᶜ Alexander also calls them chame-leons, Socr. i. 6 p. 12. Athanasius so calls the Meletians, Hist. Arian. § 79. Cyril compares them to " the leopard which cannot change his spots." Dial. ii. init Naz. Or 28. 2. On the fickleness of the Arians, vid. infra, § 4. &c. Orat. ii. 40 He says, ad Ep. Æg. 6. that they considered Creeds as yearly covenants; and de Synod. § 3. 4. as State Edicts. vid. also §. 14. and *passim*. " What wonder that they fight against their fathers, when they fight against themselves ᴰ" §. 37.

ᵈ ἐπιχείρημα. and so Orat. 1.§. 44. init.

but infra, §. 25. ἐπιχειρήματα means more definitely reasonings or argu-mentations.

ᵉ ἀλογίας, an allusion, frequent in Athanasius, to the judicial consequence of their denying the Word of God. Thus, just below, n. 3. " Denying the Word" or Reason " of God, reason have they none " Also Orat. i. §. 35. fin §. 40. init. §. 62. Orat. ii. §. 7. init. Hence he so often calls the Arians " mad " and " deranged;" e. g. " not aware how *mad* their *reason* is." Orat. 1 § 37.

goodness of the Father, and admire the Son's economy for our sakes. However, this they did not say; no, nor liked to witness what He was doing; or they witnessed indeed, for this they could not help, but they changed their ground of complaint again, "Why healest Thou the paralytic, why makest Thou the born-blind to see, on the sabbath day?" But this too was an excuse, and mere murmuring; for on other days as well did the Lord heal *all manner of sickness,* Mat. 4, *and all manner of disease,* but they complained still accord- 23. ing to their wont, and by calling Him Beelzebub, preferred the suspicion of Atheism[f], to a recantation of their own wickedness. And though in such sundry times and diverse manners the Saviour shewed His Godhead and preached the Father to all men, nevertheless, as kicking against the pricks, they contradicted in the language of folly, and this they did,

CHAP. I.

---

[f] or ungodliness, ἀθιότητες. Thus Aetius was called ὁ ἄθιος, the ungodly. de Synod. §. 6; and Arius complains that Alexander had expelled him and his from Alexandria, ὡς ἀνθρώπους ἀθίους. Theodor. Hist. 1. 4 "Atheism" and "Atheist" imply intention, system, and profession, and are so far too strong a rendering of the Greek. Since Christ was God, to deny Him was to deny God. The force of the term, however, seems to be, that, whereas the Son had revealed the "unknown God," and destroyed the reign of idols, the denial of the Son was bringing back idolatry and its attendant spiritual ignorance. Thus in the Orat. contr. Gent. §. 29 fin. written before the Arian controversy, he speaks of "the Greek idolatry as full of all Atheism" or ungodliness, and contrasts with it the knowledge of "the Guide and Framer of the Universe, the Father's Word," "that through Him *we may discern His Father,* and the Greeks may know *how far they have separated themselves from the truth.*" And Orat. ii. 43. he classes Arians with the Greeks, who "though they have the name of God in their mouths, incur the charge of *Atheism,* because they know not the real and true God, *the Father of our Lord Jesus Christ.*" (vid. also Basil in Eunom. ii. 22.) Shortly afterwards he gives a further reason for the title, observing that Arianism was worse than previous heresies, such as Manicheism, inasmuch as the latter denied the Incarnation, but it tore from God's substance His connatural Word, and, as far as its words went, infringed upon the perfections and being of the First Cause. And so ad Ep. Æg. §. 17. fin. he says, that it alone, beyond other heresies, "has been bold against the Godhead Itself in a mad way, (μανικώτερον, vid. foregoing note,) denying that there is a Word, and that the Father was always Father." Elsewhere, he speaks more generally, as if Arianism introduced "an Atheism or rather Judaism *against the Scriptures,* being next door to Heathenism, so that its disciple cannot be even named Christian, for all such tenets are *contrary to the Scriptures;*" and he makes this the reason why the Nicene Fathers stopped their ears and condemned it. ad Ep. Æg. §. 13. For the same reason he calls the heathen ἄθιοι, atheistical or ungodly, "who are arraigned of irreligion by Divine Scripture." Orat. contr. Gent. §. 14. vid. εἰδώλων ἀθιότητα §. 46. init. Moreover, he calls the Arian persecution worse than the pagan *cruelties,* and therefore "a Babylonian Atheism," Ep. Encycl. §. 5. as not allowing the Catholics the use of prayer and baptism, with a reference to Dan. vi. 11, &c. Thus too he calls Constantius atheist, for his treatment of Hosius, οὔτε τὸν Θεὸν φοβηθεὶς ὁ ἄθιος. Hist. Arian. 45. Another reason for the title seems to have lain in the idolatrous character of Arian worship *on its own shewing,* viz. as worshipping One whom they yet maintained to be a creature.

4   *And, like the Jews, have recourse to violence.*

NICEN. DEF.
§. 2.

according to the divine proverb, that by finding occasions, they might separate themselves from the truth [g].

3. As then the Jews of that day, for acting thus wickedly and denying the Lord, were with justice deprived of their laws and of the promise made to their fathers, so the Arians, Judaizing now, are, in my judgment, in circumstances like those of Caiaphas and the contemporary Pharisees. For, perceiving that their heresy is utterly unreasonable, they invent excuses, " Why was this defined, and not that?" Yet wonder not if now they practise thus; for in no long time they will turn to outrage, and next will threaten *the band and the captain* [h]. Forsooth in these their heterodoxy has such consistence as we see; for denying the Word of God, reason have they none at all, as is equitable. Aware then of this, I would have made no reply to their interrogations; but, since thy friendliness [i] has asked to know the transactions of the Council, I have without any delay related at once what then took place, shewing in few words, how destitute Arianism is of a religious spirit, and how its very business is to frame evasions.

John 18, 12.

[g] A reference to Prov. 18, 1. which runs in the Septuagint, " a man seeketh occasions, when desirous of separating himself from friends."

[h] Apparently an allusion to the text in the margin. Elsewhere, he speaks of " the chief captain" and " the governor," with an allusion to Acts 23, 22—24. &c. &c. Hist. Arian. §. 66. fin. vid. also § 2. Speaking of the Council of Tyre, A.D. 335. he asks, Apol. contr. Arian. §. 8. " How venture they to call that a Council in which a Count presided, and an executioner was present, and a registrar [or jailer] introduced us instead of the deacons of the Church?" vid. also §. 10. and 45. Orat. ii. §. 43. Ep. Encycl. §. 5. Against the use of violence in religion, vid. Hist. Arian. §. 33. 67. (Hil. ad Const. i. 2.) On the other hand, he observes, that at Nicæa, "it was not necessity which drove the judges to" their decision, " but all vindicated the Truth from deliberate purpose." ad Ep. Æg. 13.

[i] διάθεσις. vid. also Hist Arian. § 45. Orat. ii. §. 4. where Parker maintains without reason that it should be translated, " external condition." vid. also Theod. Hist. i. 4. init.

CHAP. II.

CONDUCT OF THE ARIANS TOWARDS THE NICENE COUNCIL.

Ignorant as well as irreligious to attempt to reverse an Ecumenical Council; proceedings at Nicæa, Eusebians then signed what they now complain of; on the unanimity of true teachers and the process of tradition; changes of the Arians.

1. AND do thou, beloved, consider whether it be not so. If, the devil having sowed their hearts with this perverseness[k], they feel confidence in their bad inventions, let them defend themselves against the proofs of heresy which have been advanced, and then will be the time to find fault, if they can, with the definition framed against them[l]. For no one, on being convicted of murder or adultery, is at liberty after the trial to arraign the sentence of the judge, why he spoke in this way and not in that[m]. For this does not exculpate the convict, but rather increases the crime on the score of petulance and audacity. In like manner, let these either prove that their sentiments are religious, (for they were then accused and convicted, and their complaints are since, and

---

[k] ἐπισπείραντος τοῦ διαβόλου, the allusion is to Matt 13, 25. and is very frequent in Athan. chiefly with a reference to Arianism. He draws it out at length, Orat. ii. §. 34. Elsewhere, he uses the image for the evil influences introduced into the soul upon Adam's fall, contr. Apoll. 1. §. 15. as does S. Irenæus, Hær. iv. 40. n. 3. using it of such as lead to backsliding in Christians, ibid. v. 10. n. 1. Gregory Nyssen, of the natural passions and of false reason misleading them, de An. et Resurr. p. 640. vid. also Leon. Ep. 156. c. 2.

[l] The Council did two things, anathematize the Arian positions, (at the end of the Creed,) and establish the true doctrine by the insertion of the phrases, " of the substance" and " one in substance," Athan. says that the Arians must not criticise the latter before they had cleared themselves of the former. Thus he says presently, that they were at once irreligious in their faith and ignorant in their criticism; and speaks of the Council negativing their formulæ, and substituting those which were " sound and ecclesiastical." vid. also n. 4.

[m] And so St. Leo *passim* concerning the Council of Chalcedon, " Concord will be easily established, if the hearts of all concur in that faith which &c. *no discussion* being allowed whatever concerning any retractation," Ep. 94. He calls such an act a " magnum sacrilegium," Ep. 157. c. 3. " To be seeking for what has been disclosed, to retract what has been perfected, to tear up what has been laid down, (definita,) what is this but to be unthankful for what we gained?" Ep. 162 vid. the whole of it. He says that the attempt is " no mark of a peace-maker but a rebel." Ep. 164. c. 1. fin. vid. also Epp. 145, and 156, where he says, none can assail what is once determined, but " aut antichristus aut diabolus." c. 2.

6 Equivocations and variations of the Arians.

it is just that those who are under a charge should confine themselves to their own defence,) or if they have an unclean conscience, and are aware of their own irreligion, let them not complain of what they do not understand, or they will bring on them a double imputation, of irreligion and of ignorance. Rather let them investigate the matter in a docile spirit, and learning what hitherto they have not known, cleanse their irreligious ears with the spring of truth and the doctrines of religion[1].

2. Now it happened to the Eusebians in the Nicene Council as follows:—while they stood out in their irreligion, and attempted their fight against God[n], the terms they used were replete with irreligion; but the assembled Bishops, who were more than three hundred, mildly and charitably required of them to explain and defend themselves on religious grounds. Scarcely, however, did they begin to speak, when they were convicted[o], and one differed from another; then perceiving the straits in which their heresy lay, they remained dumb, and by their silence confessed the disgrace which came upon their heterodoxy. On this the Bishops, having negatived the terms they had invented, published against them the sound and ecclesiastical faith; and, whereas all subscribed it, the Eusebians subscribed it also in those very words, of which they are now complaining, I mean, "of the substance" and "one in substance," and that "the Son of God is neither creature or work, nor in the number of things generated, but that the Word is an offspring from the substance of the Father." And, what is strange indeed, Eusebius of Cæsarea in Palestine, who had denied the day before[2], but afterwards subscribed, sent to his Church a letter, saying that this was the Church's faith, and the tradition of the Fathers; and made a public profession that they were before in error, and were rashly contending against the truth. For though he was ashamed at that time to

---

[1] vid. Orat. iii. §. 28. Socr p 11. c. §. 3.

γενητῶν

[2] πρὸ μιᾶς

[n] διομαχεῖν, διομάχοι vid. Acts 5, 39. 23, 9. are of very frequent use in Athan. as is χριστόμαχοι, in speaking of the Arians, vid. infra passim. also ἀντιμαχόμενοι τῷ σωτῆρι Ep. Encycl. §. 5. And in the beginning of the controversy, Alexander ap. Socr. i. 6. p. 10. b. c. p. 12. p. 13. Theod. Hist. 1. 3. p. 729. And so διομάχος γλῶσσα Basil. contr. Eunom. ii. 27. fin. χριστομάχων. Ep. 236. init. vid. also Cyril. Thesaur. p. 19. e. p. 24. e. διόμαχοι is used of other heretics, e. g. the Manichees, by Greg. Naz. Orat. 45. §. 8.

[o] i. e. "convicted themselves," infr. §. 18. init. ἑαυτῶν ἀεὶ κατήγοροι, ad Ep. Æg. §. 6. ι. e. by their variations, vid. Tit. iii. 11. αὐτοκατάκριτος.

adopt these phrases, and excused himself to the Church in his own way, yet he certainly means to imply all this in his Epistle, by his not denying the " one in substance," and " of the substance." And in this way he got into a difficulty; for while he was excusing himself, he went on to attack the Arians, as stating that " the Son was not before His generation," and thereby hinting at a denial of His existence before His birth in the flesh. And this Acacius is aware of also, though he too through fear may pretend otherwise because of the times and deny the fact. Accordingly I have subjoined at the end of these remarks the letter of Eusebius, that thou mayest know from it the inconsiderateness towards their own doctors, shewn by Christ's enemies, and singularly by Acacius himself [p].

3. Are they not then committing a crime, in their very thought to gainsay so great and ecumenical a Council? are they not in transgression, when they dare to confront that good definition against Arianism, acknowledged, as it is, by those who had in the first instance taught them irreligion? And supposing, even after subscription, the Eusebians did change again, and return like dogs to their own vomit of irreligion, do not the present gainsayers deserve still greater detestation, because they thus sacrifice [1] their souls' liberty to others, and are willing to take these persons, as masters of their heresy, who are, as James has said, double-minded men, and unstable in all their ways, not having one opinion, but changing to and fro, and now recommending certain statements, but soon dishonouring them, and in turn recommending what just now they were blaming. But this, as the Shepherd has said, is " the child of the devil [q]," and the note of dealers rather

§. 4.

[1] προαιρούντες
vid.
de Syn.
§. 14
James 1, 8

---

[p] The party he is writing against is the Acacian, of whom he does not seem to have had much distinct knowledge. He contrasts them again and again in the passages which follow with the Eusebians of the Nicene Council, and says that he is sure that the ground they take when examined will be found substantially the same as the Eusebian vid. §. 6. *init. et alib.* § 7. *init.* § 9. *cir. fin.* §. 10 *cir. fin.* §. 13. *init.* τότε καὶ νῦν. §. 18 *circ. fin.* §. 28. *fin.* Acacius was a pupil of Eusebius's, whom he succeeded in the see of Cæsarea. He attempted to defend Arianism neither under the cloak of Semiarianism, nor with the bold logic of the Anomœans, but by a pretended adherence to Scripture. His formula was the ὅμοιον (like,) as the Semiarian was the ὁμοιούσιον, (like in substance,) and the Anomœan, as the word signifies, the ἀνόμοιον, or unlike.

[q] Hermas. Pastor. ii. 9. who is speaking immediately, as St. James, of wavering in prayer.

than of doctors. For, what our Fathers have delivered, this is truly doctrine; and this is truly the token of doctors, to confess the same thing with each other, and to vary neither from themselves nor from their fathers; whereas they who have not this character, are not to be called true doctors but evil. Thus the Greeks, as not witnessing to the same doctrines, but quarrelling one with another, have no truth of teaching; but the holy and veritable heralds of the truth agree together, not differ. For though they lived in different times, yet they one and all tend the same way, being prophets of the one God, and preaching the same Word harmoniously[r].

§. 5. 4. And thus what Moses taught, that Abraham observed; and what Abraham observed, that Noe and Enoch acknowledged, discriminating pure for impure, and becoming acceptable to God. For Abel too in this way witnessed, having knowledge in the truths which he had learned from Adam, who himself had learned from that Lord, who said, when He came at the end of the ages for the abolishment of sin, " I give no new commandment unto you, but an old commandment, which ye have heard from the beginning." Wherefore also the blessed Apostle Paul, who had learned it from Him, when describing ecclesiastical functions, forbade that deacons, not to say bishops, should be *double-tongued;* and in his rebuke of the Galatians, he made a broad declaration, *If any one preach any other Gospel unto you than that ye have received, let him be anathema, as I have said, so say I again. If even an Angel from heaven should preach unto you any other Gospel than that ye have received, let him be anathema.* Since then the Apostle thus speaks, let these men either anathematize the party of Eusebius, at least as changing round and professing what is contrary to their subscriptions; or, if they acknowledge that their subscriptions were good, let them not utter complaints against so great a Council. But if they do neither the one nor the other, they are themselves too plainly at the sport of every wind and surge, and are influenced by opinions, not their own, but

---

[r] Thus S. Basil says the same of the Grecian Sects, "We have not the task of refuting their tenets, for they suffice for the overthrow of each other." Hexaem. 1. 2. vid. also Theod. Græc. Affect. 1. p. 707. &c. August. Civ. Dei, xviii. 41. and Vincentius's celebrated Commonitorium *passim.*

of others, and being such, are as little worthy of deference now as before, in what they allege. Rather let them cease to carp at what they understand not; lest so it be that not knowing to discriminate, they at hazard call evil good and good evil, and think that bitter is sweet and sweet bitter. Doubtless, they desire that doctrines which have been judged wrong and have been reprobated should gain the ascendancy, and they make violent efforts to prejudice what was rightly defined. Nor is there reason on our part for any further explanation, or answer to their excuses, or for further resistance on theirs, but for an acquiescence in what the leaders of their heresy subscribed; for though the subsequent change of those Eusebians was suspicious and immoral, their subscription, when they had the opportunity of at least some little defence of themselves, is a certain proof of the irreligion of their doctrine. For they did not subscribe without thereby condemning the heresy, nor did they condemn it, without being encompassed with difficulty and shame; so that to change back again is a proof of their contentious zeal for irreligion. There is reason then, as I have said, that the present men should keep quiet; but since from an extraordinary want of modesty, they hope perhaps to be able to advocate this diabolical[a] irreligion better than the others, therefore, though in my former letter written to thee, I have already argued at length against them, notwithstanding, come let us now also examine them, in each of their separate statements, as their predecessors; for now not less than then their heresy shall be shewn to have no soundness in it, but to be from evil spirits.

[a] This is Athan.'s deliberate judgment. vid. de Sent. Dion. fin. where he says, "Who then will continue to call these men Christians, whose leader is the devil, and not rather diabolical?" and he adds, "not only Christ's foes, χριστομάχοι, but diabolical also." In §. 24. he speaks of Arius's "hatred of the truth." Again, "though the diabolical men rave," Orat. iii. §. 8. "friends of the devil, and his spirits." Ad Ep. Æg.

5. Another reason of his so accounting them, was their atrocious cruelty towards Catholics; this leads him elsewhere to break out. "O new heresy, that has put on the whole devil in irreligious doctrine *and conduct!*" Hist. Arian. § 66 also Alexander, "diabolical," ap. Theod. Hist. i. 3. p. 731. "satanical," ibid. p. 741. vid. also Socr. i. 9. p. 30. fin. Hilar. contr. Const. 17.

CHAP. III.

THE MEANING OF THE WORD SON AS APPLIED TO OUR LORD.

Two senses of the word, 1. adoptive, 2. substantial; attempts of Arians to find a third meaning between these; e. g. that our Lord only was created immediately by God; Asterius's view; or that our Lord alone partakes the Father. The second and true sense; God begets as He makes, really; though His creation and generation not like man's; His generation independent of time; generation implies an internal, and therefore an eternal, act in God; explanation of Prov. 8, 22.

NICEN. DEF. §. 6.
1. THEY say then what the others held and dared to maintain before them; "Not always Father, always Son; for the Son was not before His generation, but, as others, came to be from nothing; and in consequence God was not always Father of the Son; but, when the Son came to be and was created, then was God called His Father. For the Word is a creature and work, and foreign and unlike the Father in substance; and the Son is neither by nature the Father's true Word, nor His only and true Wisdom; but being a creature and one of the works, He is by a strong figure[s] called Word and Wisdom; for by the Word which is in God was He made, as were all things. Wherefore the Son is not true God[t]."

2. Now it may serve to make them understand what they are saying, to ask them first this, what in fact a son is, and of what is that name significant[u]. In truth, Divine Scripture

---

[s] καταχρηστικῶς. This word is noticed and protested against by Alexander, Socr. Hist. i. 6. p. 11. a. by the Semiarians at Ancyra, Epiph. Hær. 73. n. 5. by Basil, contr. Eunom. ii. 23. and by Cyril, Dial. ii. p. 432, 3.

[t] vid. ad Ep. Æg. 12. Orat. 1. §. 5, 6. de Synod. 15, 16. Athanas. seems to have had in mind Socr. 1. 6. p. 10, 11, or the like.

[u] vid. Orat. 1. §. 38. The controversy turned on the question what was meant by the word "Son." Though the Arians would not allow with the Catholics that our Lord was Son *by nature*, and maintained that the word implied *a beginning of existence*, they did not dare to say that He was Son merely in the sense in which we are sons, though, as Athan. contends, they necessarily tended to this conclusion, directly they receded from the Catholic view. Thus Arius said that He was a creature, "but not as one of the creatures." Orat. ii. §. 19. Valens at Ariminum said the same. Jerom. adv. Lucifer. 18 Hilary says, that, not daring directly to deny that He was God, the Arians merely asked "whether He was a Son." de Trin. viii. 3. Athanasius remarks upon this reluctance to speak

Our Lord's Sonship is not the reward of virtue. 11

acquaints us with a double sense of this word:—one which CHAP. III.
Moses sets before us in the Law, *When thou shalt hearken to the voice of the Lord thy God, to keep all His commandments which I command thee this day, to do that which is right in the eyes of the Lord thy God, ye shall be children of the Lord your God;* as also in the Gospel, John says, *But as many as received Him, to them gave He power to become the sons of God:*—and the other sense, that in which Isaac is son of Abraham, and Jacob of Isaac, and the Patriarchs of Jacob. Now in which of these two senses do they understand the Son of God in such fables as the foregoing? for I feel sure they will issue in the same irreligious tenet with the Eusebians.

Deut. 13, 18; 14, 1.

John 1, 12.

3. If in the first, which belongs to those who gain the name by grace from moral improvement, and receive power to become sons of God, (for this is what their predecessors said,) then He would seem to differ from us in nothing; no, nor would He be Only-begotten, as having obtained the title of Son as others from His virtue. For granting what they say, that, whereas His qualifications were foreknown[1], He therefore received grace from the first, the name, and the glory of the name, from His very first beginning, still there will be no difference between Him and those who receive the name upon their actions, so long as this is the ground on which He as others has the character of son. For Adam too, though he received grace from the first, and upon his creation was at once placed in paradise, differed in no respect either from Enoch, who was translated thither after his birth on his pleasing God, or from the Apostle who likewise was caught up to paradise after his actions, nay, not from the thief, who on the ground of his confession, received a promise that he should be forthwith in paradise.

[1] Theod. Hist. 1. 3. p.732.

---

out, challenging them to present "the heresy naked," de Sent. Dionys. 2. *init.* "No one," he says elsewhere, "puts a light under a bushel; let them shew the world their heresy naked." ad Ep. Æg. 18. vid. ibid. 10. In like manner, Basil says that (though Arius was really like Eunomius, in faith, contr. Eunom. 1. 4.) Aetius his master was the first to teach openly, (φανερῶς) that the Father's substance was unlike, ἀνόμοιος, the Son's.

ibid. i. 1. Epiphanius too, Hær. 76. p. 949. seems to say that the elder Arians held the divine generation in a sense in which Aetius did not; that is, they were not so consistent and definite as he. Athan. goes on to mention some of the attempts of the Arians to find some theory short of orthodoxy, yet short of that extreme heresy, on the other hand, which they felt ashamed to avow.

12 *Nor does it mean that He was created to create others*

NICEN. DEF. §. 7.

γίγοιι

δι' ὑπουρ-γοῦ

Is. 40, 28

Ps. 100, 2.

Διά

4. When thus pressed, they will perhaps make an answer which has brought them into trouble many times already; " We consider that the Son has this prerogative over others, and therefore is called Only-begotten, because He alone was brought to be by God alone, and all other things were created by God through the Son ˣ." Now I wonder who it was ʸ that suggested to you so futile and novel an idea as that the Father alone wrought with His own hand the Son alone, and that all other things were brought to be by the Son as by an under-worker. If for the toil-sake God was content with making the Son only, instead of making all things at once, this is an irreligious thought, especially in those who know the words of Esaias, *The everlasting God, the Lord, the Creator of the ends of the earth, hungereth not, neither is weary; there is no searching of His understanding.* Rather it is He who gives strength to the hungry, and through His Word refreshes the labouring. Again, it is irreligious to suppose that He disdained, as if a humble task, to form the creatures Himself which came after the Son; for there is no pride in that God, who goes down with Jacob into Egypt, and for Abraham's sake corrects Abimelec because of Sara, and speaks face to face with Moses, himself a man, and descends upon Mount Sinai, and by His secret grace fights for the people against Amalec. However, you are false in your fact, for we are told, *He made us, and not we ourselves.* He it is who through His Word made all things small and great, and we may not divide the creation, and say this is the Father's, and this the Son's, but they are of one God, who uses His proper Word as a Hand ᶻ, and in Him does all things. As God Himself shews us, when He says,

---

ˣ This is celebrated as an explanation of the Anomœans. vid. Basil. contr. Eunom. ii. 20, 21. though Athan. speaks of it as belonging to the elder Arians. vid. Socr. Hist. i. 6. p. 11.

ʸ i. e. what is your *authority?* is it not a *novel,* and therefore a wrong doctrine? vid. infr. §. 13. ad Serap. i. 3. Also Orat. i. §. 8. " Who ever *heard* such doctrine? or *whence* or *from whom* did they hear it? who, *when they were under catechising, spoke* thus to them? If they themselves confess that they now hear it for the first time, they must grant that their heresy is alien, and *not from the Fathers.*" vid. ii. §. 34. and Socr. i. 6. p. 11. c.

ᶻ vid. infr. §. 17. Orat. ii. §. 31. 71. Irenæus calls the Son and Holy Spirit the Hands of God. Hær. iv *præf.* vid. also Hilar. de Trin vii. 22. This image is in contrast to that of *instrument,* ὄργανον, which the Arians would use of the Son, vid. Socr. i. 6. p. 11. as implying He was external to God, whereas the word *Hand* implies His consubstantiality with the Father.

Nor that He alone could endure God's creative hand. 13

All these things hath My Hand made; and Paul taught us as he had learned[a], that *There is one God, from whom all things; and one Lord Jesus Christ, through whom all things.* Thus He, always as now, speaks to the sun and it rises, and commands the clouds and it rains upon one place; and where it does not rain, it is dried up. And He bids the earth to bear fruit, and fashions Jeremias in the womb. But if He now does all this, assuredly at the beginning also He did not disdain to make all things Himself through the Word; for these are but parts of the whole.

CHAP. III.
Is. 66, 2.
1 Cor. 8,6.

5. But let us suppose that the other creatures could not endure to be wrought by the absolute Hand of the Ingenerate[1], and therefore the Son alone was brought into being by the Father alone, and other things by the Son as an underworker and assistant, for this is what Asterius the sacrificer[b] has written, and Arius has transcribed[2] and bequeathed to his own friends, and from that time they use this form of words, broken reed as it is, being ignorant, the bewildered men, how brittle it is. For if it was impossible for things generated to bear the hand of God, and you hold the Son to be one of their number, how was He too equal to this formation by God alone? and if a Mediator became necessary that things generated might come to be, and you hold the Son to be generate, then must there have been some medium before Him, for His creation; and that Mediator himself again being a creature, it follows that he too needed another Mediator for his own constitution. And though we were to devise another, we must first devise his Mediator, so that we shall never come to an end. And thus a Mediator being ever in request, never will the creation be constituted, because nothing generate, as you say, can bear the absolute hand of the Ingenerate[c]. And if, on your perceiving the extravagance of this, you begin to say that the Son, though a creature, was made capable of

§. 8.
¹ ἀκράτου, ἀγενήτου
¹ Orat. ii.
§. 24. fin.
² vid. also infr. §. 20. de Synod. §. 17.

---

[a] μαθὼν ἐδίδασκεν implying the traditional nature of the teaching And so St. Paul himself, 1 Cor. 15, 3. vid. for an illustration, *supr.* §. 5. init. also note y.

[b] Asterius is one of the most famous of the elder Arians, and his work in defence of the heresy is frequently quoted by Athanasius. vid. infr. 20.

Orat. i. §. 31. ii. §. 24. 28. 37. 40. iii. §. 2. 60. de Synod. §. 18. 19. He was by profession a Sophist, and a pupil of Lucian's. He lapsed in the persecution of Maximian, and sacrificed, as intimated in the text.

[c] vid. infr. §. 24. Orat. i. §. 15. fin. ii. §. 29. Epiph. Hær. 76. p. 951.

being made by the Ingenerate, then it follows that other things also, though generated, are capable of being wrought immediately by the Ingenerate; for the Son too is but a creature in your judgment, as all of them. And accordingly the generation of the Word is superfluous, according to your irreligious and futile imagination, God being sufficient for the immediate formation of all things, and all things generate being capable of sustaining His absolute hand.

6. These irreligious men then having so little mind amid their madness, let us see whether this particular sophism be not even more irrational than the others. Adam was created alone by God alone through the Word; yet no one would say that Adam had any prerogative over other men, or was different from those who came after him, granting that he alone was made and fashioned by God alone, and we all spring from Adam, and consist according to succession of the race, so long as he was fashioned from the earth as others, and at first not being, afterwards came to be. But though we were to allow some prerogative to the Protoplast as having been vouchsafed the hand of God, still it must be one of honour not of nature. For he came of the earth, as other men; and the hand which then fashioned Adam, now also and ever is fashioning and giving entire consistence to those who come after him. And God Himself declares this to Jeremias, as I said before; *Before I formed thee in the womb, I knew thee;* and so He says of all, *All those things hath My hand made;* and again by Esaias, *Thus saith the Lord, thy redeemer, and He that formed thee from the womb, I am the Lord that maketh all things; that stretcheth forth the heavens alone; that spreadeth abroad the earth by Myself.* And David, knowing this, says in the Psalm, *Thy hands have made me and fashioned me*; and He who says in Esaias, *Thus saith the Lord who formed Me from the womb to be His servant,* signifies the same. Therefore, in respect of nature, he differs nothing from us though he precede us in time, so long as we all consist and are created by the same hand. If then these be your thoughts, O Arians, about the Son of God too, that thus He subsists and came to be, then in your judgment He will differ nothing on the score of nature from others, so long as He too was not, and came to be,

and the name was by grace united to Him in His creation for His virtue's sake. For He Himself is one of those, from what you say, of whom the Spirit says in the Psalms, *He spake the word, and they were made; He commanded, and they were created.* If so, who was it to whom God gave command[d] for the Son's creation? for a Word there must be to whom God gave command, and in whom the works are created; but ye have no other to shew than the Word ye deny, unless indeed you should devise again some new notion.

7. "Yes," they will say, "we have another;" (which indeed I have formerly heard the Eusebians use,) " on this score do we consider that the Son of God has a prerogative over others, and is called Only-begotten, because He alone partakes the Father, and all other things partake the Son." Thus they weary themselves in changing and varying their professions, like so many hues; however, this shall not save them from an exposure, as men who speak words to no purpose out of the earth, and wallow as in the mire of their own devices. For If He were called God's Son, and we the Son's sons, their fiction were plausible; but if we too are said to be sons of that God, of whom He is Son, then we too partake the Father[e], who says, *I have begotten and exalted children.* For if we did not partake Him, He had not said, *I have begotten;* but if He Himself begat us, no other than He is our Father[f]. And, as before, it matters not, whether the Son has something more and was made first, but

---

[d] In like manner, "Men were made through the Word, when the Father Himself *willed.*" Orat. i. 63. 'The Word forms matter as injoined by, and ministering to, God." προστατσί-μενος καὶ ὑπουργῶν ibid. ii. §. 22. contr. Gent. 46.

[e] His argument is, that if the Son but partook the Father in the sense in which we partake the Son, then the Son would not impart to us the Father, but Himself, and would be a separating as well as uniting medium between the Father and us; whereas He brings us so near to the Father, that we are the Father's children, not His, and therefore He must be Himself one with the Father, or the Father must be in Him with an incomprehensible completeness.

vid. de Synod. §. 51. contr. Gent. 46. fin. Hence St. Austin says, "As the Father has life in Himself, so hath He given also to the Son to have life in Himself, *not by participating,* but in Himself. For we have not life in ourselves, but in our God. But that Father, who has life in Himself, begat a Son such, as to have life in Himself, not to become partaker of life, but *to be Himself life; and of that life to make us partakers.*" Serm. 127. de Verb. Evang. 9.

[f] "To say God is *wholly partaken,* is the same as saying that *God begets.*" Orat. i. §. 16. And in like manner, our inferior participation involves such sonship as is vouchsafed to us.

16 *No sense of Sonship can be maintained but the Catholic.*

NICEN. DEF. we something less, and were made afterwards, so long as we all partake, and are called sons, of the same Father [g]. For the more or less does not indicate a different nature; but attaches to each according to the practice of virtue; and one is placed over ten cities, another over five; and some sit on twelve thrones judging the twelve tribes of Israel; and others hear the words, *Come, ye blessed of My Father*, and, *Well done, good and faithful servant*. With such ideas, however, no wonder they imagine that of such a Son God was not always Father, and such a Son was not always in being, but was generated from nothing as a creature, and was not before His generation; for such an one is other than the True Son of God.

Mat.25, 34. ib.5,32.

8. But to persist in such teaching does not consist with piety[h], for it is rather the tone of thought of Sadducees and Samosatene[i]; it remains then to say that the Son of God is so called according to the other sense, in which Isaac was son of Abraham; for what is naturally begotten from any one and does not accrue to him from without, that in the nature of things is a son, and that is what the name implies[k]. Is then the Son's generation one of human[1] af-

[1] ἀνθρω- ποπαθής

---

[g] And so in Orat. ii. §. 19—22. "Though the Son surpassed other things on a comparison, yet He were equally a creature with them; for even in those things which are of a created nature, we may find some things surpassing others. Star, for instance, differs from star in glory, yet it does not follow that some are superior, and others serve, &c." ii. §. 20. And so Gregory Nyssen contr. Eunom. iii. p. 132. D. Epiph. Hær. 76. p. 970.

[h] i. e. since it is impossible they can persist in evasions so manifest as these, nothing is left but to take the other sense of the word.

[i] Paul of Samosata is called Samosatene, as John of Damascus Damascene, from the frequent adoption of the names Paul and John. Hence also John Chrysostom, Peter Chrysologus, John Philoponus. Paul was Bishop of Antioch in the middle of the third century, and was deposed for a sort of Sabellianism. He was the friend of Lucian, from whose school the principal Arians issued. His prominent tenet, to which Athan. seems here to allude, was that our Lord became the Son by προκοπή, or growth in holiness, (vid. Luke 2, 52 προίκοπτε,) "advancing as a man." Orat. iii. §. 51. Or he may be alluding to his doctrine of our Lord's predestination, referred to *supr.* §. 6. *cir. fin.* for Paul spoke of Him as "God predestined before ages, but from Mary receiving the origin of His existence." contr. Apoll. i. 20.

[k] The force lies in the word φύσει, "naturally," which the Council expressed still more definitely by "substance." Thus Cyril says, "the term 'Son' denotes the substantial origin from the Father." Dial. 5. p. 573. And Gregory Nyssen, "the title 'Son' does not simply express the being *from* another," (vid. infra, §. 19.) but *relationship according to nature*. contr. Eunom. ii. p.91. Again St. Basil says, that Father is "a term of relationship," οἰκειώσεως. contr. Eunom. ii. 24. init. And hence he remarks, that we too are properly, κυρίως, sons of God, as becoming related to Him through works of the Spirit. ii 23. So also Cyril, *loc. cit.* Elsewhere, St. Basil defines father "one

fection? (for this perhaps, as their predecessors[1], they too will be ready to object in their ignorance;)—in no wise; for God is not as man, nor man as God Men are created of matter, and that passible[1]; but God is immaterial and incorporeal. And if so be the same terms are used of God and man in divine Scripture, yet the clear-sighted, as Paul injoins, will study it, and thereby discriminate, and dispose of what is written according to the nature of each subject, and avoid any confusion of sense, so as neither to conceive of the things of God in a human way, nor to ascribe the things of man to God[m]. For this were to mix wine with water[2], and to place upon the altar strange fire with that which is divine.

9. For God creates, and to create is also ascribed to men; and God has being[3], and men are said to be, having received from God this gift also. Yet does God create as men do? or is His being as man's being? Perish the thought; we understand the terms in one sense of God, and in another of men. For God creates, in that He calls what is not into being, needing nothing thereunto; but men work some existing material, first praying, and so gaining the wit to make, from that God who has framed all things by His proper Word. And again men, being incapable of self-existence, are inclosed in place, and consist in the Word of God; but

---

[1] παθητι-κῆς
[2] vid. Orat. iii. §. 35.
[3] ὤν ἔστι

§. 11.

---

who gives to another the origin of being according to a nature like his own," and a son "one who possesses the origin of being from another by generation." contr. Eun. ii 22 On the other hand, the Arians at the first denied that "by nature there was any Son of God." Theod Hist. i. 3 p 732.

[l] vid Eusebius, in his Letter subjoined also Socr. Hist. i. 8. Epiphan. Hær. 69. n. 8. and 15.

[m] One of the characteristic points in Athanasius is his constant attention to the *sense* of doctrine, or the *meaning* of writers, in preference to the words used. Thus he scarcely uses the symbol ὁμοούσιον, one in substance, throughout his Orations, and in the de Synod. acknowledges the Semiarians as brethren. Hence infr. §. 18. he says, that orthodox doctrine "is revered by all, though expressed in strange language, provided the speaker means religiously, and wishes to convey by it a religious sense." vid. also §. 21 He says, that Catholics are able to "speak freely," or to expatiate, παρρησιαζόμεθα, "out of Divine Scripture" Orat. i. §. 9. vid. de Sent Dionys. §. 20. init. Again· " The devil spoke from Scripture, but was silenced by the Saviour; Paul spoke from profane writers, yet, being a saint, he has a religious meaning." de Syn. §. 39. also ad Ep. Æg. 8. Again, speaking of the apparent contrariety between two Councils, " It were unseemly to make the one conflict with the other, for all their members are fathers; and it were profane to decide that these spoke well and those ill, for all of them have slept in Christ." §. 43. also §. 47. Again: " Not the phrase, but the meaning and the religious life, is the recommendation of the faithful." ad Ep. Æg §. 9.

NICEN. DEF.
God is self-existent, inclosing all things, and inclosed by none; within all according to His own goodness and power, yet without all in His proper nature[n]. As then men create not as God creates, as their being is not such as God's being, so men's generation is in one way, and the Son is from the Father in another[o]. For the offspring of men are portions of their fathers, since the very nature of bodies is not uncompounded, but transitive[p], and composed of parts;

[1] ἀπορρί-
ουσι

and men lose their substance[1] in begetting, and again they gain substance from the accession of food. And on this account men in their time become fathers of many children;

---

[n] Vid. also Incarn. §. 17. This contrast is not commonly found in ecclesiastical writers, who are used to say that God is present every where, in substance as well as by energy or power. S. Clement, however, expresses himself still more strongly in the same way, " In substance far off, (for how can the generate come close to the Ingenerate?) but most close in power, in which the universe is embosomed." Strom. 2. circ. init. but the parenthesis explains his meaning vid. Cyril. Thesaur. 6. p. 44. The common doctrine of the Fathers is, that God is present every where in *substance.* vid. Petav. de Deo, iii. 8. and 9. It may be remarked, that S. Clement continues " *neither inclosing* nor inclosed."

[o] In Almighty God is the perfection and first pattern of what is seen in shadow in human nature, according to the imperfection of the subject matter; and this remark applies, as to creation, so to generation. Athanasius is led to state this more distinctly in another connection in Orat 1. §. 21. fin. " It belongs to the Godhead alone, *that the Father is properly* (κυρίως) *Father, and the Son properly* (κυρίως) *Son;* and in Them and Them only does it hold that the Father is ever Father, and the Son ever Son." Accordingly he proceeds, shortly afterwards, as in the text, to argue, " [The heretics] ought in creation also to supply God with materials, and so to deny Him to be Creator; but if the bare idea of God transcends such thoughts, and a man believes that He is in being, not as we are, and yet in being, as God, and that He creates not as man creates, but yet creates as God, therefore He begets also not as men beget, but begets as God. For God does not make men His pattern, but rather we men, for that God *is properly* and alone truly Father of His Son, are also called fathers of our own children, for ' of Him is every fatherhood in heaven and on earth named.' §. 23. The Semiarians at Ancyra quote the same text for the same doctrine. Epiphan. Hær. 73. 5. As do Cyril. in Joan. iii. p. 24. Thesaur. 32. p. 281. and Damascene de Fid. Orth. i. 8. The same parallel, as existing between creation and generation, is insisted on by Isidor. Pel. Ep. iii. 355. Basil. contr. Eun. iv. p. 280. A. Cyril Thesaur 6. p. 43. Epiph. Hær. 69. 36. and Gregor. Naz. Orat. 20. 9. who observes that God creates with a *word*, Ps. 148, 5. which evidently transcends human creations. Theodorus Abucara with the same object, draws out the parallel of life, ζωὴ, as Athan. that of being, εἶναι. Opusc. iii. p. 420— 422.

[p] vid. de Synod. §. 51. Orat. i. §. 15. 16. ῥευστὴ vid. Orat. 1. §. 28. Bas. in. Eun. 11. 23. φύσιν. Bas. in Eun. ii. 6. Greg. Naz. Orat. 28. 22. Vid. contr. Gentes, §. 41. where Athan. without reference to the Arian controversy, draws out the contrast between the Godhead and human nature. " The nature of things generated, as having its subsistence from nothing, is of a *transitive* (ῥευστὴ) and feeble and mortal sort, considered by itself; seeing then that it was *transitive* and dissoluble, lest this should take place, and it should be resolved into its original nothing, God governs and sustains it all, by His own Word, who is Himself God," and who, as he proceeds, §. 42. " remaining Himself immoveable with the Father, moves all things in His own consistence, as each may seem fit to His Father."

Divine generation is not material, but spiritual. 19

but God, being without parts, is Father of the Son without CHAP.
partition or passion; for there is neither effluence[19] of the III.
Immaterial, nor accession from without, as among men; and
being uncompounded in nature, He is Father of One Only
Son. This is why He is Only-begotten, and alone in the
Father's bosom, and alone is acknowledged by the Father to
be from Him, saying, *This is My beloved Son, in whom I am* Mat. 3,
well pleased. And He too is the Father's Word, from which [17.]
may be understood the impassible and impartitive nature of
the Father, in that not even a human word is begotten with
passion or partition, much less the Word of God[r]. Wherefore also He sits, as Word, at the Father's right hand; for
where the Father is, there also is His Word; but we, as
His works, stand in judgment before Him; and He is
adorable, because He is Son of the adorable Father, but we
adore, confessing Him Lord and God, because we are
creatures and other than He.

10. The case being thus, let who will among them consider §. 12.
the matter, so that one may abash them by the following question; Is it right to say that what is God's offspring and proper
to Him is out of nothing? or is it reasonable in the very idea,
that what is from God has accrued to Him, that a man should
dare to say that the Son was not always? For in this again
the generation of the Son exceeds and transcends the
thoughts of man, that we become fathers of our own children
in time, since we ourselves first were not and then came into
being; but God, in that He ever is, is ever Father of the Son[s].

---

[q] S Cyril, Dial iv. init. p. 505, E. speaks of the θρυλλουμένη ἀπόρροη, and disclaims it, Thesaur. 6. p. 43. Athanasius disclaims it, Expos. §. 1. Orat. 1. §. 21. So does Alexander, ap. Theod. Hist. i. 3. p. 743. On the other hand, Athanasius quotes it in a passage which he adduces from Theognostus, *infra*, §. 25 and from Dionysius, de Sent. D. §.23. and Origen uses it, Periarchon, 1 2. It is derived from Wisd vii. 25.

[r] The title "Word" implies the ineffable mode of the Son's generation, as distinct from *material* parallels, vid. Gregory Nyssen, contr. Eunom. iii. p. 107. Chrysostom in Joan. Hom. 2. §. 4. Cyril Alex. Thesaur. 5. p. 37. Also it implies that there is but One Son. vid. infra, §. 16. " As the Origin is one substance, so its Word and Wisdom is one, substantial and subsisting." Athan. Orat iv. 1. fin.

[s] " Man," says S. Cyril, inasmuch as He had a beginning of being, also has of necessity a beginning of begetting, as what is from Him is a thing generate, but....if God's substance transcend time, or origin, or interval, His generation too will transcend these; nor does it deprive the Divine Nature of the power of generating, that it doth not this in time. For other than human is the manner of divine generation; and together with God's existing is His generating implied, and the Son was in Him by generation, nor did His generation precede His existence, but He was always, and that by generation." Thesaur. v. p. 35.

20 *As is symbolized by the words Light, Fountain, Life, &c.*

NICEN. DEF. Mat. 11, 27.
And the generation of mankind is brought home to us from things that are parallel; but, since *no one knoweth the Son but the Father, and no one knoweth the Father but the Son, and he to whomsoever the Son will reveal Him*, therefore the sacred writers to whom the Son has revealed Him, have given us a certain image from things visible, saying, *Who is the brightness of His glory, and the Expression of His Person;* and again, *For with Thee is the well of life, and in Thy light shall we see light;* and when the Word chides Israel, He says, *Thou hast forsaken the Fountain of wisdom;* and this Fountain it is which says, *They have forsaken Me the fountain of living waters*[t]. And mean indeed and very dim is the illustration[1] compared with what we desiderate; but yet it is possible from it to understand something above man's nature, instead of thinking the Son's generation to be on a level with ours. For who can even imagine that the radiance of light ever was not, so that he should dare to say that the Son was not always, or that the Son was not before His generation? or who is capable of separating the radiance from the sun, or to conceive of the fountain as ever void of life, that he should madly say, "The Son is from nothing," who says, *I am the life*, or "alien to the Father's substance," who says, *He that hath seen Me, hath seen the Father?* for the sacred writers wishing us thus to understand, have given these illustrations; and it is indecent and most irreligious, when Scripture contains such images, to form ideas concerning our Lord from others which are neither in Scripture, nor have any religious bearing.

Heb 1. Ps 36, 9.
Bar. 3, 12.
Jer. 2, 13.
1 vid Ep. 1 ad Serap. 20 p 669. a. b.

John 14, 6.
Ib. v. 9.

§. 13. 11. Therefore let them tell us, from what teacher or by what tradition they derived these notions concerning the Saviour? "We have read," they will say, "in the Proverbs, *The Lord hath created Me a beginning of His ways unto His works*[2]; this the Eusebians used to insist on[u], and you write me word,

Prov. 8, 22.
2 vid.
Orat. II. throughout.

[t] vid *infra passim*. All these titles, "Word, Wisdom, Light," &c. serve to guard the title "Son" from any notions of parts or dimensions, e. g. "He is not composed of parts, but being impassible and single, He is impassibly and indivisibly Father of the Son...for...the Word and Wisdom is neither creature, nor part of Him whose Word He is, nor an offspring passibly begotten." Orat. 1. §. 28.

[u] Eusebius of Nicomedia quotes it in his Letter to Paulinus, ap. Theodor. Hist. i. 5. And Eusebius of Cæsarea Demonstr. Evang. v. 1.

Creation is an external act, generation an internal. 21

that the present men also, though overthrown and confuted by an abundance of arguments, still were putting about in every quarter this passage, and saying that the Son was one of the creatures, and reckoning Him with things generated[1]. But they seem to me to have a wrong understanding of this passage also; for it has a religious and very orthodox sense, which, had they understood, they would not have blasphemed the Lord of glory. For on comparing what has been above stated with this passage, they will find a great difference between them [x]. For what man of right understanding does not perceive, that what are created and made are external to the maker; but the Son, as the foregoing argument has shewn, exists not externally, but from the Father who begat Him? for man too both builds a house and begets a son, and no one would mismatch things, and say that the house or the ship were begotten by the builder[2], but the Son was created and made by him; nor again that the house was an image of the maker, but the Son unlike Him who begat Him; but rather he will confess that the Son is an image of the Father, but the house a work of art, unless his mind be disordered, and he beside himself. Plainly, divine Scripture, which knows better than any the nature of every thing, says through Moses, of the creatures, *In the beginning God created the heaven and the earth;* but of the Son it introduces the Father Himself[1.] saying, *I have begotten Thee from the womb before the morning star;* and again, *Thou art My Son, this day have I begotten Thee.* And the Lord says of Himself in the Proverbs, *Before all the hills He begets Me;* and concerning things generated and created John speaks, *All things were made by Him;* but preaching of the Lord, he says, *The Only-begotten Son, who is in the bosom of the Father, He hath declared Him.* If then son, therefore not creature; if creature, not son; for great is the difference between them, and son and creature cannot be the same, unless his substance be considered to be at once from God, and external to God.

CHAP. III.

[1] γεννητοῖς

[2] Serap. ii. 6.

Gen. 1,
Ps. 110, 3.
Ps. 2, 7.

Prov. 8, 25
John 1, 3.
ver. 18.

---

[x] i. e. "Granting that the *primâ facie* impression of this text is in favour of our Lord's being a creature, yet so many arguments have been already brought, and may be added, against His creation, that we must interpret this text by them It cannot mean that our Lord was simply created, *because* we have already shewn that He is not external to His Father"

NICEN. DEF. §. 14.

12. "Has then the passage no meaning?" for this, like a swarm of gnats, they are droning about us[y]. No surely, it is not without meaning, but has a very apposite one; for it is true to say that the Son was created too, but this took place when He became man; for creation belongs to man. And any one may find this sense duly given in the divine oracles, who, instead of accounting their study a secondary matter, investigates the time and characters[z], and the object, and thus studies and ponders what he reads. Now as to the season spoken of, he will find for certain that, whereas the Lord always is, at length in fulness of the ages[1] He became man; and whereas He is Son of God, He became Son of man also. And as to the object he will understand, that, wishing to annul our death, He took on Himself a body from the Virgin Mary; that by offering this unto the Father a sacrifice for all, He might deliver us all, who by fear of death were all our life through subject to bondage. And as to the character, it is indeed the Saviour's, but is said of Him when He took a body and said, *The Lord has created Me a beginning of His ways unto His works.* For as it properly belongs to God's Son to be everlasting, and in the Father's bosom, so on His becoming man, the words befitted Him, *The Lord created Me.* For then it is said of Him, and He hungered, and He thirsted, and He asked where Lazarus lay, and He suffered, and He rose again[2]. And as, when we hear of Him as Lord and God and true Light, we understand Him as being from the Father, so on hearing, *The Lord created,* and *Servant,* and *He suffered,* we shall justly ascribe this, not to the Godhead, for it is irrelevant, but we must interpret it by that flesh which He bore for our sakes; for to it these things are proper, and this flesh was none other's than the Word's. And if we wish to know the object attained by this,

[1] αἰώνων

Heb. 2, 15.

Prov 8, 22.

[2] Sent D 9. Orat. iii. § 26—41

---

[y] περιβομβοῦσιν So in ad Afros 5. init. And Sent. D. §. 19 περιέχονται περιβομβοῦντες. And Gregory Nyssen, contr. Eun. viii. p. 234. C. ὡς ἂν τοὺς ἀπείρους ταῖς πλατωνικαῖς καλλιφωνίαις περιβομβήσειεν vid. also περιέρχονται ὡς οἱ κάνθαροι Orat. iii. fin.

[z] πρόσωπα. vid. Orat 1. §. 54. ii. §. 8. Sent. D. 4. not *persons,* but *characters;* which must also be considered the meaning of the word. contr. Apoll. ii. 2. and 10; though it there approximates (even in phrase, οὐκ ἐν διαιρέσει προσώπων) to its ecclesiastical use, which seems to have been later. Yet persona occurs in Tertull. in Prax. 27; it may be questioned, however, whether in any genuine Greek treatise till the Apollinarians.

we shall find it to be as follows; that the Word was made flesh in order to offer up this body for all, and that we, partaking of His Spirit, might be made gods, a gift which we could not otherwise have gained than by His clothing Himself in our created body [1]; for hence we derive our name of " men of God" and " men in Christ." But as we, by receiving the Spirit, do not lose our own proper substance, so the Lord, when made man for us, and bearing a body, was no less God; for He was not lessened by the envelopment of the body, but rather deified it and rendered it immortal [a].

CHAP. III.

[1] Orat. II. §. 70.

[a] " remaining Himself unalterable, and not changed by His human economy and presence in the flesh." Orat. II. 6.

CHAP IV

PROOF OF THE CATHOLIC SENSE OF THE WORD SON.

Power, Word or Reason, and Wisdom, the names of the Son, imply eternity; as well as the Father's title of Fountain. The Arians reply that these do not formally belong to the essence of the Son, but are names given Him, that God has many words, powers, &c. Why there is but one Son and Word, &c. All the titles of the Son coincide in Him.

NICEN. DEF. §. 15.
1. THIS then is quite enough to expose the infamy of the Arian heresy; for, as the Lord has granted, out of their own words is irreligion brought home to them [b]. But come now and let us on our part act on the offensive, and call on them for an answer; for now is fair time, when their own ground has failed them, to question them on ours; perhaps it may abash the perverse, and disclose to them whence they have fallen. We have learned from divine Scripture, that the Son of God, as was said above, is the very Word and Wisdom of the Father. For the Apostle says, *Christ the power of God and the Wisdom of God;* and John after saying, *And the Word was made flesh,* at once adds, *And we have seen His glory, the glory as of the Only-begotten of the Father, full of grace and truth;* so that, the Word being the Only-begotten Son, in this Word and in Wisdom heaven and earth and all that is therein were made. And of this Wisdom that God is Fountain we have learned from [1] Baruch, by Israel's being charged with having forsaken the Fountain of Wisdom. If then they deny Scripture, they are at once aliens to their name, and

1 Cor. 1, 24
John 1, 14.

[1] vid. supr. §. 12.

[b] The main argument of the Arians was that our Lord was a Son, and *therefore* was not eternal, but of a substance which had a beginning. With this Arius started in his dispute with Alexander. "Arius, a man not without dialectic skill, thinking that the Bishop was introducing the doctrine of Sabellius the Libyan, out of contention fell off into the opinion diametrically opposite,....and he says, '*If* the Father begot the Son, he that was begotten had a beginning of existence, and from this it is plain that once the Son was not; and it follows of necessity that He had His subsistence out of nothing." Socr. i. 5 Accordingly, Athanasius says, " Having argued with them as to the meaning of their own selected term, 'Son,' let us go on to others, which on the very face make for us, such as Word, Wisdom, &c "

may fitly be called of all men atheists[1], and Christ's enemies, for they have brought upon themselves these names But if they agree with us that the sayings of Scripture are divinely inspired, let them dare to say openly what they think in secret, that God was once wordless and wisdomless[c]; and let them in their madness[2] say, "There was once when He was not," and, "before His generation, Christ was not[d]," and again let them declare that the Fountain begat not Wisdom from Itself, but acquired It from without, till they have the daring to say, "The Son came of nothing;" whence it will follow that there is no longer a Fountain, but a sort of pool, as if receiving water from without, and usurping the name of Fountain[e].

2. How full of irreligion this is, I consider none can doubt who has ever so little understanding But since they whisper something about *Word* and *Wisdom*, being only names of the Son[f], we must ask then, If these are only names of

---

[c] ἄλογος, ἄσοφος. vid infra, §. 26. This is a frequent argument in the controversy, viz that to deprive the Father of His Son or substantial Word, (λόγος,) is as great a sacrilege as to deny His Reason, λόγος, from which the Son receives His name. Thus Orat 1. § 14. fin. Athan. says, "imputing to God's nature an absence of His Word, (ἀλογίαν or irrationality,) they are most irreligious" vid. §. 19 fin 24. Elsewhere, he says, " Is a man not mad himself, who even entertains the thought that God is word-less and wisdom-less ᵖ for such illustrations and such images Scripture hath proposed, that, considering the inability of human nature to comprehend concerning God, we might even from these, however poorly and dimly, discern as far as is attainable." Orat ii 32. vid also iii 63. iv. 14. Serap. ii. 2.

[d] These were among the original positions of the Arians, the former is mentioned by Socrates, vid. note b. the latter is one of those specified in the Nicene Anathema

[e] And so πηγὴ ξηρά Serap. ii. 2. Orat. 1 § 14. fin. also ii. §. 2 where Athanasius speaks as if those who deny that Almighty God is Father, cannot really believe in Him as a Creator. "If He be not a Son, let Him be called a work, and let God be called, not Father, but Framer only and Creator, and not of a generative nature. But if the divine substance be not fruitful, (καρπογόνος,) but barren, as they say, as a light which enlightens not, and a dry fountain, are they not ashamed to maintain that He possesses the creative energy ᵖ" vid also πηγὴ θεότητος Pseudo-Dion Div. Nom. c 2. πηγὴ ἐκ πηγῆς, of the Son Epiphan Ancor. 19. And Cyril, " It thou take from God His being Father, thou wilt deny the generative power (καρπόγονον) of the divine nature, so that It no longer is *perfect*. This then is a token of its perfection, and the Son who went forth from Him apart from time, is a pledge (σφραγὶς) to the Father that He is perfect " Thesaur p 37.

[f] Arius said, as the Eunomians after him, that the Son was not really, but only called, Word and Wisdom, which were simply attributes of God, and the prototypes of the Son vid Socr. 1. 6. p 11 Theod. Hist.1, 3 p.731. Athan asks, Is the Son then more than wisdom ᵖ if on the other hand He be less, still He must be so called because of some gift or quality in Him, analogous to wisdom, or of the nature of wisdom, and admitting of improvement and growth. But this was the notorious doctrine of Christ's προκοπὴ or advancement " I am in wonder," he says,

NICEN. the Son, He must be something else beside them. And if
DEF. He is higher than the names, it is not lawful from the lesser to
denote the higher; but if He be less than the names, yet He
surely must have in Him the principle of this more honourable appellation; and this implies His advance, which is an
irreligion equal to any thing that has gone before. For He
who is in the Father, and in whom also the Father is, who says,
John 10, *I and the Father are one,* whom He that hath seen, hath seen
30.
¹βελτιοῦ- the Father, to say that He has been improved¹ by any thing
σθαι external, is the extreme of madness.

3. However, when they are beaten hence, and like the Eusebians are in these great straits, then they have this remaining
² vid. plea, which Arius too in ballads, and in his own Thalia²,
Syn.
§. 15. fabled, as a new difficulty: " Many words speaketh God;
which then of these are we to call Son and Word, Only-
begotten of the Father ᵍ ?" Insensate, and any thing but Chris-

Orat. II. §. 37. " how, whereas God is one, these men introduce after their private notions, many images, and wisdoms, and words, and say that the Father's proper and natural Word is other than the Son, by whom He even made the Son, and that the real Son is but notionally called Word, as vine, and way, and door, and tree of life, and Wisdom also only in name,—the proper and true Wisdom of the Father, which co-exists with Him without generation, being other than the Son, by which He even made the Son, and named Him Wisdom as partaking of it." He goes on to observe in § 38. that to be consistent they should explain away not only word, wisdom, &c. but the title of *being* as applied to Him; " and then what is He ᵖ for He is none of these Himself, if they are but His names, and He has but a semblance of being, and is decorated with these names by us."

ᵍ As the Arians took the title Son in that part of its earthly sense in which it did not apply to our Lord, so they misinterpreted the title Word also; which denoted the Son's immateriality and indivisible presence in the Father, but did not express His perfection. vid. Orat. II. §. 34—36. which precedes the passage quoted in the last note. " As our word is proper to us and from us, and not a work external to us, so also the Word of God is proper to Him

and from Him, and is not made, *yet not as the word of man,* else one must consider God as man. Men have many words, and after those many, not any one of them all, for the speaker has ceased, and thereupon his word fails. But God's Word is one and the same, and, as it is written, "remaineth for ever," not changed, not first one and then another, but existing the same always. For it behoved that God being one, one should be His Image, one His Word, one His Wisdom." § 36. vid. contr. Gent 41. ad Ep. Æg. 16. Epiph. Hær. 65 3. Nyss. in Eun XII. p. 349. Origen, (in a passage, however, of questionable doctrine,) says, " As there are gods many, but to us one God the Father, and many lords, but to us one Lord Jesus Christ, so then are many words, but we pray that in us may exist the Word that was in the beginning, with God, and God." in Joan. tom. II. 3.
" Many things, it is acknowledged, does the Father speak to the Son," say the Semiarians at Ancyra, " but the words which God speaks to the Son, are not sons. They are not substances of God, but vocal energies; but the Son, though a Word, is not such, but, being a Son, is a substance" Epiph. Hær. 73. 12. The Semiarians are speaking against Sabellianism, which took the same ground here as Arianism; so did the heresy of Samosatene, who, according to

If our Lord is the Word, He is the Son and the Image. 27

tians[h]! for first, on using such language about God, they conceive of Him almost as a man, speaking and reversing His first words by His second, just as if one Word from God were not sufficient for the framing of all things at the Father's will, and for His providential care of all. For His speaking many words would argue a feebleness in them all, each needing the service of the other. But that God should have one Word, which is the true doctrine, both shews the power of God, and the perfection of the Word that is from Him, and the religious understanding of them who thus believe.

4. O that they would consent to confess the truth from this their own statement! for if they once grant that God produces words, they plainly know Him to be a Father; and acknowledging this, let them consider that, while they are loth to ascribe one Word to God, they are imagining that He is Father of many; and while they are loth to say that there is no Word of God at all, yet they do not confess that He is the Son of God,—which is ignorance of the truth, and inexperience in divine Scripture. For if God is altogether Father of the Word, wherefore is not He a Son that is begotten? And again, Son of God who should be, but His Word? For there are not many Words, or each would be imperfect, but one is the Word, that He only may be perfect, and because, God being one, His image too must be one, which is the Son. For the Son of God, as may be learnt from the divine oracles themselves, is Himself the Word of God, and the Wisdom, and the Image, and the Hand, and the Power; for God's offspring is one, and of the generation from the Father these titles are tokens[1]. For if you say the

---

Epiphanius, considered our Lord, the internal Word, or thought. Hær. 65. The term word in this inferior sense is often in Greek ῥῆμα. Epiph. supr. and Cyril. de Incarn. Unig. init p. 679.

[h] "If they understood and acknowledged the characteristic idea (χαρακτῆρα) of Christianity, they would not have said that the Lord of glory was a creature" ad Serap. ii. 7. In Orat. i. §. 2. he says, Arians are not Christians *because* they are Arians, for Christians are called, not from Arius, but from Christ, who is their only Master vid. also de Syn. §. 38. init. Sent. D. fin. Ad Afros. 4. Their cruelty and cooperation with the heathen populace was another reason. Greg. Naz. Orat. 25. 12.

[1] All the titles of the Son of God are consistent with each other, and variously represent one and the same Person. "Son" and "Word," denote His derivation, "Word" and "Image," His Similitude; "Word" and "Wisdom," His immateriality; "Wisdom" and "Hand", His co-existence. "If He is not Son, neither is He Image." Orat. ii §. 2. "How is there Word and Wisdom, unless there be a proper offspring of His substance?" ii. §. 22. vid. also Orat. i. §. 20, 21. and at great length Orat. iv. §. 20. &c. vid. also Naz. Orat. 30. n. 20. Basil. contr. Eunom. i. 18. Hilar. de Trin. vii. 11. August. in Joann. xlviii. 6. and in Psalm 44, (45,) 5.

NICEN. Son, you have declared what is from the Father by nature; and
DEF. if you imagine the Word, you are thinking again of what is
from Him, and what is inseparable, and, speaking of Wisdom,
again you mean just as much, what is not from without, but
from Him and in Him; and if you name the Power and the
Hand, again you speak of what is proper to substance;
and, speaking of the Image, you signify the Son; for what else
is like God but the offspring from Him? Doubtless the things,
which came to be through *the Word*, these are *founded in
Wisdom;* and what are *laid in Wisdom*, these are all made by
the Hand, and came to be through the Son. And we have proof
of this, not from external sources, but from the Scriptures;
Is. 48, for God Himself says by Esaias the Prophet; *My hand also
13. hath laid the foundation of the earth, and My right hand
Is. 51, hath spanned the heavens.* And again, *And I have covered
16. them in the shadow of My Hand, that I may plant the
heavens, and lay the foundations of the earth.* And David
being taught this, and knowing that the Lord's Hand was nothing
Ps. 104, else than Wisdom, says in the Psalm, *In wisdom hast Thou
24. made them all; the earth is full of Thy riches.* Solomon
Prov. 3, also received the same from God, and said, *The Lord by
19. wisdom hath founded the earth;* and John, knowing that
John 1, the Word was the Hand and the Wisdom, thus preached, *In
1. the beginning was the Word, and the Word was with God,
and the Word was God; the same was in the beginning
with God: all things were made by Him, and without Him
was not any thing made.* And the Apostle, understanding
that the Hand and the Wisdom and the Word was nothing else
Heb. 1, than the Son, says, *God, who at sundry times and in divers
1. 2. manners spake in time past unto the Fathers by the Prophets,
hath in these last days spoken unto us by His Son, whom He
hath appointed Heir of all things, by whom also He made
1 Cor. 8, the ages.* And again, *There is one Lord Jesus Christ,
6. through whom are all things, and we through Him.* And
knowing also that the Word, the Wisdom, the Son was the
Image Himself of the Father, He says in the Epistle to the
Col. 1, Colossians, *Giving thanks to God and the Father, which
12—17. hath made us meet to be partakers of the inheritance of the
Saints in light, who hath delivered us from the power of
darkness, and hath translated us into the kingdom of His

dear Son; in whom we have redemption[1], even the remission of sins; who is the Image of the Invisible God, the First-born of every creature; for by Him were all things created, that are in heaven, and that are in earth, visible and invisible, whether they be thrones, or dominions, or principalities, or powers; all things were created by Him and for Him; and He is before all things, and in Him all things consist. For as all things are created by the Word, so, because He is the Image, are they also created in Him[k]. And thus any one who directs His thoughts to the Lord, will avoid stumbling upon the stone of offence, but rather will go forward to that brightness which is reflected from the light of truth; for this is really the doctrine of truth, though these contentious men burst with spite[l], neither religious towards God, nor abashed at their confutation

CHAP. IV.
[1] through His blood, rec. t.

[k] vid a beautiful passage, contr Gent. 42. &c. Again, of men, "He made them after His own image, imparting to them of the power of His proper Word, that, having as it were *certain shadows of the* Word, and becoming rational, λογικοὶ, they might be enabled to continue in blessedness." Incarn. 3. vid. also Orat. ii. 78. where he speaks of Wisdom as being infused into the world on its creation, that it might possess " a type and semblance of Its Image."

[l] διαῤῥαγῶσιν, and so Serap ii. fin διαῤῥηγνύωνται. de Syn. 34. διαῤῥηγνύωσιν ἑαυτούς Orat ii. § 23. σπαραττίτωσαν ἑαυτούς Orat. ii. §. 64. τρίζιτο τοὺς ὀδόντας. Sent. D. 16.

CHAP. V.

DEFENCE OF THE COUNCIL'S PHRASES, "FROM THE SUBSTANCE," AND "ONE IN SUBSTANCE."

Objection that the phrases are not scriptural; we ought to look at the sense more than the wording; evasion of the Eusebians as to the phrase "of God" which is in Scripture; their evasion of all explanations but those which the Council selected, which were intended to negative the Arian formulæ; protest against their conveying any material sense.

NICEN. DEF. §. 18.

1. Now the Eusebians were at the former period examined at great length, and convicted themselves, as I said before; on this they subscribed; and after this change of mind they kept in quiet and retirement[m]; but since the present party, in the fresh arrogance of irreligion, and in dizziness about the truth, are full set upon accusing the Council, let them tell us what are the sort of Scriptures from which they have learned, or who is the Saint[1] by which they have been taught, that they have heaped together the phrases, "out of nothing[2]," and "He was not before His generation," and "once He was not," and "alterable," and "pre-existence," and "at the will;" which are their fables in mockery of the Lord. For the blessed Paul in his Epistle to the Hebrews says, *By faith we understand that the ages were framed by the Word of God, so that things which are seen were not made of things which do appear.* But nothing is common to the Word with the ages[n]; for He it

[1] v. sup. p. 12. note y.
[2] ἐξ οὐκ ὄντων
Heb. 11, 3.

---

[m] After the Nicene Council, the Eusebians did not dare avow their heresy in Constantine's lifetime, but merely attempted the banishment of Athanasius, and the restoration of Arius. Their first Council was A.D. 341, four years after Constantine's death.

[n] By αἰών, age, seems to be meant duration, or the measure of duration, before or independent of the existence of motion, which is the measure of time. As motion, and therefore time, are creatures, so are the ages. Considered as the measure of duration, an age has a sort of positive existence, though not an οὐσία or substance, and means the same as "world," or an existing system of things viewed apart from time and motion. vid. Theodor. in Hebr. 1. 2. Our Lord then is the Maker of the ages thus considered, as the Apostle also tells us, Hebr. 11, 3. and God is the King of the ages, 1 Tim. 1, 17. or is before all ages, as being eternal, or προαιώνιος. However, sometimes the word is synonymous with eternity; "as time is to things which are under time, so ages to things which are everlasting." Damasc. Fid. Orth. ii. 1. and "ages of ages" stands

The Son before all ages, because their Creator. 31

is who is in existence before the ages, by whom also the ages came to be. And in the Shepherd[1], it is written, (since they allege this book also, though it is not of the Canon[o],) "First of all believe, that God is one, who created all things, and arranged them, and brought all things from nothing into being;" but this again does not relate to the Son, for it speaks concerning all things which came to be through Him, from whom He is distinct; for it is not possible to reckon the Framer of all with the things made by Him, unless a man is so beside himself as to say that the architect also is the same as the buildings which he rears.

2. Why then, when they have invented on their part unscriptural phrases, for the purposes of irreligion, do they accuse those who are religious in their use of them[p]? For irreligiousness is utterly forbidden, though it be attempted to

---

[marginal notes: CHAP. V. [1] Herm. [o] Herm. [1] vid. ad Afr. 5.]

---

for eternity; and then the "ages" or measures of duration, may be supposed to stand for the ἴδιαι or ideas in the Divine Mind, which seems to have been a Platonic or Gnostic notion Hence Synesius, Hymn iii addresses the Almighty as αἰωνότοκε, parent of the ages. Hence sometimes God Himself is called the Age, Clem. Alex Hymn. Pæd. iii fin. or, the Age of ages, Pseudo-Dion de Div. Nom. 5. p. 580. or again, αἰώνιος. Theodoret sums up what has been said thus " Age is not any subsisting substance, but is an interval indicative of time, now infinite, when God is spoken of, now commensurate with creation, now with human life." Hær. v. 6. If then, as Athan. says in the text, the Word is Maker of the ages, He is independent of duration altogether, He does not come to be in time, but is above and beyond it, or eternal. Elsewhere he says, " The words addressed to the Son in the 144th Psalm, ' Thy kingdom is a kingdom of all ages,' forbid any one to imagine any interval at all in which the Word did not exist For if every interval is measured by ages, and of all the ages the Word is King and Maker, therefore, whereas no interval at all exists prior to Him, it were madness to say, ' There was once when the Everlasting (αἰώνιος) was not.'" Orat. i. 12. And so Alexander; " Is it not unreasonable that He who made times, and ages, and seasons, to all of which belongs ' was not,'

should be said not to be? for, if so, that interval in which they say the Son was not yet begotten by the Father, precedes that Wisdom of God which framed all things.'" Theod. Hist. i. 3. p. 736. vid. also Basil. de Sp. S. n. 14. Hilar. de Trin. xii. 34.

[o] And so in Ep. Fest. fin. he enumerates it with Wisdom, Ecclesiasticus, Esther, Judith, Tobit, and others, "not canonized but appointed by the Fathers to be read by late converts and persons under teaching " He calls it elsewhere a most profitable book Incarn. 3.

[p] Athan. here retorts the charge brought against the Council, as it was obvious to do, which gave occasion for this Treatise. If the Council went beyond Scripture in the use of the word " substance," (which however can hardly be granted,) who made this necessary, but they who had already introduced the phrases, " the Son was out of nothing," &c. &c. [p] " Of the substance," and " one in substance," were directly intended to contradict and supplant the Arian unscriptural innovations, as he says below, §. 20. fin. 21 init. vid also ad Afros. 6 de Synod. §. 36, 37 He observes in like manner that the Arian ἀγένητος, though allowable as used by religious men, de Syn. §. 46. was unscriptural, Orat. 1. §. 30, 34. Also Epiph. Hær. 76. p. 941 Basil. contr. Eunom. 1. 5. Hilar. contr. Const. 16. Ambros. Incarn. 80.

32 *History of the Nicene symbol, "Of the Substance."*

NICEN. DEF.
disguise it with artful expressions and plausible sophisms; but religiousness is confessed by all to be lawful, even though presented in strange phrases[1], provided only they are used with a religious view, and a wish to make them the expression of religious thoughts. Now the aforesaid grovelling phrases of Christ's enemies, have been shewn in these remarks to be both formerly and now replete with irreligion; whereas the definition of the Council against them, if accurately examined, will be found to be altogether a representation of the truth, and especially if diligent attention be paid to the occasion which gave rise to these expressions, which was reasonable, and was as follows:—

[1] vid. p. 17. note m.

§. 19.   3. The Council[2] wishing to negative the irreligious phrases of the Arians, and to use instead the acknowledged words of the Scriptures, that the Son is not from nothing but *from God*, and is *Word* and *Wisdom*, nor creature or work, but the proper offspring from the Father, the party of Eusebius, out of their inveterate heterodoxy, understood the phrase *from God* as belonging to us, as if in respect to it the Word of God differed nothing from us, and that because it is written, *There is one God, from whom all things;* and again, *Old things are passed away, behold, all things are new, and all things are from God.* But the Fathers, perceiving their craft and the cunning of their irreligion, were forced to express more distinctly the sense of the words *from God.* Accordingly, they wrote "from the substance of God[q]," in order that *from God*

[2] vid. ad Afr. 5.
1 Cor. 8, 6.
2 Cor. 5, 17.

---

[q] Hence it stands in the Creed, "from the Father, *that is*, from the substance of the Father." vid. Eusebius's Letter, *infra*. According to the received doctrine of the Church all rational beings, and in one sense all beings whatever, are "from God," over and above the fact of their creation; and of this truth the Eusebians made use to deny our Lord's proper divinity. Athan. lays down elsewhere that nothing remains in consistence and life, except from a participation of the Word, which is to be considered a gift from Him, additional to that of creation, and separable in idea from it. vid. above, note k. Thus he says that the all-powerful and all-perfect, Holy Word of the Father, pervading all things, and developing every where His power, and illuminating all things visible and invisible, gathers them within Himself and knits them in one, leaving nothing destitute of His power, but quickening and preserving all things and through all, and each by itself, and the whole altogether." contr. Gent. 42. Again, "God *not only* made us of nothing, *but also* vouchsafed to us a life according to God, and *by the grace of the Word.* But men, turning from things eternal to the things of corruption at the devil's counsel, have brought on themselves the corruption of death, who were, as I said, *by nature corrupted*, but by *the grace of the participation of the Word*, had escaped their natural state, had they remained good." Incarn. 5. Man thus considered is, in his first estate a son of God and born of

Necessity of it, to explain " of God." 33

might not be considered common and equal in the Son and in things generate, but that all others might be acknowledged as creatures, and the Word alone as from the Father. For though all things be said to be from God, yet this is not in the sense in which the Son is from Him; for as to the creatures, "*of God*" is said of them on this account, in that they exist not at random or spontaneously, nor come to be by chance [1], according to those philosophers who refer them to the combination of atoms, and to elements of similar structure,—nor as certain heretics speak of a distinct Framer,—nor as others again say that the constitution of all things is from certain Angels;— but in that, whereas God is, it was by Him that all things were brought into being, not being before, through His Word, but as to the Word, since He is not a creature, He alone is both called and is *from the Father*; and it is significant of this sense to say that the Son is " from the substance of the Father," for to no creature does this attach. In truth, when Paul says that *all things are from God*, he immediately adds, *and one Lord Jesus Christ, through whom all things*, by way of shewing all men, that the Son is other than all these things which came to be from God, (for the things which came to be from God, came to be through His Son;) and that he had used his foregoing words with reference to the world as framed by God [r],

CHAP. V.

[1] vid. de Syn §. 35.

1 Cor. 8, 6.

God, or, to use the term which occurs so frequently in the Arian controversy, in the number, not only of the creatures, but of *things generate*, γενητά This was the sense in which the Arians said that our Lord was Son of God, whereas, as Athan. says, " things generate, *being works*, cannot be called generate, except so far as, *after* their making, they partake of the begotten Son, and are therefore *said* to have been generated also; not at all in their own *nature*, but because of their participation of the Son in the Spirit." Orat. 1. 56. The question then was, as to the *distinction* of the Son's divine generation over that of holy men; and the Catholics answered that He was ἐξ οὐσίας, from the substance of God; not by participation of grace, not by resemblance, not in a limited sense, but really and simply, and therefore by an internal divine act. vid. below, §. 22. and infr. §. 31. note k.

[r] When characteristic attributes and prerogatives are ascribed to God, or to the Father, this is done only to the exclusion of creatures, or of false gods, not to the exclusion of His Son who is implied in the mention of Himself. Thus when God is called only wise, or the Father the only God, or God is said to be ingenerate, ἀγένητος, this is not in contrast to the Son, but to all things which are distinct from God. vid. Athan. Orat. III. 8. Naz. Orat. 30, 13. Cyril Thesaur. p. 142. " The words ' one' and ' only' ascribed to God in Scripture," says S Basil, " are not used in contrast to the Son or the Holy Spirit, but with reference to those who are not God, and falsely called so." Ep. 8. n. 3. On the other hand, when the Father is mentioned, the other Divine Persons are implied in Him, " The Blessed and Holy Trinity," says S. Athan "is indivisible and one in itself; and when the Father is mentioned, His Word is added, and the Spirit in the Son, and if the Son is named, in the Son is the Father, and the Spirit is not external to the Word." ad Serap. 1. 14.

D

NICEN. and not as if all things were from the Father as the Son is.
DEF. For neither are other things as the Son, nor is the Word one among others, for He is Lord and Framer of all; and on this account did the Holy Council declare expressly that He was of the substance* of the Father, that we might believe the Word to be other than the nature of things generate, being alone truly from God; and that no subterfuge should be left open to the irreligious. This then was the reason why the Council wrote " of the substance."

§. 20. 4. Again, when the Bishops said that the Word must be described as the True Power and Image of the Father, like ¹ἀπαράλ-λακτον to the Father in all things and unvarying¹, and as unalterable, and as always, and as in Him without division; (for never was the Word not, but He was always, existing everlastingly with the Father, as the radiance of light,) the party of Eusebius endured indeed, as not daring to contradict, being put to shame by the arguments which were urged against them; but withal they were caught whispering to each other and winking with their eyes, that " like," and " always," and " power," and " in Him," were, as before, common to us and the Son, and that it was no difficulty to agree to these. As to " like," they said that it is written of us, *Man is the image* 1 Cor. 11, 7. *and glory of God;* " always," that it was written, *For we* 2 Cor. 4, 11. *which live are alway;* " in Him," *In Him we live and* Acts 17, 28. *move and have our being;* " unalterable," that it is written, Rom. 8. *Nothing shall separate us from the love of Christ;* as to who shall " power," that the caterpillar and the locust are called separate *power,* and *great power,* and that it is often said of the Joel 2, 25. people, for instance, *All the power of the Lord came out of* Ex. 12, *the land of Egypt;* and others are heavenly powers, for 41. Ps 46,8. Scripture says, *The Lord of powers is with us, the God*

---

* Vid. also ad Afros. 4. Again, "' I am,' τὸ ὂν, is really proper to God and is a whole, bounded or mutilated neither by aught before Him, nor after Him, for He neither was, nor shall be " Naz. Orat. 30. 18 fin. Also Cyril Dial i. p. 392. Damasc. Fid. Orth 1. 9. and the Semiarians at Ancyra, Epiph. Hær. 73. 12 init. By the " essence," however, or " substance" of God, the Council did not mean any thing distinct from God, vid. note a, infr. but God Himself viewed in His self-existing nature, (vid. Tert. in Hermog. 3) nay, it expressly meant to negative the contrary notion of the Arians, that our Lord was from something distinct from God, and in consequence of created substance. Moreover the term expresses the idea of God *positively,* in contradistinction to negative epithets, such as infinite, immense, eternal, &c. Damasc. Fid. Orthod. i 4. and as little implies any thing distinct from God as those epithets do.

of Jacob is our refuge Indeed Asterius, by title the sophist, had said the like in writing, having taken it from them, and before Him Arius[1] having taken it also, as has been said. But[1] the Bishops, discerning in this too their simulation, and whereas it is written, *Deceit is in the heart of the irreligious that imagine evil*, were again compelled on their part to concentrate the sense of the Scriptures, and to re-say and re-write what they had said before, more distinctly still, namely, that the Son is " one in substance[t]" with the Father; by way of signifying that the Son was from the Father, and not merely like, but is the same in likeness[u], and of shewing that the Son's likeness and unalterableness was different from such copy of the same as is ascribed to us, which we acquire from virtue on the ground of observance of the commandments.

CHAP. V.

[1] vid. supr. p. 13.ref.2.

Prov 12, 20.

5. For bodies which are like each other, may be separated and become at distances from each other, as are human sons relatively to their parents, (as it is written concerning Adam and Seth, who was begotten of him, that he was like him after his own pattern;) but since the generation of the Son from the[3]

Gen. 5,

---

[t] vid. ad Afros. 5. 6. ad Serap. 11. 5. S. Ambrose tells us, that a Letter written by Eusebius of Nicomedia, in which he said, " If we call Him true Son of the Father and uncreate, then are we granting that He is one in substance, ὁμοούσιον," determined the Council on the adoption of the term. de Fid iii. n. 125. He had disclaimed "of the substance," in his Letter to Paulinus Theod. Hist. 1. 4. Arius, however, had disclaimed ὁμοούσιον already. Epiph Hær. 69. 7. It was a word of old usage in the Church, as Eusebius of Cæsarea confesses in his Letter, infr Tertullian in Prax. 13. fin. has the translation " unius substantiæ," (vid. Lucifer de non Parc. p. 218.) as he has " de substantia Patris," in Prax. 4. and Origen perhaps used the word, vid. Pamph. Apol. 5. and Theognostus and the two Dionysius's, *infra*, §. 25 26. And before them Clement had spoken of the ἕνωσις τῆς μοναδικῆς οὐσίας, " the union of the single substance," vid. Le Quien in Damasc. Fid. Orth 1. 8. Novatian too has " per substantiæ communionem," de Trinit. 31

[u] The Eusebians allowed that our Lord was like and the image of the Father, but in the sense in which a picture is like the original, differing from it in substance and in fact. In this sense they even allowed the strong word ἀπαράλλακτος *unvarying* image, vid beginning of § 20. which had been used by the Catholics, (vid. Alexander, ap. Theod. Hist. 1. 3. p 740) as by the Semiarians afterwards, who even added the words κατ' οὐσίαν, or " according to substance " Even this strong phrase, however, κατ' οὐσίαν ἀπαράλλακτος εἰκών, or ἀπαραλλάκτως ὅμοιος, did not appear to the Council an adequate safeguard of the doctrine. Athan notices de Syn. that " like" applies to qualities rather than to substance, §. 53 Also Basil. Ep 8. n. 3. " while in itself," says the same Father, " it is frequently used of faint similitudes, and falling very far short of the original." Ep. 9 n. 3. Accordingly, the Council determined on the word ὁμοούσιον as implying, as the text expresses it, " *the same* in likeness," ταὐτὸν τῇ ὁμοιώσει, that the likeness might not be analogical. vid. the passage about gold and brass, p. 40 below. Cyril. in Joan. l. v. p. 302.

NICEN. Father is not according to the nature of men, and not only
DEF. like, but also inseparable from the substance of the Father,
and He and the Father are one, as He has said Himself, and
the Word is ever in the Father and the Father in the Word,
as the radiance stands towards the light, (for this the phrase
itself indicates,) therefore the Council, as understanding
this, suitably wrote "one in substance," that they might both
defeat the perverseness of the heretics, and shew that the
Word was other than generated things. For, after thus
writing, they at once added, " But they who say that the
Son of God is from nothing, or created, or alterable, or a
work, or from other substance, these the Holy Catholic
¹ vid. Church anathematizes¹." And in saying this, they shewed
Euseb's clearly that " of the substance," and " one in substance," do
Letter,
infr. negative² those syllables of irreligion, such as " created,"
² vid. p.
31. not. and " work," and " generated," and " alterable," and " He
p. was not before His generation." And he who holds these,
contradicts the Council; but he who does not hold with
Arius, must needs hold and comprehend the decisions of the
Council, suitably regarding them to signify the relation of the
radiance to the light, and from thence gaining the illustration
of the truth.

§. 21.   6. Therefore if they, as the others, make an excuse that the
terms are strange, let them consider the sense in which the
Council so wrote, and anathematize what the Council anathematized; and then, if they can, let them find fault with
the expressions. But I well know that, if they hold the
sense of the Council, they will fully accept the terms in which
³ vid p. it is conveyed; whereas if it be the sense³ which they wish to
17. note
m. complain of, all must see that it is idle in them to discuss the
wording, when they are but seeking handles for irreligion.

7. This then was the reason of these expressions; but if
they still complain that such are not scriptural, that very complaint is a reason why they should be cast out, as talking idly
and disordered in mind; and next why they should blame
themselves in this matter, for they set the example, beginning
their war against God with words not in Scripture. However,
if a person is interested in the question, let him know, that, even
if the expressions are not in so many words in the Scriptures,
yet, as was said before, they contain the sense of the Scriptures,

and expressing it, they convey it to those who have their
hearing unimpaired for religious doctrine. Now this circumstance it is for thee to consider, and for those illinstructed men to learn. It has been shewn above, and must be believed as true, that the Word is from the Father, and the only Offspring[x] proper to Him and natural. For whence may one conceive the Son to be, who is the Wisdom and the Word, in whom all things came to be, but from God Himself? However, the Scriptures also teach us this, since the Father says by David, *My heart was bursting of a good Word,* and, *From the womb before the morning star I begat Thee;* and the Son signifies to the Jews about Himself, *If God were your Father, ye would love Me; for I proceeded forth from the Father.* And again; *Not that any one has seen the Father, save He which is from God, He hath seen the Father.* And moreover, *I and My Father are one,* and, *I in the Father and the Father in Me,* is equivalent with saying, " I am from the Father, and inseparable from Him." And John, in saying, *The Only-begotten Son, which is in the bosom of the Father, He hath declared Him,* spoke of what he had learned from the Saviour. Besides, what else does *in the bosom* intimate, but the Son's genuine generation from the Father?

8. If then any man conceives as if God were compound, so as to have accidents in His substance[y], or any external

---

[x] γέννημα, offspring; this word is of very frequent occurrence in Athan. He speaks of it, Orat. IV. 3. as virtually Scriptural "If any one declines to say ' offspring,' and only says that the Word exists with God, let such a one fear lest, *declining an expression of Scripture* (τὸ λεγόμενον) he fall into extravagance, &c." Yet Basil, contr. Eunom. II. 6—8. explicitly disavows the word, as an unscriptural invention of Eunomius. "That the Father begat we are taught in many places· that the Son is an offspring we never heard up to this day, for Scripture says, ' unto us a *child* is born, unto us a *son* is given.' " c. 7. He goes on to say that " it is fearful to give Him names of our own, to whom God has given a name which is above every name," and observes that offspring is not the word which even a human father would apply to his son, as for instance we read, " Child, (τέκνον,) go into the vineyard," and " Who art thou, my son?" moreover that fruits of the earth are called offspring, ("I will not drink of the offspring of this vine,") rarely animated things, except indeed in such instances as, " O generation (offspring) of vipers " Nyssen defends his brother, contr Eunom. Orat III. p. 105. In the Arian formula " an offspring, but not as *one of the offsprings,"* it is synonymous with " work" or " creature." On the other hand Epiphanius uses it, e. g. Hær. 76. n. 8. and Naz. Orat. 29 n. 2. Eusebius, Demonstr. Ev. IV. 2. Pseudo-Basil. adv. Eunom. IV. p. 280. fin

[y] συμβεβηκός. And so elsewhere, when resisting the Arian and Sabellian notion that the wisdom of God is only a quality in the Divine nature, "In that case God will be compounded of substance and quality; for every quality is in the substance. And at this rate, whereas the Divine

envelopement[x], and to be encompassed, or as if there is aught about Him which completes the substance, so that when we say " God," or name " Father," we do not signify the invisible and incomprehensible substance, but something about it, then let them complain of the Council's stating that the Son was from the substance of God; but let them reflect, that in thus considering they commit two blasphemies; for they make God material, and they falsely say that the Lord is not Son of the very Father, but of what is about Him[1]. But if God be simple, as He is, it follows that in saying " God" and naming " Father," we name nothing as if about Him, but signify His substance itself. For though to comprehend what the substance of God is be impossible, yet if we only understand that God is, and if Scripture indicates Him by means of these titles, we, with the intention of indicating Him and none else, call Him God and Father and Lord. When then He says, *I am that I am*, and *I am the Lord God*, or when Scripture says, *God*, we understand nothing else by it but the intimation of His incomprehensible substance Itself, and that He Is, who is spoken of[a]. Therefore

[margin: NICEN. DEF.]
[margin: 1 περὶ αὐ-τὸν]
[margin: Ex. 3, 14. 15.]

Unity (μονὰς) is indivisible, it will be considered compound, being separated into substance and accident" Orat iv. 2 vid also Orat. 1. 36. This is the common doctrine of the Fathers. Athenagoras, however, speaks of God's goodness as an accident, " as colour to the body," " as flame is ruddy and the sky blue," Legat. 24. This, however, is but a verbal difference, for shortly before he speaks of His being, τὸ ὄντως ὄν, and His unity of nature, τὸ μονοφυὲς, as in the number of ἐπισυμβιβηκότα αὐτῷ Eusebius uses the word συμβιβηκὸς in the same way, Demonstr Evang. iv. 3. And hence St. Cyril, in controversy with the Arians, is led by the course of their objections to observe, " There are cogent reasons for considering these things *as accidents συμβιβηκότα* in God, though they be not." Thesaur. p. 263 vid. the following note.

[x] περιβολὴ, and so de Synod. §. 34. which is very much the same passage. Some Fathers, however, seem to say the reverse. E. g. Nazianzen says that " neither the immateriality of God nor ingenerateness, present to us His substance." Orat. 28. 9. And St. Augustine, arguing on the word ingenitus, says,

that " not every thing which is said to be in God is said according to substance." de Trin. v. 6. And hence, while Athan. in the text denies that there are qualities or the like belonging to Him, περὶ αὐτὸν, it is still common in the Fathers to speak of qualities, as in the passage of S Gregory just cited, in which the words περὶ θεὸν occur. There is no difficulty in reconciling these statements, though it would require more words than could be given to it here. Petavius has treated the subject fully in his work de Deo 1 7—11. and especially ii. 3. When the Fathers say that there is no difference between the divine ' proprietates' and essence, they speak of the fact, considering the Almighty as He is; when they affirm a difference, they speak of Him as contemplated by us, who are unable to grasp the idea of Him as one and simple, but view His Divine Nature as if *in projection*, (if such a word may be used,) and thus divided into substance and quality as man may be divided into genus and difference.

[a] In like manner de Synod. §. 34. Also Basil, " The substance is not any one of things which do not attach, but is the very being of God." contr. Eunom.

"*Of the substance*" *only brings out the meaning of* "*Son.*" 39

let no one be startled on hearing that the Son of God is from the substance of the Father, rather let him accept the explanation of the Fathers, who in more explicit but equivalent language have for *from God* written " of the substance." For they considered it the same thing to say that the Word was *of God* and " of the substance of God," since the word " God," as I have already said, signifies nothing but the substance of Him Who Is If then the Word is not in such sense from God, as to be Son, genuine and natural, from the Father, but only as creatures because they are framed, and as *all things are from God*, then neither is He from the substance of the Father, nor is the Son again Son according to substance, but in consequence of virtue, as we who are called sons by grace. But if He only is from God, as a genuine Son, as He is, then let the Son, as is reasonable, be called from the substance of God.

CHAP. V.

9. Again, the illustration of the Light and the Radiance has this meaning. For the Saints have not said that the Word was related to God as fire kindled from the heat of the sun, which is commonly put out again, for this is an external work and a creature of its author, but they all preach of Him as Radiance[b], thereby to signify His being from the substance, proper and[1] indivisible, and His oneness with the Father. This also will secure His true[2] unalterableness and immutability; for how can these be His, unless He be proper

§. 23.

[1] ἀδιαίρε-τον
[2] τὸ ἄ-τρεπτον καὶ ἀναλ-λοίωτον

---

1. 10 fin. " The nature of God is no other than Himself, for He is simple and uncompounded." Cyril Thesaur p. 59. " When we say the power of the Father, we say nothing else than the substance of the Father." August. de Trin. vii. 6. And so Numenius in Eusebius, " Let no one deride, if I say that the name of the Immaterial is substance and being." Præp. Evang. xi. 10.

b Athan.'s ordinary illustration is, as here, not from " fire," but from " radiance," ἀπαύγασμα, after St. Paul and the Author of the Book of Wisdom, meaning by radiance the light which a light diffuses by means of the atmosphere. On the other hand Arius in his letter to Alexander, Epiph. Hær. 69. 7. speaks against the doctrine of Hieracas that the Son was from the Father as a light from a light or as a lamp divided into two, which after all was Arian doctrine. Athanasius refers to fire, Orat. iv. §. 2 and 10. but still to fire and its radiance. However, we find the illustration of fire from fire, Justin. Tryph 61. Tatian contr. Græc. 5. At this early day the illustration of radiance might have a Sabellian bearing, as that of fire in Athan 's had an Arian. Hence Justin protests against those who considered the Son as "like the sun's light in the heaven," which " when it sets, goes away with it," whereas it is as " fire kindled from fire." Tryph. 128 Athenagoras, however, like Athanasius, says " as light from fire," using also the word ἀπόῤῥοια, effluence vid. also Orig. Periarch. 1. 2. n. 4. Tertull. Ap. 21. Theognostus infr. §. 25.

NICEN. Offspring of the Father's substance? for this too must be
DEF. taken to confirm His ¹ identity with His own Father.
¹ ταυτό-
τητα   10. Our explanation then having so religious an aspect,
Christ's enemies should not be startled at the " One in
substance" either, since this term also admits of being soundly
expounded and defended. Indeed, if we say that the
Word is from the substance of God, (for after what has been
said this must be a phrase admitted by them,) what does this
mean but the truth and eternity of the substance from which
He is begotten? for it is not different in kind, lest it be
combined with the substance of God, as something foreign
and unlike it. Nor is He like only outwardly, lest He
seem in some respect or wholly to be other in substance, as
brass shines like gold and silver like tin. For these are foreign
and of other nature, and are separated off from each other in
nature and qualities, nor is brass proper to gold, nor is the
² vid. de pigeon born from the dove²; but though they are considered
Syn §.
41. Hyp. like, yet they differ in substance. If then it be thus with the
Mel. et Son, let Him be a creature as we are, and not One in sub-
Euseb.
stance; but if the Son is Word, Wisdom, Image of the Father,
Radiance, He must in all reason be One in substance. For
³ si i. e. unless³ it be proved that He is not from God, but an instru-
si μη
⁴ ὄργανον ment⁴ different in nature and different in substance, surely
the Council was sound in its doctrine and apposite in its
decree ᶜ.

§. 24.   11. Further, let every corporeal thought be banished on this
subject; and transcending every imagination of sense, let us,
with the pure understanding and with mind alone, apprehend
⁵ γνήσιον the Son's genuine ⁵ relation towards the Father, and the Word's
⁶ἰδιότητα proper⁶ relation towards God, and the unvarying⁷ likeness
⁷ ἀπα-
ράλλακ- of the radiance towards the light: for as the words " Offspring"
τον   and " Son" bear, and are meant to bear, no human sense, but
one suitable to God, in like manner when we hear the phrase
" one in substance," let us not fall upon human senses, and
imagine partitions and divisions of the Godhead, but as
having our thoughts directed to things immaterial, let us

ᶜ As " of the substance" declared " likeness," even " like in substance"
that our Lord was *uncreate*, so " one answering for this purpose, for such
in substance" declared that He was *equal* phrases might all be understood of *re-*
with the Father; no term derived from *semblance* or *representation*. vid. note t.

preserve undivided the oneness of nature and the identity of light; for this is proper to the Son as regards the Father, and in this is shewn that God is truly Father of the Word. Here again, the illustration of light and its radiance is in point[d]. Who will presume to say that the radiance is unlike and foreign from the sun? rather who, thus considering the radiance relatively to the sun, and the identity of the light, would not say with confidence, " Truly the light and the radiance are one, and the one is manifested in the other, and the radiance is in the sun, so that whoso sees this, sees that also?" but such a oneness and natural possession[1], [ἰδιότητα] what should it be named by those who believe and see aright, but Offspring one in substance? and God's Offspring what should we fittingly and suitably consider, but the Word, and Wisdom, and Power? which it were a sin to say was foreign from the Father, or a crime even to imagine as other than with Him everlastingly.

12. For by this Offspring the Father made all things, and extending His Providence unto all things, by Him He exercises His love to man, and thus He and the Father are one, as has been said; unless indeed these perverse men make a fresh attempt, and say that the substance of the Word is not the same as the Light which is in Him from the Father, as if the Light in the Son were one with the Father, but He Himself foreign in substance as being a creature. Yet this is simply the belief of Caiaphas and Samosatene, which the Church cast out, but they now are disguising; and by this they fell from the truth, and were declared to be heretics. For if He partakes in fulness the light from the Father, why is He not rather that which others partake[2], that there be no medium introduced between Himself and the Father? Otherwise, it is no longer clear that all things were generated by the Son, but by Him, of whom He too partakes[e]. And if

[2] vid. p. 15. note c.

---

[d] Athan. has just used the illustration of radiance in reference to " of the substance:" and now he says that it equally illustrates " one in substance;" the light diffused from the sun being at once contemporaneous and homogeneous with its original.

[e] The point in which perhaps all the ancient heresies concerning our Lord's divine nature agreed, was in considering His different titles to be those of different beings or subjects, or not really and properly to belong to one and the same person; so that the Word was not the Son, or the Radiance not the Word, or our Lord was the Son, but only improperly the Word, not the true Word, Wisdom, or Radiance. Paul of Samosata, Sabellius, and Arius, agreed in considering that the Son was a creature,

NICEN. DEF. this is the Word, the Wisdom of the Father, in whom the Father is revealed and known, and frames the world, and without whom the Father doth nothing, evidently He it is who is from the Father: for all things generated partake of Him, as partaking of the Holy Ghost. And being such, He cannot be from nothing, nor a creature at all, but rather the proper Offspring from the Father as the radiance from light.

and that He was called, made after, or inhabited by the impersonal attribute called the Word or Wisdom. When the Word or Wisdom was held to be personal, it became the doctrine of Nestorius.

CHAP. VI.

AUTHORITIES IN SUPPORT OF THE COUNCIL.

Theognostus; Dionysius of Alexandria, Dionysius of Rome; Origen.

1. THIS then is the sense in which the Fathers at Nicæa made use of these expressions; but next that they did not invent them for themselves, (since this is one of their excuses,) but spoke what they had received from their predecessors, proceed we to prove this also, to cut off even this excuse from them. Know then, O Arians, foes of Christ, that Theognostus[a], a learned man, did not decline the phrase "of the substance," for in the second book of his Hypotyposes, he writes thus of the Son:—

"The substance of the Son is not any thing procured from without, nor accruing out of nothing[b], but it sprang from the Father's substance, as the radiance of light, as the vapour[c] of water; for neither the radiance, nor the vapour, is the water itself or the sun itself, nor is it alien; but it is an effluence of the Father's substance, which, however, suffers no partition. For as the sun remains the same, and is not impaired by the rays poured forth by it, so neither does the Father's substance suffer change, though it has the Son as an Image of Itself[d]."

Theognostus then, after first investigating in the way of an

[a] Athanasius elsewhere calls him "the admirable and excellent." ad Serap. iv. 9. He was Master of the Catechetical school of Alexandria towards the end of the 3d century, being a scholar, or at least a follower of Origen. His seven books of Hypotyposes treated of the Holy Trinity, of angels, and evil spirits, of the Incarnation, and the Creation. Photius, who gives this account, Cod 106, accuses him of heterodoxy on these points; which Athanasius in a measure admits, as far as the wording of his treatise went, when he speaks of his "investigating by way of exercise." Eusebius does not mention him at all.

[b] Vid above §. 15. fin. " God was alone," says Tertullian, "because there was nothing external to Him, *extrinsecus*, yet not even then alone, for He had with Him, what He had in Himself, His Reason" in Prax. 5 Non per adoptionem spiritus filius fit *extrinsecus*, sed naturâ filius est. Origen. Periarch. 1. 2. n. 4.

[c] From Wisdom 7, 25 and so Origen. Periarch. 1. 2. n. 5. and 9. and Athan. de Sent. Dionys. 15.

[d] It is sometimes erroneously supposed that such illustrations as this are intended to *explain* how the Sacred Mystery in question is possible, whereas they are merely intended to shew that the words we use concerning it are not *self-contradictory*, which is the objec-

exercise [e], proceeds to lay down his sentiments in the foregoing words.

2. Next, Dionysius, who was Bishop of Alexandria, upon his writing against Sabellius and expounding at large the Saviour's economy according to the flesh, and thence proving against the Sabellians that not the Father but His Word was made flesh, as John has said, was suspected of saying that the Son was a thing made and generated, and not one in substance with the Father; on this he writes to his namesake Dionysius, Bishop of Rome, to explain that this was a slander upon him [f]. And he assured him that he had not called the Son made, nay, did confess Him to be even one in substance. And his words run thus:—

" And I have written in another letter a refutation of the false

---

tion most commonly brought against them. To say that the doctrine of the Son's generation does not intrench upon the Father's perfection and immutability, or negative the Son's eternity, seems at first sight inconsistent with what the words Father and Son mean, till another image is adduced, such as the sun and radiance, in which that alleged inconsistency is seen to exist in fact. Here one image corrects another; and the accumulation of images is not, as is often thought, the restless and fruitless effect of the mind to *enter into the Mystery*, but is a *safeguard* against any one image, nay, any collection of images being supposed *sufficient*. If it be said that the language used concerning the sun and its radiance is but popular not philosophical, so again the Catholic language concerning the Holy Trinity may, nay, must be economical, not adequate, conveying the truth, not in the tongues of angels, but under human modes of thought and speech.

[e] ἐν γυμνασίᾳ ἐξέτασις. And so §. 27. of Origen, ζητῶν καὶ γυμνάζων Constantine too, writing to Alexander and Arius, speaks of altercation, φυσικῆς τινος γυμνασίας ἕνεκα Socr. 1. 7. In somewhat a similar way, Athanasius speaks of Dionysius writing κατ' οἰκονομίαν, economically, or with reterence to certain persons addressed or objects contemplated, de Sent. D. 6. and 26.

[f] It is well known that the great development of the power of the See of Rome was later than the age of Athanasius, but it is here in place, to state historically some instances of an earlier date in which it interfered in the general conduct of the Church. S. Clement of Rome wrote a pastoral letter to the Corinthians, at a time when they seem to have been without a Bishop. The heretic Marcion, on his excommunication at home, came to Rome upon the death of Hyginus the ninth Bishop, and was repulsed by the elders of the see. Epiph Hær. 42. n. 1. Polycarp came to Anicetus on the question of Easter. Euseb. Hist. iv. 14. Soter, not only sent alms to the Churches of Christendom generally, according to the primitive custom of his Church, but " exhorted affectionately the brethren who came up thither as a father his children." ibid. iv. 23. Victor denounced the Asian Churches for observing Easter after the Jewish custom. ibid. v. 24. Paul of Samosata was put out of the see house at Antioch by the civil power, on the decision of " the Bishops of Italy and of Rome." ibid. vii. 30. For a consideration of this subject, as far as it is an objection to the Anglican view of ecclesiastical polity, the reader is referred to Mr Palmer's Treatise on the Church, vii. 3 and 4. where five reasons are assigned for the early pre-eminence of the Roman Church, the number of its clergy and people, its wealth and charity. its apostolical origin, the purity of its faith, and the temporal dignity of the city of Rome.

charge they bring against me, that I deny that Christ was one in substance with God. For though I say that I have not found this term any where in Holy Scripture, yet my remarks which follow, and which they have not noticed, are not inconsistent with that belief. For I instanced a human production as being evidently homogeneous, and I observed that undeniably parents differed from their children only in not being the same individuals, otherwise there could be neither parents nor children. And my letter, as I said before, owing to present circumstances I am unable to produce; or I would have sent you the very words I used, or rather a copy of it all, which, if I have an opportunity, I will do still. But I am sure from recollection that I adduced parallels of things kindred with each other; for instance, that a plant grown from seed or from root, was other than that from which it sprang, yet was altogether one in nature with it [g]: and that a stream flowing from a fountain, gained a new name, for that neither the fountain was called stream, nor the stream fountain, and both existed, and the stream was the water from the fountain."

3. And that the Word of God is not a work or creature, but an offspring proper to the Father's substance and indivisible, as the great Council wrote, here you may see in the words of Dionysius, Bishop of Rome, who, while writing against the Sabellians, thus inveighs against those who dared to say so:—

§. 26.

"Next, I reasonably turn to those who divide and cut into pieces and destroy that most sacred doctrine of the Church of God, the Divine Monarchy [h], making it certain three powers and partitive [i] ¹μιμιριςμίνας

---

[g] The Eusebians at Nicæa objected to this image, Socr. 1. 8. as implying that the Son was a προβολὴ, issue or development, as Valentinus taught. Epiph Hær. 69. 7. Athanasius elsewhere uses it himself.

[h] By the Monarchy is meant the doctrine that the Second and Third Persons in the Ever-blessed Trinity are ever to be referred in our thoughts to the First as the Fountain of Godhead, vid. p. 25. note e. and p. 33. note r. It is one of the especial senses in which God is said to be one. "We are not introducing three origins or three Fathers, as the Marcionites and Manichees, just as our illustration is not of three suns, but of sun and its radiance." Orat. iii. §. 15. vid. also iv. §. 1 "The Father is union, ἕνωσις," says S. Greg. Naz. "from whom and unto whom are the others." Orat 42.

15. also Orat. 20. 7. and Epiph. Hær. 57. 5. Tertullian, before Dionysius, uses the word Monarchia, which Praxeas had perverted into a kind of Unitarianism or Sabellianism, in Prax. 3. Irenæus too wrote on the Monarchy, i. e against the doctrine that God is the author of evil. Eus. Hist. v. 20. And before him was Justin's work de Monarchiâ, where the word is used in opposition to Polytheism. The Marcionites, whom Dionysius presently mentions, are also specified in the above extract by Athan. vid. also Cyril. Hier. Cat. xvi. 4. Epiphanius says that their three origins were God, the Creator, and the evil spirit. Hær. 42, 3 or as Augustine says, the good, the just, and the wicked, which may be taken to mean nearly the same thing. Hær. 22. The Apostolical Canons denounce those who baptize into Three Unoriginate; vid.

NICEN. DEF.

¹ ἐμφιλο-χωρεῖν

subsistences¹ and godheads three. I am told that some among you who are catechists and teachers of the Divine Word, take the lead in this tenet, who are diametrically opposed, so to speak, to Sabellius's opinions; for he blasphemously says that the Son is the Father, and the Father the Son, but they in some sort preach three Gods, as dividing the Holy Unity into three subsistences foreign to each other and utterly separate For it must needs be that with the God of the Universe, the Divine Word is one, and the Holy Ghost must repose¹ and habitate in God; thus in one as in a summit, I mean the God of the Universe, must the Divine Trinity ᵏ be gathered up and brought together For it is the doctrine of the presumptuous Marcion, to sever and divide the Divine Monarchy into three origins,—a devil's teaching, not that of Christ's true disciples and lovers of the Saviour's lessons For they know well that a Trinity is preached by divine Scripture, but that neither Old Testament nor New preaches three Gods.

4. Equally must one censure those who hold the Son to be a work, and consider that the Lord has come into being, as one of things which really came to be; whereas the divine oracles witness to a generation suitable to Him and becoming, but not to any fashioning or making. A blasphemy then is it, not ordinary, but

---

also Athan. Tom ad Antioch. 5. Naz. Orat. 20. 6. Basil denies τρεῖς ἀρχικαὶ ὑποστάσεις, de Sp. S. 38. which is a Platonic phrase.

¹ And so Dionysius of Alexandria in a fragment preserved by S. Basil, " If because the subsistences are three, they say that they are partitive, μεμερισμένας, still three there are, though these persons dissent, or they utterly destroy the Divine Trinity." de Sp. S. n. 72. Athan. expresses the same more distinctly, οὐ τρεῖς ὑποστάσεις μεμερισμένας, Expos. Fid. §. 2. In S. Greg. Naz. we find ἀμέριστος ἐν μεμερισμένοις ἡ θεότης Orat. 31. 14. Elsewhere for μιμ. he substitutes ἀτιῤῥήγνυμαι Orat 20. 6. ἀτιξινω-μέναις ἀλλήλων καὶ διισπασμέναις Orat. 23. 6. as infra ξένας ἀλλήλων πανταπασι κεχω-ρισμένας The passage in the text comes into question in the controversy about the ἐξ ὑποστάσεως ἢ οὐσίας of the Nicene Creed, of which infra on the Creed itself in Eusebius's Letter

ᵏ The word τριὰς translated Trinity is first used by Theophilus, ad Autol. II. 15 Gibbon remarks that the doctrine of " a numerical rather than a generical unity," which has been explicitly put forth by the Latin Church, is "favoured by the Latin language; τριὰς seems to excite the idea of substance, trinitas of qualities." ch. 21 note 74. It is certain that the Latin view of the sacred truth, when perverted, becomes Sabellianism; and that the Greek, when perverted, becomes Arianism; and we find Arius arising in the East, Sabellius in the West. It is also certain that the word Trinitas is properly abstract, and expresses τριὰς or " a three," only in an ecclesiastical sense. But Gibbon does not seem to observe that Unitas is abstract as well as Trinitas; and that we might just as well say in consequence, that the Latins held an abstract unity or a unity of qualities, while the Greeks by μονὰς taught the doctrine of " a one" or a numerical unity. " Singularitatem hanc dico, says S Ambrose, quod Græcè μονότης dicitur, singularitas ad personam pertinet, unitas ad naturam." de Fid. v. 1. It is important, however, to understand, that " Trinity" does not mean the *state* or *condition* of being three, as humanity is the condition of being man, but is synonymous with " three persons" Humanity does not exist and cannot be addressed, but the Holy Trinity is a three, or a unity which exists in three. Apparently from not considering this, Luther and Calvin objected to the word Trinity, " It is a common prayer," says Calvin, " Holy Trinity, one God, have mercy on us It displeases me, and savours throughout of barbarism." Ep. ad Polon. p. 796.

Heresy of making the Son a creature. 47

even the highest, to say that the Lord is in any sort a handiwork. For if He came to be Son, once He was not; but He was always, if (that is) He be in the Father, as He says Himself, and if the Christ be Word and Wisdom and Power, (which, as ye know, divine Scripture says,) and these attributes be powers of God If then the Son came into being once, these attributes were not; consequently there was a time, when God was without them ; which is most extravagant. And why say more on these points to you, men full of the Spirit and well aware of the extravagances which come to view from saying that the Son is a work? Not attending, as I consider, to this circumstance, the authors of this opinion have entirely missed the truth, in explaining, contrary to the sense of divine and prophetic Scripture in the passage, the words, *The Lord hath created Me a beginning of His ways unto His works.* For the sense of *He created,* as ye know, is not one, for we must understand *He created* in this place, as ' He set over the works made by Him,' that is, 'made by the Son Himself.' And *He created* here must not be taken for *made,* for creating differs from making; *Is not He Thy Father that hath bought thee? hath He not made thee and created thee?* says Moses in his great song in Deuteronomy. And one may say to them, O men of great hazard, is He a work, who is *the First-born of every creature, who is born from the womb before the morning star,* who said, as Wisdom, *Before all the hills He begets Me?* And in many passages of the divine oracles is the Son said to have been [1] generated, but now here to have [2] come into being; which manifestly convicts those of misconception about the Lord's generation, who presume to call His [1] divine and ineffable generation a making [1] Neither then may we divide into three Godheads the wonderful and divine Unity , nor [2] disparage with the name of ' work' the dignity and exceeding majesty of the Lord ; but we must believe in God the Father Almighty, and in Christ Jesus His Son, and in the Holy Ghost, and hold that to the God of the universe the Word is united. For *I*, says He, *and the Father are one* , and, *I in the Father and the*

CHAP. VI.

Prov. 8, 22.

Deut. 32, 6.

Col 1, 15.

Ps. 110, 3.
Prov. 8, 25.

γίγνεσθαι
γεγονέναι

---

[1] This extract discloses to us, (in connexion with the passages from Dionysius Alex here and in the de Sent. D.) a remarkable anticipation of the Arian controversy in the third century. 1. It appears that the very symbol of ἦν ὅτε οὐκ ἦν, " once He was not," was asserted or implied ; vid also the following extract from Origen, §. 27. and Origen Periarchon, iv. 28. where mention is also made of the ἐξ οὐκ ὄντων, " out of nothing," which was the Arian symbol in opposition to " of the substance." Allusions are made besides, to " the Father not being always Father," de Sent D. 15. and " the Word being brought to be by the true Word, and Wisdom by the true Wisdom;" ibid. 25. 2. The same special text is used in defence of the heresy, and that not at first sight an obvious one, which is found among the Arians, Prov 8, 22. 3. The same texts were used by the Catholics, which occur in the Arian controversy. e. g. Deut. 32, 6. against Prov. 8, 22. and such as Ps. 110, 3. Prov. 8, 25. and the two John 10, 30. and 14, 10. 4. The same Catholic symbols and statements are found, e. g. " begotten not made," " one in substance," " Trinity," ἀδιαίρετον, ἄναρχον, ἀΐδιος, light from light, &c. Much might be said on this circumstance, as forming part of the proof of the very early date of the development and formation of the Catholic theology, which we are at first sight apt to ascribe to the 4th and 5th centuries.

NICEN. DEF. *Father in Me.* For thus both the Divine Trinity, and the holy preaching of the Monarchy, will be preserved."

§. 27. 5. And concerning the everlasting co-existence of the Word with the Father, and that He is not of another substance or subsistence, but proper to the Father's, as the Bishops in the Council said, hear again from the labour-loving[m] Origen also. For what he has written as if inquiring and exercising himself, that let no one take as expressive of his own sentiments, but of parties who are disputing in the investigation, but what he[n] definitely declares, that is the sentiment of the labour-loving man. After his exercises[1] then against the heretics, straightway he introduces his personal belief, thus:—

[1] vid. p. 44, note e.

"If there be an Image of the Invisible God, it is an invisible Image; nay, I will be bold to add, that, as being the likeness of the Father, never was it not For else was that God, who, according to John, is called Light, (for *God is Light,*) without the radiance of His proper glory, that a man should presume to assert the Son's origin of existence, as if before He was not. But when was not that Image of the Father's Ineffable and Nameless and Unutterable subsistence, that Expression and Word, and He that knows the Father? for let him understand well who dares to say, 'Once the Son was not,' that he is saying, 'Once Wisdom was not,' and 'Word was not,' and 'Life was not.'"

6. And again elsewhere he says:—

"But it is not innocent nor without peril, if because of our weakness of understanding we deprive God, as far as in us lies, of the Only-begotten Word ever co-existing with Him; and the Wisdom in which He rejoiced; else He must be conceived as not always possessed of joy."

See, we are proving that this view has been transmitted from father to father; but ye, O modern Jews and disciples of Caiaphas, how many fathers can ye assign to

---

[m] φιλοπόνου. and so Serap. IV. 9.

[n] ἃ μὲν ὡς ζητῶν καὶ γυμνάζων ἔγραψι, ταῦτα μὴ ὡς αὐτοῦ φρονοῦντος δεχέσθω τις ἀλλὰ τῶν πρὸς ἔριν φιλονεικούντων ἐν τῷ ζητεῖν, ἀδιῶς ὁρίζων ἀποφαίνεται, τοῦτο

τοῦ φιλοπόνου τὸ φρόνημά ἐστι "ἀλλά. Certè legendum ἀλλ' ἅ, idque omnino exigit sensus" Montfaucon. Rather for ἀδιῶς read ἃ δὲ ὡς, and put the stop at ζητεῖν instead of δεχέσθω τις

The Nicene Council did but consign tradition to writing 49

your phrases? Not one of the understanding and wise; for all abhor you, but the devil alone[1]; none but he is your father in this apostasy, who both in the beginning scattered on you the seed of this irreligion, and now persuades you to slander the Ecumenical Council[o], for committing to writing, not your doctrines, but that which from the beginning those who were eye-witnesses and ministers of the Word have handed down to us[p]. For the faith which the Council has confessed in writing, that is the faith of the Catholic Church; to assert this, the blessed Fathers so expressed themselves while

CHAP. VI.
―――
[1] supr. p.
9. note s.

---

[o] vid. supr. §. 4. Orat. 1. §. 7. Ad Afros. 2 twice. Apol. contr. Arian. 7. ad Ep. Æg. 5. Epiph. Hær. 70. 9. Euseb. Vit Const. iii. 6. The Council was more commonly called μεγάλη vid. supr. § 26. The second General Council, A.D. 381, took the name of ecumenical. vid. Can. 6 fin. but incidentally. The Council of Ephesus so styles itself in the opening of its Synodical Letter.

[p] The profession under which the decrees of Councils come to us is that of setting forth in writing what has ever been held orally or implicitly in the Church. Hence the frequent use of such phrases as ἐγγραφῶς ἐξετέθη with reference to them. Thus Damasus, Theod. Hist. v. 10. speaks of that "apostolical faith, which was *set forth in writing* by the Fathers in Nicæa." On the other hand, Ephrem of Antioch, speaks of the doctrine of our Lord's perfect humanity being "inculcated by our Holy Fathers, but not as yet [i. e. till the Council of Chalcedon] being *confirmed* by the decree of an ecumenical Council" Phot. 229. p. 801. (ἐγγραφῶς, however, sometimes relates to the act of subscribing. Phot *ibid* or to Scripture, Clement. Strom. 1. init. p. 321.) Hence Athan. says ad Afros. 1 and 2. that "the Word of the Lord which was given through the ecumenical Council in Nicæa *remaineth for ever;*" and uses against its opposers the texts, "Remove not the ancient landmark which thy fathers have set," (vid. also Dionysius in Eus Hist. vii 7.) and "He that curseth his father or his mother, shall surely be put to death." Prov 22, 28. Ex. 21, 17. vid. also Athan. ad Epict. 1. And the Council of Chalcedon professes to "drive away the doctrines of error by a common decree, and *renew* the unswerving faith of the fathers,"

Act. v. p. 452. "as," they proceed, "from of old the prophets spoke of Christ, and He Himself instructed us, and the creed of the Fathers has delivered to us," whereas "other faith it is not lawful for any to bring forth, or to write, or to draw up, or to hold, or to teach." p 456. vid. S. Leo. supr. p. 5. note m. This, however, did not interfere with their *adding* without *undoing*. "For," says Vigilius, "if it were unlawful to receive aught further after the Nicene statutes, on what authority venture we to assert that the Holy Ghost is of one substance with the Father, which it is notorious was there omitted p." contr. Eutych v. init. he gives other instances, some in point, others not. vid also Eulogius, apud Phot Cod 23. pp. 829. 853 Yet to add to the *confession* of the Church is not to add to the *faith*, since nothing can be added to the faith Leo, Ep. 124. p. 1237. Nay, Athan. says that the Nicene faith is sufficient to refute every heresy, ad Max 5. fin. also Leo. Ep. 54. p. 956. and Naz. Ep 102. init. excepting, however, the doctrine of the Holy Spirit, which explains his meaning. The Henoticon of Zeno says the same, but with the intention of dealing a blow at the Council of Chalcedon. Evagr. iii. 14. p. 345. Aetius at Chalcedon says that at Ephesus and Chalcedon the Fathers did not profess to draw up an exposition of faith, and that Cyril and Leo did but *interpret the Creed.*" Conc t. 2 p. 428. Leo even says that the Apostles' Creed is sufficient against all heresies, and that Eutyches erred on a point "of which our Lord wished no one of either sex in the Church to be ignorant," and he wishes Eutyches to take the plenitude of the Creed "pure et simplici corde." Ep. 31. p 857, 8.

E

condemning the Arian heresy; and this is a chief reason why these apply themselves to calumniate the Council. For it is not the terms which trouble them[1], but that those terms prove them to be heretics, and presumptuous beyond other heresies.

CHAP VII

ON THE ARIAN SYMBOL "INGENERATE."

This term afterwards adopted by them; and why; three senses of it. A fourth sense Ingenerate denotes God in contrast to His creatures, not to His Son; Father the scriptural title instead, Conclusion.

1 THIS in fact was the reason, when the unsound nature of their phrases had been exposed at that time, and they were henceforth open to the charge of irreligion, that they proceeded to borrow of the Greeks the term Ingenerate [a], that, under shelter of it, they might reckon among the things generate and the creatures, that Word of God, by whom these very things came to be, so unblushing are they in their irreligion, so obstinate in their blasphemies against the Lord. If then this want of shame arises from ignorance of the term, they ought to learn of those who gave it them, and who have not scrupled to say that even intellect, which they derive from Good, and the soul which proceeds from intellect, though their respective origins be known, are notwithstanding ingenerate, for they understand that by so saying they do not disparage that first Origin of which the others come [b]. This being the case, let them

---

[a] ἀγένητον Opportunity will occur for noticing this celebrated word on Orat. 1. 30—34 where the present passage is partly re-written, partly transcribed. Mention is also made of it in the De Syn. 46, 47. Athanasius would seem to have been but partially acquainted with the writings of the Anomœans, whose symbol it was, and to have argued with them from the writings of the elder Arians, who had also made use of it.

[b] Montfaucon quotes a passage from Plato's Phædrus, in which the human soul is called "ingenerate and immortal," but Athan is referring to another subject, the Platonic, or rather the Eclectic Trinity Thus Theodoret, " Plotinus, and Numenius, explaining the sense of Plato, say, that he taught Three principles beyond time and eternal, Good, Intellect, and the Soul of all," de Affect. Cur. 11. p. 750. And so Plotinus himself, " It is as if one were to place Good as the centre, Intellect like an immoveable circle round, and Soul a moveable circle, and moveable by appetite." 4 Ennead. iv. c. 16. vid. Porphyry in Cyril. contr. Julian. viii. p. 271. vid. ibid. 1. p. 32. Plot. 3 Ennead.

52 *Arians used phrases, neither in nor according to Scripture.*

NICEN. DEF.
say the like themselves, or else not speak at all, of what they do not know. But if they consider they are acquainted with the subject, then they must be interrogated; for ^c the expression is not from divine Scripture[1], but they are contentious, as elsewhere, for unscriptural positions. Just as I have related the reason and sense, with which the Council and the Fathers before it defined and published " of the substance," and " one in substance," agreeably to what Scripture says of the Saviour; so now let them, if they can, answer on their part what has led them to this unscriptural phrase, and in what sense they call God Ingenerate?

[1] supr. p. 31. note p

2. In truth, I am told^d, that the name has different senses; philosophers say that it means, first, " what has not yet, but may, come to be;" next, " what neither exists, nor can come into being;" and thirdly, " what exists indeed, but was neither generated nor had origin of being, but is everlasting and indestructible^e." Now perhaps they will wish to pass over the

---

v. 2 and 3. Athan.'s testimony that the Platonists considered their three ὑποστάσεις all ingenerate is perhaps a singular one. In 5 Ennead. iv. 1. Plotinus says what seems contrary to it, ἡ δὲ ἀρχὴ ἀγέννητος, speaking of His τἀγαθόν. Yet Plato, quoted by Theodoret, ibid. p. 749, speaks of εἴτε ἀρχὴν εἴτε ἀρχάς

^c ἐπεὶ μάλιστα, ὅτι μάλιστα, Orat. 1. § 36. de Syn. §. 21. fin. ὅταν μάλιστα Apol. ad Const. 23. καὶ μάλιστα, de Syn. §. 42. 54.

^d And so de Syn. §. 46. " we have on *careful inquiry* ascertained, &c." Again, " I have acquainted myself on their account [the Arians'] with the meaning of ἀγέννητον." Orat. 1. §. 30. This is remarkable, for Athan. was a man of liberal education, as his Orat. contr. Gent and de Incarn. shew, especially his acquaintance with the Platonic philosophy. Sulpicius too speaks of him as a jurisconsultus, Sacr Hist. ii. 50. St. Gregory Naz. says, that he gave some attention, but not much, to the subjects of general education, τῶν ἐγκυκλίων, that he might not be altogether ignorant, of what he nevertheless despised, Orat. 21. 6. In the same way S. Basil, whose cultivation of mind none can doubt, speaks slightingly of his own philosophical knowledge. He writes of his " neglecting his own weakness, and being utterly unexercised in such disquisitions," contr. Eunom. init. And so in de Sp. §. 5. he says, that " they who have given time" to vain philosophy, " divide causes into principal, co-operative," &c. Elsewhere he speaks of having " expended much time on vanity, and wasted nearly all his youth in the vain labour of pursuing the studies of that wisdom which God has made foolishness," Ep. 223. 2. In truth, Christianity has a philosophy of its own. Thus in the commencement of his Viæ Dux Anastasius says, " It is a first point to be understood, that the tradition of the Catholic Church does not proceed upon, or follow, the philosophical definitions in all respects, and especially as regards the mystery of Christ, and the doctrine of the Trinity, but a certain rule of its own, evangelical and apostolical " p. 20.

^e Four senses of ἀγέννητον are enumerated, Orat. i. §. 30. 1. What is not as yet, but is possible; 2. what neither has been, nor can be; 3. what exists, but has not come to be from any cause; 4. what is not made, but is ever. Only two senses are specified in the de Syn. §. 46. and in these the question really lies; 1. what is, but without a cause, 2. uncreate.

The equivocation of the word Ingenerate.

first two senses, from the absurdity which follows; for according to the first, things that already have come to be, and things that are expected to be, are ingenerate; and the second is more extravagant still; accordingly they will proceed to the third sense, and use the word in it: though here, in this sense too, their irreligion will be quite as great. For if by Ingenerate they mean what has no origin of being, nor is generated or created, but eternal, and say that the Word of God is contrary to this, who comprehends not the craft of these foes of God? who but would stone[f] such madmen? for, when they are ashamed to bring forward again those first phrases which they fabled, and which were condemned, the bad men have taken another way to signify them, by means of what they call Ingenerate. For if the Son be of things generate, it follows, that He too came to be from nothing; and if He has an origin of being, then He was not before His generation; and if He is not eternal, there was once when He was not[g]. If these are their sentiments, they ought to signify their heterodoxy in their own phrases, and not to hide their perverseness under the cloke of the Ingenerate. But instead of this, the evil-minded men are busy with their craftiness after their father, the devil; for as he attempts to deceive in the guise of others, so these have broached the term Ingenerate, that they might pretend to speak piously of

§. 29.

---

[f] Βαλλιέθωσαν παρὰ πάντων, Orat. ii. §. 28. An apparent allusion to the punishment of blasphemy and idolatry under the Jewish Law. vid. reference to Ex 21, 17, in page 49, note p. Thus, e.g. Nazianzen "While I go up the mount with good heart, that I may become within the cloud, and may hold converse with God, for so God bids; if there be any Aaron, let him go up with me and stand near. And if there be any Nadab or Abiud, or of the elders, let him go up, but stand far off, according to the measure of his purification.... But if any one is an evil and savage beast, and quite incapable of science and theology; let him stand off still further, and depart from the mount; *or he will be stoned* and crushed, for the wicked shall be miserably destroyed. For as stones for the bestial are true words and strong. Whether he be leopard, let him die spots and all," &c. &c. Orat. 28. 2.

[g] The Arians argued that the word *Ingenerate* implied *generate* or *creature* as its correlative, and therefore indirectly signified *Creator;* so that the Son being not ingenerate, was not the Creator. Athan answers, that in the use of the word, whether there be a Son does not come into the question. As the idea of Father and Son does not include creation, so that of creator and creature does not include generation; and it would be as illogical to infer that there are no creatures because there is a Son, as that there is no Son because there are creatures. Or, more closely, as a thing generate, though not the Father, is not therefore Son, so the Son though not Ingenerate is not therefore a thing generate. vid. p. 33, note r.

God, yet might cherish a concealed blasphemy against the Lord, and under this covering might teach it to others.

3. However, on the detecting of this sophism, what remains to them? "We have found another," say the evil-doers; and then proceed to add to what they have said already, that Ingenerate means what has no author of being, but stands itself in this relation to things generate. Unthankful, and in truth deaf to the Scriptures! who do every thing, and say every thing, not to honour God, but to dishonour the Son, ignorant that he who dishonours the Son, dishonours the Father. For first, even though they denote God in this way, still the Word is not proved to be of things generated. For if He be viewed as offspring of the substance of the Father, He is of consequence with Him eternally. For this name of offspring does not detract from the nature of the Word, nor does Ingenerate take its sense from contrast with the Son, but with the things which come to be through the Son; and as he who addresses an architect, and calls him framer of house or city, does not under this designation allude to the son who is begotten from him, but on account of the art and science which he displays in his work, calls him artificer, signifying thereby that he is not such as the things made by him, and while he knows the nature of the builder, knows also that he whom he begets is other than his works; and in regard to his son calls him father, but in regard to his works, creator and maker; in like manner he who says in this sense that God is ingenerate, names Him from His works, signifying, not only that He is not generate, but that He is maker of things which are so; yet is aware withal that the Word is other than the things generate, and alone a proper[1] offspring of the Father, through whom all things came to be and consist [h].

[1] ἴδιον

§. 30. 4. In like manner, when the Prophets spoke of God as Allpowerful, they did not so name Him, as if the Word were included in that All[2], (for they knew that the Son was other than things generate, and Sovereign over them Himself, according to His likeness to the Father;) but because He is Sovereign over all things which through the Son He has made, and

[2] ἵνα τῶν πάντων

[h] The whole of this passage is repeated in Orat. 1. 33. &c. vid. for this particular argument, Basil also, contr. Eunom. 1. 16.

has given the authority of all things to the Son, and having given it, is Himself once more the Lord of all things through the Word. Again, when they called God, Lord of the powers[1], they said not this as if the Word was one of those powers, but because, while He is Father of the Son, He is Lord of the powers which through the Son have come to be. For again, the Word too, as being in the Father, is Lord of them all, and Sovereign over all; for all things, whatsoever the Father hath, are the Son's. This then being the force of such titles, in like manner let a man call God ingenerate, if it so please him; not however as if the Word were of generate things, but because, as I said before, God not only is not generate, but through His proper Word is He the maker of things which are so. For though the Father be called such, still the Word is the Father's Image and one in substance with Him; and being His Image, He must be distinct from things generate, and from every thing; for whose Image He is, to Him hath He it to be proper[2] and to be like: so that he who calls the Father ingenerate and almighty, perceives in the Ingenerate and the Almighty, His Word and His Wisdom, which is the Son. But these wondrous men, and prompt for irreligion, hit upon the term Ingenerate, not as caring for God's honour, but from malevolence towards the Saviour; for if they had regard to honour and blessing, it rather had been right and good to acknowledge and to call God Father, than to give Him this name; for in calling God ingenerate, they are, as I said before, calling Him from things which came to be, and as a Maker only, that so they may imply the Word to be a work after their own pleasure; but he who calls God Father, in Him withal signifies His Son also, and cannot fail to know that, whereas there is a Son, through this Son all things that came to be were created.

5. Therefore it will be much more accurate to denote God from the Son and to call Him Father, than to name Him and call Him Ingenerate from His works only; for the latter term refers to the works that have come to be at the will of God through the Word, but the name of Father points out the proper offspring from His substance. And whereas the Word surpasses things generate, by so much and more also doth calling God Father surpass the calling Him Ingenerate;

[1] i. e. of hosts.
[2] τὴν ἰδιότητα

NICEN. DEF.

for the latter is unscriptural and suspicious, as it has various senses; but the foimer is simple and scriptural, and more accurate, and alone implies the Son. And " Ingenerate" is a word of the Greeks who know not the Son: but " Father" has been acknowledged and vouchsafed by our Lord; for He, John 14, knowing Himself whose Son He was, said, *I in the Father* 10, 9. *and the Father in Me;* and, *He that hath seen Me hath* John 10, 30. *seen the Father;* and, *I and the Father are one;* but no where is He found to call the Father Ingenerate. Moreover, when He teaches us to pray, He says not, " When ye pray, Mat. 6, say, O God Ingenerate," but rather, *When ye pray, say, Our* 9. *Father, which art in heaven.* And it was His Will, that the Summary of our faith should have the same bearing. For He has bid us be baptized, not in the name of Ingenerate and generate, not into the name of uncreate and creature, but into the name of Father, Son, and Holy Ghost [1]; for with such an initiation we too are made sons verily [k], and using the

---

[1] And so St. Basil, " Our faith was not in Framer and Work, but in Father and Son were we sealed through the grace in baptism." contr, Eunom. 11. 22. And a somewhat similar passage occurs Orat. 11 §. 41.

[k] υἱοποιούμεθα ἀληθῶς This strong term " truly" or " verily" seems taken from such passages as speak of the " grace and truth" of the Gospel, John 1. 12—17. Again St. Basil says, that we are sons, κυρίως, " properly," and πρώτως " primarily," in opposition to τροπικῶς, " figuratively," contr Eunom. 11. 23. St Cyril too says, that we are sons "naturally" φυσικῶς as well as κατὰ χάριν, vid. Suicer Thesaur v υἱός 1 3 Of these words, ἀληθῶς, φυσικῶς, κυρίως, and πρώτως, the first two are commonly reserved for our Lord, e g. τὸν ἀληθῶς υἱόν, Orat 11. § 37 ἡμεῖς υἱοὶ, οὐκ ὡς ἐκεῖνος φύσει καὶ ἀληθείᾳ, 111 §. 19. Hilary seems to deny us the title of " proper" sons, de Trin. xii 15, but his " proprium" is a translation of ἴδιον, not κυρίως. And when Justin says of Christ, ὁ μόνος λεγόμενος κυρίως υἱὸς, Apol. 11. 6 κυρίως seems to be used in reference to the word κύριος Lord, which he has just been using, κυριολογεῖν, being sometimes used by him as others in the sense of " naming as Lord," like θεολογεῖν. vid. Tryph. 56

There is a passage in Justin's ad Græc. 21. where he (or the writer) when speaking of ἐγώ εἰμι ὁ ὤν, uses the word in the same ambiguous sense; οὐδὲν γὰρ ὄνομα ἐπὶ θεοῦ κυριολογεῖσθαι δυνατὸν, 21, as if κύριος, the Lord, by which " I am" is translated, were a sort of symbol of that proper name of God which cannot be given. But to return, the true doctrine then is, that, whereas there is a primary and secondary sense in which the word Son is used, primary when it has its formal meaning of continuation of nature, and secondary when it is used nominally, or for an external resemblance to the first meaning, it is applied to the regenerate, not in the secondary sense, but in the primary. St. Basil and St. Gregory Nyssen consider Son to be " a term of *relationship* according to *nature*," (vid. supr. p. 16, note k,) also Basil in Psalm 28, 1. The actual presence of the Holy Spirit in the regenerate in *substance*, (vid. Cyril. Dial. 7. p 638.) constitutes this relationship of nature; and hence after the words quoted from St. Cyril in the beginning of this note, in which he says, that we are sons, φυσικῶς, he proceeds, " naturally, because *we are in Him*, and in Him alone." vid. Athan.'s

Novel terms of heresy met by new terms of orthodoxy. 57

name of the Father, we acknowledge from that name, the Word in the Father. But if He wills that we should call His own Father our Father, we must not on that account measure ourselves with the Son according to nature, for it is because of the Son that the Father is so called by us; for since the Word bore our body and came to be[1] in us, therefore by reason of the Word in us, is God called our Father. For the Spirit of the Word in us, names through us His own Father as ours, which is the Apostle's meaning when he says, *God hath sent forth the Spirit of His Son into your hearts, crying, Abba, Father.*

CHAP. VII

[1] γίγονε ἐν ἡμῖν

Gal. 4, 6.

6. But perhaps being refuted as touching the term Ingenerate also, they will say, according to their evil nature, "It behoved, as regards our Lord and Saviour Jesus Christ also, to state from the Scriptures[2] what is there written of Him, and not to introduce unscriptural expressions." Yes, it behoved, say I too; for the tokens of truth are more exact as drawn from Scripture, than from other sources[1]; but the ill disposition and the versatile and crafty irreligion of the Eusebians, compelled the Bishops, as I said before, to publish more distinctly the terms which overthrow their irreligion; and what the Council did write has already been shewn to have an orthodox sense, while the Arians have been shewn to be corrupt in their expressions, and evil in their dispositions.

§. 32.

[2] supr p. 52.

---

words which follow in the text at the end of §. 31. And hence Nyssen lays down, as a received truth, that "to none does the term 'proper,' κυριώτατον, apply, but to one in whom the name responds with truth to the nature," contr Eunom. III. p. 123. And he also implies, p 117, the intimate association of our sonship with Christ's, when he connects together regeneration with our Lord's eternal generation, neither being διὰ ταθοὺς, or, by the will of the flesh. If it be asked, what the *distinctive* words are which are incommunicably the Son's, since so much is man's, it is obvious to answer, ἴδιος υἱός and μονογενής, which are in Scripture, and the symbols " of the substance," and " one in substance," of the Council; and this is the value of the Council's phrases, that, while they guard the Son's divinity, they allow full scope, without risk of entrenching on it, to the Catholic doctrine of the fulness of the Christian privileges. vid. supr. p. 32. note q.

[1] " The holy and inspired Scriptures are sufficient of themselves for the preaching of the truth; yet there are also many treatises of our blessed teachers composed for this purpose." contr. Gent. init. " For studying and mastering the Scriptures, there is need of a good life and a pure soul, and virtue according to Christ," Incarn. 57. " Since divine Scriptures is more sufficient than any thing else, I recommend persons who wish to know fully concerning these things," (the doctrine of the blessed Trinity,) " to read the divine oracles," ad Ep. Æg. 4. " The Scriptures are sufficient for teaching; but it is good for us to exhort each other in the faith, and to refresh each other with discourses." Vit. S. Ant. 16. And passim in Athan.

NICEN. DEF. The term Ingenerate, having its own sense, and admitting of a religious use, they nevertheless, according to their own idea, and as they will, use for the dishonour of the Saviour, all for the sake of contentiously maintaining, like giants [m], their fight with God. But as they did not escape condemnation when they adduced these former phrases, so when they misconceive of the Ingenerate which in itself admits of being used well and religiously, they were detected, being disgraced before all, and their heresy every where proscribed.

7. This then, as I could, have I related, by way of explaining what was formerly done in the Council; but I know that the contentious among Christ's foes will not be disposed to change even after hearing this, but will ever search about for other pretences, and for others again after those. For as the Prophet speaks, *If the Ethiopian change his skin, or the leopard his spots*, then will they be willing to think religiously, who have been instructed in irreligion. Thou however, Beloved, on receiving this, read it by thyself; and if thou approvest of it, read it also to the brethren who happen to be present, that they too on hearing it, may welcome the Council's zeal for the truth, and the exactness of its sense; and may condemn that of Christ's foes, the Arians, and the futile pretences, which for the sake of their irreligious heresy they have been at the pains to frame for each other; because to God and the Father is due the glory, honour, and worship with His co-existent Son and Word, together with the All-holy and Life-giving Spirit, now and unto endless ages of ages. Amen.

Jer. 13, 23.

[m] And so, Orat. ii. §. 32. κατὰ τοὺς μυθευομένους γίγαντας And so Nazianzen, Orat. 43. 26. speaking of the disorderly Bishops during the Arian ascendancy. Also Socr. v. 10. p. 268. d. Sometimes the Scripture giants are spoken of, sometimes the mythological

APPENDIX.

LETTER OF EUSEBIUS OF CÆSAREA TO THE PEOPLE OF HIS DIOCESE [a].

1. WHAT was transacted concerning ecclesiastical faith at the Great Council assembled at Nicæa, you have probably learned, Beloved, from other sources, rumour being wont to precede the accurate account of what is doing. But lest in such reports the circumstances of the case have been misrepresented, we have been obliged to transmit to you, first, the formula of faith presented by ourselves, and next, the second, which the Fathers put forth with some additions to our words. Our own paper then, which was read in the presence of our most pious [b] Emperor, and declared to be good and unexceptionable, ran thus:—

2. As we have received from the Bishops who preceded, us and in our first catechisings, and when we received the Holy Laver,

---

[a] This Letter is also found in Socr. Hist. 1. 8. Theod. Hist. 1. Gelas. Hist. Nic. 11. 34. p. 442. Niceph Hist viii. 22.

[b] And so infr. "most pious," § 4. "most wise and most religious," ibid. "most religious," §. 8. §. 10. Eusebius observes in his Vit. Const. the same tone concerning Constantine, and assigns to him the same office in determining the faith (being as yet unbaptized) E. g. "When there were differences between persons of different countries, as if some common bishop appointed by God, he convened Councils of God's ministers; and not disdaining to be present and to sit amid their conferences," &c. 1. 44. When he came into the Nicene Council, " it was," says Eusebius, " as some heavenly Angel of God," iii. 10. alluding to the brilliancy of the imperial purple. He confesses, however, he did not sit down until the Bishops bade him. Again at the same Council, " with pleasant eyes looking serenity itself into them all, collecting himself, and in a quiet and gentle voice" he made an oration to the Fathers upon peace. Constantine had been an instrument in conferring such vast benefits, humanly speaking, on the Christian body, that it is not wonderful that other writers of the day besides Eusebius should praise him. Hilary speaks of him as " of sacred memory," Fragm. 5. init. Athanasius calls him " most pious," Apol. contr. Arian. 9. " of blessed memory," ad Ep Æg. 18. 19 Epiphanius " most religious and of ever-blessed memory," Hær. 70. 9. Posterity, as was natural, was still more grateful.

NICEN. DEF.
and as we have learned from the divine Scriptures, and as we believed and taught in the presbytery, and in the Episcopate itself, so believing also at the time present, we report to you our faith, and it is this ᶜ:—

§. 3. We believe in One God, the Father Almighty, the Maker of all things visible and invisible.

And in One Lord Jesus Christ, the Word of God, God from God, Light from Light, Life from Life, Son Only-begotten, first-born of every creature, before all the ages, begotten from the Father, by whom also all things were made; who for our salvation was made flesh, and lived among men, and suffered, and rose again the third day, and ascended to the Father, and will come again in glory to judge quick and dead.

And we believe also in One Holy Ghost; believing each of These to be and to exist, the Father truly Father, and the Son truly Son, and the Holy Ghost truly Holy Ghost, as also our Mat. 28, Lord, sending forth His disciples for the preaching, said, *Go,* 19. *teach all nations, baptizing them in the Name of the Father, and of the Son, and of the Holy Ghost.* Concerning whom we confidently affirm that so we hold, and so we think, and so we have held aforetime, and we maintain this faith unto the death, anathematizing every godless heresy. That this we have ever thought from our heart and soul, from the time we recollect ourselves, and now think and say in truth, before God Almighty and our Lord Jesus Christ do we witness, being able by proofs to shew and to convince you, that, even in times past, such has been our belief and preaching.

§. 4. 3. On this faith being publicly put forth by us, no room for

ᶜ " The Children of the Church have received from their holy Fathers, that is, the holy Apostles, to guard the faith, and witho to deliver and preach it to their own children.... Cease not, faithful and orthodox men, thus to speak, and to teach the like from the divine Scriptures, and to walk, and to catechise, to the confirmation of yourselves and those who hear you; namely, that holy faith of the Catholic Church, as the holy and only Virgin of God received its custody from the holy Apostles of the Lord; and thus, in the case of each of those who are under catechising, who are to approach the Holy Laver, ye ought not only to preach faith to your children in the Lord, but also to teach them expressly, as your common mother teaches, to say ' We believe in One God,' " &c. Epiph. Ancor. 119 fin. who thereupon proceeds to give at length the Niceno-Constantinopolitan Creed. And so Athan. speaks of the orthodox faith, as " issuing from Apostolical teaching and the Fathers' tradition, and confirmed by New and Old Testament." ad Adelph. 6. init. Cyril Hier. too as " declared by the Church and established from all Scripture." Cat. v. 12. " Let us guard with vigilance what we have *received*.... What then have we received from the *Scriptures* but altogether this? that God made the world by the Word," &c. &c. Procl. ad Armen. p. 612. " That God, the Word, after the union remained such as He was, &c. so clearly hath divine Scripture, and moreover the doctors of the Churches, and the lights of the world taught us." Theodor. Dial. 3. init. " That it is the tradition of the Fathers is not the whole of our case, for they too followed the meaning of Scripture, starting from the testimonies, which just now we laid before you from Scripture." Basil de Sp. §. 16. vid. also a remarkable passage in de Synod. §. 6. fin. infra.

contradiction appeared; but our most pious Emperor, before any one else, testified that it comprised most orthodox statements. He confessed moreover that such were his own sentiments, and he advised all present to agree to it, and to subscribe its articles and to assent to them, with the insertion of the single word, One in substance, which moreover he interpreted as not in the sense of the affections of bodies, nor as if the Son subsisted from the Father, in the way of division, or any severance; for that the immaterial, and intellectual, and incorporeal nature could not be the subject of any corporeal affection, but that it became us to conceive of such things in a divine and ineffable manner. And such were the theological remarks of our most wise and most religious Emperor; but they, with a view to the addition of One in substance, drew up the following formula:—

4. *The Faith dictated in the Council.*

"We believe in One God, the Father Almighty, Maker of all things visible and invisible:—

"And in One Lord Jesus Christ, the Son of God, begotten of the Father, Only-begotten, that is, from the Substance of the Father; God from God, Light from Light, Very God from Very God, begotten not made, One in substance with the Father, by whom all things were made, both things in heaven and things in earth; who for us men and for our salvation came down and was made flesh, was made man, suffered, and rose again the third day, ascended into heaven, and cometh to judge quick and dead.

"And in the Holy Ghost.

"But those who say, 'Once He was not,' and 'Before His generation He was not,' and 'He came to be from nothing,' or those who pretend that the Son of God is 'Of other subsistence or substance [d],' or 'created,' or 'alterable,' or 'mutable,' the Catholic Church anathematizes."

5. On their dictating this formula, we did not let it pass without inquiry in what sense they introduced "of the substance of the Father," and "one in substance with the Father." Accordingly questions and explanations took place,

---

[d] The only clauses of the Creed which admit of any question in their explanation, are the "He was not before His generation," and "of other subsistence or substance." Of these the former shall be reserved for a later part of the volume; the latter is treated of in a note at the end of this Treatise; infr. p. 66.

and the meaning of the words underwent the scrutiny of reason. And they professed, that the phrase " of the substance" was indicative of the Son's being indeed from the Father, yet without being as if a part of Him And with this understanding we thought good to assent to the sense of such religious doctrine, teaching, as it did, that the Son was from the Father, not however a part of His substance[e]. On this account we assented to the sense ourselves, without declining even the term " One in substance," peace being the object which we set before us, and stedfastness in the orthodox view.

§. 6. 6. In the same way we also admitted " begotten, not made ;" since the Council alleged that " made" was an appellative common to the other creatures which came to be through the Son, to whom the Son had no likeness. Wherefore, said they, He was not a work resembling the things which through Him came to be[f], but was of a substance

---

[e] Eusebius does not commit himself to any positive sense in which the formula " of the substance" is to be interpreted, but only says what it does not mean. His comment on it is " of the Father, but not as a part," where, what is not negative, instead of being an explanation, is but a recurrence to the original words of Scripture, of which ἐξ οὐσίας itself is the explanation, a curious inversion. Indeed it is very doubtful whether he admitted the ἐξ οὐσίας at all. He says, that the Son is not like the radiance of light so far as this, that the radiance is an inseparable accident of substance, whereas the Son is by the Father's will, κατὰ γνώμην καὶ προαίρεσιν, Demostr Ev. iv, 3. And though he insists on our Lord being alone, ἐκ θεοῦ, yet he means in the sense which Athan. refutes, supr. § 7. viz. that He alone was created immediately from God, vid. next note f. It is true that he plainly condemns with the Nicene Creed the ἐξ οὐκ ὄντων of the Arians, " out of nothing," but an evasion was at hand here also ; for he not only adds, according to Arian custom, " as others," (vid. note following,) but he has a theory that no being whatever is out of nothing, for non-existence cannot be the cause of existence. God, he says, " proposed His own will and power as a sort of matter and substance of the production and constitution of the universe, so that it is not reasonably said, that any thing is out of nothing. For what is from nothing cannot be at all. How indeed can nothing be to any thing a cause of being [p] but all that is, takes its being from One who only is, and was, who also said, ' I am that I am.'" Demostr. Ev. iv. 1. Again, speaking of our Lord, " He who was from nothing would not truly be Son of God, as neither is any other of things generate." Eccl. Theol. 1. 9. fin.

[f] Eusebius distinctly asserts, Dem. Ev. iv, 2. that our Lord is a creature. " This offspring," he says, " did He first produce Himself from Himself as a foundation of those things which should succeed, the perfect handywork, δημιούργημα, of the Perfect, and the wise structure, ἀρχιτεκτόνημα, of the Wise," &c. Accordingly his avowal in the text is but the ordinary Arian evasion of " an offspring, not as the offsprings." E. g " It is not without peril to say recklessly that the Son is generate out of nothing similarly to the other generates." Dem. Ev. v. 1. vid also Eccl. Theol. 1. 9. iii. 2. And he considers our Lord the only Son by a divine provision similar to that by which there is only one sun in the firmament,

to the people of his Diocese. 63

which is too high for the level of any work[1], and which the Divine oracles teach to have been generated from the Father[g], the mode of generation being inscrutable and incalculable to every generated nature.

APPEN-
DIX.
[1] ποίημα

7. And so too on examination there are grounds for saying, that the Son is "one in substance" with the Father; not in the way of bodies, nor like mortal beings, for He is not such by division of substance, or by severance[2], no nor by any affection[3], or alteration, or changing of the Father's substance and power[h], (since from all such the ingenerate nature of

§. 7.

[2] κατ' ἀποτομὴν
[3] πάθος

---

as a *centre* of light and heat " Such an Only-begotten Son, the excellent artificer of His will and operator, did the supreme God and Father of that operator Himself first of all beget, through Him and in Him giving subsistence to the operative words (ideas or causes) of things which were to be, and casting in Him the seeds of the constitution and governance of the universe;...Therefore the Father being one, it behoved the Son to be one also, but should any one object that He constituted not more, it is fitting for such a one to complain that He constituted not more suns, and moons, and worlds, and ten thousand other things " Dem. Ev iv. 5. fin. vid. also iv. 6.

g Eusebius does not say that our Lord is *from the substance of* the Father, but has *a substance from* the Father. This is the Semi-arian doctrine, which, whether confessing the Son from the substance of the Father or not, implied that His substance was not the Father's substance, but a second substance. The same doctrine is found in the Semi-arians of Ancyra, though they seem to have confessed, " of the substance." And this is one object of the ὁμοούσιον, to hinder the confession " of the substance" from implying a second substance, which was not obviated or was even encouraged by the ὁμοιούσιον. The Council of Ancyra, quoting the text " As the Father hath life in Himself, so," &c. says, " since the life which is in the Father means substance, and the life of the Only-begotten which is begotten from the Father means substance, the word ' so' implies a likeness of substance to substance." Hær. 73. 10 fin   Hence Eusebius does not scruple to speak of " two substances," and other writers of

three substances, contr Marc. 1. 4. p. 25. He calls our Lord " a second substance." Dem. Ev. vi. Præf. Præp. Ev. vii, 12. p. 320. and the Holy Spirit a third substance, ibid. 15 p. 325. This it was that made the Latins so suspicious of three hypostases, because the Semi-arians, as well as they, understood ὑπόστασις to mean substance. Eusebius in like manner calls our Lord " another God," " a second God." Dem. Ev. v. 4 p. 226. v fin. " second Lord." ibid. 3 init. 6 fin. " second cause." Dem. Ev, v. Præf. vid. also ἕτερον ἔχουσα τὸ κατ' οὐσίαν ὑποκείμενον, Dem. Ev. v. 1. p. 215. καθ' ἑαυτὸν οὐσιωμένος. ibid. iv 3. And so ἕτερος παρὰ τὸν πατέρα. Eccl. Theol. 1. 20. p 90. and ζωὴν ἰδίαν ἔχων ibid. and ζῶν καὶ ὑφιστὼς καὶ τοῦ πατρὸς ὑπάρχων ἕκτος. ibid. Hence Athan insists so much, as in this treatise, on our Lord *not* being external to the Father. Once admit that He is in the Father, and we may call the Father, the *only* God, for He is included. And so again as to the Ingenerate, the term does not exclude the Son, for He is generate in the Ingenerate.

h This was the point on which, as we have partly seen already, the Semi-arians made their principal stand against the " one in substance," though they also objected to it as being of a Sabellian character. E. g. Euseb Demonstr. iv. 3. p. 148. d. p. 149. a, b. v. 1. p 213—215. contr. Marcell. 1. 4. p. 20. Eccl. Theol. 1. 12. p. 73. in laud. Const. p 525. de Fide i. ap. Sirmond. tom 1. p. 7. de Fide ii. p. 16. and apparently his de Incorporali. And so the Semi-arians at Ancyra, Epiph. Hær. 73. 11. p. 858. a, b. And so Meletius, ibid. p. 878 fin. and Cyril Hier. Catech. vii, 5. xi, 18. though of

the Father is alien,) but because " one in substance with the Father" suggests that the Son of God bears no resemblance to the generated creatures, but that to His Father alone who begat Him is He in every way assimilated, and that He is not of any other subsistence and substance, but from the Father[j]. To which term also, thus interpreted, it appeared well to assent; since we were aware that even among the ancients, some learned and illustrious Bishops and writers[k] have used the term " one in substance," in their theological teaching concerning the Father and Son.

§. 8.

8. So much then be said concerning the faith which was published; to which all of us assented, not without inquiry, but according to the specified senses, mentioned before the most religious Emperor himself, and justified by the forementioned considerations. And as to the anathematism published by them at the end of the Faith, it did not pain us, because it forbade to use words not in Scripture, from which almost all the confusion and disorder of the Church have come. Since then no divinely inspired Scripture has used the phrases, " out of nothing," and " once He was not," and the rest which follow, there appeared no ground for using or teaching them; to which also we assented as a good decision, since it had not been our custom hitherto to use these terms.

§. 9.

9. Moreover to anathematize " Before His generation He was not," did not seem preposterous, in that it is confessed

---

course Catholics would speak as strongly on this point as their opponents.

[j] Here again Eusebius does not say " from the Father's substance," but " not from other substance, but from the Father." According to note e. supr. he considered the will of God a certain matter or substance. Montfaucon in loc. and Collect. Nov. Præf p. xxvi. translates without warrant " ex Patris hypostasi et substantiâ." As to the Son's perfect likeness to the Father which he seems here to grant, it has been already shewn, p. 35. note u, how the admission was evaded. The likeness was but a likeness after its own kind, as a picture is of the original. " Though our Saviour Himself teaches," he says, " that the Father is the ' only true God,' still let me not be backward to confess Him also the true God, *as in an image*, and that possessed, so that the addition of ' only' may belong to the Father alone as archetype of the image ....As, supposing one king held sway, and his image was carried about into every quarter, no one in his right mind would say that those who held sway were two, but one who was honoured through His image, in like manner," &c. de Eccles. Theol. ii, 23. vid. ibid. 7. pp. 109. 111.

[k] Athanasius in like manner, ad Afros. 6. speaks of " testimony of ancient Bishops about 130 years since;" and in de Syn §. 43. of " long before" the Council of Antioch, A. D. 269. viz. the Dionysii, &c. vid. supra p. 35. note t.

by all, that the Son of God was before the generation according to the flesh[1]. Nay, our most religious Emperor did at the time prove, in a speech, that He was in being even according to His divine generation which is before all ages, since even before He was generated in energy, He was in virtue [m] with the Father ingenerately, the Father being always Father, as King always, and Saviour always, having all things in virtue, and being always in the same respects and in the same way.

10. This we have been forced to transmit to you, Beloved, as making clear to you the deliberation of our inquiry and assent, and how reasonably we resisted even to the last minute as long as we were offended at statements which differed from our own, but received without contention what no longer pained us, as soon as, on a candid examination of the sense of the words, they appeared to us to coincide with what we ourselves have professed in the faith which we have already published.

---

[1] Socrates, who advocates the orthodoxy of Eusebius, leaves out the heterodox paragraph altogether. Bull, however, Defens. F. N. III 9. n. 3 thinks it an interpolation Athanasius alludes to the early part of the clause, supr. p 7 and ad Syn. § 13. where he says, that Eusebius implied that the Arians denied even our Lord's existence before His incarnation. As to Constantine, he seems to have been used on these occasions by the court Bishops who were his instructors, and who made him the organ of their own heresy. Upon the first rise of the Arian controversy he addressed a sort of pastoral letter to Alexander and Arius, telling them that they were disputing about a question of words, and recommending them to drop it and live together peaceably. Euseb. vit. C. ii. 69. 72.

[m] Theognis, another of the Nicene Arians, says the same, according to Philostorgius; viz " that God even before He begat the Son was a Father, as having the power, δύναμις of begetting." Hist. ii. 15. Though Bull pronounces such doctrine to be heretical, as of course it is, still he considers that it expresses what *otherwise* stated may be orthodox, viz. the doctrine that our Lord was called the Word from eternity, and the Son upon His descent to create the worlds. And he acutely and ingeniously interprets the Arian formula, " Before His generation He was not," to support this view. Another opportunity will occur of giving an opinion upon this question; meanwhile, the *parallel* on which the heretical doctrine is supported in the text is answered by many writers, on the ground that Father and Son are words of nature, but Creator, King, Saviour, are external, or what may be called accidental to Him Thus Athanasius observes, that Father actually implies Son, but Creator only the power to create, as expressing a δύναμις, " a maker is before his works, but he who says Father, forthwith in Father implies the existence of the Son " Orat. iii. §. 6. vid. Cyril too, Dial. ii. p. 459. Pseudo-Basil. contr. Eun. iv. 1. fin. On the other hand Origen argues the reverse way, that since God is eternally a Father, therefore eternally Creator also. " As one cannot be father without a son, nor lord without possession, so neither can God be called Allpowerful, without subjects of His power;" Periarch. 1. 2. n. 10. hence he argued for the eternity of matter.

NOTE on page 61.

On the meaning of the phrase ἐξ ἑτέρας ὑποστάσεως ἢ οὐσίας *in the Nicene Anathema.*

NICEN. DEF. Bishop Bull has made it a question, whether these words in the Nicene Creed mean the same thing, or are to be considered distinct from each other, advocating himself the latter opinion against Petavius. The history of the word ὑπόστασις is of too intricate a character to enter upon here; but a few words may be in place in illustration of its sense as it occurs in the Creed, and with reference to the view taken of it by the great divine, who has commented on it

Bishop Bull, as I understand him, (Defens. F. N. ii. 9. §. 11.) considers that two distinct ideas are intended by the words οὐσία and ὑπόστασις, in the clause ἐξ ἑτέρας ὑποστάσεως ἢ οὐσίας; as if the Creed condemned those who said that the Son was not from the Father's substance, and those also who said that He was not from the Father's hypostasis or subsistence, as if a man might hold at least one of the two without holding the other. And in matter of fact, he does profess to assign two parties of heretics, who denied this or that proposition respectively.

Petavius, on the other hand, (de Trin. iv. 1.) considers that the word ὑπόστασις, is but another term for οὐσία, and that not two but one proposition is contained in the clause in question; the word ὑπόστασις not being publicly recognised in its present meaning till the Council of Alexandria, in the year 362. Coustant. (Epist. Pont. Rom. pp. 274 290 462.) Tillemont, (Memoires S. Denys. d'Alex. §. 15) Huet, (Origenian. ii. 2. n. 3.) Thomassin, (de Incarn. iii. 1) and Morinus, (de Sacr. Ordin. ii. 6) take substantially the same view; while Maranus (Præf. ad S. Basil. §. 1. tom. 3. ed. Bened.) Natalis Alexander, Hist. (Sæc. 1. Diss. 22 circ. fin.) Burton, (Testimonies to the Trinity, No. 71.) and the President of Magdalen, (Reliqu. Sacr. vol. iii. p. 189.) differ from Petavius, if they do not agree with Bull.

Bull's principal argument lies in the strong fact, that S. Basil expressly asserts, that the Council did mean the two terms to be distinct, and this when he is answering the Sabellians, who grounded their assertion that there was but one ὑπόστασις, on the alleged fact, the Council had used οὐσία and ὑπόστασις indifferently.

Bull refers also to Anastasius, Hodeg. 21. (22. p. 343.?) who says, that the Nicene Fathers defined that there are three hypostases or Persons in the Holy Trinity. Petavius considers that he derived this from Gelasius of Cyzicus, a writer of no great authority; but, as the passage occurs in Anastasius, they are the words of Andrew of Samosata. But what is more important, elsewhere Anastasius quotes a passage from Amphilochius to something of the same effect.

Note on the word Hypostasis in the Nicene Anathema

c 10. p 164 He states it besides himself, c. 9 p. 150 and c. 24. Νοττ. p. 364 In addition, Bull quotes passages from S. Dionysius of Alexandria, S. Dionysius of Rome, (vid above, pp 44—48 and note i. p 46) Eusebius of Cæsarea, and afterwards Origen; in all of which three hypostases being spoken of, whereas, antiquity early or late, never speaks in the same way of three οὐσίαι, it is plain that ὑπόστασις then conveyed an idea which οὐσία did not. To these may be added a passage in Athanasius, in Illud, Omnia, &c. §. 6.

Bishop Bull adds the following explanation of the two words as they occur in the Creed: he conceives that the one is intended to reach the Arians, and the other the Semi-arians, that the Semi-arians did actually make a distinction between οὐσία and ὑπόστασις, admitting in a certain sense that the Son was from the ὑπόστασις of the Father, while they denied that He was from His οὐσία. They then are anathematized in the words ἐξ ἑτέρας οὐσίας, and, as he would seem to mean, the Arians in the ἐξ ἑτέρας ὑποστάσεως.

Now I hope it will not be considered any disrespect to so great an authority, if I differ from this view, and express my reasons for doing so.

1. First then, supposing his account of the Semi-arian doctrine ever so free from objection, granting that they denied the ἐξ οὐσίας, and admitted the ἐξ ὑποστάσεως, yet *who* are they who, according to his view, *denied* the ἐξ ὑποστάσεως, or said that the Son was ἐξ ἑτέρας ὑποστάσεως? he does not assign any parties, though he implies the Arians. Yet though, as is notorious, they denied the ἐξ οὐσίας, there is nothing to shew that they or any other party of Arians maintained specifically that the Son was not of the ὑπόστασις, or subsistence of the Father. That is, the hypothesis supported by this eminent divine, does not answer the very question which it raises. It professes that those who denied the ἐξ ὑποστάσεως, were not the same as those who denied the ἐξ οὐσίας; yet it fails to tell us who did deny the ἐξ ὑποστάσεως, in a sense distinct from ἐξ οὐσίας

2 Next, his only proof that the Semi-arians did hold the ἐξ ὑποστάσεως as distinct from the ἐξ οὐσίας, lies in the circumstance, that the three (commonly called) Semi-arian confessions of A.D 341, 344, 351, known as Mark's of Arethusa, the Macrostiche, and the first Sirmian, anathematize those who say that the Son is ἐξ ἑτέρας ὑποστάσεως καὶ μὴ ἐκ τοῦ θεοῦ, not anathematizing the ἐξ ἑτέρας οὐσίας, which he infers thence was their own belief. Another explanation of this passage will be offered presently; meanwhile, it is well to observe, that Hilary, in speaking of the confession of Philippopolis which was taken from Mark's, far from suspecting that the clause involved an omission, defends it on the *ground of its retaining the Anathema*. de Synod. 35. thus implying that ἐξ ἑτέρας ὑποστάσεως καὶ μὴ ἐκ τοῦ θεοῦ was equivalent to ἐξ ἑτέρας ὑποστάσεως ἢ οὐσίας. And it may be added, that Athanasius in like manner, in his account of the Nicene Council above translated, (de Decret §. 20. fin.) when repeating its anathema, drops the ἐξ ὑποστάσεως altogether, and reads τοὺς δὲ λέγοντας ἐξ οὐκ ὄντων, ... ἢ ποίημα, ἢ ἐξ ἑτέρας οὐσίας, τούτους ἀναθεματίζει κ. τ. λ

NICEN. DEF.

3. Further, Bull gives us no proof whatever that the Semi-arians did deny the ἐξ οὐσίας; while it is very clear, if it is right to contradict so great a writer, that most of them did not deny it. He says that it is " certissimum" that the heretics who wrote the three confessions above noticed, that is, the Semi-arians, "*nunquam fassos*, nunquam fassuros fuisse filium ἐξ οὐσίας, è substantiâ, Patris progenitum." His reason for not offering any proof for this naturally is, that Petavius, with whom he is in controversy, maintains it also, and he makes use of Petavius's admission against himself. Now it may seem bold in a writer of this day to differ not only with Bull but with Petavius; but the reason for doing so is simple; it is because Athanasius asserts the very thing which Petavius and Bull deny, and Petavius admits that he does; that is, he allows it by implication when he complains that Athanasius had not got to the bottom of the doctrine of the Semi-arians, and thought too favourably of them. " Horum Semi-arianorum, quorum antesignanus fuit Basilius Ancyræ episcopus, prorsus obscura fuit hæresis . . . . . ut ne ipse quidem Athanasius satis illam exploratam habuerit." de Trin. i. x. §. 7.

Now S. Athanasius's words are most distinct and express ; " As to those who receive all else that was defined at Nicæa, but dispute about the ' One in substance' only, we must not feel as towards enemies .... for, as *confessing that the Son is from the substance of the Father* and not of other subsistence, ἐκ τῆς οὐσίας τοῦ πατρὸς εἶναι, καὶ μὴ ἐξ ἑτέρας ὑποστάσεως τὸν υἱὸν, . . . they are not far from receiving the phrase ' One in substance' also. Such is Basil of Ancyra, in what he has written about the faith." de Syn. §. 41;—a passage, not only express for the matter in hand, but remarkable too, as apparently using ὑπόστασις and οὐσία as synonymous, which is the main point which Bull denies. What follows in Athanasius is equally to the purpose: he urges the Semi-arians to accept the ὁμοούσιον, in consistency, *because* they maintain the ἐξ οὐσίας and the ὁμοιούσιον would not sufficiently secure it.

Moreover Hilary, while defending the Semi-arian decrees of Ancyra or Sirmium, says expressly, that according to them, among other truths, "non creatura est Filius genitus, sed *à naturâ Patris* indiscreta substantia est " de Syn. 27.

Petavius, however, in the passage to which Bull appeals, refers in proof of his view of Semi-arianism, to those Ancyrene documents, which Epiphanius has preserved, Hær. 73, and which he considers to shew, that according to the Semi-arians the Son was not ἐξ οὐσίας τοῦ πατρός. He says, that it is plain from their own explanations that they considered our Lord to be, not ἐκ τῆς οὐσίας, but ἐκ τῆς ὁμοιότητος [he does not say ὑποστάσεως, as Bull wishes] τοῦ πατρὸς and that, ἐνεργείᾳ γεννητικῇ, which was one of the divine ἐνέργειαι, as creation, ἡ κτιστικὴ, was another. Yet surely Epiphanius does not bear out this representation better than Athanasius; since the Semi-arians, whose words he reports, speak of " υἱὸν ὅμοιον καὶ κατ' οὐσίαν ἐκ τοῦ πατρὸς, p. 825. b. ὡς ἡ σοφία τοῦ σοφοῦ υἱός, οὐσία οὐσίας. p 853. c. κατ' οὐσίαν υἱὸν τοῦ Θεοῦ καὶ πατρός. p. 854. c ἐξουσίᾳ ὁμοῦ καὶ οὐσίᾳ πατρὸς μονογενοῦς υἱοῦ.

p. 858. d. besides the strong word γνήσιο,, ibid. and Athan. de Syn §. 41. not to insist on other of their statements.

The same fact is brought before us even in a more striking way in the conference at Constantinople, A. D. 360, before Constantius, between the Anomœans and Semi-arians, where the latter, according to Theodoret, shew no unwillingness to acknowledge even the ὁμοούσιον, *because* they acknowledge the ἐξ οὐσίας. When the Anomœans wished the former condemned, Silvanus of Tarsus said, " If God the Word be not out of nothing, nor a creature, *nor of other substance, οὐσίας*, therefore is He one in substance, ὁμοούσιος, with God who begot Him, as God from God, and Light from Light, and He has the same nature with His Father." Hist ii 23. Here again it is observable, as in the passage from Athanasius above, that, while apparently reciting the Nicene Anathema, he omits ἐξ ἑτέρης ὑποστάσεως, as if it were superfluous to mention a synonyme.

At the same time there certainly is reason to suspect that the Semi-arians approximated towards orthodoxy as time went on; and perhaps it is hardly fair to determine what they held at Nicæa by their statements at Ancyra, though to the latter Petavius appeals. Several of the most eminent among them, as Meletius, Cyril, and Eusebius of Samosata conformed soon after; on the other hand in Eusebius, who is their representative at Nicæa, it will perhaps be difficult to find a clear admission of the ἐξ οὐσίας. But at any rate he does not maintain the ἐξ ὑποστάσεως, which Bull's theory requires.

On various grounds then, because the Semi-arians as a body did not deny the ἐξ οὐσίας, nor confess the ἐξ ὑποστάσεως, nor the Arians deny it, there is reason for declining Bishop Bull's explanation of these words as they occur in the Creed; and now let us turn to the consideration of the authorities on which that explanation rests.

As to Gelasius, Bull himself does not insist upon his testimony, and Anastasius is too late to be of authority. The passage indeed which he quotes from Amphilochius is important, but as he was a friend of St. Basil, perhaps it does very much increase the weight of St. Basil's more distinct and detailed testimony to the same point, and no one can say that that weight is inconsiderable.

Yet there is evidence the other way which overbalances it. Bull, who complains of Petavius s rejection of St. Basil's testimony concerning a Council which was held before his birth, cannot maintain his own explanation of its Creed without rejecting Athanasius's testimony respecting the doctrine of his contemporaries, the Semi-arians ; and moreover the more direct evidence, as we shall see, of the Council of Alexandria, A. D. 362, S. Jerome, Basil of Ancyra, and Socrates.

First, however, no better comment upon the sense of the Council can be required than the incidental language of Athanasius and others, who in a foregoing extract exchanges οὐσία for ὑπόστασις in a way which is natural only on the supposition that he used them as synonymes. Elsewhere, as we have seen, he omits the word ἢ ὑποστάσεως in the Nicene Anathema, while Hilary considers the Anathema sufficient *with* that omission.

70 *Note on the word Hypostasis in the Nicene Anathema.*

NICEN. DEF. In like manner Hilary expressly translates the clause in the Creed by ex alterâ substantiâ vel essentiâ. Fragm. ii. 27. And somewhat in the same way Eusebius says in his letter, ἐξ ἑτέρας τινὸς ὑποστάσεως τε καὶ οὐσίας.

But further, Athanasius says expressly, ad Afros.—" Hypostasis is substance, οὐσία, and means nothing else than simply being, which Jeremiah calls existence when he says," &c. §. 4. It is true, he elsewhere speaks of three Hypostases, but this only shews that he attached no fixed sense to the word. This is just what I would maintain; its sense must be determined by the context, and, whereas it always stands in all Catholic writers for the Una Res, (as the 4th Lateran speaks,) which οὐσία denotes, when Athanasius says, " three hypostases," he takes the word to mean οὐσία in that particular sense in which it is three, and when he makes it synonymous with οὐσία, he uses it to signify Almighty God in that sense in which He is one.

Leaving Athanasius, we have the following evidence concerning the history of the word ὑπόστασις. St. Jerome says, " The whole school of secular learning understanding nothing else by hypostasis than usia, substance" Ep. xv. 4. Where, speaking of the Three Hypostases he uses the strong language, " If you desire it, then be a *new* faith framed *after* the Nicene, and let the orthodox confess in terms like the Arian."

In like manner, Basil of Ancyra, George, and the other Semiarians, say distinctly, " This hypostasis our Fathers called substance," οὐσία Epiph. Hær 74 12. fin.; in accordance with which is the unauthorized addition to the Sardican Epistle, " ὑπόστασιν, ἣν αὐτοὶ οἱ αἱρετικοὶ οὐσίαν προσαγορεύουσι." Theod. Hist. ii. 6.

If it be said that Jerome from his Roman connection, and Basil and George as Semi-arians, would be led by their respective theologies for distinct reasons thus to speak, it is true, and may have led them to too broad a statement of the fact; but then on the other hand it was in accordance also with the theology of St. Basil, so strenuous a defender of the formula of the Three Hypostases, to suppose that the Nicene Fathers meant to distinguish ὑπόστασις from οὐσία in their anathema.

Again, Socrates informs us that, though there was some dispute about hypostasis at Alexandria shortly before the Nicene Council, yet the Council itself " devoted not a word to the question." Hist. iii. 7.; which hardly consists with its having intended to rule that ἐξ ἑτέρας ὑποστάσεως was distinct from ἐξ ἑτέρας οὐσίας.

And in like manner the Council of Alexandria, A D. 362, in deciding that the sense of Hypostasis was an open question, not only from the very nature of the case goes on the supposition that the Nicene Council had not closed it, but says so in words again and again in its Synodal Letter. If the Nicene Council had already used " hypostasis" in its present sense, what remained to Athanasius at Alexandria but to submit to it?

Indeed the history of this Council is perhaps the strongest argument against the supposed discrimination of the two terms by the Council of Nicæa. Bull can only meet it by considering that an innovation upon the " veterem vocabuli usum" began at the date of the Council of Sardica, though Socrates mentions the dispute as existing at Alexandria before the Nicene Council, Hist. iii. 4. 5 while the supposititious confession of Sardica professes to have received the doctrine of the one hypostasis by tradition as Catholic.

Nor is the use of the word in earlier times inconsistent with these testimonies, though it occurs so seldom, in spite of its being a word of St. Paul, that testimony is our principal evidence. Socrates's remarks deserve to be quoted; " Those among the Greeks who have treated of the Greek philosophy, have defined substance, οὐσία, in many ways, but they had made no mention at all of hypostasis. Irenæus the Grammarian, in his alphabetical Atticist, even calls the term barbarous, because it is not used by any of the ancients, and if any where found, it does not mean what it is now taken for. Thus in the Phœnix of Sophocles it means an ' ambush ,' but in Menander, ' preserves,' as if one were to call the wine-lees in a cask ' hypostasis.' However it must be observed, that, in spite of the old philosophers being silent about the term, the more modern continually use it for substance, οὐσίας." Hist. iii. 7. The word principally occurs in Origen among Ante-Nicene writers, and he, it must be confessed, uses it, as far as the context decides its sense, to mean subsistence or person. In other words, it was the word of a certain school in the Church, which afterwards was accepted by the Church; but this proves nothing about the sense in which it was used at Nicæa. The three Hypostases are spoken of by Origen, his pupil Dionysius, as afterwards by Eusebius of Cæsarea, (though he may notwithstanding have considered hypostasis synonymous with substance,) and Athanasius; (Origen in Joan. ii. 6 Dionys. ap. Basil de Sp S. n. 72. Euseb. ap. Socr. i. 23 Athan. in Illud Omnia, &c. 6.) and the Two Hypostases of the Father and the Son, by Origen, Ammonius, and Alexander, (Origen in Cels. viii. 2 Ammon ap. Caten. in Joan. x. 30. Alex. ap. Theod. i 3. p. 740.) As to the passage in which two hypostases are spoken of in Dionysius's letter to Paul of Samosata, that letter certainly is not genuine, as might be shewn on a fitting occasion, though it is acknowledged by very great authorities.

I confess that to my mind there is an antecedent probability that the view which has here been followed is correct Judging by the general history of doctrine, one should not expect that the formal ecclesiastical meaning of the word should have obtained every where so early. Nothing is more certain than that the doctrines themselves of the Holy Trinity and the Incarnation were developed, or, to speak more definitely, that the propositions containing them were acknowledged, from the earliest times; but the particular terms which now belong to them are almost uniformly of a later date. Ideas were brought out, but technical phrases did not obtain. Not that these phrases did not exist, but either not as technical, or in use in a particular School or Church, or with a particular writer, or as ἅπαξ λεγόμενα, as words discussed, nay resisted, perhaps used by some local Council, and then at length accepted generally from their

72 *Note on the word Hypostasis in the Nicene Anathema.*

NICEN. DEF. obvious propriety. Thus the words of the Schools pass into the service of the Catholic Church. Instead then of the word ὑπόστασις being, as Maran says, received in the East " summo consensu," from the date of Noetus or at least Sabellius, or of Bull's opinion " apud *Catholicos* Dionysii ætate *ratum et fixum* illud fuisse, tres esse in divinis hypostases," I would consider that the present use of the word was in the first instance Alexandrian, and that it was little more than Alexandrian till the middle of the 4th century.

Lastly, it comes to be considered how the two words are to be accounted for in the Creed, if they have not distinct senses. Coustant supposes that ἐξ οὐσίας was added to explain ἐξ ὑποστάσεως, lest the latter should be taken in a Sabellian sense. On which we may perhaps remark besides, that the reason why ὑπόστασις was selected as the principal term was, that it was agreeable to the Westerns as well as admitted by the Orientals. Thus, by way of contrast, we find the second General Council, at which there were no Latins, speaking of Three Hypostases, and Pope Damasus and the Roman Council speaking a few years sooner of the Holy Ghost as of the same hypostasis and usia with the Father and the Son. Theod. Hist. ii. 17. Many things go to make this probable. For instance, Coustant acutely points out, though Maran and the President of Magdalen dissent, that this probably was a point of dispute between the two Dionysii; the Bishop of Alexandria asserting, as we know he did assert, Three Hypostases, the Bishop of Rome protesting in reply against " Three *partitive* Hypostases," as involving tritheism, and his namesake rejoining, " If because there are Three Hypostases, any say that they are partitive, three there are, though they like it not " Again, the influence of the West shews itself in the language of Athanasius, who, contrary to the custom of his Church, of Origen, Dionysius, and his own immediate patron and master Alexander, so varies his own use of the word, as to make his writings almost an example of that freedom which he vindicated in the Council of Alexandria. Again, when Hosius went to Alexandria before the Nicene Council, and a dispute arose with reference to Sabellianism about the words ὑπόστασις and οὐσία, what is this too, but the collision of East and West? It should be remembered moreover that Hosius presided at Nicæa, a Latin in an Eastern city; and again at Sardica, where, though the decree in favour of the One Hypostasis was not passed, it seems clear from the history that he was resisting persons with whom in great measure he agreed. Further, the same consideration accounts for the omission of the ἐξ οὐσίας from the Confession of Mark and the two which follow, on which Bull relies in proof that the Semi-arians rejected this formula. These three Semi-arian Creeds, and these only, were addressed to the Latins, and therefore their compilers naturally select that synonyme which was most pleasing to them, as the means of securing a hearing; just as Athanasius on the other hand in his de Decretis, writing to the Greeks, omits ὑποστάσεως, and writes οὐσίας.

EPISTLE OF S. ATHANASIUS,

ARCHBISHOP OF ALEXANDRIA,

CONCERNING THE COUNCILS HELD AT ARIMINUM IN ITALY AND AT SELEUCIA IN ISAURIA.

CHAP I.

HISTORY OF THE COUNCILS.

Reason why two Councils were called Inconsistency and folly of calling any; and of the style of the Arian formularies; occasion of the Nicene Council, proceedings at Ariminum, Letter of the Council to Constantius; its decree. Proceedings at Seleucia; reflections on the conduct of the Arians.

1. PERHAPS news has reached even yourselves concerning the Council, which is at this time the subject of general conversation; for letters both from the Emperor and the Prefects[a] were circulated far and wide for its convocation. However, you take that interest in the events which have occurred, that I have determined upon giving you an account of what I have seen myself[b] or have ascertained, which may save you from the suspense attendant on the reports of others; and this the more, because there are parties who are in the practice of misrepresenting what is going on.

2. At Nicæa then, which had been fixed upon, the Council did not meet, but a second edict[c] was issued, convening the

---

[a] There were at this time four prætorian præfects, who divided between them this administration of the Empire. They had been lately made merely civil officers, Constantine having suppressed the celebrated troops which they used to command. At Ariminum, one of them, Taurus, was present, and was the instrument of the Emperor in overawing the Council.

[b] From these words Tillemont and Gibbon infer that Athanasius was present at least at Seleucia, but, as Montfaucon observes, such a supposition is not required by the words, and is in itself improbable.

[c] The Council was originally to have been held at Nicæa, but the party of Basil did not like a second meeting in the same place, and Nicomedia was

74 Circumstances of the calling of the Two Councils.

Counc Western Bishops at Ariminum in Italy, and the Eastern at
Arim. Seleucia the Rugged, as it is called, in Isauria. The professed
and
Seleu reason of such a meeting was to treat of the faith touching our
Lord Jesus Christ; and those who alleged it, were Ursacius,
Valens[d], and one Germinius[e] from Pannonia; and from Syria,
Acacius, Eudoxius[f], and Patrophilus of Scythopolis[g]. These
men who had always been of the Arian party, and *understood
neither how they believe or whereof they affirm*, and were
silently deceiving first one and then another, and scattering
[1] supr. the second sowing[1] of their heresy, influenced some persons of
p. 5.
note k. consequence, and the Emperor Constantius among them,
[2] infr. being a heretic[2], on some pretence about the Faith, to call a
p. 90.
note p. Council; under the idea that they should be able to put into

substituted. The greater number of Bishops had set out, when an earthquake threw the city into ruins. Nicæa was then substituted again at Basil's wish, Soz iv. 16. but it was considered too near the seat of the earthquake to be safe Then the Eusebian or Acacian influence prevailed, and the Council was divided into two, but at first Ancyra, Basil's see, was to have been one of them, (where a celebrated Council of Semi-arians actually was held at the time) Hil de Syn 8. but this was changed for Seleucia A delegacy of Bishops from each Province was summoned to Nicomedia, but to Nicæa, all Bishops whatever, whose health admitted of the journey, according to Sozomen, but Hilary says, only one or two from each province of Gaul were summoned to Ariminum, he himself was at Seleucia, under compulsion of the local magistrate, being in exile there for the faith, Sulp. Sev ii 57.

[d] Ursacius, Bishop of Singidon, and Valens, Bishop of Mursa, are generally mentioned together. They were pupils of Arius, and as such are called young by Athan. ad Ep. Æg. 7. by Hilary ad Const 1. 5. (imperitis et improbis duobus *adolescentibus*,) and by the Council of Sardica, ap Hilar. Fragm. ii. 12. They first appear at the Council of Tyre, A D 335. The Council of Sardica deposed them; in 349, they publicly retracted their charges against Athanasius, who has preserved their letters. Apol. contr. Arian 58 Valens was the more prominent of the two; he was a favourite Bishop of Con-

stantius, was an extreme Arian in his opinions, and the chief agent at Ariminum in effecting the lapse of the Latin Fathers.

[e] Germinius was made Bishop of Sirmium by the Eusebians in 351, instead of Photinus whom they deposed for a kind of Sabellianism. However, he was obliged in 358 to sign the Semi-arian formula of Ancyra, yet he was an active Eusebian again at Ariminum. At a later date he approached very nearly to Catholicism.

[f] Acacius has been mentioned, p. 7. note p. Eudoxius is said to have been a pupil of Lucian, Arius's Master, though the dates scarcely admit it. Eustathius, Catholic Bishop of Antioch, whom the Eusebians subsequently deposed, refused to admit him into orders. Afterwards he was made Bishop of Germanicia in Syria, by his party. He was present at the Council of Antioch in 341, spoken of infra, § 22. and carried into the West in 345, the fifth Confession, called the Long, μακρόστιχος infr. § 26. He afterwards passed in succession to the sees of Antioch, (vid. supr. p. 1. note a) and Constantinople, and baptized the Emperor Valens into the Arian profession.

[g] Patrophilus was one of the original Arian party, and took share in all their principal acts, but there is nothing very distinctive in his history. Sozomen assigns to these six Bishops the scheme of dividing the Council into two, Hist. iv. 16. and Valens undertook to manage the Latins, Acacius the Greeks.

the shade the Nicene Council, and prevail upon all to turn round, and to establish irreligion every where instead of the Truth.

3. Now here I marvel first, and think that I shall carry every thinking man whatever with me, that, whereas a Catholic Council had been fixed, and all were looking forward to it, it was all of a sudden divided in two, so that one part met here, and the other there. However, this would seem providential, in order in the respective Councils to exhibit the faith without guile or corruption of the one party, and to expose the dishonesty and duplicity of the other. Next, this too was on the mind of myself and my true brethren here, and made us anxious, the impropriety of this great gathering which we saw in progress; for what pressed so much, that the whole world was to be put into confusion, and those who at the time bore the profession of clerks, should run about far and near, seeking how best to learn to believe in our Lord Jesus Christ? Certainly, if they were believers already, they would not have been seeking, as though they were not. And to the catechumens, this was no small scandal; but to the heathen, it was something more than common, and even furnished broad merriment[h], that Christians, as if waking out of sleep at this time of day, should be making out how they were to believe concerning Christ; while their professed clerks, though claiming deference from their flocks, as teachers, were infidels on their own shewing, in that they were seeking what they had not. And the party of Ursacius, who were at the bottom of all this, did not understand what wrath they were storing up against themselves, as our Lord says by His saints, *Woe unto them, through whom My Name is blasphemed among the Gentiles;* and by His own mouth in the Gospels, *Whoso shall offend one of these little ones, it were better for him that a millstone were hanged about his neck, and that he were drowned in the depth of the sea,*

Is 52,5.
Rom. 2, 24.
Mat 18, 6.

---

[h] The heathen Ammianus speaks of "the troops of Bishops hurrying to and fro at the public expense," and "the Synods, in their efforts to bring over the whole religion to their side, being the ruin of the posting establishments." Hist. xxi. 16 " The spectacle proceeded to that pitch of indecency," says Eusebius, "that at length in the very midst of the theatres of the unbelievers, the solemn matters of divine teaching were subjected to the basest mockery." in vit Const ii 61. Heathen Philosophers attended the Nicene Council, "from an interest to learn what the Christian doctrine was." Soz. i. 18.

Counc. *than, as Luke adds, that he should offend one of these little*
Arim.
and *ones.*
Seleu.

§. 3. 4. What defect of teaching was there for religious truth in the Catholic Church¹, that they should search after faith now, and should prefix this year's Consulate to their profession of it? Yet Ursacius, and Valens, and Germinius, and their friends have done, what never took place, never was heard of among Christians. After putting into writing what it pleased them to believe, they prefix to it the Consulate, and the month and the day of the current year ᵏ; thereby to shew all thinking men, that their faith dates, not from of old, but now, from the reign of Constantius ¹; for whatever they write has a view to their own heresy. Moreover, though pretending to write

---

¹ "Who is there, who when he heard, upon his first catechisings, that God had a Son, and had made all things in His proper Word, did not so understand it in that sense which we now intend? who, when the vile Arian heresy began, but at once, on hearing its teachers, was startled, as if they taught strange things?" Orat. ii. § 34 And Hilary with the same sense, " I call the God of heaven and earth to witness, that, before I had heard either term, I always felt concerning the two words that by ' one in substance' ought to be understood 'like in substance,' that is, that nothing can be like Him in nature, but That which is of the same nature. Regenerated long since, and for a while a Bishop, yet I never heard the Nicene Creed till I was in exile, the Gospels and Apostles intimated to me the meaning of ' one in substance' and ' like in substance.'" de Syn. 91. vid. also ad Const ii. 7.

ᵏ " Faith is made a thing of dates rather than Gospels, while it is written down by years, and is not measured by the confession of baptism " ad Const ii. 4. " We determine yearly and monthly creeds concerning God, we repent of our determinations, we defend those who repent, we anathematize those whom we have defended, we condemn our own doings in those of others, or others in us, and gnawing each other, we are well nigh devoured one of another " ibid. 5.

¹ " Who are you? whence and when came ye? what do ye on my property being none of mine? by what right, O Marcion, cuttest thou my wood? by what license, O Valentinus, turnest thou my springs? by what power, O Apelles, movest thou my landmarks? Mine is possession... I possess of old, I have prior possession... I am heir of the Apostles." Tertull. de Præscr 37 Tardily for me hath this time of day put forth these, in my judgment, most impious doctors. Full late hath that faith of mine, which Thou hast instructed, encountered these Masters Before these names were heard of, I thus believed in Thee, I thus was new born by Thee, and thenceforth I thus am Thine." Hil. de Trin. vi. 21. ' What heresy hath ever burst forth, but under the name of some certain men, in some certain place, and at some certain time? who ever set up any heresy, who first divided not himself from the consent of the universality and antiquity of the Catholic Church?" Vincent Lir. Commonit. 24 " I will tell thee my mind briefly and plainly, that thou shouldest remain in that Church which, being founded by the Apostles, endures even to this day. When thou hearest that those who are called Christ's, are named, not after Jesus Christ, but after some one, say Marcionites, Valentinians, &c. know then it is not Christ's Church, but the synagogue of Antichrist. For by the very fact that they are formed afterwards, they shew that they are those who the Apostle foretold should come." Jerom in Lucif. 27. " If the Church was not.... whence hath Donatus appeared? from what soil has he sprung? out of what sea hath he emerged? from what heaven hath he fallen?" August. de Bapt. contr. Don. iii. 3.

about the Lord, they nominate another sovereign for themselves, Constantius, who has bestowed on them this reign of irreligion [m]; and they who deny that the Son is everlasting, have called him Eternal Emperor; such foes of Christ are they in behalf of irreligion.

5. But perhaps the dates in the holy Prophets form their excuse for the Consulate, so bold a pretence, however, will serve but to publish more fully their ignorance of the subject. For the prophecies of the sacred writers do indeed specify their times; (for instance, Esaias and Osee lived in the days of Ozias, Joatham, Achaz, and Ezekias; Jeremias, in the days of Josias, Ezekiel and Daniel prophesied unto Cyrus and Darius; and others in other times;) yet they were not laying the foundations of divine religion; it was before them, and was always, for before the foundation of the world had God prepared it for us in Christ. Nor were they signifying the respective dates of their own faith; for they had been believers before these dates, which did but belong to their own preaching. And this preaching chiefly related to the Saviour's coming, and secondarily to what was to happen to Israel and the nations; and the dates denoted not the commencement of faith, as I said before, but of the prophets themselves, that

---

[m] Athan. says, that after Eusebius had taken up the patronage of the heresy, he made no progress till he had gained the Court, Hist. Arian. 66. shewing that it was an act of external power by which Arianism grew, not an inward movement in the Church. which indeed loudly protested against the Emperor's proceeding. "If Bishops are to judge," he says shortly before, "what has the Emperor to do with this matter? if the Emperor is to threaten, what need of men styled Bishops? where in the world was such a thing heard of? where had the Church's judgment its force from the Emperor, or his sentence was at all recognised? many Councils have been before this, many judgments of the Church, but neither the Fathers ever argued with the Emperor about them, nor the Emperor meddled with the concerns of the Church. Paul the Apostle had friends of Cæsar's household, and in his Epistle he saluted the Philippians in their name, but he took them not to him as partners in his judgments. But now a new spectacle, and this the discovery of the Arian heresy," &c § 52. Again, "In what then is he behind Antichrist? what more will he do when he comes? or rather, on his coming will he not find the way by [Constantius] prepared for him unto his deceiving without effort? for he too is to claim the judgments for the court instead of the Churches, and of these he is to become head " § 76. And so Hosius to Constantius, "Cease, I charge thee, and remember that thou art a mortal man. Fear the day of judgment, keep thyself clear against it. Interfere not with things ecclesiastical, nor be the man to charge us in a matter of the kind, rather learn them thyself from us. God has put into thy hand the kingdom; to us He hath intrusted the things of the Church, and as he who is traitorous to thy rule speaks against God who has thus ordained, so fear thou, lest drawing to thyself the things of the Church, thou fallest beneath a great accusation." Apud Athan. ibid. 44. vid. infr. p. 90. note p.

78 *Difference between decree of faith and rule of discipline.*

CouNC. ARIM. AND SELEU.
is, when it was they thus prophesied. But our modern sages, not in historical narration, nor in prediction of the future, but, after writing, "The Catholic Faith was published," immediately add the Consulate and the month and the date; that, as the sacred writers specified the dates of their histories, and of their own ministries, so these may mark the date of their own faith. And would that they had written, touching " their own[n];" (for it does date from to-day;) and had not made their essay as touching "the Catholic," for they did not write, " Thus we believe," but " the Catholic Faith was published."

§. 4. 6. The boldness then of their design shews how little they understand the subject; while the novelty of their phrase befits their heresy. For thus they shew, when it was they began their own faith, and that from that same time present they would have it proclaimed. And as according to the Evangelist Luke, there *was made a decree* concerning the taxing, and this decree before was not, but began from those days in which it was made by its framer, they also in like manner, by writing, "The Faith is now published," shewed that the sentiments of their heresy are young, and were not before. But if they add " of the Catholic Faith," they fall before they know it into the extravagance of the Phrygians, and say with them, " To us first was revealed," and " from us dates the Faith of Christians." And as those inscribe it with the names of Maximilla and Montanus[1], so do these with " Constantius, Sovereign," instead of Christ. If, however, as they would have it, the faith dates from the present Consulate, what must the Fathers do, and the blessed Martyrs? nay, what will they themselves do with their own catechumens, who departed to rest before this Consulate? how will they wake them up, that so they may obliterate their former lessons, and may sow in turn the seeming discoveries which they have now put into writing[o]? So ignorant they are on

[1] vid. infr. Orat. iii. §. 47.

---

[n] " He who speaketh of his own, ἐκ τῶν ἰδίων, speaketh a lie." Athan contr Apoll 1. fin. "They used to call the Church a virgin," says Hegesippus, " for it was not yet defiled by profane doctrines....the Simonists, Dositheans, &c....each privately (ἰδίως) and separately has brought in a private opinion." ap. Euseb. Hist. iv. 22. Sophronius at Seleucia cried out, " If to publish day after day our own private (ἰδίαν) will, be a profession of faith, accuracy of truth will fail us." Socr. ii. 40.

[o] " However the error was, certainly error reigned so long as heresies were not. Truth needed a rescue, and looked out for Marcionites and Valentinians.

the subject; with no knowledge but that of making excuses, CHAP. I.
and those unbecoming and unplausible, and carrying with
them their own refutation.

7. As to the Nicene Council, it was not a common meeting, §. 5.
but convened upon a pressing necessity, and for a reasonable
object. The Syrians, Cilicians, and Mesopotamians, were
out of order in celebrating the Feast, and kept Easter with
the Jews [p]; on the other hand, the Arian heresy had risen up
against the Catholic Church, and found supporters in the
Eusebians, who were both zealous for the heresy, and conducted the attack upon religious people. This gave occasion
for an Ecumenical[1] Council, that the feast might be every [1 supr.
where celebrated on one day, and that the heresy which was p 49 note o.
springing up might be anathematized. It took place then;
and the Syrians submitted, and the Fathers pronounced the
Arian heresy to be the forerunner of Antichrist[q], and drew up

Meanwhile, gospelling was nought, faith was nought, nought was the baptism of so many thousand thousand, so many works of faith performed, so many virtues, so many gifts displayed, so many priesthoods, so many ministries exercised, nay, so many martyrdoms crowned." Tertull Præscr 29 "'Profane novelties,' which if we receive, of necessity the faith of our blessed ancestors, either all or a great part of it must be overthrown; the faithful people of all ages and times, all holy saints, all the chaste, all the continent, all the virgins, all the Clergy, the Deacons, the Priests, so many thousands of confessors, so great armies of martyrs, so many famous populous cities and commonwealths, so many islands, provinces, kings, tribes, kingdoms, nations, to conclude, almost now the whole world, incorporated by the Catholic Faith to Christ their head, must needs be said, so many hundred years, to have been ignorant, to have erred, to have blasphemed, to have believed they knew not what." Vinc. Comm 24. "O the extravagance [r] the wisdom, hidden after Christ's coming, they announce to us to-day, which is a thing to draw tears For if the faith began thirty years since, while near four hundred are past since Christ was manifested, nought hath been our gospel that long while, and nought our faith, and fruitlessly have martyrs been martyred, and fruitlessly have such and so great rulers ruled the people. Greg. Naz. ad Cledon. Ep. 102 p 97.

p This seems to have been an innovation in these countries of about fifty years old, or from about the year 276. It is remarkable, that the Quartodeciman custom had come to an end in Proconsular Asia, where it had existed from St. John's time, before it began in Syria. Tillemont refers the change to Anatolius of Laodicea, the writer of this note has attempted in a former work to prove Paul of Samosata the author of it.

q πρόδρομος, præcursor, is almost a received word for the predicted apostasy or apostate, (vid. note on St Cyril's Cat. xv. 9. also infr. note p) but the distinction was not always carefully drawn between the apostate and the Antichrist. Constantius is called Antichrist by Athan. Hist. Arian. 67. his acts are the προοίμιον καὶ παρασκευὴ of Antichrist Hist Arian. 70 fin 71 and 80. Constantius is the image, εἴκων, of Antichrist. 74 and 80 and shews the likeness, ὁμοίωμα, of the malignity of Antichrist. 75 vid also 77 πρόδρομος 77 "Let Christ be expected, for Antichrist is in possession" Hilar. contr. Const. init. Constantius, Antichrist. ibid. 5. Speaking of Auxentius, the Arian Bishop of Milan, he says, " Of one thing I warn you, beware of Antichrist; it is ill that

COUNC. ARIM AND SELEU

a suitable formula against it. And yet in this, many as they are, they ventured on nothing like the proceedings of these three or four men˚. Without prefixing Consulate, month, and day, they wrote concerning the Easter, " It seemed good as follows," for it did then seem good that there should be a general compliance; but about the faith they wrote not, " It seemed good," but, " Thus believes the Catholic Church;" and thereupon they confessed how the faith lay, in order to shew that their own sentiments were not novel, but Apostolical; and what they wrote down, was no discovery of theirs, but is the same as was taught by the Apostles[1].

[1] infr. p. 84. note c.

---

a love of walls has seized you, it is ill that your veneration for God's Church lies in houses and edifices, it is ill that under this plea ye insinuate the name of peace. Is there any doubt that Antichrist is to sit in these? Mountains and woods and lakes and prisons and pits are to me more safe, for in these did prophets, sojourning or sunk, still by God's spirit prophesy." contr. Aux. 12. Lucifer calls Constantius præcursor Antichristi. p 89. possessed with the spirit of Antichrist, p. 219. friend of Antichrist, p. 259. Again, S. Jerome, writing against Jovinian, says that he who so says that there are no differences of rewards is Antichrist, ii. 21. S Leo, alluding to 1 John 4, 10. calls Nestorius and Eutyches, Antichristi præcursores. Ep. 75. p. 1022. Again, Antichrist, whoever opposes what the Church has once settled, with an allusion to opposition to the see of St. Peter. Ep. 156 c. 2. Anastasius speaks of the ten horns of Monophysitism, Hodeg. 6. also 8. and 24. and calls Severus, Monophysite Bp. of Antioch, Antichrist, for usurping the judicial powers of Christ and His Church. ibid. p. 92.

r " They know not to be reverent even to their leaders. And this is why commonly schisms exist not among heretics, because while they are, they are not visible. Schism is their very unity. I am a liar if they do not dissent from their own rules, while every man among them equally alters at his private judgment (suo arbitrio) what he has received, just as he who gave to them composed it at his private judgment. The progress of the thing is true to its nature and its origin. What was a right to Valentinus, was a right to Valentinians, what

to Marcion was to the Marcionites, to innovate on the faith at their private judgment. As soon as any heresy is thoroughly examined, it is found in many points dissenting from its parent. Those parents for the most part have no Churches; they roam about without Mother, without see, bereaved of the faith, without a country, without a home." Tertull. Præscr. 42. At Seleucia Acacius said, " If the Nicene faith has been altered once and many times since, no reason why we should not dictate another faith now." Eleusius the Semi-arian answered, " This Council is called, not to learn what it does not know, not to receive a faith which it does not possess, but walking in the faith of the Father," (meaning the Semiarian Council of the Dedication, A.D. 341 vid. infr. §. 22.) " it swerves not from it in life or death." On this Socrates (Hist. ii. 40.) observes, " How call you those who met at Antioch Fathers, O Eleusius, you who deny their Fathers? for those who met at Nicæa, and unanimously professed the Consubstantial, might more properly receive the name, &c. But if the Bishops at Antioch set at nought their own fathers, those who come after are blindly following parricides; and how did they receive a valid ordination from them, whose faith they set at nought as reprobate? But if those had not the Holy Ghost, which cometh through laying on of hands, neither did these receive the priesthood; for did they receive from those who have not wherewith to give?"

ˢ ὀλίγοι τινές, says Pope Julius, ap. Athan. Apol. 34. ἐγραψάν τινες περὶ πίστεως, says Athan. ad Ep Æg. 5.

New Councils for new heresies. 81

8. But the Councils which they have set in motion, what colourable pretext have they[1]? If any new heresy has risen since the Arian, let them tell us the positions which it has devised, and who are its inventors? and in their own formula, let them anathematize the heresies antecedent to this Council of theirs, among which is the Arian, as the Nicene Fathers did, that it may be made appear that they too have some cogent reason for saying what is novel[2]. But if no such event has happened, and they have it not to shew, but rather they themselves are uttering heresies, as holding Arius's irreligion, and are exposed day by day, and day by day shift their ground[t], what need is there of Councils, when the Nicene is sufficient, as against the Arian heresy, so against the rest, which it has condemned one and all by means of the sound faith? For even the notorious Aetius, who was surnamed godless[3], vaunts not of the discovering of any mania of his own, but under stress of weather has been wrecked upon Arianism, himself and the persons whom he has beguiled. Vainly then do they run about with the pretext that they have demanded Councils for the faith's-sake; for divine Scripture is sufficient above all things; but if a Council be needed on the point, there are the proceedings of the Fathers, for the Nicene Bishops did not neglect this matter, but stated the doctrine so exactly, that persons reading their words honestly, cannot but be reminded by them of the religion towards Christ announced in divine Scripture[4].

9. Having therefore no reason on their side, but being in difficulty whichever way they turn, in spite of their pretences, they have nothing left but to say; " Forasmuch as we contradict

CHAP. I.
[1] ad Ep. Æg. 10.
[2] vid. infr. notes b and c.
[3] vid. p. 3. note f.
[4] vid. p. 57. note l, p. 60. note c.
§. 7.

---

[t] vid de Decr. init. and §. 4. and p 2. note c. We shall have abundant instances of the Arian changes as this Treatise proceeds. " It happens to thee," says S. Hilary to Constantius, " as to unskilful builders, always to be dissatisfied with what thou hast done, thou art ever destroying what thou art ever building." contr. Constant. 23. " O miserable state ! with what seas of cares, with what storms, are they tossed ! for now at one time, as the wind driveth them, they are carried away headlong in error; at another time, coming again to themselves, they are beaten back like contrary waves; sometimes with rash presumption, they allow such things as seem uncertain, at another time of pusillanimity they are in fear even about those things which are certain, doubtful which way to take, which way to return, what to desire, what to avoid, what to hold, what to let go, &c." Vincent. Comm. 20. " He writes," says Athan. of Constantius, " and while he writes repeats, and while he repeats is exasperated, and then he grieves again, and not knowing how to act, he shews how bereft the soul is of understanding " Hist Arian. 70. vid. also ad Ep. Æg. 6.

G

our predecessors, and transgress the traditions of the Fathers, therefore we have thought good that a Council should meet[u]; but again, whereas we fear lest, should it meet at one place, our pains will be thrown away, therefore we have thought good that it be divided into two; that so when we put forth our articles to these separate portions, we may overreach with more effect, with the threat of Constantius the patron of this irreligion, and may abrogate the acts of Nicæa, under pretence of their simplicity." If they have not put this into words, yet this is the meaning of their deeds and their disturbances. Certainly, many and frequent as have been their speeches and writings in various Councils, never yet have they made mention of the Arian heresy as unchristian[1]; but, if any present happened to accuse the heresies, they always took up the defence of the Arian, which the Nicene Council had anathematized; nay, rather, they cordially welcomed the professors of Arianism. This then is in itself a strong argument, that the aim of the present Councils was not truth, but the annulling of the acts of Nicæa; but the proceedings of them and their friends in the Councils themselves, make it equally clear that this was the case:—So that it follows to relate every thing as it occurred.

§. 8. 10. When all were in expectation that they were to assemble in one place, whom the Emperor's letters convoked, and to form one Council, they were divided into two: and, while some betook themselves to Seleucia called the Rugged, the others met at Ariminum, to the number of those four hundred bishops and more, among whom were Germinius, Auxentius, Valens, Ursacius, Demophilus, and Caius[x]. And, while the whole

---

[u] "The Emperor [Theodosius] had a conversation with Nectarius, Bishop [of Constantinople], in what way to make Christendom concordant, and to unite the Church. This made Nectarius anxious; but Sisinnius, a man of ready speech and of practical experience, and throughly versed in the interpretation of the sacred writings and in the doctrines of philosophy, having a conviction that disputations would but aggravate the party spirit of the heresies instead of reconciling schisms, advises him to avoid dialectic engagements, and to appeal to the statements of the ancients, and to put the question to the heresiarchs from the Emperor, whether they made any sort of account of the doctors who belonged to the Church before the division, or came to issue with them as aliens from Christianity, for if they made their authority null, therefore let them venture to anathematize them. But if they did venture, then they would be driven out by the people." Socr. v. 10.

[x] There were two Arian Bishops of Milan of the name of Auxentius, but little is known of them besides. S. Hilary wrote against the elder; the other came into collision with St Ambrose Demophilus, Bishop of Berea,

Third Confession of Sirmium, Homœan in doctrine.

assembly was discussing the matter from the divine Scriptures, these men produced a paper, and, reading the Consulate, they demanded that the whole Council should acquiesce in it, and that no questions should be put to the heretics beyond it, nor inquiry made into their meaning, but that it should be sufficient;—and it ran as follows [y]:

11. The Catholic Faith was published in the presence of our Sovereign the most religious and gloriously victorious Emperor, Constantius, Augustus, the eternal and majestic, in the Consulate of the most illustrious Flavians, Eusebius, and Hypatius, in Sirmium on the 11th of the Calends of June [z].

viii. Confession, or 3rd Sirmian. of 359. vid. §. 29 infr.

We believe in one Only and True God, the Father Almighty, Creator and Framer of all things:

And in one Only-begotten Son of God, who, before all ages, and before all origin, and before all conceivable time, and before all comprehensible substance, was begotten impassibly from God; through whom the ages were disposed and all things were made; and Him begotten as the Only-begotten, Only from the Only Father, God from God, like to the Father who begat Him, ὅμοιον according to the Scriptures; whose generation no one knoweth save the Father alone who begat Him. We know that He, the Only-begotten Son of God, at the Father's bidding came from the heavens for the abolishment of sin, and was born of the Virgin Mary, and conversed with the disciples, and fulfilled the economy according to the Father's will, and was crucified, and died and descended into the parts beneath the earth, and had the economy of things there, whom the gate-keepers of hell saw and shuddered; and He rose from the dead the third day, and conversed with the disciples, and fulfilled the economy, and when the forty days were full ascended into the heavens, and sitteth on the right hand of the Father, and is coming in the last day of the resurrection in the glory of the Father, to render to every one according to his works.

And in the Holy Ghost, whom the Only-begotten of God Himself, Jesus Christ, had promised to send to the race of men, the Paraclete, as it is written, " I go to the Father, and I will ask the Father, and He shall send unto you another Paraclete, even the Spirit of Truth," He shall take of Mine and shall teach and bring to your remembrance all things.

---

was one of those who carried the long Confession into the West, though not mentioned by Athan. below. He was afterwards claimed by Aetius, as agreeing with him. Of Caius, an Illyrian Bishop, nothing is known except that he sided throughout with the Arian party.

[y] The Creed which follows had been prepared at Sirmium shortly before, and is the third, or, as some think, the fourth, drawn up at Sirmium. It was the composition of Mark of Arethusa, yet it was written in Latin; and though Mark was a Semi-arian, it distinctly abandons the word substance. But this point of history is involved in much obscurity. As it stands it is a patchwork of two views. It will be observed, that it is the Creed on which Athanasius has been animadverting above.

[z] May 22, 359, Whitsun-Eve.

COUNC. ARIM AND SELEU
But whereas the term "substance," has been adopted by the Fathers in simplicity, and gives offence as being misconceived by the people, and is not contained in the Scriptures, it has seemed good to remove it, that it be never in any case used of God again, because the divine Scriptures no where use it of Father and Son. But we say that the Son is like the Father in all things, as all the Holy Scriptures say and teach [a].

§. 9.   12. When this had been read, the dishonesty of its framers was soon apparent. For on the Bishops proposing that the Arian heresy should be anathematized together with the other heresies [b], and all assenting, Ursacius and Valens and their friends refused; till in the event the Fathers condemned them, on the ground that their confession had been written, not in sincerity, but for the annulling of the Acts of Nicæa, and the introduction instead of their miserable heresy. Marvelling then at the deceitfulness of their language and their unprincipled intentions, the Bishops said; "Not as if in need of faith have we come hither; for we have within us faith, and that in soundness: but that we may put to shame those who gainsay the truth and attempt novelties. If then ye have drawn up this formula, as if now beginning to believe, ye are not so much as clerks, but are starting with school; but if you meet us with the same views, with which we have come hither, let there be a general unanimity, and let us anathematize the heresies, and preserve the teaching of the Fathers. Thus pleas for Councils will not longer circulate about, the Bishops at Nicæa having anticipated them once for all, and done all that was needful for the Catholic Church [c]." However, even then, in

[a] This clause shews the presence and influence of the Acacian party; but the confession is raised towards the end by the introduction of the phrase, "like in all things," κατὰ πάντα ὅμοιον, which was added by Constantius himself, Epiph. Hær. 73. 22. and which in the minds of the more orthodox included "substance," vid. S. Cyril, Catech. IV. 7. xi. 18. a sense, however, which is contradictory to what goes before. It is impossible to go into this subject without being involved in historical difficulties, which there would be no room for discussing.

[b] The Eusebian party began after the Nicene Council by attacking Athanasius; then they held Councils to explain the faith; then they attacked the received terms of theology, and thereby the Nicene Creed, professing to adhere to Scripture. At Seleucia, as described infra, they openly attacked the Creed. But they did not dare avow the Arian heresy; the first step then on the part of the Catholics was to demand of them a condemnation of it. The Anomœans perplexed the Eusebians by letting out the secret of their real Arianism.

[c] It need scarcely be said, that the great object of the Arians was to obtain a *consideration* of the doctrine settled at Nicæa by a new Council.

spite of this general agreement of the Bishops, still the above-mentioned refused. So at length the whole Council, condemning them as ignorant and deceitful men, or rather as heretics, gave their suffrages in behalf of the Nicene Council, and gave judgment all of them that it was enough; but as to the forenamed Ursacius and Valens, Germanicus, Auxentius, Caius, and Demophilus, they pronounced them to be heretics, deposed them as not really Christians[1], but Arians, and wrote against them in Latin what has been translated in its substance[2] into Greek, thus:—

[1] supr. p. 27.
[2] κατὰ δύναμιν

§. 10.

13. *Copy of an Epistle from the Council to Constantius, Augustus*[d].—

" We believe it has been ordered by God's command, upon the mandate[e] of your religiousness, that we, the Bishops of the Western Provinces, came from all parts to Ariminum, for the manifestation of the Faith to all Catholic Churches and the detection of the heretics. For upon a discussion, in which we all took part who are right-minded, it was resolved to adhere to that faith which, enduring from antiquity we have ever received from Prophets, Gospels, and Apostles, from God Himself, and our Lord Jesus Christ, the upholder of your dominion, and the author of your welfare For we deemed it to be a sin, to mutilate any work of the saints, and in particular of those who in the case of the Nicene for-

---

This Athan. all through his works strenuously resists. In the Letter which follows, the Council observes, that the Emperor had commanded " to treat of the faith," under which ambiguous phrase the Arians attempted to " propose," as they say, " something novel for their consideration." And so at Sardica the Council writes to Pope Julius, that the Emperors Constantius and Constans had proposed three subjects for its consideration; first, " that all points in discussion should be debated afresh (de integro), and above all concerning the holy faith and the integrity of the truth which [the Arians] had violated." Hil. Fragm. ii. 11. Enemies of the Arians seem to have wished this as well as themselves; and the Council got into difficulty in consequence. Hosius the president and Protogenes Bishop of the place wrote to the Pope to explain, " from fear," says Sozomen, " lest some might think that there was any innovation upon the Nicene decrees." iii. 12. From his way of stating the matter, Sozomen seems to have himself believed

that the Council did publish a creed And, as has been alluded to in a former note, p 70. a remarkable contession, and attributed to the Council, does exist. Accordingly Athanasius, Eusebius of Vercellæ, and the Council of Alexandria, A.D 362, protest against the idea. "It is true that certain persons wished to add to the Nicene Council as if there was something wanting, but the Holy Council was displeased," &c. Tom. ad Antioch. However, Vigilius of Thapsus repeats the report. contr. Eutych. v. init.

[d] The same version of the Letter which follows is found in Socr. ii 39. Soz iv. 10. Theod. Hist. ii 19. Niceph l. 40. On comparison with the Latin original, which is preserved by Hilary, Fragm. viii. it appears to be so very freely executed, that it has been thought better here to translate it from the text of Hilary

[e] Ex præcepto Præceptum becomes a technical word afterwards for a royal deed, charter, or edict; and it has somewhat of that meaning even here.

COUNC. mulary, held session together with Constantine of glorious memory,
ARIM. the Father of your religiousness. Which formulary was put abroad
AND and gained entrance into the minds of the people, and being at
SELEU. that time drawn up against Arianism, is found to be such, that
heresies are overthrown by it; from which, if aught were subtracted, an opening is made to the poison of the heretics.
 Accordingly Ursacius and Valens formerly came into suspicion
of the said Arian heresy, and were suspended from Communion,
¹ supr and asked pardon according to their letters¹, and obtained it then
p 74. at the Council of Milan, in the presence of the legates of the Roman
note d. Church. And since Constantine was at the Nicene Council, when the
formulary was drawn up with great deliberation, and after being
baptized with the profession of it, departed to God's rest, we think
it a crime to mutilate aught in it, and in any thing to detract
from so many Saints, and Confessors, and Successors of Martyrs who drew it up; considering that they in turn preserved all
doctrine of the Catholics who were before them, according to the
Scriptures, and that they remained unto these times in which thy
religiousness has received the charge of ruling the world from
God the Father through our God and Lord Jesus Christ. For them,
they were attempting to pull up what had been reasonably laid down.
For, whereas the letters of your religiousness commanded to treat of
the faith, there was proposed to us by the aforenamed troublers
of the Churches, Germinius being associated with Auxentius ᶠ and
Caius, something novel for our consideration, which contained
many particulars of perverse doctrine Accordingly, when they
found that what they proposed publicly in the Council was un-
acceptable, they considered that they must draw up another
statement Indeed it is certain that they have often changed these
formularies in a short time. And lest the Churches should have
a recurrence of these disturbances, it seemed good to keep the
ancient and reasonable institutions. For the information therefore of your clemency, we have instructed our legates to acquaint
you of the judgment of the Council by our letter, to whom we
have given this sole direction, not to execute the legation otherwise than for the stability and permanence of the ancient decrees;
that your wisdom also might know, that peace would not be
accomplished by the removal of those decrees, as the aforesaid
Valens and Ursacius, Germinius and Caius, engaged. On the
contrary, troubles have in consequence been excited in all regions
and the Roman Church.
 On this account we ask your clemency to regard and hear all
our legates with favourable ears and a serene countenance, and

---

ᶠ Auxentius, omitted in Hilary's copy, is inserted here, and in the Decree which follows, from the Greek, since Athanasius has thus given his sanction to the fact of his being condemned at Ariminum. Yet Auxentius appeals to Ariminum triumphantly Hil contr. Aux. fin. Socrates, Hist. ii. 37. says, that Demophilus also was deposed, but he was an Eastern Bishop, if he be Demophilus of Berea. vid. Coustant. on Hil. Fragm vii. p. 1342. Yet he is mentioned also by Athanasius as present, supra, §. 9. A few words are wanting in the Latin in the commencement of one of the sentences which follow.

not to suffer aught to be abrogated to the dishonour of the ancients; so that all things may continue which we have received from our forefathers, who, as we trust, were prudent men, and acted not without the Holy Spirit of God; because by these novelties not only are faithful nations troubled, but the infidels also are deterred from believing. We pray also that you would give orders that so many Bishops, who are detained at Ariminum, among those are numbers who are broken with age and poverty, may return to their own country, lest the members of their Churches suffer, as being deprived of their Bishops. This, however, we ask with earnestness, that nothing be innovated, nothing withdrawn; but that all remain incorrupt which has continued in the times of the Father of your sacred piety and in your own religious days; and that your holy prudence will not permit us to be harassed, and torn from our sees; but that the Bishops may in quiet give themselves always to the prayers, which they do always offer for your own welfare and for your reign, and for peace, which may the Divinity bestow on you, according to your merits, profound and perpetual! But our legates will bring the subscriptions and names of the Bishops or Legates, as another letter informs your holy and religious prudence.

14. *Decree of the Council* [g].   § 11.

As far as it was fitting, dearest brethren, the Catholic Council has had patience, and has so often displayed the Church's forbearance towards Ursacius and Valens, Germinius, Caius, and Auxentius; who by so often changing what they had believed, have troubled all the Churches, and still are endeavouring to introduce their heretical spirit into Christian minds. For they wish to annul the formulary passed at Nicæa, which was framed against the Arian and other heresies. They have presented to us besides a creed drawn up by themselves, which we could not lawfully receive. Even before this have they been pronounced heretics by us, and it has been confirmed by a long period, whom we have not admitted to our communion, but condemned them in their presence by our voices. Now then, what seems good to you, again declare, that it may be ratified by the subscription of each.

All the Bishops answered, It seems good that the aforenamed heretics should be condemned, that the Church may remain in unshaken faith, which is truly Catholic, and in perpetual peace

15. Matters at Ariminum then had this speedy issue; for

---

[g] This Decree is also here translated from the original in Hilary, who has besides preserved the "Catholic Definition" of the Council, in which it professes its adherence to the Creed of Nicæa, and in opposition to the Sirmian Confession which the Arians had proposed, acknowledges in particular both the word and the meaning of "substance;" " substantiæ nomen et rem, à multis sanctis Scripturis insinuatam mentibus nostris, obtinere debere sui firmitatem." Fragm. vii. 3.

COUNC. there was no disagreement there, but all of them with one
ARIM. accord both put into writing what they decided upon, and
AND
SELEU. deposed the Arians[h]. Meanwhile the transactions in Seleucia
§. 12. the Rugged were as follows: it was in the month called by the
Romans September, by the Egyptians Thoth, and by the
Macedonians Gorpiæus[i], and the day of the month according
to the Egyptians the 16th, upon which all the members of the
Council assembled together. And there were present about
a hundred and sixty; and whereas there were many who
were accused among them, and their accusers were crying
out against them, Acacius, and Patrophilus, and Uranius of
Tyre, and Eudoxius, who usurped the Church of Antioch,
and Leontius, and Theodotus, and Evagrius, and Theodulus,
and George who has been driven from the whole world[k], adopt
an unprincipled course. Fearing the proofs which their accusers had to shew against them, they coalesced with the rest of
the Arian party[l], (who were mercenaries in the cause of irreligion
as if for this purpose, and were ordained by Secundus who had

[h] Athanasius seems to have known no more of the proceedings at Arimi-num, which perhaps were then in pro-gress, when he wrote this Treatise; their termination, as is well known, was very unhappy, " Ingemuit totus orbis," says St. Jerome, " et Arianum se esse miratus est." ad Lucif. 19 A deputation of ten persons was sent from the Coun-cil to Constantius, to which Valens op-posed one of his own. Constantius pre-tended the barbarian war, and delayed an answer till the beginning of October, the Council having opened in July. The Postscript to this Treatise con-tained the news of this artifice and of the Council's distress in consequence, which Athanasius had just heard. He also seems to have inserted into his work, §. 30 and 31, upon the receipt of the news of the mission of Valens to Constantinople, a mission which ended in the submission of the Catholic dele-gacy. Upon this returning to Ariminum with the delegates and the Arian creed they had signed, (vid. infr. §. 30.) Valens, partly by menaces and partly by sophistry, succeeded in procuring the subscriptions of the Council also to the same formula.

[i] Gorpiæus was the first month of the Syro-Macedonic year among the Greeks, dating according to the era of the Seleu-cidæ. The Roman date of the meeting of the Council was the 27th of Septem-ber. The original transactions at Ari-minum had at this time been finished as much as two months, and its deputies were waiting for Constantius in Constantinople.

[k] There is little to observe of these Acacian Bishops in addition to what has been said of several of them, except that George is the Cappadocian, the notorious intruder into the see of S. Athanasius. The charges which lay against them were of various kinds. Socrates says that the Acacian party consisted in all of 34; others increase it by a few more.

[l] The Eusebian or Court party are here called Acacian, and were Anomœ-ans and Semi-arians alternately, or more properly as they may be called Homœan or Scriptural; for Arians, Semi-arians, and Anomœans, all used theological terms as well as the Catho-lics. The Semi-arians numbered about 100, the remaining dozen might be the Egyptian Bishops who were zealous supporters of the Catholic cause. How-ever, there were besides a few Anomœ-ans or Arians, as Athan. calls them, with whom the Acacians now coa-lesced.

been deposed by the great Council,) the Libyan Stephen, and Seras, and Pollux, who were under accusation upon various charges, next Pancratius, and one Ptolemy a Meletian [m]. And they made a pretence of entering upon the question of faith, but it was clear [n] they were doing so from fear of their accusers; and they took the part of the heresy, till at length they were left by themselves. For, whereas supporters of the Acacians lay under suspicion and were very few, but the others were the majority; therefore the Acacians, acting with the boldness of desperation, altogether denied the Nicene formula, and censured the Council, while the others, who were the majority, accepted the whole proceedings of the Council, except that they complained of the word "Consubstantial," as obscure and open to suspicion. When then time passed, and the accusers pressed, and the accused put in pleas, and thereby were led on further by their irreligion and blasphemed the Lord, thereupon the majority of Bishops became indignant [o], and deposed Acacius, Patrophilus, Uranius, Eudoxius, and George the contractor [1], and others from Asia, Leontius, and Theodosius, Evagrius and Theodoret, and excommunicated Asterius, Eusebius, Augerus, Basilicus, Phœbus, Fidelius, Eutychius, and Magnus. And this they did on their non-appearance, when summoned to defend themselves on charges which numbers preferred against them. And they decreed that so they should remain, until they made their defence and

[1] pork-con-tractor to the troops, ὑποδιάκ- την, Hist. Arian. 75. vid. Naz. Orat. 21. 16.

[m] The Meletian schismatics of Egypt had formed an alliance with the Arians from the first. Athan. imputes the alliance to ambition and avarice in the Meletians, and to zeal for their heresy in the Arians. Ad Ep. Æg. 22. vid. also Hist. Arian. 78. After Sardica the Semi-arians attempted a coalition with the Donatists of Africa. Aug. contr. Cresc. iii 38.

[n] Acacius had written to the Semi-arian Macedonius of Constantinople in favour of the κατὰ πάντα ὅμοιον, and of the Son's being τῆς αὐτῆς οὐσίας, and this the Council was aware of. Soz. iv. 22. Acacius made answer that no one ancient or modern was ever judged by his writings. Socr. ii 40.

[o] They also confirmed the Semi-arian Confession of the Dedication, 341. of which infr. §. 22. Basil of Ancyra, the leading Semi-arian, was not present; and he and Mark of Arethusa were both parties to the Acacian third Sirmium Confession, which had been proposed at Ariminum. George of Laodicea, however, who was with him at the Council of Ancyra in the foregoing year, acted as the leader of the Semi-arians. After this the Acacians drew up another Confession, which Athan. has preserved, infra, §. 29. in which they persist in their rejection of all but Scripture terms. This the Semi-arian majority rejected, and proceeded to depose its authors. There is nothing to remark as regards the names of Arian Bishops here introduced into the text.

Counc. cleared themselves of the offences imputed to them. And
Arim. after despatching the sentence pronounced against them to
and
Seleu. the diocese of each, they proceeded to Constantius, that most
irreligious ᴾ Augustus, to report to him their proceedings, as
they had been ordered And this was the termination of the
Council in Seleucia.

§. 13. 16. Who then but must approve of the conscientious conduct
of the Bishops at Ariminum? who endured such labour of
journey and perils of sea, that by a sacred and canonical
resolution they might depose the Arians, and guard inviolate
the definitions of the Fathers. For each of them deemed
that, if they undid the acts of their predecessors, they were
affording a pretext to their successors to undo what they
¹ supr. themselves then were enacting¹. And who but must condemn
p. 80, the fickleness of the party of Eudoxius and Acacius, who
note r.
² προτί- sacrifice² the honour due to their own fathers to partizan-
νουσι
infr. §.
16. fin.

ᴾ Up to the year 356, Athanasius had treated Constantius as a member of the Church, but at that date the Eusebian or Court party abandoned the Semi-arians for the Anomœans, George of Cappadocia was sent as Bishop to Alexandria, Athanasius was driven into the desert, St. Hilary and other Western Bishops were sent into banishment, Hosius was persecuted into signing an Arian confession, and Pope Liberius into communicating with the Arians Upon this Athanasius changed his tone and considered that he had to deal with an Antichrist. We have seen above, note g, the language both of himself and others in consequence In his Apol. contr. Arian. init. (A.D. 350) ad Ep Æg. 5. (356.) and his Apol. ad Constant. passim. (356) he calls the Emperor most pious, religious, &c. At the end of the last-mentioned work, § 27. the news comes to him while in exile of the persecution of the Western Bishops and the measures against himself. He still in the peroration calls Constantius, " blessed and divinely favoured Augustus," and urges on him that he is a "Christian, φιλόχριστος, Emperor." In the works which follow, Apol. de fuga, §. 26. (357) he calls him an heretic; and Hist. Arian. § 45, &c. (358.) speaking of the treatment of Hosius, &c. he calls him " Ahab,"

" Belshazzar," " Saul," " Antichrist." The passage at the end of the Apol. contr. Arian. in which he speaks of the " much violence and tyrannical power of Constantius," is an addition of Athan.'s at a later date, vid. Montfaucon's note on §. 38. fin. This is worth mentioning, as it shews the unfairness of the following passage from Gibbon, ch. xxi. note 116. " As Athanasius dispersed secret invectives against Constantius, see the Epistle to the monks," [i. e Hist. Arian. ad Monach A. D. 358] " at the same time that he assured him of his profound respect, we might distrust the professions of the Archbishop. tom. 1. p. 677." [i. e. apparently Apol. ad Const. A.D 356.] Again in a later part of the chapter, " In his public Apologies, which he addressed to the Emperor himself, he sometimes affected the praise of moderation; whilst at the same time in secret and vehement invectives he exposed Constantius as a weak and wicked prince, the executioner of his family, the tyrant of the republic, and the Antichrist of the Church." He offers no proof of this assertion It may be added that S. Greg. Naz. praises Constantius, but it is in contrast with Julian. Orat. iv. 3 v. 6 And S. Ambrose, but it is for his enmity to paganism. Ep. 1. 18 n. 32.

and the Acacians 91

ship and patronage of the Ario-maniacs ^q? for what confidence CHAP.
can be placed in their acts, if the acts of their fathers be I.
undone? or how call they them fathers and themselves successors, if they set about impeaching their judgment? and especially what can Acacius say of his own master, Eusebius, who not only gave his subscription in the Nicene Council, but even in a letter ¹ signified to his flock, that that was true ¹ Vid. faith, which the Council had declared? for, if he explained supr. de Decr. §. 3.

---

^q " The dumb ass forbade the *madness* of the prophet," παραφρονίαν. On the word 'Αρειομανῖται, Gibbon observes, " The ordinary appellation with which Athanasius and his followers chose to compliment the Arians, was that of Ariomanites," ch. xxi. note 61. Rather, the name originally was a state title, injoined by Constantine, vid. Petav. de Trin. 1. 8. fin. Naz. Orat. p. 794. note e. and thenceforth used by the general Church, e. g. Eustathius of Antioch, ap. Theod. Hist. 1 7 Constant ap. Concil. t. 1 p 456 b. Hilar. de Trin. vi. Julius ap. Athan. Apol. 23. Council of Egypt, ibid. 6. Phæbadius, contr. Arian. circ. fin. Epiph. Hær. 69 19 (ὁ μανιώδης 'Άρειος) Greg. Naz. Orat 11. 37 τῆς 'Αρείου καλῶς ὀνομασθείσαν μανίαν and so ὁ τῆς μανίας ἐπώνυμος. Orat. 43. 30 vid. also Orat. 20. 5. and so Proclus, τὴν 'Αρείου μανίαν ad Armen p 618 fin. And Athan. e g μανίαν διαβόλου ad Serap. 1 1. also ad Serap. 1. 17 fin. 19 init 20 d 24. e. 29 e. 11 1 fin. iv. 5 init. 6 fin. 15 fin. 16 fin. In some of these the denial of the divinity of the Holy Ghost is the madness. In like manner Hilary speaks continually of their " furor." de Trin. e. g. 1. 17. Several meanings are implied in this title; the real reason for it was the fanatical fury with which it spread and maintained itself, e. g. ὁ μανικὸς ἐραστὴς τοῦ χριστοῦ, enthusiastic. Chrysost. in Esai. vi. 1 Hom. iv. 3. p. 124. Thus Athan. contrasts the Arian hatred of the truth, with the mere worldliness of the Meletians, supr. p. 89. note m. Hence they are ἀσεβεῖς, χριστόμαχοι, and governed by κακόνοια and κακοφροσύνη. Again, Socrates speaks of it as a flame which ravaged, ἐπινέμετο, provinces and cities. 1. 6. And Alexander cries out ὦ ἀνοσίου τύφου καὶ ἀμέτρου μανίας Theod. Hist. 1. 3. p 741. vid. also pp. 735, 6. 747. And we read much of their eager spirit of proselytism. Theod. ibid. The original word *mania* best expresses it in English. Their cruelty came into this idea of their " mania;" hence Athan. in one place calls the Arian women, in the tumult under George of Cappadocia, *Mœnades.* " They running up and down like Bacchanale and furies, μαινάδες καὶ ἐριννυες, thought it a misfortune not to find opportunity for injury, and passed that day in grief in which they could do no harm " Hist Arian. 59. Also " profana Ariorum novitas velut quædam Bellona aut Furia." Vincent. Commin. 6. Eustathius speaks of οἱ παράδοξοι τῆς ἀρείου θυμέλης μισόχοροι ap. Phot. 225. p 759. And hence the strange paronomasia of Constantine, 'Άρεις, ἄρεις, with an allusion to Hom Il. v. 31. A second reason, or rather sense, of the appellation was what is noted, supr p. 2. note e. that, denying the Word, they have forfeited the gift of reason, e. g. τῶν 'Αρειομανιτῶν τὴν ἀλογίαν de Sent. Dion. init. vid ibid 24. fin. Orat. 11. §. 32. c. iii. § 63. throughout. Hence in like manner Athan. speaks of the heathen as mad who did not acknowledge God and His Word. contr. Gent. fin also 23. fin. Hence he speaks of εἰδωλομανία contr. Gent. 10. and 21 fin. Again, Incarn. 47. he speaks of the *mania* of oracles, which belongs rather to the former sense of the word. Other heresies had the word *mania* applied to them, e. g. that of Valentinus Athan. Orat. 11. §. 70 κἂν μαινῆται. Epiphanius speaks of the ἐμμανὴς διδασκαλία of the Noetians. Hær. 57. 2. Nazianzen contrasts the sickness, νόσος, of Sabellius with the madness of Arius; Orat. 20. 5. but Athan. says, μαίνεται μὲν 'Άρειος, μαίνεται δὲ Σαβέλλιος, Orat. iv. 25. But this note might be prolonged indefinitely.

himself in that letter in his own way[r], yet he did not contradict the Council's terms, but even charged it upon the Arians, that, their position that the Son was not before His generation, was not even consistent with His being before Mary. What then will they proceed to teach the people who are under their teaching? that the fathers erred? and how are they themselves to be trusted by those, whom they teach to disobey their Teachers? and with what faces too will they look upon the sepulchres of the Fathers whom they now name heretics? And why do they defame the Valentinians, Phrygians, and Manichees, yet give the name of saint to those whom they themselves suspect of making parallel statements? or how can they any longer be Bishops, if they were ordained by persons whom they accuse of heresy[1]? But if their sentiments were wrong and their writings seduced the world, then let their memory perish altogether; when, however, you cast out their books, go and cast out their relics too from the cemeteries, so that one and all may know that they are seducers, and that you are parricides. The blessed Apostle approves of the Corinthians because, he says, *ye remember me in all things, and keep the traditions as I delivered them to you;* but they, as entertaining such views of their predecessors, will have the daring to say just the reverse to their flocks: " We praise you not for remembering your fathers, but rather we make much of you, when you hold not their traditions." And let them go on to cast a slur on their own ignoble birth, and say, " We are sprung not of religious men but of heretics." For such language, as I said before, is consistent in those who barter[2] their Father's fame and their own salvation for Arianism, and fear not the words of the divine proverb, *There is a generation that curseth their father,* and the threat lying in the Law against such.

17. They then, from zeal for the heresy, are of this obstinate temper; you, however, be not troubled at it, nor take their audacity for truth. For they dissent from each other, and, whereas they have revolted from their Fathers, are not of one and the same mind, but float about with various and discordant changes. And, as quarrelling with the Council of Nicæa, they

---

[r] ὡς ἠθέλησεν vid. also de Decr. §. 3. ὡς ἠθέλησαν ad Ep. Æg. 5.

have held many Councils themselves, and have published a faith with in each of them, and have stood to none[1], nay, they will never do otherwise, for perversely seeking, they will never find that Wisdom which they hate. I have accordingly subjoined, portions both of Arius's writings and of whatever else I could collect, of their publications in different Councils; whereby you will learn to your surprise with what object they stand out against an Ecumenical[2] Council and their own Fathers[3] without blushing.

CHAP. II.

HISTORY OF ARIAN OPINIONS.

Arius's own sentiments; his Thalia and Letter to S. Alexander; corrections by Eusebius and others; extracts from the works of Asterius; letter of the Council of Jerusalem, first Creed of Arians at the Dedication at Antioch; second, Lucian's on the same occasion; third, by Theophronius; fourth, sent to Constans in Gaul; fifth, the Macrostiche sent into Italy; sixth, at Sirmium; seventh, at the same place; and eighth also, as given above in Chapter 1; ninth, at Seleucia; tenth, at Constantinople; eleventh, at Antioch.

COUNC. ARIM. AND SELEU.

§. 15.

¹ ὡς ἐν θαλίᾳ

1. ARIUS and his friends thought and professed thus: "God made the Son out of nothing, and called Him His Son;" "The Word of God is one of the creatures;" and "Once He was not," and "He is alterable; capable, when it is His will, of altering." Accordingly they were expelled from the Church by Alexander of blessed memory. However, after his expulsion, when he was with the Eusebians, he drew up his heresy upon paper, and imitating, as if in festivity¹, no grave writer, but the Egyptian Sotades, in the dissolute tone of his metre*, he writes at great length, for instance as follows:—

2. *Blasphemies of Arius.*

God Himself then, in His own nature, is ineffable by all men.
Equal or like Himself He alone has none, or one in glory.

ᵃ Again, Orat. 1. §. 2—5. he calls him the Sotadean Arius; and speaks of the "dissolute manners," and "the effeminate tone," and the "jests" of the Thalia; a poem which, he says shortly before, "is not even found among the more respectable Greeks, but among those only who sing songs over their wine, with noise and revel." vid. also de Sent. D. 6 Constantine also after the "Ἄρεις Ἄρεις, proceeds, ἐπισχέτω δὲ εἰ ἡ γοῦν Ἀφροδίτης ὁμιλία. Epiph. Hær. 69. 9 fin. Socrates too says that "the character of the book was gross and dissolute." Hist. i. 9. The Arian Philostorgius tells us that "Arius wrote songs for the sea and for the mill and for the road, and then set them to suitable music," Hist. ii. 2. It is remarkable that Athanasius should say the *Egyptian* Sotades, and again in Sent. D. 6. There were two Poets of the name; one a writer of the Middle Comedy, Athen. Deipn. vii. 11; but the other, who is here spoken of, was a native of Maronea in Crete, according to Suidas, (in voc.) under the successors of Alexander, Athen. xiv. 4. He wrote in Ionic metre, which was of infamous name from the subjects to which he and others applied it. vid. Suid. ibid. Some read "Sotadicos" for "Socraticos," Juv. Satir. ii. 10. vid. also Martial Ep. ii. 86. The characteristic of the metre was the recurrence of the same cadence, which virtually destroyed the division into verses, Turneb. in Quinct. 1. 8. and thus gave the composition that lax and slovenly air to which Athanasius

And Ingenerate we call Him, because of Him who is generate
             by nature.
We praise Him as Unoriginate because of Him who has an origin
And adore Him as everlasting, because of Him who in time
             has come to be.
The Unoriginate made the Son an origin of things generated;
And advanced Him as a Son to Himself by adoption.
He has nothing proper to God in proper subsistence.
For He is not equal, no, nor one in substance [b] with Him.
Wise is God, for He is the teacher of Wisdom [c].
There is full proof that God is invisible to all beings,
Both to things which are through the Son, and to the Son He is
             invisible.
I will say it expressly, how by the Son is seen the Invisible;
By that power by which God sees, and in His own measure,
The Son endures to see the Father, as is lawful.
Thus there is a Three, not in equal glories
Not intermingling with each other [d] are their subsistences.
One more glorious than the other in their glories unto immensity.
Foreign from the Son in substance is the Father, for He is
             Unoriginate.

alludes. Horace's Ode, " Miserarum est nec amori, &c." is a specimen of this metre, and some have called it Sotadic; but Bentley shews in loc that Sotades wrote in the Ionic à majore, and that his verse had somewhat more of system than is found in the Ode of Horace. Athenæus implies that all Ionic metres were called Sotadic, or that Sotades wrote in various Ionic metres. The Church adopted the Doric music, and forbade the Ionic and Lydian. The name "Thalia" commonly belonged to convivial songs; Martial contrasts the "lasciva Thalia" with "carmina sanctiora," Epigr. vii 17. vid. Thaliarchus, "the master of the feast," Horat. Od. 1. 9. If one were to attempt to form a judgment on the nature of Arius's proceeding, it would be this, that he attempted to popularize his heresy by introducing it into the common employments and recreations of life, and having no reverence, he fell into the error of modern religionists, who, with a better creed, sing spiritual songs at table, and use in their chapels glees and opera airs. This would be more offensive of old even than now, in proportion to the keener sensibilities of the South and the more definite ideas which music seems to have conveyed to their minds; and more especially in a case where the metre Arius employed had obtained so shocking a reputation, and was associated in the minds of Christians with the deeds of darkness, in the midst of which in those heathen times the Church lived and witnessed.

[b] This passage ought to have been added to note t, p. 35. supr. as containing a more direct denial of the ὁμοούσιον, so incorrect is Gibbon's assertion, that on Eusebius's "ingenuously confessing that it was incompatible with the principles of their theological system, the *fortunate opportunity* was eagerly embraced by the Bishops," as if they were bent at all hazards, and without reference to the real and substantial agreement or disagreement of themselves and the Arians, to find some word which might accidentally serve to exclude the latter from communion.

[c] That is, Wisdom, or the Son, is but the *disciple* of Him who is Wise, and not the *attribute* by which He is Wise, which is what the Sabellians said, vid. Orat. iv. § 2. and what Arius imputed to the Church.

[d] ἀνεπίμικτοὶ, that is, he denied the περιχώρησις, vid. infra, Orat. iii. 3, &c.

Understand that the One was; but the Two was not, before it was in existence.
It follows at once that, though the Son was not, the Father was God.
Hence the Son, not being, (for He existed at the will of the Father,)
Is God Only-begotten, and He is alien from either.
Wisdom existed as Wisdom by the will of the Wise God.
Hence He is conceived in numberless conceptions[e].
Spirit, Power, Wisdom, God's glory, Truth, Image, and Word.
Understand that He is conceived to be Radiance and Light.
One equal to the Son, the Superior is able to generate.
But more excellent, or superior, or greater, He is not able.
At God's will the Son is what and whatsoever He is
And when and since He was, from that time He has subsisted from God.
He, being a strong God, praises in His degree the Superior.
To speak in brief, God is ineffable by His Son.
For He is to Himself what He is, that is, unspeakable.
So that nothing which is called comprehensible[f]
Does the Son know to speak about; for it is impossible for Him
To investigate the Father, who is by Himself.
For the Son does not know His own substance,
For, being Son, He really existed, at the will of the Father.
What argument then allows, that He who is from the Father
Should know His own parent by comprehension?
For it is plain that, for That which hath origin
To conceive how the Unoriginate is,
Or to grasp the idea, is not possible.

§. 16.   3. And what they wrote by letter to Alexander of blessed memory, the Bishop, runs as follows:—

To Our Blessed Pope[g] and Bishop, Alexander, the Presbyters and Deacons, send health in the Lord.

Our faith from our forefathers, which also we have learned from

---

[e] ἐπινοίαις, that is, our Lord's titles are but *names*, or *figures*, not properly belonging to Him but only existing in our minds.

[f] κατὰ κατάληψιν, that is, there is nothing comprehensible in the Father for the Son to know and declare. On the other hand the doctrine of the Anomœans, who in most points agreed with Arius, was, that all men could know Almighty God perfectly; according to Socrates, who says, "Not to seem to be slandering, listen to Eunomius himself, what words he dares to use in sophistry concerning God; they run thus —' God knows not of His substance more than we do; nor is it known to Him more, to us less; but whatsoever we may know of it, that He too knows; and what again He, that you will find without any distinction in us.'" Hist. iv. 7.

[g] Alexander is also so called, Theod. Hist. 1. 4. p. 749. Athanasius, Hieron. contr. Joan. 4. Heraclas, also of Alex-

thee, Blessed Pope, is this :—We acknowledge One God, alone Ingenerate, alone Everlasting, alone Unoriginate, alone True, alone having Immortality, alone Wise, alone Good, alone Sovereign; Judge, Governor, and Providence of all, unalterable and unchangeable, just and good, God of Law and Prophets and New Testament; who generated an Only-begotten Son before eternal times, through whom He has made both the ages and the universe, and generated Him, not in semblance, but in truth; and that He made Him subsist at His own will unalterable and unchangeable; perfect creature of God, but not as one of the creatures, offspring, but not as one of things generated; nor as Valentinus pronounced that the offspring of the Father was an issue[h]; nor as Manichæus taught that the offspring was a portion of the Father, one in substance[i]; or as Sabellius, dividing the One, speaks of a Son-and-Father[k]; nor as Hieracas, of one torch from another, or as a lamp divided into two[l], nor of Him who was before, being afterwards generated or new-created into a Son[m], as thou too thyself, Blessed

andria, by Dionysius apud Euseb. Hist vii. 7 Epiphanius of Cyprus, Hieron. Ep. 57, 2. John of Jerusalem, Hier. contr. Joan. 4. Cyprian of Carthage, Ep. ap Cypr. 31. Augustine of Hippo, Hier. Ep 141 init. Lupus, Pragmatius, Leontius, Theoplastus, Eutropius,&c of Gaul, by Sidon. Apoll Ep. vi. Eutyches, Archimandrite, Abraham Abbot, are called by the same name, in the Acts of Chalcedon

[h] What the Valentinian προβολὴ was, is described in Epiph Hær.31, 13. The Æons, wishing to shew thankfulness to God, contributed together (ἐρανισαμένους) whatever was most beautiful of each of them, and moulding these several excellencies into one, formed this Issue, προβαλέσθαι προβλημα, to the honour and glory of the Profound, βύθος, and they called this star and flower of the Pleroma, Jesus, &c. And so Tertullian " a joint contribution, ex ære collatitio, to the honour and glory of the Father, ex omnium defloratione constructum," contr. Valent. 12. Accordingly Origen protests against the notion of προβολὴ, Periarch iv. p. 190. and Athanasius Expos § 1. The Arian Asterius too considers προβολὴ to introduce the notion of τεκνογονία, Euseb. contr. Marc.1.4. p 20. vid. also Epiph. Hær.72.7. Yet Eusebius uses the word προβάλλεσθαι. Eccles. Theol 1 8. On the other hand Tertullian uses it with a protest against the Valentinian sense. Justin has προβληθὲν γέννημα, Tryph. 62. And Nazianzen calls the Almighty Father προβολεὺς of the Holy Spirit. Orat. 29. 2. Arius introduces the word here as an *argumentum ad invidiam*. Hil de Trin. vi 9.

[i] The Manichees adopting a material notion of the divine substance, considered that it was divisible, and that a portion of it was absorbed by the power of darkness, vid. Appendix to Translation of St. Augustine's Confessions, ii.

[k] υἱοπατόρα. This word is made the symbol of the Noetians or Sabellians by both Catholics and Arians, as if their doctrine involved or avowed Patripassianism, or that the Father suffered. Without entering upon the controversy raised by Beausobre, (Hist Manich. iii. 6. §. 7, &c.) Mosheim, (Ant. Constant. sæc. ii. §. 68. iii. 32) and Lardner, (Cred. part ii. ch. 41.) on the subject, we may refer to the following passages for the use of the term. It is ascribed to Sabellius, Ammon. in Caten Joan. i. 1. p. 14. to Sabellius and Marcellus, Euseb Eccl. Theol. ii. 5. to Marcellus, Cyr Hier. Catech. xv. 9. also iv. 8. xi 16. Epiph. Hær. 73 11 fin. to Sabellians, Athan. Expos. F. 2. and 7 Can. Constant and Greg. Nyssen. contr. Eum xii p 305. to certain heretics, Cyril Alex. in Joann. p. 243. to Praxeas and Montanus Mar. Merc. p. 128. to Sabellius, Cæsar. Dial 1. p. 550. to Noetus, Damasc. Hær. 57.

[l] Hieracas was a Manichæan. He compared the Two Divine Persons to the two lights of one lamp, where the oil is common and the flame double, thus implying a substance distinct from Father and Son, or to a flame divided into two by (for instance) the papyrus which was commonly used instead of a wick. vid. Hilar. de Trin. vi 12.

[m] Bull considers that the doctrine of such Fathers is here spoken of as held that

98   *Arius's letter to Alexander.*

COUNC. Pope, in the midst of the Church and in Session hast often con-
ARIM. demned; but, as we say, at the will of God, created before times
AND and before ages, and gaining life and being from the Father, who
SELEU. gave subsistence to His glories together with Him. For the
Father did not, in giving to Him the inheritance of all things,
deprive Himself, of what He has ingenerately in Himself; for He
is the Fountain of all things.
Thus there are Three Subsistences. And God, being the cause
of all things, is Unoriginate and altogether Sole, but the Son being
generated apart from time by the Father, and being created and
founded before ages, was not before His generation, but being
generated apart from time before all things, alone was made to
subsist by the Father. For He is not eternal or co-eternal or co-
ingenerate with the Father, nor has He His being together with the
Father, as some speak of relations[n], introducing two ingenerate
origins, but God is before all things as being a One and an
Origin of all. Wherefore also He is before the Son; as we have
Rom. learned also from Thy preaching in the midst of the Church. So
11, 36. far then as from God He has being, and glories, and life, and all
Ps. 110, things are delivered unto Him, in such sense is God His origin.
3. For He is above Him, as being His God and before Him. But
John if the terms *from Him,* and *from the womb,* and *I came forth from*
16, 28. *the Father, and I am come*[1], be understood by some to mean as if a
¹ ἥκω part of Him, one in substance, or as an issue, then the Father is
and so according to them compounded and divisible and alterable and
Chrys. material, and, as far as their belief goes, has the circumstances of
Hom. 3. a body, who is the Incorporeal God.
Hebr.
init.
Epiph.
Hær.73. This is a part of what the Arians cast out from their
31. and heretical hearts.
36.
§. 17. 4. And before the Nicene Council took place, similar state-

our Lord's συγκατάβασις to create the
world was a γέννησις, and certainly such
language as that of Hippol. contr.
Noet. §. 15. favours the supposition.
But one class of the Sabellians may
more probably be intended, who held
that the Word became the Son on His
incarnation, such as Marcellus, vid.
Euseb. Eccles. Theol. i. 1. contr. Marc.
ii. 3. vid. also Eccles. Theol. ii. 9.
p. 114. b. μηδ' ἄλλοτε ἄλλην κ τ λ
Also the Macrostich says, " We anathematize those who call Him the
mere Word of God, not allowing
Him to be Christ and Son of God before
all ages, but from the time He took on
Him our flesh, such are the followers
of Marcellus and Photinus, &c." infra,
§. 26. Again, Athanasius, Orat. iv. 15.
says that, of those who divide the Word
from the Son, some called our Lord's
manhood the Son, some the two Natures
together, and some said " that the Word

Himself became the Son when He was
made man." It makes it more likely
that Marcellus is meant, that Asterius
seems to have written against him before
the Nicene Council, and that Arius
in other of his writings borrowed from
Asterius. vid. de Decret. §. 8.

[n] Eusebius's letter to Euphration,
which is mentioned just after, expresses
this more distinctly—" If they co-exist,
how shall the Father be Father and the
Son Son? or how the One first, the Other
second? and the One ingenerate and
the Other generate?" Acta Conc. 7.
p. 301. The phrase τὰ πρός τι Bull well
explains to refer to the Catholic truth
that the Father or Son being named,
the Other is therein implied without
naming. Defens. F. N. iii. 9. §. 4.
Hence Arius, in his Letter to Eusebius, complains that Alexander says,
ἀεὶ ὁ θεὸς, ἀεὶ ὁ υἱός· ἅμα πατήρ, ἅμα υἱός.
Theod. Hist. 1. 4.

ments were made by Eusebius's party, Narcissus, Patrophilus, Maris, Paulinus, Theodotus, and Athanasius of Nazarbi º. And Eusebius of Nicomedia wrote over and above to Arius, to this effect, " Since your sentiments are good, pray that all may adopt them; for it is plain to any one, that what has been made was not before its generation; but what came to be, has an origin of being." And Eusebius of Cæsarea in Palestine, in a letter to Euphration the Bishop, did not scruple to say plainly that Christ was not true God ᵖ. And Athanasius of Nazarbi uncloked the heresy still further, saying that the Son of God was one of the hundred sheep. For writing to Alexander the Bishop, he had the extreme audacity to say: " Why complain of the Arians, for saying, The Son of God is made as a creature out of nothing, and one among others? For all that are made being represented in parable by the hundred sheep, the Son is one of them. If then the hundred are not created and generated, or if there be beings beside that hundred, then may the Son be not a creature nor one among others; but if those hundred are all generate, and there is nothing besides the hundred save God alone, what extravagance do the Arians utter, when, as comprehending and reckoning Christ in the hundred, they say that He is one among others?" And George who now is in Laodicea, and then was presbyter of Alexandria, and was staying at Antioch, wrote to Alexander the Bishop; " Do not complain of the Arians, for saying, ' Once the Son of God was not,' for Esaias came to be son of Amos, and, whereas Amos was before Esaias came to be, Esaias was not before, but came to be afterwards." And he wrote to the Arians, " Why complain of Alexander the Pope¹, saying, that the Son is from the Father? for you too need not fear to say that the Son was from God. For if the Apostle wrote, *All things are*

¹ p. 96, note g.

l Cor. 11, 12.

º Most of these original Arians were attacked in a work of Marcellus's which Eusebius answers. " Now he replies to Asterius," says Eusebius, " now to the great Eusebius," [of Nicomedia,] " and then he turns upon that man of God, that indeed thrice blessed person Paulinus, [of Tyre.] Then he goes to war with Origen ... Next he marches out against Narcissus, and pursues the other Eusebius," himself. " In a word, he counts for nothing all the Ecclesiastical Fathers, being satisfied with no one but himself." contr. Marc. i. 4. There is little to be said of Maris and Theodotus. Nazarbi is more commonly called Anazarbus, and is in Cilicia.

ᵖ This is quoted, among other passages from Eusebius, in the 7th General Council, Act. 6. p. 409. " The Son Himself is God, but not Very God."

COUNC. *from God*, and it is plain that all things are made of nothing,
ARIM. though the Son too is a creature and one of things made,
AND
SELEU. still He may be said to be from God in that sense in which
all things are said to be from God." From him then the
Arians learned to pretend to the phrase *from God*, and to use
it indeed, but not in a good meaning. And George himself
was deposed by Alexander for certain reasons, and among
them for manifest irreligion; for he was himself a presbyter,
as has been said before.

§. 18. 5. On the whole then such were their statements, as if they
all were in dispute and rivalry with each other, which should
make the heresy more irreligious, and display it in a more
naked form. And as for their letters I have them not at hand,
to dispatch them to you; else I would have sent you copies;
but, if the Lord will, this too I will do, when I get possession of
them. And one Asterius[q] from Cappadocia, a many-headed
Sophist, one of the Eusebians, whom they could not advance
into the Clergy, as having done sacrifice in the former persecution in the time of Constantius's grandfather, writes, with the
countenance of the Eusebians, a small treatise, which was on
a par with the crime of his sacrifice, yet answered their
wishes; for in it, after comparing, or rather preferring, the
locust and the caterpillar to Christ, and saying that Wisdom
in God was other than Christ, and was the Framer as well of
Christ as of the world, he went round the Churches in Syria
and elsewhere, with introductions from the Eusebians, that
as he once had been at pains to deny the truth, so now he

---

[q] Asterius has been mentioned above, p. 13 note b. Philostorgius speaks of him as adopting Semi-arian terms, and Acacius gives an extract from him containing them. ap. Epiph. Hær. 72. 6. and doubtless both he (to judge by his fragments) and Eusebius write with much less of revolting impiety than others of their party. Thus in one of the extracts made in the text he distinguishes after the manner of the Semi-arians between the γεννητική and the δημιουργική δύναμις. Again, the illustration of the Sun in another much resembles Euseb. Demonstr. iv. 5. So does his doctrine, supr. de Decr. §. 8. that the Son was generated to create other beings, and that, because they could not bear the hand of the Al-mighty. also vid. Orat ii 24 cf Demonstr. iv. 4. Eccl Theol. 1. 8. 13 Præp. vii. 15. but especially Eusebius's avowal, "not that the Father was not able, did He beget the Son, but because those things which were made were not able to sustain the power of the Ingenerate, therefore speaks He through a Mediator. contr. Sabell. 1. p. 9. At the same time if he is so to be considered, it is an additional proof that the Semi-arians of 325 were far less Catholic than those of 359. He seems to be called many-headed with an allusion to the Hydra, and to his activity in the Arian cause and his fertility in writing. He wrote comments on Scripture.

might make free with it. The bold man intruded himself into forbidden places, and seating himself in the place of Clerks, he used to read publicly this treatise of his, in spite of the general indignation. The treatise is written at great length, but portions of it are as follows:—

"For the Blessed Paul said not that he preached Christ, His, that is, God's, 'proper Power' or 'Wisdom,'" but without the article, *God's Power and God's Wisdom*, preaching that the proper power of God Himself was distinct, which was connatural and co-existent with Him ingenerately, generative indeed of Christ, creative of the whole world; concerning which he teaches in his Epistle to the Romans, thus, *The invisible things of Him from the creation of the world are clearly seen, being understood by the things which are made, even His eternal power and godhead*. For as no one would say that the Godhead there mentioned was Christ, but the Father Himself, so, as I think, His eternal power is also not the Only-begotten God, but the Father who begat Him. And he tells us of another Power and Wisdom of God, namely, that which is manifested through Christ, and made known through the works themselves of His Ministry.

And again :—

Although His eternal Power and Wisdom, which truth argues to be Unoriginate and Ingenerate, would appear certainly to be one and the same, yet many are those powers which are one by one created by Him, of which Christ is the First-born and Only-begotten. All however equally depend upon their Possessor, and all His powers are rightly called His, who has created and uses them, for instance, the Prophet says that the locust, which became a divine punishment of human sin, was called by God Himself, not only the power of God, but the great power. And the blessed David too in most of the Psalms, invites, not Angels alone, but Powers also to praise God. And while he invites them all to the hymn, He presents before us their multitude, and is not unwilling to call them ministers of God, and teaches them to do His will.

6. These bold words against the Saviour did not content him, but he went further in his blasphemies, as follows :

The Son is one among others; for He is first of things generated, and one among intellectual natures, and as in things visible the sun is one among what is apparent, and it shines upon the

---

r None but the Clergy might enter the Chancel, i. e. in Service time. Hence Theodosius was made to retire by St Ambrose. Theod v. 17. The Council of Laodicea, said to be held A.D. 372, forbids any but persons in orders, ἱερατικοὶ, to enter the Chancel and then communicate Can 19. vid. also 44. Conc. t. l. p 788, 789. It is doubtful what orders, the word ἱερατικοὶ is intended to include vid. Bingham Antiqu. viii 6. §. 7.

whole world according to the command of its Maker, so the Son, being one of the intellectual natures, also enlightens and shines upon all that are in the intellectual world.

And again he says, Once He was not, writing thus:—" And before the Son's generation, the Father had pre-existing knowledge how to generate; since a physician too, before he cured, had the science of curing[1]." And he says again: " The Son was created by God's beneficent earnestness; and the Father made Him by the superabundance of His Power." And again: " If the will of God has pervaded all the works in succession, certainly the Son too, being a work, has at His will come to be and been made." Now though Asterius was the only person to write all this, the Eusebians felt the like in common with him.

§. 20. 7. These are the doctrines for which they are contending; for these they assail the Ancient Council, because its members did not propound the like, but anathematized the Arian heresy instead, which they were so eager to recommend. On this account they put forward, as an advocate of their irreligion, Asterius who sacrificed, a sophist too, that he might not spare to speak against the Lord, or by a shew of reason to mislead the simple. And they were ignorant, the shallow men, that they were doing harm to their own cause. For the ill savour of their advocate's idolatrous sacrifice, betrayed still more plainly that the heresy is Christ's foe. And now again, the general agitations and troubles which they are exciting, are in consequence of their belief, that by their numerous murders and their monthly Councils, at length they will undo the sentence which has been passed against the Arian heresy[2]. But here too they seem ignorant, or to pretend ignorance, that even before Nicæa that heresy was held in detestation, when Artemas* was laying its foundations, and before him Caiaphas's assembly and that of the Pharisees his contemporaries. And at all times is this school of Christ's foes detestable, and will not cease to be hateful,

---

* Artemas or Artemon was one of the chiefs of a school of heresy at Rome at the end of the second century. Theodotus was another, and the more eminent. They founded separate sects. Their main tenet is what would now be called Unitarianism, or that our Lord was a mere man. Artemas seems to have been more known in the East; at least is more frequently mentioned in controversy with the Arians, e. g. by Alexander, Theod. Hist. 1. 3. p. 739.

Council of Jerusalem

the Lord's Name being full of love, and the whole creation bending the knee, and confessing *that Jesus Christ is Lord, to the glory of God the Father.* Phil. 2, 11.

8. Yet so it is, they have convened successive Councils §. 21. against that Ecumenical One¹, and are not yet tired ᵗ. After the ¹ p. 49, Nicene, the Eusebians had been deposed; however, in course note o. of time they intruded themselves without shame upon the Churches, and began to plot against the Bishops who withstood them, and to substitute in the Church men of their own heresy. Thus they thought to hold Councils at their pleasure, as having those who concurred with them, whom they had ordained on purpose for this very object². Accord- ² p. 84, ingly, they assemble at Jerusalem, and there they write note b. thus :—

The Holy Council assembled in Jerusalem ᵘ by the grace of God, to the Church of God which is in Alexandria, and to all throughout Egypt, Thebais, Libya, and Pentapolis, also to the Bishops, Priests, and Deacons throughout the world, health in the Lord.

To all of us who have come together into one place from different provinces, to the great celebration, which we have held at the consecration of the Saviour's Martyry ˣ, built to God the

---

ᵗ It will be observed, that the Eusebian or court party from 341 to 358, contained in it two elements, the more religious or Semi-arian which tended to Catholicism, and ultimately coalesced with it, the other the proper Arian or Anomœan which was essentially heretical. During the period mentioned, it wore for the most part the Semi-arian profession. Athanasius as well as Hilary does justice to the Semi-arians; but Athanasius does not seem to have known or estimated the quarrel between them and the Arians as fully as Hilary. Accordingly, while the former is bent in this treatise in bringing out the great fact of the variations of the heretical party, Hilary, wishing to commend the hopeful Semi-arians to the Gallic Church, makes excuses for them, on the ground of the *necessity* of explanations of the Nicene formulary, "necessitatem hanc furor hereticus imponit." Hil. de Syn. 63. vid. also 62. and 28. At the same time, Hilary himself bears witness quite as strongly as Athan. to the miserable variations of the heretical party, vid. supr. p. 76, note k. as Ammianus in p. 75, note h. The same thing is meant in Nazianzen's well-known declaration against Councils, "Never saw I Council brought to a useful issue, nor remedying, but rather increasing existing evils." Ep. 130.

ᵘ This Council at Jerusalem was a continuation of one held at Tyre at which Athan was condemned It was very numerously attended; by Bishops, (as Eusebius says, Vit. Const iv. 43.) from Macedonia, Pannonia, Thrace, Asia Minor, Syria, Arabia, Egypt, and Libya. One account speaks of the number as being above 200. He says that "an innumerable multitude from all provinces accompanied them." It was the second great Council in Constantine's reign, and is compared by Eusebius (invidiously) to the Nicene, c. 47. At this Council Arius was solemnly received, as the Synodal Letter goes on to say.

ˣ This Church, called the Martyry or Testimony, was built over the spot

King of all, and to His Christ, by the zeal of the most religious Emperor Constantine, the grace of Christ provided a higher gratification, in the conduct of that most religious Emperor himself, who, by letters of his own, banishing from the Church of God all jealousy, and driving far away all envy, by means of which, the members of Christ had been for a long season in dissention, exhorted us, what was our duty, with open and peaceable mind to receive Arius and his friends, whom for a while jealousy which hates virtue had contrived to expel from the Church. And the most religious Emperor bore testimony in their behalf by his letter to the exactness of their faith, which, after inquiry of them, and personal communication with them by word of mouth, he acknowledged, and made known to us, subjoining to his own letters their orthodox teaching in writing [y], which we all confessed to be sound and ecclesiastical. And he reasonably recommended that they should be received and united to the Church of God, as you will know yourselves from the transcript of the same Epistle, which we have transmitted to your reverences. We believe that yourselves also, as if recovering the very members of your own body, will experience great joy and gladness, in acknowledging and recovering your own bowels, your own brethren and fathers; since not only the Presbyters who are friends of Arius are given back to you, but also the whole Christian people and the entire multitude, which on occasion of the aforesaid men have a long time been in dissension among you. Moreover it were fitting, now that you know for certain what has passed, and that the men have communicated with us and have been received by such a Holy Council, that you should with all readiness hail this your coalition and peace with your own members, specially since the articles of the faith which they have published preserve indisputable the universally confessed apostolical tradition and teaching.

§ 22. 9. This was the first of their Councils, and in it they were speedy in divulging their views, and could not conceal them.

---

made sacred by our Lord's death, burial, and resurrection, in commemoration of the discovery of the Holy Cross, and has been described from Eusebius in the preface to the Translation of S. Cyril's Catechetical Lectures, p. xxiv. It was begun A. D. 326, and dedicated at this date, A.D. 335, on Saturday the 13th of September. The 14th however is the feast of the Exaltatio S. Crucis both in East and West.

[y] This is supposed to be the same Confession which is preserved by Socr. i 26. and Soz. ii 27. and was presented to Constantine by Arius in 330. It says no more than " And in the Lord Jesus Christ His Son, who was begotten from Him before all the ages God and Word, through whom all things were made, both in the heavens and upon earth ;" afterwards it professes to have " received the faith from the holy Evangelists," and to believe " as all the Catholic Church and as the Scriptures teach." The Synodal Letter in the text adds " apostolical tradition and teaching." Arius might safely appeal to Scripture and the Church for a creed which did not specify the point in controversy. In his letter to Eusebius of Nicomedia before the Nicene Council where he does state the distinctive articles of his heresy he appeals to him as a fellow pupil in the School of Lucian, not to tradition. Theod. Hist. i. 4.

Council at Antioch, and first creed of Eusebians. 105

For when they said that they had banished all jealousy, and, after the expulsion of Athanasius, Bishop of Alexandria, recommended the reception of Arius and his friends, they shewed, that their measures against Athanasius himself then, and before against all the other Bishops who withstood them, had for their object their receiving Arius's party, and introducing the heresy into the Church. But although they had approved in this Council all Arius's malignity, and had ordered to receive his party into communion, as they had set the example, yet feeling that even now they were short of their wishes, they assembled a Council at Antioch under colour of the so-called Dedication[z]; and, since they were in general and lasting odium for their heresy, they publish different letters, some of this sort, and some of that; and what they wrote in one letter was as follows:—

CHAP. I.

We have not been followers of Arius,—how could Bishops, such as we, follow a Presbyter?—nor did we receive any other faith beside that which has been handed down from the beginning[a]. But, after taking on ourselves to examine and to verify his faith, we have admitted him rather than followed him; as you will understand from our present avowals

1st Confession or 1st of Antioch, A.D. 341.

For we have been taught from the first, to believe in one God, the God of the Universe, the Framer and Preserver of all things both intellectual and sensible.

And in One Son of God, Only-begotten, existing before all ages, and being with the Father who begat Him, by whom all things were made, both visible and invisible, who in the last days according to the good pleasure of the Father came down,

---

[z] i. e. the dedication of the Dominicum Aureum, which had been ten years in building. vid. the description of it in Euseb. Vit. Const. III. 50. This Council is one of great importance in the history, though it was not attended by more than 90 Bishops according to Ath. infr. or 97 according to Hilary de Syn. 28. The Eusebians had written to the Roman see against Athan. and eventually called on it to summon a Council. Accordingly, Julius proposed a Council at Rome; they refused to come, and instead held this meeting at Antioch. Thus in a certain sense it is a protest of the East against the Pope's authority. Twenty-five Canons are attributed to this Council, which have been received into the Code of the Catholic Church,
though not as *from* this Council, which took at least some of them from more ancient sources. It is remarkable that S. Hilary calls this Council an assembly of Saints. de Syn. 32. but it is his course throughout to look at these Councils on their hopeful side. vid. note t.

[a] The Council might safely appeal to antiquity, since, with Arius in the Confession noticed supr. note y, they did not touch on the point in dispute. The number of their formularies, three or four, shews that they had a great difficulty in taking any view which would meet the wishes and express the sentiments of one and all. The one that follows, which is their first, is as meagre as Arius's, quoted note y.

Counc. and took flesh of the Virgin, and fulfilled all His Father's will;
Arim. and suffered and rose again, and ascended into heaven, and
AND sitteth on the right hand of the Father, and cometh again to
Seleu. judge quick and dead, and remaineth King and God unto all
ages.

And we believe also in the Holy Ghost; and if it be necessary to add, we believe concerning the resurrection of the flesh, and the life everlasting.

§. 23. 10. Here follows what they published next at the same Dedication in another Epistle, being dissatisfied with the first, and devising something newer and fuller:

IId Con- We believe [b], conformably to the evangelical and apostolical
fession tradition, in One God, the Father Almighty, the Framer, and
or 2d Maker, and Preserver of the Universe, from whom are all
of An-
tioch, things
A. D. And in One Lord Jesus Christ, His Only-begotten Son, God,
341. by whom are all things, who was begotten before all ages from
¹ Vid. the Father, God from God, whole from whole, sole from sole [1],
xthCon- perfect from perfect, King from King, Lord from Lord, Living
fession, Word, Living Wisdom, true Light, Way, Truth, Resurrection,
infr. Shepherd, Door, both unalterable and unchangeable [c]; unvarying
§. 30. image [d] of the Godhead, Substance, Will, Power, and Glory of the

[b] This formulary is that known as *the* Formulary of the Dedication It is quoted as such by Socr. II. 39, 40. Soz. iv. 15. and infr. §. 29. Sozomen says that the Eusebians attributed it to Lucian, alleging that they had found a copy written by his own hand; but he decides neither for or against it himself. Hist. III. 5. And the Auctor de Trinitate, (in Theodoret's works, t. 5) allows that it is Lucian's, but interpolated Dial III. init. vid. Routh, Reliqu. Sacr. vol. III. p. 294—6. who is in favour of its genuineness; as are Bull, Cave, and S. Basnage. Tillemont and Co Ι-stant take the contrary side, the latter observing (ad Hilar. de Synod. 28) that Athanasius, infr. §. 36, speaks of parts of it as Acacius's, and that Acacius attributes its language to Asterius The Creed is of a much higher cast of doctrine than the two former, (§. 22 and note y,) containing some of the phrases which in the fourth century became badges of Semi-arianism.

[c] These strong words and those which follow, whether Lucian's or not, mark the great difference between this confession and the foregoing. It would seem as if the Eusebians had at first tried the assembled Bishops with a negative confession, and finding that they would not accept it, had been forced upon one of a more orthodox character. It is observable too that even the Council of Jerusalem, but indirectly received the Confession on which they re-admitted Arius, though they gave it a real sanction. The words "unalterable and unchangeable" are formal Anti-arian symbols, as the τρεπτὸν or alterable was one of the most characteristic part of Arius's creed vid. Orat. I. §. 35. &c.

[d] On ἀπαράλλακτος εἰκὼν κατ' οὐσίαν, which was synonymous with ὁμοούσιος, vid. infr. §. 38. and one of the symbols of Semi-arianism, (not as if it did not express truth, but because it marked the limit of Semi-arian approximation to the absolute truth,) something has been said, supr. p 35, note u It was in order to secure the true sense of ἀπαράλλακτον that the Council adopted the word ὁμοούσιον 'Απαράλλακτον is accordingly used as a familiar word by Athan. de Decr. supr. §. 20. 24. Orat. III. §. 36. contr. Gent. 41. 46 fin. Philostorgius ascribing it to Asterius, and Acacius quotes a passage from his

Father; the first born of every creature, who was in the beginning
with God, God the Word, as it is written in the Gospel, *and the
Word was God;* by whom all things were made, and in whom
all things consist; who in the last days descended from above,
and was born of a Virgin according to the Scriptures, and was
made Man, Mediator[e] between God and man, and Apostle of our
faith, and Prince of life, as He says, *I came down from heaven,
not to do Mine own will, but the will of Him that sent Me;* who
suffered for us and rose again on the third day, and ascended
into heaven, and sat down on the right hand of the Father, and
is coming again with glory and power, to judge quick and dead.

And in the Holy Ghost, who is given to those who believe for
comfort, and sanctification, and initiation, as also our Lord Jesus
Christ enjoined His disciples, saying, *Go ye, teach all nations,
baptizing them in the Name of the Father, and the Son, and the
Holy Ghost;* that of Father being truly Father, and of Son
being truly Son, and of the Holy Ghost being truly Holy Ghost,
the names not being given without meaning or effect, but denoting accurately the peculiar subsistence, rank, and glory of
each that is named, so that they are three in subsistence, and in
agreement one[f].

writings containing it. (vid. supr. note q.) Acacius at the same time forcibly expresses what is meant by the word, τὸ ἔκτυπον καὶ τρανὲς ἐκμαγεῖον τοῦ θεοῦ τῆς οὐσίας, and S Alexander before him, τὴν κατὰ πάντα ὁμοιότητα αὐτοῦ ἐκ φύσεως ἀπομαξάμενος. Theod. Hist. 1. 3 (as, in the legend, the impression of our Lord's face on the cloth at His crucifixion) Χαρακτὴρ, Hebr. i. 3. contains the same idea. "An image not inanimate, not framed by the hand, nor work of art and imagination, (ἐπίνοιας,) but a living image, yea, the very life (αὐτοοῦσα); ever preserving the unvarying (τὸ ἀπαράλλακτον), not in likeness of fashion, but in its very substance." Basil. contr. Eunom i. 18. The Auctor de Trinitate says, speaking of the word in this very creed, "Will in nothing varying from will (ἀπαράλλακτος) is the *same* will, and power nothing varying from power is the *same* power; and glory nothing varying from glory is the *same* glory." The Macedonian replies "Unvarying I say, the same I say not" Dial. iii. p. 993. Athan. de Decr. l. c. seems to say the same. That is, in the Catholic sense, the image was not ἀπαράλλακτος, if there was *any* difference, unless He was one with Him of whom He was the image. vid. Hil. supra. p 76 note 1.

[e] This statement perhaps is the most Catholic in the Creed, not that the former are not more explicit in themselves, or that in a certain true sense our Lord may not be called a Mediator before He became incarnate, but because the Arians, even Eusebius, seem to have made His mediatorship consist essentially in His divine nature, whereas this Confession speaks of our Lord as made Mediator when He came in the flesh. On the other hand, Eusebius, like Philo and the Platonists, considers Him as made in the beginning, the "Eternal Priest of the Father," Demonst. v. 3. de Laud. C. p. 503 fin. "an intermediate divine power," p. 525. "mediating and joining generated substance to the Ingenerate," p. 528 vid. infr. pp. 115. and 119. notes f. and o.

[f] This phrase, which is of a more Arian character than any other part of the Confession, is justified by S Hilary on the ground, that when the Spirit is mentioned, agreement is the best symbol of unity. de Syn. 32. It is protested against in the Sardican Confession. Theod. Hist. ii. 6. p. 846. A similar passage occurs in Origen, contr. Cels viii. 12 to which Huet. Origen ii 2. n 3. compares Novatian de Trin. 22. The Arians insisted on the "oneness in agreement" as a fulfilment of such texts as "I and my Father are one," but this subject will come before us in Orat. iii. §. 10. vid. infr § 48.

108 *Creed of Theophronius, at Antioch,*

COUNC. ARIM. AND SELEU.

Holding then this faith, and holding it in the presence of God and Christ, from beginning to end, we anathematize every heretical heterodoxy[g]. And if any teaches, beside the sound and right faith of the Scriptures, that time, or season, or age[h], either is or has been before the generation of the Son, be he anathema. Or if any one says, that the Son is a creature as one of the creatures[i], or an offspring as one of the offsprings, or a work as one of the works, and not the aforesaid articles one after another, as the divine Scriptures have delivered, or if he teaches or preaches beside what we received, be he anathema. For all that has been delivered in the divine Scriptures, whether by Prophets or Apostles, do we truly and conscientiously both believe and follow[i].

[1] vid. p. 10, note u.

§. 24. 11. And one Theophronius[k], Bishop of Tyana, put forth before them all the following statement of his personal faith. And they subscribed it, accepting the faith of this man:—

IId Confession or 3d of Antioch, A D. 341.

God knows, whom I call as a witness upon my soul, that so I believe:—in God the Father Almighty, the Creator and Maker of the Universe, from whom are all things:
And in His Only-begotten Son, God, Word, Power, and Wisdom, our Lord Jesus Christ, through whom are all things; who was begotten from the Father before the ages, perfect God from perfect God[l] and being with God in subsistence, and in the

---

[g] The whole of these anathemas are an Eusebian addition. The Council anathematizes " *every* heretical heterodoxy ," *not*, as Athanasius observes, supra, §. 7 the Arian.

[h] The introduction of these words " time," " age," &c allows them still to hold the Arian formula " once He was not," for our Lord was, as they held, *before* time, but still created.

[i] This emphatic mention of Scripture is also virtually an Arian evasion, to hold certain truths, " *as* Scripture has delivered," might either mean *because* and *as in fact*, or *so far as*, and admitted of a silent reference to themselves, as interpreters of Scripture.

[k] Nothing is known of Theophronius; his Confession is in great measure a relapse into Arianism proper; that is, as far as the absence of characteristic symbols is a proof of a wish to introduce the heresy. The phrase " perfect God" will be mentioned in the next note

[l] It need scarcely be said, that " perfect from perfect" is a symbol on which the Catholics laid stress, Athan. Orat. II 35. Epiph. Hær 76 p 945. but it admitted of an evasion. An especial reason for insisting on it in the previous centuries had been the Sabellian doctrine, which considered the title " Word" when applied to our Lord to be adequately explained by the ordinary sense of the term, as a word spoken by us. vid. on the λόγος προφορικὸς, infr. p. 113, note z In consequence they insisted on His τὸ τέλειον, perfection, which became almost synonymous with His personality. Thus the Apollinarians, e. g. denied that our Lord was *perfect* man, because His *person* was not human. Athan. contr. Apoll 1. 2. Hence Justin, Tatian, are earnest in denying that our Lord was a portion divided from the Divine Substance, οὐ κατ' ἀποτομὴν, &c. &c. Just. Tryph 128 Tatian. contr. Græc. 5. And Athen. condemns the notion of " the λόγος ἐν τῷ θεῷ ἀτελὴς, γεννηθεὶς τέλειος Orat. IV 11. The Arians then, as being the especial opponents of the Sabellians, insisted on nothing so much as our Lord's being a real, living, substantial, Word. vid. Eusebius passim. " The Father," says Acacius against Marcellus, " begat the Only-begotten, alone alone, and perfect perfect , for there is nothing

last days descended, and was born of the Virgin according to the Scriptures, and was made man, and suffered, and rose again from the dead, and ascended into the heavens, and sat down on the right hand of His Father, and cometh again with glory and power to judge quick and dead, and remaineth for ever·

And in the Holy Ghost, the Paraclete, the Spirit of truth, which also God promised by His Prophet to pour out upon His servants, and the Lord promised to send to His disciples: which also He sent, as the Acts of the Apostles witness.

But if any one teaches, or holds in his mind, aught beside this faith, be he anathema, or with Marcellus of Ancyra[m], or Sabellius, or Paul of Samosata, be he anathema, both himself and those who communicate with him.

12. Ninety Bishops met at the Dedication under the Consulate of Marcellinus and Probinus, in the 14th of the Indiction[n], Constantius the most irreligious[1] being present. Having thus conducted matters at Antioch at the Dedication, thinking that their composition was deficient still, and fluctuating moreover in their own views, again they draw up afresh another formulary, after a few months, professedly concerning the faith, and despatch Narcissus, Maris, Theodorus, and

---

imperfect in the Father, wherefore neither is there in the Son, but the Son's perfection is the genuine offspring of His perfection, and superperfection" ap. Epiph Hær 72 7 Τέλειος then was a relative word, varying with the subject-matter, vid. Damasc. F. O 1. 8 p 138. and when the Arians said that our Lord was perfect God, they meant, "perfect, *in that sense in which* He is God"—1. e. as a secondary divinity.—Nay, in one point of view they would use the term of His divine Nature more freely than the Catholics sometimes had. For, Hippolytus, e g. though of course really holding His perfection from eternity as the Son, yet speaks of His *condescension* in coming upon earth as a kind of completion of His Sonship, He becoming thus a Son a second time, whereas the Arians holding no real condescension or assumption of a really new state, could not hold that our Lord was in any respect essentially other than He had been before the incarnation. " Nor was the Word," says Hippolytus, " before the flesh and by Himself, perfect Son, though being perfect Word,

Only-begotten, nor could the flesh subsist by itself without the Word, because that in the Word it has its consistence thus then He was manifested One perfect Son of God." contr. Noet. 15.

[m] Marcellus wrote his work against Asterius in 335, the year of the Arian Council of Jerusalem, which at once took cognizance of it, and cited Marcellus to appear before them The same year a Council held at Constantinople condemned and deposed him, about the time that Arius came thither for re-admission into the Church. From that time his name is frequently introduced into the Arian anathemas, vid Macrostich, §. 26. By adding those " who communicate with him," the Eusebians intended to strike at the Roman see, which had acquitted Marcellus in a Council held in June of the same year.

[n] The commencement and the origin of this mode of dating are unknown. It seems to have been introduced between A.D. 313 and 315. The Indiction was a cycle of 15 years, and began with the month of September. S. Athanasius is the first ecclesiastical author who adopts it

110   *Creed sent into Gaul,*

CCOUNC. Mark into Gaul°. And they, as being sent from the Council, ARIM AND deliver the following document to Constans Augustus of SELEU. blessed memory P, and to all who were there:

ivthCon- We believe q in One God, the Father Almighty, Creator and
fession, Maker of all things; from whom the whole family in heaven and
or 4th of on earth is named.
Antioch,
A.D. And in His Only-begotten Son, our Lord Jesus Christ, who
342. before all ages was begotten from the Father, God from God,
Light from Light, by whom all things were made in the heavens
and on the earth, visible and invisible, being Word, and Wisdom,
and Power, and Life, and True Light; who in the last days was
made man for us, and was born of the Holy Virgin; who was
crucified, and dead, and buried, and rose again from the dead the
third day, and was taken up into heaven, and sat down on the
right hand of the Father; and is coming at the end of the world,
to judge quick and dead, and to render to every one according
to his works; whose Kingdom endures indissolubly into infinite
ages r; for He shall be seated on the right hand of the Father,
not only in this world but in that which is to come.

° This deputation had it in purpose to gain the Emperor Constans to the Eusebian party. They composed a new Confession with this object Theodore of Heraclea, (who made commentaries on Scripture and is said to have been an elegant writer,) Maris and Narcissus, were all Eusebians, but Mark was a Semi-arian. As yet the Eusebian party were making use of the Semi-arians, but their professed Creed had already much degenerated from Lucian's at the Dedication.

P Constans had lately become master of two thirds of the Empire by the death of his elder brother Constantine, who had made war upon him and fallen in an engagement. He was at this time only 22 years of age. His enemies represent his character in no favourable light, but, for whatever reason, he sided with the Catholics, and S. Athanasius, who had been honourably treated by him in Gaul, speaks of him in the language of gratitude. In his apology to Constantius, he says, " thy brother of blessed memory filled the Churches with offerings," and he speaks of " the grace given him through baptism." §. 7. Constans was murdered by Magnentius in 350, and one of the calumnies against Athanasius was that he had sent letters to the murderer.

q The fourth, fifth, and sixth Confessions are the same, and with them agree the Creed of Philippopolis (A. D. 347, or 344 according to Mansi). These extend over a period of nine years, A.D. 342—351, (or 15 or 16 according to Baronius and Mansi, who place the 6th Confession, i. e. the 1st Sirmian, at 357, 358 respectively,) and make the stationary period of Arianism. The two parties of which the heretical body was composed were kept together, not only by the court, but by the rise of the Sabellianism of Marcellus (A D. 335) and Photinus (about 342). This too would increase their strength in the Church, and is the excuse, which Hilary himself urges, for their frequent Councils. Still they do not seem to be able to escape from the argument of Athanasius, that, whereas new Councils are for new heresies, if but one new heresy had risen, but one new Council was necessary. If these four Confessions say the same thing, three of them must be superfluous vid. infr. §. 32. However, in spite of the identity of the Creed, the difference in their Anathemas is very great, as we shall see.

r These words, which answer to those afterwards added at the second General Council (381—3) are directed against the doctrine of Marcellus, who taught that the Word was but a divine energy, manifested in Christ and retiring from Him at the consummation of all things, when the manhood or flesh of Christ would consequently no *being fourth creed of Eusebians, negative.* 111

And in the Holy Ghost, that is, the Paraclete; which, having CHAP. promised to the Apostles, He sent forth after His ascension into I. heaven, to teach them and to remind of all things; through whom also shall be sanctified the souls of those who sincerely believe in Him.

But those who say, that the Son was from nothing, or from other subsistence and not from God, and, there was time when He was not, the Catholic Church regards as aliens ˢ.

13. As if dissatisfied with this, they hold their meeting §. 26. again after three years, and dispatch Eudoxius, Martyrius, and Macedonius of Cilicia ᵗ, and some others with them, to the parts of Italy, to carry with them a faith written at great length, with numerous additions over and above those which have gone before. They went abroad with these, as if they had devised something new.

We believe in One God, the Father Almighty, the Creator and vth Con-
Maker of all things, from whom the whole family in heaven and fession
on earth is named. or Ma-
crostich,
A. D.
345.

longer reign. " How can we admit," says Marcellus in Eusebius, " that that flesh, which is from the earth and profiteth nothing, should co-exist with the Word in the ages to come as serviceable to Him?" de Eccl. Theol. iii. 8. Again, " If He has received a beginning of His Kingdom not more than four hundred years since, it is no paradox that He who gained that Kingdom so short a while since, should be said by the Apostle to deliver it up to God What are we told of the human flesh, which the Word bore for us, not four hundred years since? will the Word have it in the ages to come, or only to the judgment season?" iii. 17. And, " Should any ask concerning that flesh which is in the Word having become immortal, we say to him, that we count it not safe to pronounce on points of which we learn not for certain from divine Scripture." cont. Marc. ii. 4.

ˢ S. Hilary, as we have seen above, p. 67. by implication calls this the Nicene Anathema; and so it is in the respects in which he speaks of it; but it omits many of the Nicene clauses, and with them the condemnation of many of the Arian articles. The especial point which it evades is our Lord's eternal existence, substituting for " once He was not," " there was

time when He was not," and leaving out " before His generation He was not," " created," " alterable" and " mutable." It seems to have been considered sufficient for Gaul, as used now, for Italy as in the 5th Confession or Macrostich, and for Africa as in the creed of Philippopolis.

ᵗ Little is known of Macedonius who was Bishop of Mopsuestia, or of Martyrius; and too much of Eudoxius. This Long Confession, or Macrostich, which follows, is remarkable for the first signs of the presence of that higher party of Semi-arians who ultimately joined the Church. It is observable also that the more Catholic portions occur in the Anathemas, as if they were forced in indirectly, and that with an inconsistency with the other statements, for not only the word " substance" does not occur, but the Son is said to be made. At this date the old Semi-arians, as Eusebius Asterius, and Acacius were either dying off, or degenerating into most explicit impiety; the new school of Semi-arians consisting for the most part of a younger generation. St. Cyril delivered his Catechetical Lectures two or three years later than this Creed, viz. 347 or 348. Silvanus, Eleusius, Meletius, Eusebius of Samosata are later still.

Counc.
Arim.
and
Self U.

And in His Only-begotten Son our Lord Jesus Christ, who before all ages was begotten from the Father, God from God, Light from Light, by whom all things were made, in heaven and on the earth, visible and invisible, being Word and Wisdom and Power and Life and True Light, who in the last days was made man for us, and was born of the Holy Virgin, crucified and dead and buried, and rose again from the dead the third day, and was taken up into heaven, and sat down on the right hand of the Father, and is coming at the end of the world to judge quick and dead, and to render to every one according to His works, whose Kingdom endures unceasingly unto infinite ages; for He sitteth on the right hand of the Father not only in this world, but also in that which is to come.

And we believe in the Holy Ghost, that is, the Paraclete, which, having promised to the Apostles, He sent forth after the ascension into heaven, to teach them and to remind of all things; through whom also shall be sanctified the souls of those who sincerely believe in Him.

But those who say, (1) that the Son was from nothing, or from other subsistence and not from God; (2) and that there was a time or age when He was not, the Catholic and Holy Church regards as aliens. Likewise those who say, (3) that there are three Gods: (4) or that Christ is not God; (5) or that before the ages He was neither Christ nor Son of God; (6) or that Father and Son, or Holy Ghost, are the same; (7) or that the Son is Ingenerate; or that the Father generated the Son, not by choice or will; the Holy and Catholic Church anathematizes.

(1.) For neither is safe to say that the Son is from nothing, (since this is no where spoken of Him in divinely inspired Scripture,) nor again of any other subsistence before existing beside the Father, but from God alone do we define Him genuinely to be generated. For the divine Word teaches that the Ingenerate and Unoriginate, the Father of Christ, is One [u].

(2.) Nor may we, adopting the hazardous position, "There was once when He was not," from unscriptural sources, imagine any interval of time before Him, but only the God who generated Him apart from time; for through Him both times and ages came to be. Yet we must not consider the Son to be co-unoriginate and co-ingenerate with the Father; for no one can be properly called Father or Son of one who is co-unoriginate and co-ingenerate with Him [x]. But we acknowledge that the Father who alone

[u] It is observable that here and in the next paragraph the only reasons they give against using the only two Arian formulas which they condemn is that they are not found in Scripture, which leaves the question of their truth untouched Here, in their explanation of the ἐξ οὐκ ὄντων, or from nothing, they do but deny it with Eusebius's evasion, that nothing can be from nothing, and every thing must be from God. vid p 62, note e

[x] They argue, after the usual Arian manner, that the term "Son" essentially implies beginning, and excludes the title "co-unoriginate," whereas the Catholics contended (as alluded to supr p. 98, note n) that the word Father implied a continuity of nature, that is, a co-eternal existence with the Father vid p. 10, note u.

is Unoriginate and Ingenerate, hath generated inconceivably and incomprehensibly; and that the Son hath been generated before ages, and in no wise to be ingenerate Himself like the Father, but to have the Father who generated Him as His origin; for the *Head of Christ is God*.

CHAP. II.

1 Cor. 11, 3.

(3.) Nor again, in confessing three realities¹ and three Persons, ¹ πράγ- of the Father and the Son and the Holy Ghost according to the ματα Scriptures, do we therefore make Gods three; since we acknowledge the Self-complete and Ingenerate and Unoriginate and Invisible God to be one only ʸ, the God and Father of the Only- begotten, who alone hath being from Himself, and alone vouchsafes this to all others bountifully.

ᵠ p. 123, note u.

(4.) Nor again in saying that the Father of our Lord Jesus Christ is the one only God, the only Ingenerate; do we therefore deny that Christ also is God before ages. as the disciples of Paul of Samosata, who say that after the incarnation He was by advance³ made God, from being made by nature a mere man. For we acknowledge, that though He be subordinate to His Father and God, yet, being before ages begotten of God, He is God perfect according to nature and true, and not first man and then God, but first God and then becoming man for us, and never having been deprived of being ʸ.

³ ¹ ἐκ προ- κοπῆς p. 16, note l.

(5.) We abhor besides, and anathematize those who make a pretence of saying that He is but the mere word of God and unexisting, having His being in another,—now as if pronounced, as some speak, now as mental ᶻ,—holding that He was not Christ or Son of God or

---

ʸ These strong words, θιὸν κατὰ φύσιν τέλειον καὶ ἀληθῆ are of a different character from any which have occurred in the Arian Confessions They can only be explained away by considering them used *in contrast* to the Samosatene doctrine; Paul saying that that dignity, which the Arians ascribed to our Lord before His birth in the flesh, was bestowed on Him after it. vid. p 115, ref. 1. Thus " perfect according to nature" and " true," will not be directly connected with " God' so much as opposed to, " by advance," " by adoption." &c. p. 108, note 1

ᶻ The use of the words ἐνδιάθετος and προφορικὸς, *mental* and *pronounced*, to distinguish the two senses of λόγος, *reason* and *word*, came from the school of the Stoics, and is found in Philo, and was under certain limitations allowed in Catholic theology. Damasc. F. O. ii. 21. To use either absolutely and to the exclusion of the other would have involved some form of Sabellianism, or Arianism as the case might be ; but each might correct the defective sense of either S. Theophilus speaks of our Lord as at once

ἐνδιάθετος and προφορικὸς. ad Autol. ii. 10 and 22. S. Cyril as ἐνδιάθετος, in Joann. p 39 on the other hand he says, " This pronounced word of ours, προφορικὸς, is generated from mind and unto mind, and seems to be other than that which stirs in the heart, &c &c .. so too the Son of God proceeding from the Father without division, is the expression and likeness of what is proper to Him, being a subsistent Word, and living from a Living Father." Thesaur p 47 When the Fathers deny that our Lord is the προφορικὸς λόγος, they only mean that that title is not, even as far as its philosophical idea went, an adequate representative of Him, a word spoken being insubstantive, vid. Athan. Orat. ii 35. Hil. de Syn. 46. Cyr. Catech. xi. 10. Damas. Ep. ii. p 203. nec prolativum ut generationem ei demas, for this was the Arian doctrine. " The Son [says Eunomius] is other than the Mental Word, or Word in intellectual action, of which partaking and being filled He is called the Pronounced Word, and expressive of the Father's substance, that is, the Son." Cyril in Joann. p. 31 The Gnostics seem to have held the

114   *The Macrostich Creed, sent into Italy,*

COUNC. ARIM. AND SELEU
[1] p. 107, note e

mediator[1] or image of God before ages; but that He first became Christ and Son of God, when He took our flesh from the Virgin, not four hundred years since. For they will have it that then Christ began His Kingdom, and that it will have an end after the consummation of all and the judgment [a]. Such are the disciples of Marcellus and Scotinus[b] of Galatian Ancyra, who, equally with Jews, negative Christ's existence before ages, and His Godhead, and unending Kingdom, upon pretence of supporting the divine Monarchy. We, on the contrary, regard Him not as simply God's pronounced word or mental, but as Living God and Word, existing in Himself, and Son of God and Christ; being and abiding with His Father before ages, and that not in foreknowledge only [c], and ministering to Him for the whole framing whether of things visible or invisible. For He it is, to whom the Father said, *Let Us make man in Our image, after Our likeness*[2], who also was seen in His own Person [d] by the patriarchs, gave the law,

Gen 1, 26.
[2] vid. p. 120, notes p and q.

λόγος προφορικός. Iren. Hær. ii. 12. n. 5. Marcellus is said by Eusebius to have considered our Lord as first the one and then the other. Eccl. Theol. ii. 15. Sabellius thought our Lord the προφορικὸς according to Epiph. Hær. p 398. Damasc Hær. 62. Paul of Samosata the ἐνδιάθετος. Epiph. Hær 65. passim. Eusebius, Eccles. Theol ii. 17. describes our Lord as the προφορικὸς while he disowns it.

[a] This passage seems taken from Eusebius, and partly from Marcellus's own words vid. supr. note r. S. Cyril speaks of his doctrine in like terms. Catech. xv. 27.

[b] i. e. Photinus of Sirmium, the pupil of Marcellus is meant, who published his heresy about 343. A similar play upon words is found in the case of other names, though Lucifer seems to think that his name was really Scotinus and that his friends changed it. de non parc. pp. 203, 220, 226. Thus Noetus is called ἀνόητος Epiph. Hær. 57. 2 fin. and 8. Eudoxius, ἀδόξιος. Lucifer. pro Athan. i. p. 65. Moriend p. 258. Eunomians among the Latins, (by a confusion with Anomœan,) ἄνομοι, or *sine lege*, Cod Can. lxi. 1. ap. Leon. Op t. 3 p. 443. Vigilantius dormitantius, Jerom. contr. Vigil. init Aerius ἀέριον πνεῦμα ἴσχιν. Epiph Hær. 75. 6 fin. Of Arius, "Ἀρεις, ἄρεις vid supr. p. 91, note q. Gregory, ὁ νυστάζων Anast. Hod. 10. p. 186. Eutyches, δυστυχὴς, &c. &c Photinus seems to have brought out more fully the heresy of Marcellus, both of whom, as all Sabellians excepting Patripassians, differed from the Arians mainly in this point alone, *when* it was that our Lord came into being, the

Arians said before the worlds, the Samosatenes, Photinians, &c said on His human birth; both parties considered Him a creature, and that the true Word and Wisdom were attributes or energies of Almighty God. This Lucifer well observes to Constantius in the course of one of the passages above quoted, " Quid interesse arbitraris inter te et Paulum Samosatenum, vel eum tum ejus discipulum tuum conscotinum, nisi quia tu *ante omnia* dicas, ille vero *post omnia?*" p. 203, 4. A subordinate difference was this, that the Samosatene, Photinian, &c. considered our Lord to be really gifted with the true Word, whereas the Arian did scarcely more than consider Him framed after the pattern of it. Photinus was condemned, after this Council, at Sardica, (347 if not 344,) and if not by Catholics at least by Eusebians, at Milan (348) by the Catholics, and perhaps again in 351, at Sirmium his see, by the Eusebians in 351, when he was deposed. He was an eloquent man and popular in his diocese, and thus maintained his ground for some years after his condemnation.

[c] " This passage of the Apostle," Rom 1. 1. " [Marcellus] I know not why perverts, instead of *declared*, ὁρισθέντος, making it *predestined*, προορισθέντος, that the Son may be such as they who are predestined at foreknowledge." Euseb. contr. Marc. 1. 2 Paul of Samosata also considered our Lord Son by foreknowledge, προγνώσει vid. Routh. Reliqu. t. 2 p 466. and Eunomius, Apol. 24.

[d] αὐτοπροσωπῶς and so Cyril. Hier. Catech. xv. 14 and 17. It means, " not in personation," and Philo contrasting divine appearances with those

being the fifth of the Eusebians, Semi-arian. 115

spoke by the prophets, and at last, became man, and manifested CHAP His own Father to all men, and reigns to never-ending ages. II For Christ has taken no recent dignity¹, but we have believed ¹ p 113, Him to be perfect from the first, and like in all things to the note y. Father ᵉ.

(6.) And those who say that the Father and Son and Holy Ghost are the same, and irreligiously take the Three Names of one and the same Reality² and Person, we justly proscribe from the ² πράγ· Church, because they suppose the illimitable and impassible ματος. Father to be limitable withal and passible through His becoming p. 113, man: for such are they whom the Latins call the Patropassians, ¹ᵉᶠ·¹· and we Sabellians ᶠ. For we acknowledge that the Father who sent, remained in the peculiar state of His unchangeable Godhead, and that Christ who was sent fulfilled the economy of the incarnation.

(7.) And at the same time those who irreverently say that the Son was generated, not by choice or will, thus encompassing God with a necessity which excludes choice and purpose, so that He begat the Son unwillingly, we account as most irreligious and alien to the Church ; in that they have dared to define such things concerning God, beside the common notions concerning Him, nay, beside the purport of divinely inspired Scripture. For we, knowing that God is absolute and sovereign over Himself, have a religious judgment that He generated the Son voluntarily and freely , yet, as we have a reverent belief in the Son's words concerning Himself, *The Lord hath created Me a beginning* Prov. 8, 22

of Angels. Leg. Alleg III 62 On the other hand, Theophilus on the text, " The voice of the Lord God walking in the garden," speaks of the Word, " assuming the person, πρόσωπον, of the Father," and " in the person of God." ad Autol II 22 the word not then having its theological sense.

ᵉ ὅμοιον κατὰ πάντα. Here again we have a strong Semi-arian or almost Catholic formula introduced by the bye, marking the presence of what may be called the new Semi-arian school. Of course it admitted of evasion, but in its fulness it included " substance " At Sirmium Constantius inserted it in the Confession which occurs supra vid. p. 84, note a. On this occasion Basil subscribed in this form. " I, Basil, Bishop of Ancyra, believe and assent to what is aforewritten, confessing that the Son is like the Father in all things; and by ' in all things,' not only that He is like in will, but in subsistence, and existence, and being ; as divine Scripture teaches, spirit from spirit, life from life, light from light, God from God, true Son from true, Wisdom from the Wise God and Father, and once for all, like the Father in all things, as a son is to a father. And if any one says that He is like in a certain respect, κατά τι, as is written afore, he is alien from the Catholic Church, as not confessing the likeness according to divine Scripture." Epiph. Hær. 73 22. S. Cyril of Jerusalem uses the κατὰ πάντα or ἐν πᾶσιν ὅμοιον, Catech IV. 7. xi. 4 and 18. and Athan. Orat. 1. §. 21. and II §. 18 and 22. Damasc. F. O 1. 8. p. 135

ᶠ Eusebius also, Eccles. Theol 1. 20 says that Sabellius held the Patropassian doctrine Epiph. however, Hær. p. 398.denies it, and imputes the doctrine to Noetus. Sabellius's doctrine will come before us infr. Orat. IV , meanwhile it should be noticed, that in the reason which the Confession alleges against that heretical doctrine it is almost implied that the divine nature of the Son suffered on the Cross. They would naturally fall into this notion directly they gave up their belief in our Lord's absolute divinity. It would as naturally follow to hold that our Lord had no human soul, but that His pre-existent nature stood in the place of it —also that His Mediatorship was no peculiarity of His Incarnation. vid p. 107, note e. p. 119, note o

I 2

COUNC. of His ways for His works, we do not understand Him to be
ARIM. generated, like the creatures or works which through Him came
AND to be. For it is irreligious and alien to the ecclesiastical faith,
SELEU to compare the Creator with handiworks created by Him, and to
think that He has the same manner of generation with the rest.
For divine Scripture teaches us really and truly that the Only-
begotten Son was generated sole and solely [g].

Yet [h], in saying that the Son is in Himself, and both lives and exists
like the Father, we do not on that account separate Him from
the Father, imagining place and interval between their union in
the way of bodies. For we believe that they are united with
[1] de   each other without mediator or distance [1], and that they exist in-
Decr.   separable; all the Father embosoming the Son, and all the Son
§.8.supr. hanging and adhering to the Father, and alone resting on the
p 13.   Father's breast continually [2]. Believing then in the All-perfect
[2] de   Trinity, the most Holy, that is, in the Father, and the Son, and the
Decr.
§ 26   Holy Ghost, and calling the Father God, and the Son God, yet
supr   we confess in them, not two Gods, but one dignity of Godhead, and
p 46   one exact harmony of dominion, the only Father being Head over
the whole universe wholly, and over the Son Himself, and the
Son subordinated to the Father, but, excepting Him, ruling
over all things after Him which through Himself have come to
be, and granting the grace of the Holy Ghost unsparingly to the
holy at the Father's will. For that such is the account of
[3] p. 45, the Divine Monarchy [3] towards Christ, the sacred oracles have
note h. delivered to us.

Thus much, in addition to the faith before published in
epitome, we have been compelled to draw forth at length, not in
any officious display, but to clear away all unjust suspicion concerning our opinions, among those who are ignorant of what we
really hold · and that all in the West may know, both the
audacity of the slanders of the heterodox, and as to the Orientals,

---

[g] The Confession does not here comment on the clause against our Lord's being Ingenerate, having already noticed it under paragraph (2) It will be remarked that it still insists upon the unscripturalness of the Catholic positions. The main subject of this paragraph is θελήσει γεννηθὶν, which forms great part of the Arian question and controversy, is reserved for Orat. III. 59, &c. in which Athanasius formally treats of it. He treats of the text Prov. viii 22 throughout Orat. II. The doctrine of the μονογενὴς has already partially come before us in de Decr. §. 7—9. p. 12, &c. Μόνως, not as the creatures. vid. p. 62, note f

[h] This last paragraph is the most curious of the instances of the presence of this new and nameless influence, which seems at this time to have been springing up among the Eusebians, and shewed itself by acts before it has a place in history. The paragraph is in its very form an interpolation or appendix, while its doctrine bears distinctive characters of something higher than the old Semiarianism. The characteristic of that, as of other shapes of the heresy, was the absolute separation which it put between the Father and the Son. They considered Them as two οὐσίαι, ὅμοιαι like, but not as ὁμοούσιοι, their very explanation of the word τέλειος was "independent" and "distinct." Language then, such as that in the text, was the nearest assignable approach to the reception of the ὁμοούσιον; all that was wanting was the doctrine of the περιχώρησις, of which infr. Orat. III. It is observable that a hint is thrown out by Athanasius about "suggestions" from without, a sentence or two afterwards. It is observable too that in the next paragraph the preceding doctrine is pointedly said to be that of "the Orientals."

their ecclesiastical judgment in the Lord, to which the divinely inspired Scriptures bear witness without violence, where men are not perverse.

14. However they did not stand even to this, for again at Sirmium[1] they met together[k] against Photinus[l], and there composed a faith again, not drawn out into such length, not so full in words; but subtracting the greater part and adding in its place, as if they had listened to the suggestions of others, they wrote as follows:—

[1] Sirmium was a city of lower Pannonia, not far from the Danube, and it was the great bulwark of the Illyrian provinces of the Empire. There Vetranio assumed the purple, and there Constantius was born. The frontier war caused it to be from time to time the Imperial residence. We hear of Constantius at Sirmium in the summer of 357. Ammian xvi. 10. He also passed there the ensuing winter. ibid. xvii. 12. In October, 358, after the Sarmatian war, he entered Sirmium in triumph, and passed the winter there xvii. 13 fin. and with a short absence in the spring, remained there till the end of May, 359. vid. p 84, note a.

[k] In the dates here fixed for the Confessions of Sirmium, Petavius has been followed, who has thrown more light on the subject than any one else. In 351, the Semi-arian party was still stronger than in 345 The leading person in this Council was Basil of Ancyra, who is generally considered their head. Basil held a disputation with Photinus Silvanus too of Tarsus now appears for the first time; while, according to Socrates, Mark of Arethusa, who was more connected with the Eusebians than any other of his party, drew up the Anathemas, the Confession used was the same as that sent to Constans, of the Council of Philippopolis, and the Macrostich.

[l] There had been no important Oriental Council held since that of the Dedication ten years before, till this of Sirmium; unless indeed that of Philippopolis requires to be mentioned, which was a secession from the Council of Sardica. S. Hilary treats its creed as a Catholic composition. de Syn. 39—63. Philastrius and Vigilius call the Council a meeting of "holy bishops" and a "Catholic Council." de Hær. 65 in Eutych. v. init. What gave a character and weight to this Council, which belonged to no other Eusebian meeting, was, that it met to set right a real evil, and was not a mere pretence with Arian objects Photinus had now been 8 or 9 years in the open avowal of his heresy, yet in possession of his see. Nothing is more instructive in the whole of this eventful history than the complication of the Oriental party, and the apparent advance yet decline of the truth Principles, good and bad, were developing on both sides with energy The fall of Hosius and Liberius, and the dreadful event of Ariminum, are close before the ruin of the Eusebian power. As to the Bishops present at this Sirmian Council, we have them described in Sulpitius, "Part of the Bishops followed Arius, and welcomed the desired condemnation of Athanasius, part, brought together by fear and faction, yielded to a party spirit, a few, to whom faith was dear and truth precious, rejected the unjust judgment" Hist ii. 52., he instances Paulinus of Treves, whose resistance, however, took place at Milan some years later. Sozomen gives us a similar account, speaking of a date a few years before the Sirmian Council "The East," he says, "in spite of its being in faction after the Antiochene Council" of the Dedication, "and thenceforth openly dissenting from the Nicene faith, in reality, I think, concurred in the sentiment of the majority, and with them confessed the Son to be of the Father's substance; but from contentiousness certain of them fought against the term ' One in substance ,' some, as I conjecture, having originally objected to the word...others from habit... others, aware that the resistance was unsuitable, leaned to this side or that to gratify parties, and many thought it weak to waste themselves in such strife of words, and peaceably held to the Nicene decision." Hist iii 13.

The first Creed of Sirmium, against Photinus,

COUNC. ARIM. AND SELEU. vi. Confession, or 1st Sirmian A.D. 351. Eph. 3, 15.

We believe in One God, the Father Almighty, the Creator and Maker of all things, *from whom the whole family in heaven and earth is named.*

And in His Only-begotten Son, our Lord Jesus the Christ, who before all the ages was begotten from the Father, God from God, Light from Light, by whom all things were made, in heaven and on the earth, visible and invisible, being Word and Wisdom and True Light and Life, who in the last days was made man for us, and was born of the Holy Virgin, and crucified and dead and buried, and rose again from the dead the third day, and was taken up into heaven, and sat down on the right hand of the Father, and is coming at the end of the world, to judge quick and dead, and to render to every one according to his works; whose Kingdom being unceasing endures unto the infinite ages; for He shall sit on the right hand of the Father, not only in this world, but also in that which is to come.

And in the Holy Ghost, that is, the Paraclete; which, having promised to the Apostles, to send forth after His ascension into heaven, to teach and to remind them of all things, He did send; through whom also are sanctified the souls of those who sincerely believe in Him.

[vid note on Nic. Anath. p. 66.]

(1) But those who say that the Son was from nothing or from other subsistence¹ and not from God, and that there was time or age when He was not, the Holy and Catholic Church regards as aliens.

(2.) Again we say, Whosoever says that the Father and the Son are two Gods, be he anathema ᵐ.

(3) And whosoever, saying that Christ is God, before ages Son of God, does not confess that He subserved the Father for the framing of the universe, be he anathema ⁿ.

ᵐ This Anathema which has occurred in substance in the Macrostich, and again infra, Anath 18 and 23. is a disclaimer on the part of the Eusebian party of the charge brought against them with reason by the Catholics, of their in fact holding a supreme and a secondary God. In the Macrostich it is disclaimed upon a simple Arian basis. The Semiarians were more open to this imputation, Eusebius, as we have seen above, distinctly calling our Lord a second and another God. vid. p 63, note g. It will be observed that this Anathema contradicts the one which immediately follows, and the 11th, in which Christ is called God, except, on the one hand, the Father and Son are One God, which was the Catholic doctrine, or, on the other, the Son is God in name only, which was the pure Arian or Anomœan.

ⁿ The language of Catholics and heretics is very much the same on this point of the Son's ministration, with this essential difference of sense, that Catholic writers mean a ministration internal to the divine substance and an instrument connatural with the Father, and Arius meant an external and created medium of operation vid. p 12. note z. Thus S Clement calls our Lord "the All-harmonious Instrument (ὄργανον) of God." Protrept. p 6 Eusebius "an animated and living instrument (ὄργανον ἔμψυχον,) nay, rather divine and vivific of every substance and nature." Demonstr. iv 4 S. Basil, on the other hand, insists that the Arians reduced our Lord to "an inanimate instrument." ὄργανον ἄψυχον, though they called Him ὑπουργὸν τελεώτατον, most perfect minister or under-worker. adv. Eunom. ii. 21. Elsewhere he says, "the nature of a cause is one, and the nature of an instrument, ὀργάνου, an-

being the sixth of the Eusebians, Semi-arian. 119

(4.) Whosoever presumes to say that the Ingenerate, or a part of Him¹ was born of Mary, be he anathema.

(5) Whosoever says that according to foreknowledge² the Son is before Mary and not that, generated from the Father before ages, He was with God, and that through Him all things were generated, be he anathema.

(6.) Whosoever shall pretend that the substance of God was enlarged or contracted³, be he anathema.

(7.) Whosoever shall say that the substance of God being enlarged made the Son, or shall name the enlargement of His substance the Son, be he anathema.

(8) Whosoever calls the Son of God the mental or pronounced Word⁴, be he anathema.

(9) Whosoever says that the Son from Mary is man only, be he anathema.

(10.) Whosoever, speaking of Him who is from Mary God and man, thereby means God the Ingenerate⁵, be he anathema.

(11.) Whosoever shall explain *I am the First and I am the Last, and besides Me there is no God*, which is said for the denial of idols and of gods that are not, to the denial of the Only-begotten, before ages God, as Jews do, be he anathema.

(12.) Whosoever, because it is said *The Word was made flesh*, shall consider that the Word was changed into flesh, or shall say that He underwent an alteration and took flesh, be he anathema°.

CHAP. II.
¹ p. 114, note c.
² p. 114, note c.
³ Orat. iv. §. 13.
⁴ p. 113, note z.
⁵ p. 112, n (2)
Is. 44, 6.
John 1, 14.

---

other;... foreign then in nature is the Son from the Father, since such is an instrument from a workman." de Sp S. n. 6 fin. vid. also n. 4 fin. and n. 20. Afterwards he speaks of our Lord as " not intrusted with the ministry of each work by particular injunctions in detail, for this were ministration," λειτουργικὸν, but as being " full of the Father's excellences," and " fulfilling not an instrumental, ὀργανικὴν, and servile ministration, but accomplishing the Father's will like a Creator, δημιουργικῶς ibid. n. 19. And so S. Gregory, " The Father signifies, the Word accomplishes, not servilely, not ignorantly, but with knowledge and sovereignty, and, to speak more suitably, in the Father's way, πατρικῶς. Orat. 30. 11 And S Cyril, " There is nothing abject in the Son, as in a minister, ὑπουργῷ, as they say; for the God and Father injoins not, ἐπιτάττει, on His Word, ' Make man,' but as one with Him, by nature, and inseparably existing in Him as a co-operator," &c. in Joann. p. 48. Explanations such as these secure for the Catholic writers some freedom in their modes of speaking, e g. we have seen, supr. p. 15. note d. that Athan speaks of the Son, as " enjoined and ministering," προστατόμενος, καὶ ὑπουργῶν,

Orat. ii. §. 22 Thus S. Irenæus speaks of the Father being well-pleased and commanding, κελεύοντος, and the Son doing and framing. Hær. iv. 75. S. Basil too, in the same treatise in which are some of the foregoing protests, speaks of " the Lord ordering, προστάσσοντα, and the Word framing." de Sp S. n 38. S Cyril of Jerusalem, of " Him who bids, ἐντέλλεται, bidding to one who is present with Him," Cat xi 16. vid. also ὑπηρετῶν τῇ βουλῇ, Justin. Tryph. 126. and ὑπουργὸν, Theoph. ad Autol. ii. 10 ἐξυπηρετῶν θελήματι, Clem. Strom. vii. p. 832

° The 12th and 13th Anathemas are intended to meet the charge which is alluded to pp 115, 123, notes f and u, that Arianism involved the doctrine that our Lord's divine nature suffered. Athanasius brings this accusation against them distinctly in his work against Apollinaris, " Idle then is the fiction of the Arians, who suppose that the Saviour took flesh only, irreligiously imputing the notion of suffering to the impassible godhead." contr. Apollin. i. 15. vid. also Ambros. de Fide, iii. 38. Salig in his de Eutychianismo ant. Eutychen takes notice of none of the passages in the text.

COUNC. ARIM. AND SELEU.
Gen 1, 26.
l p. 114, ref. 2.

Gen. 19, 24.

(13.) Whosoever, as hearing the Only-begotten Son of God was crucified, shall say that His Godhead underwent corruption, or passion, or alteration, or diminution, or destruction, be he anathema.

(14.) Whosoever shall say that *Let Us make man*[1] was not said by the Father to the Son, but by God to Himself, be he anathema[p].

(15.) Whosoever shall say that Abraham saw, not the Son, but the Ingenerate God or part of Him, be he anathema[q].

(16.) Whosoever shall say that with Jacob, not the Son as man, but the Ingenerate God or part of Him, did wrestle, be he anathema[r].

(17.) Whosoever shall explain, *The Lord rained fire from the Lord* not of the Father and the Son, and says that He rained from

---

[p] This Anathema is directed against the Sabellians, especially Marcellus, who held the very opinion which it denounces, that the Almighty spake with Himself. Euseb. Eccles. Theol. ii 15. The Jews said that Almighty God spoke to the Angels. Basil. Hexaem. fin. Others that the plural was used as authorities on earth use it in way of dignity. Theod. in Gen. 19. As to the Catholic Fathers, as is well known, they interpreted the text in the sense here given. It is scarcely necessary to refer to instances, Petavius, however, cites the following. First those in which the Eternal Father is considered to speak to the Son. Theophilus, ad Autol ii 18 Novatian, de Trin 26. Tertullian, de Carn. Christ. 5. Synod. Antioch. contr Paul. ap. Routh. Reliqu. t. 2. p 468. Basil Hexaem. fin Cyr. Hieros. Cat. x. 6. Cyril. Alex Dial. iv p. 516. Athan. contr. Gentes, 46. Orat. iii. §. 29. fin Chrysost. in Genes. Hom. viii 3. Hilar. iv. 17. v. 8. Ambros. Hexaem. vi 7. Augustin. ad Maxim ii. 26 n 2. Next those in which Son and Spirit are considered as addressed. Theoph. ad Autol. ii. 18. Pseudo-Basil. contr. Eunom. v. p. 315. Pseudo-Chrysost. de Trin. t i. p. 832. Cyril Thesaur p. 12. Theodor. in Genes. 19. Hær. v. 3. and 9. But even here, where the Arians agree with Catholics, they differ in this remarkable respect, that in this and the following Canons they place certain interpretations of Scripture under the sanction of an anathema, shewing how far less *free* the system of heretics is than that of the Church.

[q] This again, in spite of the wording, which is directed against the Catholic doctrine, and of an heretical implication, is a Catholic interpretation vid (be sides Philo de Somnus i. 12) Justin.

Tryph. 56. and 126. Iren. Hær. iv. 10. n. 1. Tertull. de carn. Christ. 6. adv. Marc iii 9 adv. Prax. 16 Novat. de Trin 18. Origen in Gen. Hom iv. 5. Cyprian adv Jud. ii. 5. Antioch. Syn. contr. Paul. apud Routh. Rell. t 2 p. 469. Athan Orat ii. 13 Epiph Ancor. 29 and 39. Hær. 71. 5. Chrysost. in Gen. Hom. 41. 7. These references are principally from Petavius; also from Dorscheus, who has written an elaborate commentary on this Council. The implication alluded to above is, that the Son is of a visible substance, and thus is naturally the manifestation of the Invisible God. Petavius maintains, and Bull denies, (Defens. F D. iv. 3) that the doctrine is found in Justin, Origen, &c. The Catholic doctrine is that the Son has condescended to become visible by means of material appearances. Augustine seems to have been the first who changed the mode of viewing the texts in question, and considered the divine appearance, not God the Son, but a created Angel. vid. de Trin ii. passim. Jansenius considers that he did so from a suggestion of St. Ambrose, that the hitherto received view had been the origo hæresis Arianæ, vid. his Augustinus, lib. procem. c. 12. t. 2. p. 12. The two views are not inconsistent with each other. It is remarkable that in this and the next anathema for " partem ejus" in Hilary, Petavius should propose to read " patrem" against the original text in Athan. μέρος αὐτοῦ, and the obvious explanation of it by the phrase μέρος ὁμοούσιον, which was not unfrequently in the mouths of Arian objectors. vid. supr. p. 97, note 1

[r] This and the following Canon are Catholic in their main doctrine, and might be illustrated, if necessary, as the foregoing.

Himself, be he anathema. For the Son Lord rained from the Father Lord.

(18.) Whosoever hearing that the Father is Lord and the Son Lord and the Father and Son Lord, for there is Lord from Lord, says there are two Gods, be he anathema. For we do not place the Son in the Father's order, but as subordinate to the Father; for He did not descend upon Sodom without the Father's will[1], nor did He rain from Himself, but from the Lord, that is, the Father authorizing it. Nor is He of Himself set down on the right hand, but He hears the Father saying, *Sit Thou on My right hand.*

(19) Whosoever says that the Father and the Son and the Holy Ghost are One Person, be he anathema.

(20.) Whosoever, speaking of the Holy Ghost as Paraclete, shall speak of the Ingenerate God, be he anathema[s].

(21.) Whosoever shall deny, what the Lord taught us, that the Paraclete is other than the Son, for He hath said, *And another Paraclete shall the Father send to you, whom I will ask*, be he anathema.

(22) Whosoever shall say that the Holy Ghost is part of the Father or of the Son[2], be he anathema.

(23.) Whosoever shall say that the Father and the Son and the Holy Ghost be three Gods, be he anathema.

(24) Whosoever shall say that the Son of God at the will of God came to be, as one of the works, be he anathema.

(25.) Whosoever shall say that the Son was generated, the Father not wishing it[3], be he anathema. For not by compulsion, forced by physical necessity, did the Father, as He wished not, generate the Son, but He at once willed, and, after generating Him from Himself apart from time and passion, manifested Him.

(26.) Whosoever shall say that the Son is ingenerate and unoriginate, as if speaking of two unoriginate and two ingenerate, and making two Gods, be he anathema For the Son is the Head, which is the origin of all. and God is the Head, which is the origin of Christ[4]; for thus to one unoriginate origin of the universe do we religiously refer all things through the Son

(27.) And in accurate delineation of the idea of Christianity we say this again; Whosoever shall not say that Christ is God, Son of God, as being before ages, and having subserved the Father in

---

[s] It was an expedient of the Macedonians to deny that the Holy Spirit was God because it was not usual to call Him Ingenerate; and perhaps to their form of heresy which was always implied in Arianism, and which began to shew itself formally among the Semiarians ten years later, this anathema may be traced. They asked the Catholics whether the Holy Spirit was *Ingenerate, generate,* or *created,* for into these three they divided all things. vid. Basil. in Sabell. et Ar. Hom. xxiv 6. But, as the Arians had first made the alternative only between *Ingenerate* and *created,* and Athan. de Decr. § 28. supr. p. 53, note g. shews that *generate* is a third idea really distinct from one and the other, so S. Greg. Naz. adds, *processive*, ἐκπορευτὸν, as an intermediate idea, contrasted with *Ingenerate,* yet distinct from *generate.* Orat. xxxi. 8. In other words, *Ingenerate* means, not only *not generate,* but *not from any origin.* vid. August. de Trin. xv. 26.

122 *The second Creed of Sirmium, subscribed by Hosius,*

Counc.
Arim.
and
Seleu. the framing of the Universe, but that from the time that he was born of Mary, from thence He was called Christ and Son, and took an origin of being God, be he anathema

§ 28.   15. Casting aside the whole of this, as if they had discovered something better, they propound another faith, and write at Sirmium in Latin what is here translated into Greek[t].

vii. Confession, or 2nd Sirmian, A.D. 357.   Whereas it has seemed good that there should be some discussion concerning faith, all points have been carefully investigated and discussed at Sirmium in the presence of Valens, and Ursacius, and Germanius, and the rest.
  It is held for certain that there is one God, the Father Almighty, as also is preached in all the world.
  And His One Only-begotten Son, our Lord Jesus Christ, generated from Him before the ages; and that we may not

John 20, 17. speak of two Gods, since the Lord Himself has said, *I go to My Father and your Father, and My God and your God* On this account

πορευ ομαι He is God of all, as also the Apostle has taught: *Is He God of the*

Rom 3, 29. *Jews only, is He not also of the Gentiles? yea of the Gentiles also: since there is one God who shall justify the circumcision from faith, and the uncircumcision through faith;* and every thing else agrees, and has no ambiguity.
  But since many persons are disturbed by questions concerning what is called in Latin "Substantia," but in Greek "Usia," that is, to make it understood more exactly, as to "One in Substance," or what is called, "Like in substance," there ought to be no mention of any of these at all, nor exposition of them in the Church, for this reason and for this consideration, that in divine Scripture nothing is written about them, and that they are above men's knowledge and above men's understanding; and because no one can declare the Son's generation, as it is written,

Is. 53, 6. *Who shall declare His generation?* for it is plain that the Father only knows how He generated the Son, and again the Son how He has been generated by the Father. And to none can it be a question that the Father is greater: for no one can doubt that the Father is greater in honour and dignity and Godhead, and in

vid.
John 10, 29.
John 14, 28. the very name of Father, the Son Himself testifying, *The Father that sent Me is greater than I.* And no one is ignorant, that it is Catholic doctrine, that there are two Persons of Father and Son, and that the Father is greater, and the Son subordinated[1] to

[1] ὑποτεταγμένον the Father together with all things which the Father has subordi-

---

[t] The Creed which follows was not put forth by a Council, but at a meeting of a few Arian Bishops, and the author was Potamius, Bishop of Lisbon. It is important as marking the open separation of the Eusebians or Acacians from the Semi-arians, and their adoption of Anomœan tenets. Hilary, who defends the Eusebian Councils up to this date, calls this a "blasphemia," and upon it followed the Semi-arian Council by way of protest at Ancyra. St. Hilary tells us that it was the Confession which Hosius was imprisoned and tortured into signing. Whether it is the one which Pope Liberius signed is doubtful, but he signed an Arian Confession at this time.

being the seventh of the Eusebians, Arian. 123

nated to Him, and that the Father has no origin, and is invisible, and immortal, and impassible; but that the Son has been generated from the Father, God from God, Light from Light, and that His generation, as aforesaid, no one knows, but the Father only. And that the Son Himself and our Lord and God, took flesh, that is, a body, that is, man, from Mary the Virgin, as the Angel heralded beforehand; and as all the Scriptures teach, and especially the Apostle Himself, the doctor of the Gentiles, Christ took man of Mary the Virgin, through which He suffered. And the whole faith is summed up¹, and secured in this, that a Trinity should ever be preserved, as we read in the Gospel, *Go ye and baptize all the nations in the Name of the Father and of the Son and of the Holy Ghost.* And entire and perfect is the number of the Trinity; but the Paraclete, the Holy Ghost, sent forth through the Son, came according to the promise, that He might teach and sanctify the Apostles and all believers ᵘ.

CHAP. II.
¹ κεφά-
λαιον
vid. de
Decr. §.
31. p 56
Orat. 1.
§ 34.
Epiph
Hær.73.
11.
Mat.28,
19.

16. After drawing up this, and then becoming dissatisfied, they composed the faith which to their shame they paraded with " the Consulate." And, as is their wont, condemning this also, they caused Martinian the notary to seize it from the parties who had the copies of it ˣ. And having got the Emperor Constantius to put forth an edict against it, they form another dogma afresh, and with the addition of certain expressions, according to their wont, they write thus in Isauria.

§. 29.

We decline not to bring forward the authentic faith published at

ix. Confession, at Seleucia A D. 359.

ᵘ It will be observed that this Confession, 1. by denying " two Gods," and declaring that the One God is the God of Christ, implies that our Lord is not God. 2. It says that the word " substance," and its compounds, ought not to be used as being unscriptural, mysterious, and leading to disturbance, 3. it holds that the Father is greater than the Son " in honour, dignity, and godhead;" 4. that the Son is subordinate to the Father *with* all other things, 5. that it is the Father's characteristic to be invisible and impassible On the last head, vid. supr. pp. 115. 119. notes f. o They also say that our Lord, hominem suscepisse per quem *compassus* est, a word which Phœbadius condemns in his remarks on this Confession, where, by the way, he uses the word " spiritus" in the sense of Hilary and the Ante-Nicene Fathers, in a connection which at once explains the obscure words of the supposititious Sardican Confession, (vid above, pp. 84, 85, note c,) and turns them into another evidence of this additional heresy involved in Arianism. " Impassibilis Deus," says Phœbadius, " quia Deus *Spiritus* . . non ergo passibilis Dei Spiritus, licet in homine suo passus." Now the Sardican Confession is thought ignorant, as well as unauthoritative, (e g. by Natalis Alex Sæc. 4. Diss. 29.) because it imputes to Valens and Ursacius the following belief, which he supposes to be Patripassianism, but which exactly answers to this aspect and representation of Arianism. ὅτι ὁ λόγος καὶ ὅτι τὸ πνεῦμα καὶ ἐσταυρώθη καὶ ἐσφάγη καὶ ἀπέθανεν καὶ ἀνέστη. Theod. Hist II. 6 p. 844

ˣ Some critics suppose that this transaction really belongs to the second instead of the third Confession of Sirmium Socrates connects it with the second. Hist. II. 30.

124 Creed of Seleucia, ninth of the Eusebians, Homœan.

COUNC. ARIM. AND SELEU.

[1] ὁμοιούσιον
[2] ἀνόμοιον

the Dedication at Antioch[y]; though certainly our fathers at that time met together for a particular subject under investigation. But since "One in substance" and "Like in substance[1]," have troubled many persons in times past and up to this day, and since moreover some are said recently to have devised the Son's "Unlikeness[2]" to the Father, on their account we reject "One in substance" and "Like in substance," as alien to the Scriptures, but "Unlike" we anathematize, and account all who profess it as aliens from the Church. And we distinctly confess the "Likeness[3]" of the Son to the Father, according to the Apostle, who says of the Son, *Who is the Image of the Invisible God.*

[3] ὅμοιον
Col. 1, 15.

And we confess and believe in one God, the Father Almighty, the Maker of heaven and earth, of all things visible and invisible.

And we believe also in our Lord Jesus Christ, His Son, generated from Him impassibly before all the ages, God the Word, God from God, Only-begotten, light, life, truth, wisdom, power, through whom all things were made, in the heavens and on the earth, whether visible or invisible. He, as we believe, at the end of the world, for the abolishment of sin, took flesh of the Holy Virgin, and was made man, and suffered for our sins, and rose again, and was taken up into heaven, and sitteth on the right hand of the Father, and is coming again in glory, to judge quick and dead

We believe also in the Holy Ghost, which our Saviour and Lord named Paraclete, having promised to send Him to the disciples after His own departure, as He did send; through whom He sanctifieth all in the Church who believe, and are baptized in the Name of Father and Son and Holy Ghost.

But those who preach aught beside this faith the Catholic Church regards as aliens. And that to this faith that is equivalent which was published lately at Sirmium, under sanction of his religiousness the Emperor, is plain to all who read it.

§ 30. 17. Having written thus in Isauria, they went up to Constantinople[z], and there, as if dissatisfied, they changed it, as is

---

[y] The Semi-arian majority in the Council had just before been confirming the Creed of the Dedication; hence this beginning. vid supr. p 89, note o. They had first of all offered to the Council the third Sirmian, or " Confession with a Date," supr. §. 3. which their coadjutors offered at Ariminum, Soz. iv. 22 and at the end of the present they profess that the two are substantially the same. They seem to mean that they are both Homœan or Scriptural Creeds, they differ in that the latter, as if to propitiate the Semi-arian majority, adds an anathema upon Anomœan as well as on the Homousion and Homœusion.

[z] These two sections seem to have been inserted by Athan. after his Letter was finished, and contain later occurrences in the history of Ariminum, than were contemplated when he wrote supra, ch. 1. n. 15. init vid. note b, in loc. In this place Athan. distinctly says, that the following Confession, which the Acacians from Seleucia adopted at Constantinople, was transmitted to Ariminum, and thereforced upon the assembled Fathers. This is not inconsistent with what seems to be the fact, that the Confession was drawn up at a Council held at Nice in Thrace near Adrianople in Oct. 359, whither the deputies from Ariminum had been summoned by Constantius. vid. Hilar. Fragm. viii. 5. There the deputies signed it, and thence they took it back to Ariminum. In the beginning of the

Creed of Nice, tenth, signed at Ariminum, Homœan. 125

their wont, and with certain additions against using even "Subsistence" of Father, Son, and Holy Ghost, they transmitted it to the Council at Ariminum, and compelled even the Bishops in those parts to subscribe it, and those who contradicted them they got banished by Constantius. And it runs thus :—

We believe in One God the Father Almighty, from whom are all things;

And in the Only-begotten Son of God, begotten from God before all ages and before every origin, by whom all things were made, visible and invisible, and begotten as only-begotten, only from the Father only [a], God from God, like to the Father that begat Him according to the Scriptures; whose generation no one knows, except the Father alone who begat Him. He as we acknowledge, the Only-begotten Son of God, the Father sending Him, came hither from the heavens, as it is written, for the undoing of sin and death, and was born of the Holy Ghost, of Mary the Virgin according to the flesh, as it is written, and conversed with the disciples, and having fulfilled the whole economy according to the Father's will, was crucified and dead and buried

Marginal note: CHAP. II. x. Confession at Nice and Constantinople. A.D. 359.360.

---

following year 360 it was confirmed by a Council at Constantinople, after the termination of that of Ariminum, and to this confirmation Athanasius refers. Socrates says, Hist. ii. 37 fin that they chose Nice in order to deceive the ignorant with the notion that it was Nicæa, and their creed the Nicene faith, and the place is actually called Nicæa, in the Acts of Ariminum preserved by Hilary, p 1346. Such a measure, whether or not adopted in matter of fact, might easily have had success, considering the existing state of the West We have seen, supr. p 76, note 1, that S. Hilary had not heard the Nicene Creed till he came into Asia Minor, A D 356 and he says of his Gallic and British brethren, "O blessed ye in the Lord and glorious, who hold the perfect and apostolic faith in the profession of your conscience, and up to this time know not creeds in writing. For ye needed not the letter, who abounded in the Spirit, nor looked for the hand's office for subscription, who believed in the heart, and professed with the mouth unto salvation. Nor was it necessary for you as bishops to read, what was put into your hands as noophytes on your regeneration. But necessity hath brought in the usage, the creeds should be expounded and subscriptions attached. For when what our conscience holds is in danger, then the letter is required, nor surely is there reason against writing what there is health in confessing." de Syn. 63. It should be added that at this Council Ulphilas the Apostle of the Goths, who had hitherto followed the Council of Nicæa, conformed, and thus became the means of spreading through his countrymen the Creed of Ariminum.

[a] μόνος ἐκ μόνου Though this is an Homœan or Acacian, not an Anomœan Creed, this phrase may be considered a symptom of Anomœan influence; μόνος παρὰ, or ὑπὸ, μόνου being one special formula adopted by Eunomius, explanatory of μονογενὴς, in accordance with the original Arian theory, mentioned de Decr. § 7. supra, p 12. that the Son was the one instrument of creation. Eunomius said that He alone was created by the Father alone, all other things being created by the Father, not alone, but *through* Him whom alone He had first created. vid. Cyril. Thesaur. 25. p. 239. St. Basil observes that, if this be a true sense of μονογενὴς, then no man is such, e. g. Isaac, as being born of two, contr. Eunom. ii 21. Acacius has recourse to Gnosticism, and illustrates the Arian sense by the contrast of the προβολὴ of the Æons, which as described supra, p. 97, note h, was ἐκ πολλῶν. ap. Epiph. Hær. 72. 7. p. 839.

Creed of Antioch,

COUNC. ARIM. AND SELEU.

and descended to the parts below the earth; at whom hell itself shuddered: who also rose from the dead on the third day, and abode with the disciples, and, forty days being fulfilled, was taken up into the heavens, and sitteth on the right hand of the Father, to come in the last day of the resurrection in the Father's glory, that He may render to every man according to his works.

And in the Holy Ghost, whom the Only-begotten Son of God Himself, Christ, our Lord and God, promised to send to the race of man, as Paraclete, as it is written, " the Spirit of truth, which He sent unto them when He had ascended into the heavens."

But the name of " Substance," which was set down by the Fathers in simplicity, and, being unknown by the people, caused offence, because the Scriptures contain it not, it has seemed good to take away, and for the future to make no mention of it at all; since the divine Scriptures have made no mention of the Substance of Father and Son. For neither ought Subsistence to be named concerning Father, Son, and Holy Ghost But we say that the Son is Like the Father, as the divine Scriptures say and teach; and all the heresies, both those which have been afore condemned already, and whatever are of modern date, being contrary to this published statement, be they anathema [b].

§. 31.
xi. Confession at Antioch.
A D. 361

18. However, they did not stand even to this, for coming down from Constantinople to Antioch, they were dissatisfied that they had written at all that the Son was " Like the Father, as the Scriptures say;" and putting their ideas upon paper, they began reverting to their first doctrines, and said that " the Son is altogether unlike the Father," and that the " Son is in no manner like the Father," and so much did they change, as to admit those who spoke the Arian doctrine nakedly and to deliver to them the Churches with licence to bring forward the words of blasphemy with impunity [c]. Because then of the extreme shamelessness of

---

[b] Here as before, instead of speaking of Arianism, the Confession anathematizes *all* heresies. vid. supr p. 108, note g. It will be observed, that for " Like in all things," which was contained in the Confession (third Sirmian) first submitted to the Ariminian Fathers, is substituted simply " Like." Moreover, they include hypostasis or subsistence, though a Scripture term, in the list of proscribed symbols. vid. also ad Afros. 4. The object of suppressing ὑπόστασις, seems to have been that, since the Creed, which was written in Latin, was to go to Ariminum, the West might be forced to deny the Latin version or equivalent of ὁμοούσιον, unius substantiæ, or hypostasis, as well as the Greek original This circumstance might be added, to those enumerated supra, p 69, &c. to shew that in the Nicene formulary *substance* and *subsistence* are synonymous.

[c] Acacius, Eudoxius, and the rest, after ratifying at Constantinople the Creed framed at Nice and subscribed at Ariminum, appear next at Antioch a year and a half later, when they throw off the mask, and, avowing the Anomœan Creed, " revert," as St Athanasius says, " to their first doctrines," 1. e. those with which Arius started. The Anomœan doctrine, it may be observed, is directly opposed rather to the Homœusian than to the Homousion, as

their blasphemy they were called by all Anomœans, having also the name of Exucontian [d], and the heretical Constantius for the patron of their ungodliness, who persisting up to the end in irreligion, and on the point of death, thought good to be baptized [e]; not however by religious men, but by Euzoius [f], who for his Arianism had been deposed, not once, but often, both when he was a deacon, and when he was in the see of Antioch.

19. The forementioned parties then had proceeded thus far, §. 32. when they were stopped and deposed. But well I know, not even under these circumstances will they stop, as many as have now dissembled [g], but they will always be making parties against

indeed the very symbols shew; "unlike in substance," being the contrary to "like in substance." It doubtless frightened the Semi-arians, and hastened their return to the Catholic doctrine.

[d] From ἐξ οὐκ ὄντων, "out of nothing," one of the original Arian positions concerning the Son. Theodoret says, that they were also called Exacionitæ, from the nature of their place of meeting, Hær. iv. 3. and Du Cange confirms it so far as to shew that there was a place or quarter of Constantinople called Exocionium or Exacionium.

[e] At this critical moment Constantius died, when the cause of truth was only not in the lowest state of degradation, because a party was in authority and vigour who could reduce it to a lower still, the Latins committed to an Anti-Catholic Creed, the Pope a renegade, Hosius fallen and dead, Athanasius wandering in the deserts, Arians in the sees of Christendom, and their doctrine growing in blasphemy, and their profession of it in boldness, every day. The Emperor had come to the throne when almost a boy, and at this time was but 44 years old. In the ordinary course of things, he might have reigned till, humanly speaking, orthodoxy was extinct. This passage shews that Athanasius did not insert these sections till two years after the composition of the work itself, for Constantius died A D. 361.

[f] Euzoius, at this time Arian Bishop of Antioch, was excommunicated with Arius in Egypt and at Nicæa, and was restored with him to the Church at the Council of Jerusalem. He succeeded at Antioch S Meletius, who on being placed in that see by the Arians

professed orthodoxy, and was forthwith banished by them.

[g] ὑπεκρίναντο *hypocrites*, is almost a title of the Arians, (with an apparent allusion to 1 Tim. iv. 2. vid. Socr. 1. p 13. Athan Orat 1 § 8) and that in various senses. The first meaning is that, being heretics, they nevertheless used orthodox phrases and statements to deceive and seduce Catholics. Thus the term is used by Alexander in the beginning of the controversy. vid Theod Hist 1 3 pp. 729. 746. Again, it implies that they agreed with Arius, but would not confess it; professed to be Catholics, but would not anathematize him vid. Athan. ad Ep Æg. 20. or alleged untruly the Nicene Council as their ground of complaint, infr § 39. Again, it is used of the hollowness and pretence of their ecclesiastical proceedings, with the Emperor at their head; which were a sort of make-belief of spiritual power, or piece of acting, δραματούργημα Ep. Encycl 2 and 6. It also means general insincerity, as if they were talking about what they did not understand, and did not realize what they said, and were blindly implicating themselves in evils of a fearful character. Thus Athan. calls them τοὺς τῆς Ἀρείου μανίας ὑποκριτάς Orat 11. § 1. init and he speaks of the evil spirit making them his sport, τοῖς ὑποκρινομένοις τὴν μανίαν αὐτοῦ. ad Serap 1 1. And hence further it is applied, as in this place, though with severity, yet to those who were near the truth, and who, though in sin, would at length come to it or not, according as the state of their hearts was. He is here anticipating the return into the Church of those whom he

the truth, until they return to themselves and say, " Let us rise and go to our fathers, and say unto them, We anathematize the Arian heresy, and we acknowledge the Nicene Council[h]:" for against this is their quarrel. Who then, with ever so little understanding, will bear them any longer? who, on hearing in every Council some things taken away and others added, but comprehends their treachery and secret depravity against Christ? who on seeing them embodying to so great a length both their profession of faith, and their own exculpation, but sees that they are giving sentence against themselves[1], and studiously writing much which may be likely by an officious display and an abundance of words to seduce the simple and hide what they are in point of heresy? But as the heathen, as the Lord said, using vain words in their prayers, are nothing profited; so they too, after all their words were spent, were not able to extinguish the judgment pronounced against the Arian heresy, but were convicted and deposed instead; and rightly; for which of their formularies is to be accepted by the hearer? or with what confidence shall they be catechists to those who come to them? for if they all have one and the same meaning, what is the need of many[2]? But if need has arisen of so many, it follows that each by itself is deficient, not complete; and they establish this point better than we can, by their innovating on them all and re-making them[3]. And the number of their Councils, and the difference of their statements is a proof that those who were present at them, while at variance with the Nicene, are yet too feeble to harm the Truth.

[1] p. 6, note o.
[2] p. 110, note q.
[3] p. 81, note t.

---

thus censures. In this sense, though with far more severity in what he says, the writer of a Tract, imputed to Athan. against the Catholicising Semiarians of 363, entitles it " on the *hypocrisy* of Meletius and Eusebius of Samosata." It is remarkable that what Athan. here predicts was fulfilled to the letter, even of the worst of these " hypocrites." For Acacius himself, who in 361 signed the Anomœan Confession above recorded, was one of those very men who accepted the Homousion with an explanation in 363.

[h] Considering that Athanasius had now been for several years among the monasteries of the deserts, in close concealment, (unless we suppose he really had issued thence and was present at Seleucia,) this is a remarkable instance of accurate knowledge of the state of feeling in the heretical party, and of foresight. From his apparent want of knowledge of the Anomœans, and his unhesitatingly classing them with the Arians, it would seem in a great measure to arise from intimate comprehension of the doctrine itself in dispute and of its bearings. There had been at that time no parallel of a great aberration and its issue.

CHAP. III.

ON THE SYMBOLS " OF THE SUBSTANCE" AND " ONE IN SUBSTANCE."

We must look at the sense not the wording. The offence excited is at the sense; meaning of the Symbols; the question of their not being in Scripture. Those who hesitate only at the latter of the two, not to be considered Arians. Reasons why " one in substance" better than " like in substance," yet the latter may be interpreted in a good sense. Explanation of the rejection of " one in substance" by the Council which condemned Samosatene; use of the word by Dionysius of Alexandria; parallel variation in the use of Ingenerate; quotation from Ignatius and another; reasons for using " one in substance," objections to it, examination of the word itself, further documents of the Council of Ariminum

1. BUT since they are thus minded both towards each other and towards those who preceded them, proceed we to ascertain from them what extravagance they have seen, or what they complain of in the received phrases, that they should thus disobey their fathers, and contend against an Ecumenical Council[a]? " The phrases ' of the substance' and ' one in substance,'" say they, " do not please us, for they are an offence to some and a trouble to many[b]." This then is what

CHAP. III. §. 33.

---

[a] The subject before us, naturally rises out of what has gone before Athan. has traced out the course of Arianism to what seemed to be its result, the resolution of it into a better element or a worse,—the precipitation of what was really unbelieving in it in the Anomœan form, and the gradual purification of that Semi-arianism which prevailed in the Eastern Sees. vid. p. 103, note t. The Anomœan creed was hopeless, but with the Semi-arians all that remained was the adjustment of phrases. They had to reconcile their minds to terms which the Church had taken from philosophy and adopted as her own. Accordingly, Athan. goes on to propose such *expla-nations* as might clear the way for a re-union of Christendom. The remainder of his work then is devoted to the consideration of the " one in substance," (as contrasted with "like in substance,") which had confessedly great difficulties in it. vid. p. 147, note u.

[b] This is only stating what the above Confessions have said again and again The objections made to it were, 1. that it was not in Scripture, 2 that it had been disowned by the Antiochene Council against Paul of Samosata; 3. that it was of a material nature, and belonged to the Manichees; 4. that it was of a Sabellian tendency; 5. that it implied that the divine substance was distinct from God.

Counc. they allege in their writings; but one may reasonably
Arim. answer them thus: If the very words were by themselves a
and
Seleu. cause of offence to them, it must have followed, not that
some only should have offended, and many troubled, but that
we also and all the rest should have been affected by them in
the same way; but if on the contrary all men are well content with the words, and they who wrote them were no
ordinary persons but men who came together from the whole
world, and to these testify in addition the 400 Bishops and
more who have now met at Ariminum, does not this plainly
prove against those who accuse the Council, that the terms
are not in fault, but the perverseness of those who misinterpret them? How many men read divine Scripture wrongly,
and as thus conceiving it, find fault with the Saints? such
were the Jews formerly, who rejected the Lord, and the
[1] vid. Manichees at present who blaspheme the Law[1]; yet are not
Orat. 1.
8. iv. 23. the Scriptures the cause to them, but their own evil humours.
If then ye can shew the terms to be actually unsound, do so
and let the proof proceed, and drop the pretence of offence
created, lest you come into the condition of the Pharisees
formerly, when, on pretending offence at the Lord's teaching,
Mat 15, He said, *Every plant, which My heavenly Father hath not
13. planted, shall be rooted up.* By which He shewed that not
the words of the Father planted by Him were really an
offence to them, but that they misinterpreted good words
and offended themselves. And in like manner they who at
that time blamed the Epistles of the Apostle, impeached,
not Paul, but their own deficient learning and distorted
minds.

§. 34. 2. For answer what is much to the purpose, Who are they
whom you pretend are offended and troubled at these terms?
of those who are religious towards Christ not one; on the
contrary they defend and maintain them. But if they are
Arians who thus feel, what wonder they should be distressed
at words which destroy their heresy? for it is not the terms
which offend them, but the proscription of their irreligion
[2] p. 32, which afflicts them[2]. Therefore let us have no more
ref. 1.
p 36, murmuring against the Fathers, nor pretence of this kind;
ref 2.
p. 138, or next[c] you will be making complaints of the Lord's Cross,
ref. 4.
[c] ἄρα vid Orat. 1. § 15. iv. § 10 Serap. ii. 1 καίροι de Decr. §. 15. init.

"*Of God,*" *if more than words, means "of His Substance.*" 131

that it is *to Jews an offence and to Gentiles foolishness*, as said the Apostle[d]. But as the Cross is not faulty, for to us who believe it is *Christ the power of God and the wisdom of God*, though Jews rave, so neither are the terms of the Fathers faulty, but profitable to those who rightly read, and subversive of all irreligion, though the Arians so often burst with rage as being condemned by them.

CHAP. III.
1 Cor 1, 23. 24.

[1] p. 29, note l.

3. Since then the pretence that persons are offended does not hold, tell us yourselves, why is it you are not pleased with the phrase " of the substance," (this must first be enquired about,) when you yourselves have written that the Son is generated from the Father? If when you name the Father, or use the word " God," you do not signify substance, or understand Him according to substance, who is that He is, but signify something else about Him[2], not to say inferior, then you should not have written that the Son was from the Father, but from what is about Him or in Him[e]; and so, shrinking from saying that God is truly Father, and making Him compound who is simple, in a material way, you will be authors of a new blasphemy. And, with such ideas, do you of necessity consider the Word and the title " Son," not as a substance but as a name[3] only, and in consequence the views ye have ye hold as far as names only, and your statements are not positive points of faith, but negative opinions.

[2] p. 38, note z

[3] p. 41, note e. p 114, note b.

4. But this is more like the crime of the Sadducees, and of those among the Greeks who had the name of Atheists It follows that you deny that creation too is the handywork of God Himself that is; at least, if " Father" and " God" do

§ 35

---

[d] " The Apostle" is a common title of St Paul in antiquity. E. g. " By partaking of the Son Himself, we are said to partake of God, and this is that which *Peter* has said, ' that ye might be partakers of the divine nature,' as says also *the Apostle,* " Know ye not that ye are the temple of God,' &c." Orat 1. §. 16 " When ' the Apostle is mentioned,' says S Augustine, if it is not specified which, Paul only is understood, because he is more celebrated from the number of his Epistles, and laboured more abundantly than all the rest." ad Bonifac. iii. 3. St. Peter is called the Apostle Orat 1. 47

[e] Vid Orat. 1 §. 15 supra, de Decr p. 38, note z Thus Eusebius calls our Lord " the light throughout the universe, moving *round* (ἀμφὶ) the Father " de Laud Const. p. 501 It was a Platonic idea, which he gained from Plotinus, whom he quotes speaking of his second Principle as " radiance around, from Him indeed, but from one who remains what He was, as the sun's bright light circling around it, (περιθέον,) ever generated from it, which nevertheless remains " Evang. Prop. xi. 17. vid. above, p. 51, note b.

k 2

not signify the very substance of Him that is, but something else, which you imagine: which is irreligious, and most shocking even to think of. But if, when we hear it said, *I am that I am*, and *In the beginning God created the heaven and the earth*, and *Hear, O Israel, the Lord our God is one Lord*, and *Thus saith the Lord Almighty*, we understand nothing else than the very simple, and blessed, and incomprehensible substance itself of Him that is, (for though we be unable to master that He is, yet hearing " Father," and " God," and " Almighty," we understand nothing else to be meant than the very substance of Him that is¹;) and if ye too have said, that the Son is from God, it follows that you have said that He is from the " substance" of the Father. And since the Scriptures precede you which say, that the Lord is Son of the Father, and the Father Himself precedes them, who says, *This is My beloved Son*, and a son is no other than the offspring from his father, is it not evident that the Fathers have suitably said that the Son is from the Father's substance? considering that it is all one to say in an orthodox sense " from God," and to say " from the substance." For all the creatures, though they be said to be generated from God, yet are not from God as the Son is; for they are not offsprings in their nature, but works. Thus, it is said, *in the beginning God*, not " generated," but *made the heaven and the earth, and all that is in them*. And not, " who generates," but *who maketh His angels spirits, and His ministers a flame of fire*. And though the Apostle has said, *One God, from whom all things*, yet he says not this, as reckoning the Son with other things ; but, whereas some of the Greeks consider² that the creation was held together by chance, and from the combination of atoms³, and spontaneously from elements of similar structure⁴, and has no cause; and others consider that it came from a cause, but not through the Word; and each heretic has imagined things at his will, and tells his fables about the creation; on this account the Apostle was obliged to introduce *from God*, that he might thereby certify the Maker, and shew that the universe was framed at His will. And accordingly he straightway proceeds. *And one Lord Jesus Christ, through whom all things*, by way of excepting the Son from that " all⁵," (for what is called God's

Objection that the Nicene Symbols are unscriptural. 133

work, is all done through the Son; and it is not possible that the things framed should have one generation with their Framer,) and by way of teaching that the phrase *of God*, which occurs in the passage, has a different sense in the case of the works, from what it bears when used of the Son, for He is offspring, and they are works: and therefore He, the Son, is the proper offspring of His substance, but they are the handywork of His will.

5. The Council, then, comprehending this[1], and aware of the different senses of the same word, that none should suppose, that the Son was said to be *from God* like the creation, wrote with greater explicitness, that the Son was "from the substance." For this betokens the true genuineness of the Son towards the Father; whereas, in its being said simply "from God," only the Creator's will concerning the framing of all is signified. If then they too had this meaning, when they wrote that the Word was "from the Father," they had nothing to complain of in the Council[2], but if they meant "of God," in the instance of the Son, as it is used of the creation, then as understanding it of the creation, they should not name the Son, or they will be manifestly mingling blasphemy with religiousness; but either they have to cease reckoning the Lord with the creatures, or at least to make statements not unworthy, and not unbecoming of the Son. For if He is a Son, He is not a creature, but if a creature, then not a Son. Since these are their views, perhaps they will be denying the Holy Laver also, because it is administered into Father and into Son; and not into Creator and Creature, as they account it.

6. "But," they say, "all this is not written: and we reject these words as unscriptural." But this, again, is an unblushing excuse in their mouths For if they think every thing must be rejected which is not written, wherefore, when the Arian party invent such a heap of phrases, not from Scripture[3], "Out of nothing," and "the Son was not before His generation," and "Once He was not," and "He is alterable," and "the Father is ineffable and invisible to the Son," and "the Son knows not even His own substance;" and all that Arius has vomited in his light and irreligious Thalia, why do not they speak against these, but rather take their part;

Chap. III.

§. 36.
de Decr.
§. 19.
p. 32.

[2] p. 130, ref 2.

[3] p. 31, note p.

134 Arian inconsistency in refusing theological terms

COUNC
ARIM.
AND
SELEU.

and on that account contend with their own Fathers? And, in what Scripture did they on their part find "Ingenerate," and the name of "substance," and "there are three subsistences," and "Christ is not very God," and "He is one of the hundred sheep," and "God's Wisdom is ingenerate and inoriginate, but the created powers are many, of which Christ is one[1]?" Or how, when in the so-called Dedication, the party of Acacius and Eusebius used expressions not in Scripture[2], and said that "the First-born of the creation" was "the unvarying Image of the divine substance, and power, and will of God," do they complain of the Fathers, for making mention of unscriptural expressions, and especially of substance? For they ought either to complain of themselves, or to find no fault with the Fathers

[1] supr § 17
[2] p 106,
[1] *te b.

§ 37

7. Now, if certain others made excuses of the expressions of the Council, it might perhaps have been set down, either to ignorance or to reverence. There is no question, for instance, about George of Cappadocia[f], who was expelled from Alexandria, a man, without character in years past, nor a Christian in any respect, but only pretending to the name to suit the times, and thinking *religion to be a* means of *gain*. And therefore reason is there, none should complain of his making mistakes about the faith, considering he knows neither what he says, nor whereof he affirms; but, according to the text, *goeth after all, as a bird* But when Acacius, and Eudoxius, and Patrophilus say this, do not they deserve the strongest reprobation? for while they write what is unscriptural

1 Tim
6, 6.

vid.
Prov 7,
22 23.

---

[f] George, whom Athanasius, Gregory Naz, and Socrates, call a Cappadocian, was born, according to Ammianus, in Epiphania of Cilicia, at a fuller's mill He was appointed pork-contractor to the army, as mentioned above, § 12 and being detected in defrauding the government, he fled to Egypt Naz Orat 21. 16 How he became acquainted with the Eusebian party does not appear Sozomen tells us that he recommended himself to the see of Alexandria, by his zeal for Arianism and his τὸ δραστήριον, and Gregory calls him the hand of the heresy as Acacius(?) was the tongue. Orat 21 21. He made himself so obnoxious to the Alexandrians, that in the reign of Julian he was torn to pieces in a rising of the heathen populace. He had laid capital informations against many persons of the place, and he tried to persuade Constantius, that as the successor of Alexander its founder he was proprietor of the soil and had a claim upon the houses built on it Ammian xxii. 11. Epiphanius tells us, Hær 76 1 that he made a monopoly of the nitre of Egypt, farmed the beds of papyrus, and the salt lakes, and even contrived a profit from the undertakers. His atrocious cruelties to the Catholics are well known Yet he seems to have collected a choice library of philosophers and poets and Christian writers, which Julian seized on, Pithæus in loc. Ammian. also Gibbon, ch 23.

themselves, and have accepted many times, the term "substance" as suitable, especially on the ground of the letter of Eusebius[1], they now blame their predecessors for using terms of the same kind. Nay, though they say themselves, that the Son is "God from God," and "Living Word," "Unvarying Image of the Father's substance;" they accuse the Nicene Bishops of saying, that He who was begotten is "of the substance" of Him who begat Him, and "One in substance" with Him. But what marvel the conflict with their predecessors and their own Fathers, when they are inconsistent to themselves, and fall foul of each other? For after publishing, in the so-called Dedication at Antioch, that the Son is unvarying Image of the Father's substance, and swearing that so they held and anathematizing those who held otherwise, nay, in Isauria, writing down, "We do not decline the authentic faith published in the Dedication at Antioch[2]," where the term "substance" was introduced, as if forgetting all this, shortly after, in the same Isauria, they put into writing the very contrary, saying, We reject the words "one in substance," and "like in substance," as alien to the Scriptures, and demolish the term "substance," as not contained therein[3].

8. Can we then any more account such men Christians? what sort of faith have they who stand neither to word nor writing, but alter and change every thing according to the times? For if, O Acacius and Eudoxius, you "do not decline the faith published at the Dedication," and in it is written that the Son is "Unvarying Image of God's substance," why is it ye write in Isauria, "we reject the Like in substance?" for if the Son is not like the Father according to substance, how is He "unvarying image of the substance?" But if you are dissatisfied at having written "Unvarying Image of the substance," how is it that ye "anathematize those who say that the Son is Unlike?" for if He be not according to substance like, He is altogether unlike: and the Unlike cannot be an Image. And if so, then it does not hold that *he that hath seen* the Son, *hath seen the Father*, there being then the greatest difference possible between Them, or rather the One being wholly Unlike the Other. And Unlike cannot possibly be called Like. By what artifice then do ye call Unlike like, and consider Like to be unlike, and so

Counc. pretend to say that the Son is the Father's Image? for if the Son
Arim. be not like the Father in substance, something is wanting to
and
Seleu. the Image, and it is not a complete Image, nor a perfect radi-
Co'oss. ance^g. How then read ye, *In Him dwelleth all the fulness of the*
2, 9. *Godhead bodily?* and *from His fulness have all we received?*
John 1,
16. how is it that ye expel the Arian Aetius as an heretic, though
ye say the same with him? for thy companion is he, O
Acacius, and he became Eudoxius's master in this so great
irreligion^h; which was the reason why Leontius the Bishop
made him deacon, that using the name of the diaconate as
a sheep's clothing, he might be able with impunity to pour
§. 39. forth the words of blasphemy. What then has persuaded you
¹ p. 81, to contradict each other¹, and to procure to yourselves so
note t. great a disgrace? You cannot give any good account of it;
this supposition only remains, that all you do is but outward
profession and pretence, to secure the countenance of Constantius and the gain from thence accruing. And ye make
nothing of accusing the Fathers, and ye complain outright of
the expressions as being unscriptural; and, as it is written,
Ez. 16, have *opened thy feet to every one that passed by;* so as to
25. change as often as they wish, in whose pay and keep you
are.

9. Yet, though a man use terms not in Scripture, it makes no
difference, so that his meaning be religiousⁱ. But the heretic,

^g Athan. here says, that when they spoke of " like," they could not consistently mean any thing short of " likeness of substance," for this is the only true likeness; and that, while they used the words ἀπαράλλακτος εἰκων, unvarying image, to exclude all essential likeness, was to suppose instead an image varying utterly from its original. It must not be supposed from this that he approves the phrase ὅμοιος κατ' οὐσίαν or ὁμοιούσιος, in this Treatise, for infr. §. 53. he rejects it on the ground that when we speak of " like," we imply qualities, not substance. According to him then the phrase " unvarying image" was, strictly speaking, self-contradictory, for every image varies from the original because it is an image Yet he himself frequently uses it, as other Fathers, and Orat. 1. §. 26. uses ὅμοιος τῆς οὐσίας. And all human terms are imperfect, and "image' itself is used in Scripture.

^h Aetius was the first to carry out Arianism in its pure Anomœan form, as Eunomius was its principal apologist. He was born in humble life, and was at first a practitioner in medicine. After a time he became a pupil of the Arian Paulinus; then the guest of Athanasius of Nazarbi, then the pupil of Leontius of Antioch, who ordained him deacon, and afterwards deposed him. This was in 350. In 351 he seems to have held a dispute with Basil of Ancyra, at Sirmium; in the beginning of 360 he was formally condemned in the Council of Constantinople, which confirmed the Creed of Ariminum, and just before Eudoxius had been obliged to anathematize his confession of faith This was at the very time Athan. wrote the present work.

ⁱ vid p 31, note p And so S Gregory in a well-known passage, " Why art thou such a slave to the letter, and takest up with Jewish wisdom, and

though he use scriptural terms, yet, as being equally dangerous and depraved, shall be asked in the words of the Spirit, *Why dost thou preach My laws, and takest My covenant in thy mouth?* Thus whereas the devil, though speaking from the Scriptures, is silenced by the Saviour, the blessed Paul, though he speaks from profane writers, *The Cretans are always liars,* and, *For we are His offspring,* and *Evil communications corrupt good manners,* yet has a religious meaning, as being holy,—is *doctor of the nations, in faith and verity,* as having *the mind of Christ,* and what he speaks, he utters religiously. What then is there even plausible, in the Arian terms, in which the *caterpillar* and the *locust*[1] are preferred to the Saviour, and He is reviled with " Once Thou wast not," and " Thou wast created," and " Thou art foreign to God in substance," and, in a word, no insult is spared against Him? On the other hand, what good word have our Fathers omitted? yea rather, have they not a lofty view and a Christ-loving religiousness? And yet these men have written, " We reject the words;" while those others they endure in their insults towards the Lord, and betray to all men, that for no other cause do they resist that great Council but that it condemned the Arian heresy. For it is on this account again that they speak against the term One in substance, about which they also entertain wrong sentiments. For if their faith was orthodox, and they confessed the Father as truly Father, believed the Son to be genuine Son, and by nature true Word and Wisdom of the Father, and as to saying that the Son is *from God,* if they did not use the words of Him as of themselves, but understood Him to be the proper offspring of the Father's substance, as the radiance is from light, they would not every one of them have found fault with the Fathers, but would have been confident that the Council wrote suitably; and that this is the orthodox faith concerning our Lord Jesus Christ.

10. " But," say they, " the sense of such expressions is ob-

CHAP. III.

Ps. 50, 16.

Tit 1, 2.

Acts 17, 28.

1 Cor. 15, 33.
1 Tim. 2, 7.

1 Cor. 2, 16.

Joel 2, 25.
1 §. 18.
p. 101.

§. 40.

---

pursuest syllables to the loss of things? For if thou wert to say, ' twice five,' or ' twice seven,' and I concluded ' ten' or ' fourteen' from your words, or from ' a reasonable mortal animal' I concluded ' man,' should I seem to you absurd? how so, if I did but give your meaning?

for words belong as much to him who demands them as to him who utters " Orat. 31. 24. vid. also Hil. contr. Constant. 16 August. Ep. 238. n. 4—6 Cyril. Dial. 1 p 391. Petavius refers to other passages. de Trin. iv. 5. §. 6.

COUNC. scure to us;" for this is another of their pretences,—" We
ARIM reject them¹," say they, " because we cannot master their
AND
SELEU. meaning." But if they were true in this profession, instead
¹ §. 8. of saying, " We reject them," they should ask instruction
from the well informed; else ought they to reject whatever
they cannot understand in divine Scripture, and to find fault
with the writers. But this were the crime of heretics rather
than of us Christians ; for what we do not understand in the
sacred oracles, instead of rejecting, we seek from persons to
whom the Lord has revealed it, and from them we ask for instruction. But since they thus make a pretence of the
obscurity of such expressions, let them at least confess what
² p. 31, is annexed to the Creed, and anathematize those who hold²
note p that " the Son is from nothing," and " He was not before
His generation," and " the Word of God is a creature and
work," and " He is alterable by nature," and " from another
subsistence ;" and in a word let them anathematize the
³ p 108, Arian heresy, which has originated such irreligion³. Nor let
note g them say any more, " We reject the terms," but that " we
do not yet understand them ," by way of having some
reason to shew for declining them. But well know I, and
am sure, and they know it too, that if they could confess all
this and anathematize the Arian heresy, they would no
⁴ p 5, longer deny those terms of the Council⁴. For on this account
note l it was that the Fathers, after declaring that the Son was
begotten from the Father's substance, and One in substance
with Him, thereupon added, " But those who say," (what has
just been quoted, the symbols of the Arian heresy,) " we
anathematize ;" I mean, in order to shew that the statements
are parallel, and that the terms in the Creed imply the disclaimers subjoined, and that all who confess the terms, will
certainly understand the disclaimers. But those who both
dissent from the latter and impugn the former, such men are
proved on every side to be foes of Christ.

§. 41. 11. Those who deny the Council altogether, are sufficiently
exposed by these brief remarks ; those, however, who accept
every thing else that was defined at Nicæa, and quarrel only
about the One in substance, must not be received as enemies;
nor do we here attack them as Ario-maniacs, nor as opponents of the Fathers, but we discuss the matter with them as

Semi-Arians not to be regarded as Arians.

brothers with brothers[1], who mean what we mean, and dispute only about the word. For, confessing that the Son is from the substance of the Father, and not from other subsistence [2], and that He is not creature nor work, but His genuine and natural offspring, and that He is eternally with the Father as being His Word and Wisdom, they are not far from accepting even the phrase " One in substance;" of whom is Basil of Ancyra, in what he has written concerning the faith[k]. For only to say " like according to substance," is very far from signifying " of the substance[3]," by which, rather, as they say themselves, the genuineness of the Son to the Father is signified. Thus tin is only like to silver, a wolf to a dog, and gilt brass to the true metal; but tin is not from silver, nor could a wolf be accounted the offspring of a dog[l]. But since they say that He is " of the substance" and " Like in substance," what do they signify by these but " One in substance[m]?" For, while to say only " Like in substance," does not necessarily convey " of the substance," on the contrary, to say " One in substance," is to signify the meaning of both terms, " Like in substance," and " of the substance." And accordingly they themselves in controversy with those who say that the Word is a creature, instead of allowing Him to be genuine Son, have taken their proofs against them from human illustrations of son and father[n], with this exception that God is not as man, nor the

CHAP. III.
[1] vid.
[2] p. 141, ref. 5.
[2] Note, p. 66.

[3] p. 64, note 1.

---

[k] Basil, who wrote against Marcellus, and was placed by the Arians in his see, has little mention in history till the date of the Council of Sardica, which deposed him Constantius, however, stood his friend, till the beginning of the year 360, when Acacius supplanted him in the Imperial favour, and he was banished into Illyricum This was a month or two later than the date at which Athan. wrote his first draught or edition of this work. He was condemned upon charges of tyranny, and the like, but Theodoret speaks highly of his correctness of life and Sozomen of his learning and eloquence. vid. Theod. Hist. ii. 20 Soz. ii. 33. A very little conscientiousness, or even decency of manners, would put a man in strong relief with the great Arian party which surrounded the Court, and a very great deal would not have been enough to secure him against their unscrupulous slanders.

[l] So also deDecr. § 23 p.40. Hyp. Mel. et Euseb Hil de Syn 89 vid p 35, note u. p 64, note 1 The illustration runs into this position, "Things that are like, cannot be the same " vid p 136, note g On the other hand, Athan himself contends for the ταυτὸν τῇ οὐσιώσει, " the same in likeness de Decr. §. 20 p. 35. vid infr note r.

[m] vid Socr. iii 25 p 204. a. b. *Una substantia* religiose prædicabitur quæ ex *nativitatis* proprietate et ex naturæ *similitudine* ita indifferens sit, ut una dicatur. Hil de Syn 67.

[m] Here at last Athan. alludes to the Ancyrene Synodal Letter, vid Epiph. Hær. 73 5 and 7 about which he has kept a pointed silence above, when tracing the course of the Arian confessions. That is, he treats the Semi-arians as tenderly as S. Hilary, *as soon as* they break company with the Arians. The

140 *The Son of God not like a human offspring.*

Counc. Arim and Seleu.
generation of the Son as offspring of man, but as one which may be ascribed to God, and it becomes us to think. Thus they have called the Father the Fount of Wisdom and Life, and the Son the Radiance of the Eternal Light, and the Offspring from the Fountain, as He says, *I am the Life*, and *I Wisdom dwell with Prudence*. But the Radiance from the Light, and Offspring from Fountain, and Son from Father, how can these be so suitably expressed as by " One in substance ?"

Prov. 8, 12.
John 14, 6.

12. And is there any cause of fear, lest, because the offspring from men are one in substance, the Son, by being called One in substance, be Himself considered as a human offspring too? perish the thought! not so; but the explanation is easy. For the Son is the Father's Word and Wisdom, whence we learn the impassibility and indivisibility[1] of such a generation from the Father[n]. For not even man's word is part of Him, nor proceeds from Him according to passion[2], much less God's Word; whom the Father has declared to be His own Son, lest, on the other hand, if we merely heard of " Word,"

[1] ἀπαθὴς ἀμέριστον
[2] de Decr. §. 10. p. 17.

Ancyrene Council of 358 was a protest against the " blasphemia" or second Sirmian Confession, which Hosius signed.

[n] It is usual with the Fathers to use the two terms " Son" and " Word" to guard and complete the ordinary sense of each other. Their doctrine is that our Lord is both, in a certain transcendent, prototypical, and singular sense, that in that high sense that are coincident with one another, that they are applied to human things by an accommodation, as far as these are shadows of Him to whom properly they really belong, that being but partially realized on earth, the ideas gained from the earthly types are but imperfect, that in consequence if any one of them is used exclusively of Him, it tends to introduce wrong ideas respecting Him, but that their respective imperfections lying on different sides, when used together they correct each other vid. p. 18, note o and p. 43, note d. The term Son, used by itself, was abused into Arianism ; and the term Word into Sabellianism, again the term Son might be accused of introducing material notions, and the term Word of imperfection and transitoriness. Each of them corrected the other. " Scripture," says Athan. " joining the two, has said ' Son,' that the natural and true offspring of the substance may be preached, but that no one may understand a human offspring, signifying His substance a second time, it calls Him Word, and Wisdom, and Radiance." Orat 1. §. 28. vid. p 20, note t. vid. also iv. § 8. Euseb. contr. Marc. ii. 4 p. 54. Isid. Pel. Ep iv. 141. So S. Cyril says that we learn " from His being called Son that He is from Him, τὸ ἐξ αὐτοῦ, from His being called Wisdom and Word, that He is in Him," τὸ ἐν αὐτῷ Thesaur. iv. p 31 However, S Athanasius observes, that properly speaking the one term implies the other, i e. in its fulness. " Since the Son's being is from the Father, therefore He is in the Father " Orat. iii. §. 3. " If not Son, not Word either ; and if not Word, not Son. For what is from the Father is Son, and what is from the Father, but the Word, &c." Orat iv §. 24 fin. On the other hand the heretics accused Catholics of inconsistency, or of a union of opposite errors, because they accepted all the Scripture images together But Vigilius of Thapsus says, that " error bears testimony to truth, and the discordant opinions of misbelievers blend in concordance in the rule of orthodoxy." contr. Eutych. ii. init Grande miraculum, ut expugnatores sui veritas confirmetur. ibid. circ. init vid. also i. init and Eulogius, ap Phot. 225 p. 759.

we should suppose Him, such as is the word of man, unsubsistent[1]; but that, hearing that He is Son, we may acknowledge Him to be a living Word and a substantive[2] Wisdom. Accordingly, as in saying "offspring," we have no human thoughts, and, though we know God to be a Father, we entertain no material ideas concerning Him, but while we listen to these illustrations and terms[3], we think suitably of God, for He is not as man, so in like manner, when we hear of "one in substance," we ought to transcend all sense, and, according to the Proverb, *understand by the understanding that is set before us;* so as to know, that not by will, but in truth, is He genuine from the Father, as Life from Fountain, and Radiance from Light. Else[4] why should we understand " offspring" and " son," in no corporeal way, while we conceive of "one in substance" as after the manner of bodies? especially since these terms are not here used about different subjects, but of whom "offspring" is predicated, of Him is " one in substance" also. And it is but consistent to attach the same sense to both expressions as applied to the Saviour, and not to interpret " offspring," as is fitting, and " one in substance" otherwise, since to be consistent, ye who are thus minded and who say that the Son is Word and Wisdom of the Father, should entertain a different view of these terms also, and understand in separate senses Word, and in distinct senses Wisdom. But, as this would be extravagant, (for the Son is the Father's Word and Wisdom, and the Offspring from the Father is one and proper to His substance,) so the sense of " offspring" and " one in substance" is one, and whoso considers the Son an offspring, rightly considers Him also as " one in substance."

13. This is sufficient to shew that the phrase of " one in substance" is not foreign nor far from the meaning of these much loved persons[5]. But since, as they allege[6], (for I have not the Epistle in question,) the Bishops who condemned Samosatene° have laid down in writing that the Son is not one in substance with the Father, and so it comes to pass that

° There were three Councils held against Paul of Samosata, of the dates of 264, 269, and an intermediate year. The third is spoken of in the text, which contrary to the opinion of Pagi, S. Basnage, and Tillemont, Pearson fixes at 265 or 266.

they, for reverence and honour towards the aforesaid, thus feel about that expression, it will be to the purpose reverently to argue with them this point also. Certainly it is unbecoming to make the one company conflict with the other; for all are fathers; nor is it religious to settle, that these have spoken well, and those ill; for all of them have gone to sleep in Christ. Nor is it right to be disputatious, and to compare the respective numbers of those who met in the Councils, or the three hundred may seem to throw the lesser into the shade; nor to compare the dates, lest those who preceded seem to eclipse those that came after. For all, I say, are Fathers; and, any how the three hundred laid down nothing new, nor was it in any self-confidence that they became champions of words not in Scripture, but they started from their Fathers, as the others, and they used their words. For there were two Bishops of the name of Dionysius, much older than the seventy who deposed Samosatene, of whom one was of Rome, and the other of Alexandria, and a charge had been laid by some persons against the Bishop of Alexandria before the Bishop of Rome, as if he had said that the Son was made, and not one in substance with the Father. This had given great pain to the Roman Council, and the Bishop of Rome expressed their united sentiments in a letter to his namesake. This led to his writing an explanation which he calls the Book of Refutation and Apology; and it runs thus .

§. 44. 14. And[1] I have written in another Letter, a refutation of the false charge which they bring against me, that I deny that Christ is one in substance with God. For though I say that I have not found or read this term any where in holy Scripture, yet my remarks[2] which follow, and which they have not noticed, are not inconsistent with that belief For I instanced a human production, which is evidently homogeneous, and I observed that undeniably fathers differed from their children, only in not being the same individuals, otherwise there could be neither parents nor children. And my Letter, as I said before, owing to present circumstances, I am unable to produce, or I would have sent you the very words I used, or rather a copy of it all; which, if I have an opportunity, I will do still. But I am sure from recollection, that I adduced many parallels of things kindred with each other, for instance, that a plant grown from seed or from root, was other than that from which it sprang, and yet altogether one in nature with it, and that a stream flowing from a fountain, changed its appearance and its name, for that neither the fountain was called stream, nor the stream fountain, but both existed, and that the fountain was as it were father, but the stream was what was generated from the fountain.

15. Thus the Bishop. If then any one finds fault with the Fathers at Nicæa, as if they contradicted the decisions of their predecessors, he may reasonably find fault also with the Seventy, because they did not keep to the statements of their own predecessors; for such were the two Dionysii and the Bishops assembled on that occasion at Rome. But neither these nor those is it religious to blame; for all were legates of the things of Christ, and all gave diligence against the heretics, and while the one party condemned Samosatene, the other condemned the Arian heresy. And rightly did both these and those define, and suitably to the matter in hand. And as the blessed Apostle, writing to the Romans, said, *The Law is spiritual, the Law is holy, and the commandment holy and just and good;* (and soon after, *What the Law could not do, in that it was weak,*) but wrote to the Hebrews, *The Law made no one perfect;* and to the Galatians, *By the Law no one is justified,* but to Timothy, *The Law is good, if a man use it lawfully;* and no one would accuse the Saint of inconsistency and variation in writing, but rather would admire how suitably he wrote to each, to teach the Romans and the others to turn from the letter to the spirit, but to instruct the Hebrews and Galatians to place their hopes, not in the Law, but in the Lord who gave the Law;—so, if the Fathers of the two Councils made different mention of the One in substance, we ought not in any respect to differ from them, but to investigate their meaning, and this will fully shew us the meaning of both the Councils. For they who deposed Samosatene, took One in substance in a bodily sense, because Paul had attempted sophistry and said, "Unless Christ has of man become God, it follows that He is One in substance with the Father; and if so, of necessity there are three substances, one the previous substance, and the other two from it," and therefore guarding against this they said with good reason, that Christ was not One in substance[p]. For the Son

CHAP. III

§. 45.

Rom. 7, 14. 12.

Rom. 8, 3.

Heb. 7.

19.

Gal. 3, 11.

1 Tim 1, 8.

---

[p] This is in fact the objection which Arius urges against the One in substance, supr. §. 16. when he calls it the doctrine of Manichæus and Hieracas,

COUNC. ARIM. AND SELEU.

is not related to the Father as he imagined. But the Bishops who anathematized the Arian heresy, understanding Paul's craft, and reflecting that the word " One in substance," has not this meaning when used of things immaterial[q], and especially of God, and acknowledging that the Word was not a creature, but an offspring from the substance, and that the Father's substance was the origin and root and fountain of the Son, and that He was of very truth[1] His Father's likeness, and not of different nature, as we are, and separate from the Father, but that, as being from Him, He exists as Son indivisible, as radiance is with respect of Light, and knowing too the illustrations used in Dionyius's case, the " fountain," and the defence of " One in substance," and before this the Saviour's saying, symbolical of unity[2], *I and the Father are one*, and *he that hath seen Me hath seen the Father*, on these grounds reasonably asserted on their part, that the Son was One in substance. And as, according to a former remark, no one would blame the Apostle, if he wrote to the Romans about the Law in one way, and to the Hebrews in another; in like manner, neither would the present Bishops find fault with the ancient, in regard to their interpretation, nor again on the view of theirs and of the need of their so writing about the Lord, would the ancient censure the present.

[margin: ¹ αὐτοαληθης ² ἐνοιδη p. 148, ref. 7. John 10, 29. John 14, 9.]

vid. p. 97, note 1. The same objection is protested against by S Basil, contr. Eunom. 1. 19. Hilar. de Trin iv. 4. Yet, while S. Basil agrees with Athan. in his account of the reason of the Council's rejection of the word, S. Hilary on the contrary reports that Paul himself accepted it,¹ e. in a Sabellian sense, and therefore the Council rejected it. " Male homousion Samosatenus confessus est, sed numquid melius Arii negaverunt." de Syn. 86.

q The Eusebians tried to establish a distinction between ὁμοούσιον and ὁμοιούσιον, " one in substance" and ' like in substance," of this sort, that the former belonged to things material, and the latter to immaterial, Soz. iii. 18. a remark which in itself was quite sufficient to justify the Catholics in insisting on the former term For the heretical party, starting with the notion in which their heresy in all its shades consisted, that the Son was a distinct being from the Father, and appealing to (what might be plausibly maintained) that spirits are incommeasurable with one another, or that each is *sui simile*, concluded that " *like* in substance" was the only term which would express the relation of the Son to the Father. Here then the word " one in substance" did just enable the Catholics to join issue with them, as exactly expressing what the Catholics wished to express, viz that there was no such distinction between Them as made the term " like" necessary, but that Their relation to Each Other was *analogous* to that of a material offspring to a material parent, or that as material parent and offspring are individuals under one common *species*, so the Eternal Father and Son are Persons under one common *individual substance*.

16. Yes surely, each Council had a sufficient reason for its own language; for since Samosatene held that the Son was not before Mary, but received from her the origin of His being, therefore the assembled Fathers deposed him and pronounced him heretic; but concerning the Son's Godhead writing in simplicity, they arrived not at accuracy concerning the One in substance, but, as they understood the word, so spoke they about it. For they directed all their thoughts to destroy the device of Samosatene, and to shew that the Son was before all things, and that, instead of becoming God from man, God had put on a servant's form, and the Word had become flesh, as John says. This is how they dealt with the blasphemies of Paul; but when the party of Eusebius and Arius said that though the Son was before time, yet was He made and one of the creatures, and as to the phrase "from God," they did not believe it in the sense of His being genuine Son from Father, but maintained it as it is said of the creatures, and as to the oneness[r] of likeness[1] between the Son and the Father, did not confess that the Son is like the Father according to substance, or according to nature, but because of Their agreement of doctrines and of teaching[2]; nay, when they drew a line and an utter distinction between the Son's substance and the Father, ascribing to Him an origin of being, other than the Father, and degrading Him to the creatures, on this account the Bishops assembled at Nicæa, with a view to the craft of the parties so thinking, and as bringing together the sense from the Scriptures, cleared up the point, by affirming the "One in substance;" that both the true genuineness of the Son might thereby be known, and that things generated might be ascribed nothing in

CHAP. III.

[1] vid Epiph. Hær.73.
[2] p. 107, note f.

---

[r] τὴν τῆς ὁμοιώσεως ἑνότητα and so ταὐτὸν τῇ ὁμοιώσει de Decr. § 20 p. 35 τὴν ἑνότητα τῆς φύσεως καὶ τὴν ταυτότητα τοῦ φωτός ibid §.24. p. 41 init also §. 23. And Basil ταυτότητα τῆς φύσεως Ep. 8. 3. ταυτότητα τῆς οὐσίας Cyril in Joan. v. p. 302. Hence it is uniformly asserted by the Catholics that the Father's godhead, θιότης, is the Son's, e g. "the Father's godhead being in the Son," infr. §. 52. ἡ πατρικὴ φύσις αὐτοῦ Orat. i. § 40. "worshipped κατὰ τὴν πατρικὴν ἰδιότητα § 42 πατρικὴν αὐτοῦ θιότητα §. 45 fin. §. 49 fin. ii § 18. § 73 fin. iii. §. 26. "the Father's godhead and propriety is the being, τὸ εἶναι of the Son." iii. § 5. fin. The Father's godhead is the Son's. τὸ πατρικὸν φῶς ὁ υἱός iii §. 53 μίαν τὴν θιότητα καὶ τὸ ἴδιον τῆς οὐσίας τοῦ πατρός §. 56. "As the water is the same which is poured from fountain into stream, so the godhead of the Father into the Son is intransitive and indivisible, ἀρρεύστως καὶ ἀδιαιρέτως. Expos §. 2. vid p. 155, note t This is the doctrine of the Una Res, which, being not defined in General Council till the fourth Lateran, many most injuriously accuse the Greek Fathers, as the two Gregories, of denying. That Council is not here referred to as of authority.

146 *As "One in Substance" so "Ingenerate" variously used.*

COUNC. ARIM. AND SELEU.
common with Him. For the precision of this phrase detects their pretence, whenever they use the phrase "from God," and gets rid of all the subtleties with which they seduce the simple. For whereas they contrive to put a sophistical construction on all other words at their will, this phrase only, as detecting their heresy, do they dread; which the Fathers did set down as a bulwark⁸ against their irreligious speculations, one and all.

§. 46. 17. Cease we then all contention, nor any longer conflict we with each other, though the Councils have differently taken the phrase " One in substance," for we have already assigned a sufficient defence of them; and to it the following may be added:—We have not derived the word " Ingenerate" from Scripture, (for no where does Scripture call God Ingenerate,) yet since it has many authorities in its favour, I was curious about the term, and found that it too has different senses¹. Some, for instance, call what is, but is neither generated, nor has any cause at all, ingenerate; and others, the increate². As then a person, having in his mind the former of these senses, viz. " that which has no cause," might say that the Son was not ingenerate, yet would not be blaming any one he perceived looking to the other meaning, "not a work or creature but an eternal offspring," and affirming accordingly that the Son was ingenerate, (for both speak suitably with a view to their own object,) so, even granting that the Fathers have spoken variously concerning the One in substance, let us not dispute about it, but take what they deliver to us in a religious way, when especially their anxiety was directed in behalf of religion.

¹ p. 52, note d.
² p. 52, note e.

§. 47. 18. Ignatius, for instance, who was appointed Bishop in Antioch after the Apostles, and became a martyr of Christ, writes concerning the Lord thus: " There is one physician, fleshly and spiritual, generate and ingenerate, God in man, true life in death, both from Mary and from God³;" whereas some teachers who followed Ignatius, write in their turn,

³ vid. Ign. ad Eph. 7.

⁸ ἰατιτείχισμα; in like manner σύνδεσμον πίστεως. Epiph. Ancor. 6. "Without the confession of the One in 'substance,'" says Epiphanius, "no heresy can be refuted; for as a serpent hates the smell of bitumen, and the scent of sesame-cake, and the burning of agate, and the smoke of storax, so do Arius and Sabellius hate the notion of the sincere profession of the ' One in substance.' " Hær. 69. 70. " That term did the Fathers set down in their formula of faith, which they perceived to be a source of dread to their adversaries; that they themselves might unsheath the sword which cut off the head of their own monstrous heresy " Ambros. de Fid III. 15.

"One is the Ingenerate, the Father, and one the genuine Son from Him, true offspring, Word and Wisdom of the Father [t]." If therefore we have hostile feelings towards these writers, then have we right to quarrel with the Councils; but if, knowing their faith in Christ, we are persuaded that the blessed Ignatius was orthodox in writing that Christ was generate on account of the flesh, (for He was made flesh,) yet ingenerate, because He is not in the number of things made and generated, but Son from Father, and are aware too that the parties who have said that the Ingenerate is One, meaning the Father, did not mean to lay down that the Word was generated and made, but that the Father has no cause, but rather is Himself Father of Wisdom, and in Wisdom hath made all things that are generated, why do we not combine all our Fathers in religious belief, those who deposed Samosatene as well as those who proscribed the Arian heresy, instead of making distinctions between them and refusing to entertain a right opinion of them? I repeat, that these, looking towards the sophistical explanation of Samosatene, wrote, "He is not one in substance [u];" and those with an apposite meaning, said that He was. For myself, I have written these brief remarks, from my feeling towards persons who were religious to Christ-ward; but were it possible to come by the Epistle which we are told that they wrote, I consider we should find further grounds for the aforesaid proceeding of these blessed men. For it is right and meet thus to feel, and to maintain a good understanding with the Fathers, if we be not spurious children, but have received the traditions from them, and the lessons of religion at their hands.

19. Such then, as we confess and believe, being the sense of the Fathers, proceed we even in their company to examine once

§. 48.

---

[t] The writer is not known. The President of Magdalen has pointed out to the Editor the following similar passage in St. Clement. ἓν μὲν τὸ ἀγέννητον, ὁ παντοκράτωρ θεός, ἓν δὲ καὶ τὸ προγεννη-θὲν δι' οὗ τὰ πάντα ἐγένετο, καὶ χωρὶς αὐτοῦ ἐγένετο οὐδὲ ἕν. Strom. vi. 7 p. 769.

[u] There is much to say on the subject of the rejection of the ὁμοούσιον at this Council of Antioch; but it branches into topics too far from the text of Athanasius to allow of its satisfactory discussion in this volume. The lamented Dr. Burton, in Mr. Faber's Apostolicity of Trinitarianism, vol. 2 p. 302. is the last writer who has denied the rejection of the symbol; but, (as appears to the present writer,) not on sufficient grounds. Reference is made to a Creed or Ecthesis, found among the acts of Ephesus, and said to have been published against Paul; and on this some remarks are made in Note p. 165

more the matter, calmly and with a good understanding, with reference to what has been said before, viz. whether the Bishops collected at Nicæa did not really exercise an excellent judgment. For if the Word be a work and foreign to the Father's substance, so that He is separated from the Father by the difference of nature, He cannot be one in substance with Him, but rather He is homogeneous by nature with the works, though He surpass them in grace[1]. On the other hand, if we confess that He is not a work but the genuine offspring of the Father's substance, it would follow that He is inseparable from the Father, being connatural[2], because He is begotten from Him. And being such, good reason He should be called One in Substance. Next, if the Son be not such from participation[3], but is in His substance the Father's Word and Wisdom, and this substance is the offspring of the Father's substance[4], and its likeness as the radiance is of the light, and the Son says, *I and the Father are One*, and *he that hath seen Me, hath seen the Father*, how must we understand these words? or how shall we so explain them as to preserve the oneness of the Father and the Son? Now as to its consisting in agreement[5] of doctrines, and in the Son's not disagreeing with the Father, as the Arians say, such an interpretation will not stand; for both the Saints and still more Angels and Archangels have such an agreement with God, and there is no disagreement among them. For he who was in disagreement, the devil, was beheld to fall from the heavens, as the Lord said. Therefore if by reason of agreement the Father and the Son are one, there would be things generate which had this agreement with God, and each of these might say, *I and the Father are One*. But if this be shocking, and so it truly is, it follows of necessity that we must conceive of Son's and Father's oneness in the way of substance. For things generated, though they have an agreement with their Maker, yet possess it only by influence[6], and by participation, and through the mind; the transgression of which forfeits heaven. But the Son, being an offspring from the substance, is one in substance, Himself and the Father that begat Him.

§. 49.

20. This is why He has equality with the Father by titles expressive of unity[7], and what is said of the Father, is said in

The Son has all things of the Father, but being the Father. 149

Scripture of the Son also, all but His being called Father[x]. Chap. III. For the Son Himself says, *All things that the Father hath are Mine;* and He says to the Father, *All Mine are Thine,* and *Thine are Mine;*—as for instance[1], the name God; for the Word was God;—Almighty, *Thus saith He that is, and that was, and that is to come, the Almighty,*—the being Light, *I am,* He says, *the Light;*—the Operative Cause, *All things were made by Him,* and *whatsoever I see the Father do, I do also;*—the being Everlasting, *His eternal power and godhead,* and *In the beginning was the Word,* and *He was the true Light, which lighteth every man that cometh into the world;*—the being Lord, for *The Lord rained fire and brimstone from the Lord,* and the Father says, *I am the Lord,* and *Thus saith the Lord, the Almighty God;* and of the Son Paul speaks thus, *One Lord Jesus Christ, through whom all things.* And on the Father Angels serve, and again the Son too is worshipped by them, *And let all the Angels of God worship Him;* and He is said to be Lord of Angels, for *the Angels ministered unto Him,* and *the Son of Man shall send His Angels.* The being honoured as the Father, for *that they may honour the Son,* He says, *as they honour the Father;*—being equal to God, *He thought it not robbery to be equal with God;*—the being Truth from the True, and Life from the Living, as being truly from the Fountain of the Father;—the quickening and raising the dead as the Father, for so we read in the Gospel. And of the Father it is written, *The Lord thy God is One Lord,* and *The God of gods the Lord hath spoken, and hath called the earth,* and of the Son, *The Lord God hath shined upon us,* and *The God of Gods shall be seen in Sion.* And again of God, Esaias says, *Who is a God like unto Thee, taking away iniquities*

John 15, 16. John 17, 10. 1 vid. Orat. iii. §. 4 John 1, 1. Apoc. 1, 8 John 8, 12. John 1, 3. John 5, 19. Rom. 1, 26. John 1, 1. John 1, 9. Gen. 19, 24. Isa. 45, 5. 1 Cor. 8, 6. Theb. Matt. 4, 11. Matt 24, 31 John 5, 23. Phil. 2, 6. Deut. 6, 4. Ps 50, 1. Ps. 118, 27. Ps. 83, 7. Sept.

---

[x] By "the Son being *equal* to the Father," is but meant that He is His "unvarying image," it does not imply any distinction of substance. "Perfectæ æqualitatis significantiam habet similitudo." Hil de Syn. 73. But though He is in all things His Image, this implies some exception, for else He would not be like or equal, but the same. "Non est æqualitas in dissimilibus, nec similitudo est intra unum." ibid. 72. Hence He is the Father's image in all things except in being the Father, εἰκὼν φυσικὴ καὶ ἀπαράλλακτος κατὰ πάντα ὅμοια τῷ πατρὶ, πλὴν τῆς ἀγεννησίας καὶ τῆς πατρότητος Damasc. de Imag. iii. 18. p. 354. vid. also Basil. contr. Eun. ii. 28 Theod Inconfus. p. 91. Basil. Ep. 38. 7 fin. For the Son is the Image of the Father, not as Father, but as God. The Arians on the other hand, objecting the phrase "unvarying image," asked why the Son was not in consequence a Father, and the beginning of a θεογονία. Athan. Orat. 1. 21. vid. infra, note z.

and passing over unrighteousness? but the Son said to whom He would, *Thy sins be forgiven Thee;* for instance, when, on the Jews murmuring, He manifested the remission by His act, saying to the paralytic, *Rise, take up thy bed, and go unto thy house.* And of God Paul says, *To the King eternal;* and again of the Son, David in the Psalm, *Lift up your heads, O ye gates, and be ye lift up ye everlasting doors, and the King of glory shall come in.* And Daniel heard it said, *His Kingdom is an everlasting Kingdom, and His Kingdom shall not be destroyed.* And in a word, all that you find said of the Father, so much will you find said of the Son, all but His being Father, as has been said.

§. 50. 24. If then any think of other origin, and other Father, considering the equality of these attributes, it is a mad thought. But if, since the Son is from the Father, all that is the Father's is the Son's as in an Image and Expression, let it be considered dispassionately, whether a substance foreign from the Father's substance admit of such attributes; and whether such a one be other in nature and alien in substance[1], and not one in substance with the Father. For we must take reverent heed, lest transferring what is proper[2] to the Father to what is unlike Him in substance, and expressing the Father's godhead by what is unlike in kind[3] and alien in substance, we introduce another substance foreign to Him, yet capable of the properties of the first substance[y], and lest we be silenced by God Himself, saying, *My glory I will not give to another,* and be discovered worshipping this alien God, and be accounted such as were the Jews of that day, who said, *Wherefore dost Thou, being a man, make Thyself God?* referring, the while, to another source the things of the Spirit, and blasphemously saying, *He casteth out devils through Beelzebub.* But if this is shocking, plainly the Son is not unlike in substance, but one in substance with the Father; for if what the Father hath is by nature the Son's, and the Son

---

[y] Arianism was placed in the perilous dilemma of denying Christ's divinity, or introducing a second God. The Arians proper went off in the former side of the alternative, the Semi-arians on the latter, and Athan., as here addressing the Semi-arians, insists on the greatness of the latter error. This of course was *the* objection which attached to the words ὁμοιούσιον, ἀπαράλλακτος εἰκών, &c. when disjoined from the ὁμοούσιον; and Eusebius's language, supr. p. 63, note g, shews us that it is not an imaginary one.

Himself is from the Father, and because of this oneness of godhead and of nature He and the Father are one, and He that hath seen the Son hath seen the Father, reasonably is He called by the Fathers "One in substance;" for to what is other in substance, it belongs not to possess such prerogatives.

22. And again, if, as we have said before, the Son is not such by participation[1], but, while all things generated have, by participation, the grace of God, He is the Father's Wisdom and Word, of which all things partake[2], it follows that He being the deifying and enlightening power of the Father, in which all things are deified and quickened, is not alien in substance from the Father, but one is substance. For by partaking[3] of Him, we partake[4] of the Father; because that the Word is proper to the Father. Whence, if He was Himself too from participation, and not from the Father His substantial Godhead and Image, He would not deify[5], being deified Himself. For it is not possible that He, who but possesses from participation, should impart of that partaking to others, since what He has is not His own, but the Giver's; and what He has received, is barely the grace sufficient for Himself.

23. However, let us fairly enquire why it is that some, as is said, decline the "One in substance," whether it does not rather shew that the Son is one in substance with the Father. They say then, as you have written, that it is not right to say that the Son is one in substance with the Father, because He who speaks of one in substance speaks of three, one substance pre-existing, and that those who are generated from it are one in substance: and they add, "If then the Son be one in substance with the Father, then a substance must be previously supposed, from which they have been generated; and that the One is not Father and the Other Son, but they are brothers together[z]." As to all this, though it be a Greek

---

[z] And so Eunomius in St. Cyril, "'Unless once the Son was not,' saith he, 'or if eternal, and co-existent with the Father, you make Him not a Son but a brother.' The Father and the Son are not from any pre-existing origin, that they should be thought brothers, but the Father is origin of the Son, and brought forth the Son, and remaineth Father, and is not called Son of any, and the Son is Son, and remaineth what He is, and is not called brother of any by nature. What place then shall brotherhood have in such?" Thesaur. pp. 22, 23. vid. Athan. Orat. 1. § 14.

152 " *One in Substance*" does not imply a whole and parts.

Counc. Arim. and Seleu.
interpretation, and what Greeks say have no claim upon us [a], still let us see whether those things which are called one in substance and are collateral, as derived from one substance pre-supposed, are one in substance with each other, or with the substance from which they are generated. For if only with each other, then are they other in substance and unlike, when referred to that substance which generated them; for other in substance is opposed to one in substance; but if each be one in substance with the substance which generated them, it is thereby confessed that what is generated from any thing, is one in substance with that which generated it; and there is no need of seeking for three substances, but merely to seek, whether it be true that this is from that [b]. For should it happen that

---

[a] vid. p. 52, note d. The word οὐσία in its Greek or Aristotelic sense seems to have stood for an individual substance, numerically one, which is predicable of nothing but itself. Improperly it stood for a species or genus. vid. Petav. de Trin iv. 1. §. 2 but as Anastasius observes in many places of his Viæ dux, Christian theology innovated on the sense of Aristotelic terms. vid. c. 1. p. 20. c. 6 p. 96. c. 9 p. 150. c. 17. p. 308. There is some difficulty in determining *how* it innovated. Anastasius and Theorian, Hodeg. 6. Legat. ad Arm. pp. 441, 2. say that it takes οὐσία to mean an universal or species, but this is nothing else than the second or improper Greek use. Rather it takes the word in a sense of its own such as we have no example of in things created, viz that of a Being numerically one, subsisting in three persons; so that the word is a predicable or in one sense *universal*, without ceasing to be individual; in which consists the mystery of the Holy Trinity. However, heretics, who refused the mystery, objected it to Catholics in its primary philosophical sense, and then, as standing for an individual substance, when applied to Father and Son, it either implied the parts of a *material* subject, or it involved no *real* distinction of persons, i. e Sabellianism. The former of these two alternatives is implied in the text by the " Greek use," the latter by the same phrase as used by the conforming Semi-arians, A D. 363. " Nor, as if any passion were supposed of the ineffable generation, is the term ' substance' taken by the Fathers, &c. nor *according to any Greek use*, Socr. iii. 25. Hence such charges against Catholicism on the part of Arians as Alexander protests against, of *either* Sabellianism *or* Valentinianism, οὐκ ... ὥσπερ Σαβιλλίῳ καὶ Βαλιττίνῳ δοκεῖ. Theod. Hist 1. 3. p. 743. In like manner, Damascene, speaking of the Jacobite use of φύσις and ὑπόστασις says, " Who of holy men ever thus spoke? unless ye introduce to us your St. Aristotle, as a thirteenth Apostle, and prefer the idolater to the divinely inspired." cont. Jacob. 10. p. 399 and so again Leontius, speaking of Philoponus, who from the Monophysite confusion of nature and hypostasis was led into Tritheism. " He thus argued, taking his start from Aristotelic principles; for Aristotle says that there are of individuals particular substances as well as one common." de Sect v. fin.

[b] The argument, when drawn out, is virtually this if, because two subjects are consubstantial, a third is presupposed of which they partake, then, since either of these two is consubstantial with that of which both partake, a new third must be supposed in which it and the pre-existing substance partake, and thus an infinite series of things consubstantial must be supposed. The only mode (which he puts first) of meeting this, is to deny that the two things are consubstantial with the supposed third, but if so, they must be different in substance from it, that is, they must differ from that, as partaking of which, they are like each other,—which is absurd vid. Basil. Ep 52. n. 2.

"*One in Substance*" *does not imply two substances.* 153

there were not two brothers, but that only one had come of that substance, he that was generated would not be called alien in substance, merely because there was no other from that substance than he; but though alone, he must be one in substance with him that begat him. For what shall we say about Jephthae's daughter; because she was only-begotten, and *he had not,* says Scripture, *other child;* and again, concerning the widow's son, whom the Lord raised from the dead, because he too had no brother, but was only-begotten, was on that account neither of these one in substance with the parent? Surely they were, for they were children, and this is a property of children with reference to their parents. And in like manner also, when the Fathers said that the Son of God was from His substance, reasonably have they spoken of Him as one in substance. For the like property has the radiance compared with the light. Else it follows that not even the creation came out of nothing. For whereas men beget with passion[1], so again they work upon an existing subject matter, and otherwise cannot make. But if we do not understand creation in a human way[c], when we attribute it to God, much less seemly is it to understand generation in a human way, or to give a corporeal sense to One in substance; instead of receding from things generate, casting away human images, nay, all things sensible, and ascending[2] to the Father[d], lest we rob the Father of the Son in ignorance, and rank Him among His own creatures.

24. Further, if, in confessing Father and Son, we spoke of two origins or two Gods, as Marcion[3] and Valentinus[4], or said that the Son had any other mode of godhead, and was not the Image and Expression of the Father, as being by nature born from

CHAP. II.

Jud. 11, 34.

[1] Orat. 1. § 28.

[2] Naz. Orat 28. 2.

§. 52.
[3] p. 45, note h.
[4] Orat. 1.
3.

---

[c] vid. de Decr. §. 11. supr. p. 18, note o. also Cyril, Thesaur. iv. p. 29. Basil. contr. Eun. ii. 23. Hil. de Syn. 17.

[d] S. Basil says in like manner that, though God is Father κυρίως properly, (vid. Ath Orat. 1. 21 fin. and p. 16, note k. p. 18, note o. p. 56, note k.) yet it comes to the same thing if we were to say that He is τροπικῶς and ἐκ μεταφορᾶς, figuratively, such; contr. Eun. ii. 24. for in that case we must, as in other metaphors used of Him, (anger, sleep, flying,) take that part of the human sense which can apply to Him. Now γέννησις implies two things,—passion, and relationship, οἰκείωσις φύσεως; accordingly we must take the latter as an indication of the divine sense of the term. On the terms Son, Word, &c. being figurative, or illustrations, and how to use them, vid. also de Decr. §. 12. supr. p. 20. Orat. 1. §. 26, 27 ii. §. 32 iii § 18. 67. Basil. contr. Eunom. ii. 17. Hil. de Trin. iv. 2. Vid. also Athan. ad Serap. 1. 20. and Basil. Ep. 38. n. 5. and what is said of the office of faith in each of these.

154 *The Father and Son not two Gods, for the Son from the Father,*

COUNC. ARIM. AND SELEU — Him, then He might be considered unlike; for such substances are altogether unlike each other. But if we acknowledge that the Father's godhead is one and sole, and that of Him the Son is the Word and Wisdom; and, as thus believing, are far from speaking of two Gods, but understand the oneness of the Son with the Father to be, not in likeness of their teaching, but according to substance and in truth, and hence speak not of two Gods but of one God; there being but one Face[e] of Godhead, as the Light is one and the Radiance; (for this was seen by the Patriarch Jacob, as Scripture says, *The sun rose upon him when the Face of God passed by;* and beholding this, and understanding of whom He was Son and Image, the holy Prophets say, *The Word of the Lord came to me;* and recognising the Father, who was beheld and revealed in Him, they were bold to say, *The God of our fathers hath appeared unto me, the God of Abraham, and Isaac, and Jacob;*) this being so, wherefore scruple we to call Him one in substance who is one with the Father, and appears as doth the Father, according to likeness and oneness of godhead? For if, as has been many times said, He has it not to be proper to the Father's substance, nor to resemble, as a Son, we may well scruple: but if this be the illuminating and creative Power, specially proper to the Father, without whom He neither frames nor is known, (for all things consist through Him and in Him;) wherefore, having cognizance of this truth, do we decline to use the phrase conveying it? For what is it to be thus connatural with the Father, but to be one in substance with Him? for God attached not to Him the Son from without[1], as needing a servant; nor are the works on a level with the Creator, and are honoured as He is, or to be thought one with the Father. Or let a man venture to make the distinction, that the sun and the radiance are two lights, or different substances; or to say that the radiance accrued to it over and above, and is not a single

Gen. 32, 31. Sept.

[1] deDecr. §. 13. and p. 14, note b.

---

[e] ἑνὸς ὄντος εἴδους ἰδιότητος; the word εἶδος, face or countenance, will come before us in Orat. III. 16. It is generally applied to the Son, as in what follows, and is synonymous with hypostasis, but it is remarkable that here it is almost synonymous with οὐσία or φύσις Indeed in one sense nature, substance, and hypostasis, are all synonymous, i. e. as one and all denoting the Una Res, which is Almighty God. They differed, in that the word hypostasis regards the One God *as* He is the Son. The apparent confusion is useful then as reminding us of this great truth, vid. the next note.

as the sun and radiance not two lights. 155

and uncompounded offspring from the sun; such, that sun and radiance are two, but the light one, because the radiance is an offspring from the Sun. But, whereas not more divisible, nay less divisible is the nature [f] of the Son towards the Father, and the godhead not accruing to the Son, but the Father's godhead being in the Son, so that he that hath seen the Son hath seen the Father in Him; wherefore should not such a one be called One in substance?

25. Even this is sufficient to dissuade you from blaming those who have said that the Son was one in substance with the Father and yet let us examine the very term "One in substance," in itself, by way of seeing whether we ought to use it at all, and whether it be a proper term, and is suitable to apply to the Son. For you know yourselves, and no one can dispute it, that Like is not predicated of substances, but of habits, and qualities; for in the case of substances we speak, not of likeness, but of identity [g]. Man, for instance, is said to be like

CHAP. III.

§. 53.

---

[f] φύσις, nature, is here used for *person.* This seems an Alexandrian use of the word. It is found in Alexander. ap. Theod Hist. i 3. p. 740. And it gives rise to a celebrated question in the Monophysite controversy, as used in S. Cyril's phrase μία φύσις σεσαρκωμένη S. Cyril uses the word both for person and for substance successively in the following passage "Perhaps some one will say, 'How is the Holy and Adorable Trinity distinguished into three Hypostases, yet issues in *one nature* of Godhead?'" Because the Same in substance necessarily following the *difference of natures*, recals the minds of believers to *one nature* of Godhead." contr. Nest. iii. p. 91. In this passage "One nature" stands for a reality, but "three Natures" is the One Eternal Divine Nature viewed in that respect in which He is Three And so S. Hilary, naturæ ex natura gignente nativitas, de Syn 17. and essentia de essentiâ, August de Trin. vii. n. 3 and de seipso genuit Deus id quod est, de Fid. et Symb. 4 i. e He is the Adorable ἰότης or Godhead viewed as begotten And Athan Orat iv. §. 1. calls the Father ἐξ οὐσίας οὐσιώδης vid. supr. p. 148. ref 4. These phrases mean that the Son *who is* the Divine Substance, is from the Father *who is* the [same] divine substance. As, (to speak of what is *analogous* not parallel,) we might say that "man is father of man," not meaning by man the same individual in both cases, but the same nature, so here we speak not of the same Person in the two cases, but the same Individuum. All these expressions resolve themselves into the original mystery of the Holy Trinity, that Person and Individuum are not equivalent terms, and we understand them neither more nor less than we understand it. In like manner as regards the incarnation, when St Paul says "God was in Christ," he does not mean absolutely the Divine Nature, which is the proper sense of the word, but the Divine Nature as existing in the Person of the Son. Hence too, (vid. Petav. de Trin. vi. 10. §. 6.) such phrases as "the Father begat the Son from *His* substance." And in like manner Athan. just afterwards, speaks of "the Father's Godhead *being in* the Son." vid. supr. p. 145, note r

[g] S. Athanasius, in saying that like is not used of substance, implies that the proper Arian senses of the ὅμοιον are more natural, and therefore the more probable, if the word came into use. These were, 1 likeness in *will* and *action*, as συμφωνία of which infr. Orat iii 11. 2. likeness to the *idea* in God's mind in which the Son was created. Cyril Thesaur. p 134. 3 likeness to the divine *act* or *energy* by which He was created. Pseudo-Basil. contr. Eun iv p 282. Cyril in Joan. c. 5.

COUNC. ARIM. AND SELEU. man, not in substance, but according to habit and character; for in substance men are one in nature. And again, man is not said to be unlike dog, but to be other in nature. Therefore, in speaking of Like according to substance, we mean like by participation[1]; (for Likeness is a quality, which may attach to substance,) and this is proper to creatures, for they, by partaking[2], are made like to God. For *when He shall appear*, says Scripture, *we shall be like Him*; like, that is, not in substance but in sonship, which we shall partake from Him. If then ye speak of the Son as being by participation[3], then indeed call Him Like in substance; but thus spoken of, He is not Truth, nor Light at all, nor in nature God. For things which are from participation, are called like, not in reality, but from resemblance to reality; so that they may fail, or be taken from those who share them. And this, again, is proper to creatures and works. Therefore, if this be extravagant, He must be, not by participation, but in nature and truth Son, Light, Wisdom, God; and being by nature, and not by sharing, He would properly be called, not Like in substance, but One in substance. But what would not be asserted, even in the case of others, (for the Like has been shewn to be inapplicable to substance,) is it not folly, not to say violence, to put forward in the case of the Son, instead of the "One in substance?"

[1] μετουσία
[2] μετοχή 1 John 3, 2.
[3] μετουσία

§. 54. 26. This justifies the Nicene Council, which has laid down, what it was becoming to express, that the Son, begotten from the Father's substance, is one in substance with Him. And if we too have been taught the same thing, let us not fight with shadows, especially as knowing, that they who have so defined, have made this confession of faith, not to misrepresent the truth, but as vindicating the truth and religiousness towards Christ, and also as destroying the blasphemies against Him of the Ario-maniacs[4]. For this must be considered and noted carefully, that, in using unlike in substance, and other in substance, we signify not the true Son, but some one of the creatures, and an introduced and adopted Son, which pleases the heretics; but when we speak uncontroversially of the One

[4] p. 91, note q.

---

iii. p. 304. 4. like *according to the Scriptures;* which of course was but an evasion. 5. like *in all things,* κατὰ πάντα, which was, as they understood it, an evasion also.

Exhortation to maintain the truth and live in unity. 157

in substance, we signify a genuine Son born of the Father; though at this Christ's enemies often burst with rage¹.

27. What then I have learned myself, and have heard men of judgment say, I have written in few words; but ye remaining on the foundation of the Apostles, and holding fast the traditions of the Fathers, pray that now at length all strife and rivalry may cease, and the futile questions of the heretics may be condemned, and all logomachy ʰ; and the guilty and murderous heresy of the Arians may disappear, and the truth may shine again in the hearts of all, so that all every where may say the same thing, and think the same thing¹; and that, no Arian contumelies remaining, it may be said and confessed in every Church, *One Lord, one faith, one baptism,* in Christ Jesus our Lord, through whom to the Father be the glory and the strength, unto ages of ages. Amen.

CHAP. III.
¹ p. 29, note l.

Eph.4,5.

ʰ And so ταῖς λογομαχίαις. Basil de Sp. S. n 16 It is used with an allusion to the fight against the Word, as χριστομαχεῖν and θεομαχεῖν. Thus λογομαχεῖν μελετήσαντες, καὶ λοιπὸν πνευματομαχοῦντες, ἔσονται μετ᾽ ὀλίγον νεκροὶ τῇ ἀλογίᾳ Serap. iv. 1.

¹ This sentiment will give opportunity for a note on the Semi-arians, which has been omitted in its proper place, § 41 and 43. vid. p.141 ref.4. There S. Athanasius calls certain of them "brethren" and "beloved," ἀγαπητοί. S. Hilary too calls them "sanctissimi viri." de Syn 80. On the other hand, Athan speaks severely of Eustathius and Basil Ep Æg. 7. and Hilary explains himself in his notes upon his de Syn. from which it appears that he had been expostulated with on his conciliatory tone. Indeed all throughout he had betrayed a consciousness that he should offend some parties. e. g. §. 6 In §. 77, he had spoken of "having expounded the faithful and religious sense of 'like in substance,' which is called Homœusion." On this he observes, note 3, "I think no one need be asked to consider why I have said in this place ' *religious* sense of like in substance,' except that I meant that there was also an *irreligious*, and that therefore I said that 'like' was not only *equal* but the ' same.' vid. p. 139, note l. In the next note he speaks of them as not more than hopeful. Still it should be observed how careful the Fathers of the day were not to mix up the question of doctrine, which rested on Catholic tradition with that of the adoption of a certain term which rested on a Catholic injunction. Not that the term was not in duty to be received, but it was to be received on account of its Catholic sense, and where the Catholic sense was held, the word might even by a sort of dispensation be waived. It is remarkable that Athanasius scarcely mentioned the word "One in substance" in his Orations or Discourses which are to follow; nor does it occur in S. Cyril's Catecheses, of whom, as being suspected of Semi-arianism, it might have been required, before his writings were received as of authority. The word was not imposed upon Ursacius and Valens, A D. 349. by Pope Julius, nor in the Council of Aquileia in 381, was it offered by St. Ambrose to Palladius and Secundianus. S. Jerome's account of the apology made by the Fathers of Ariminum is of the same kind. "We thought," they said, " the sense corresponded to the words, nor in the Church of God, where there is simplicity, and a pure confession, did we fear that one thing would be concealed in the heart, another uttered by the lips. We were deceived by our good opinion of the bad." ad Lucif. 19.

Postscript.

28. After I had written my account of the Council[1], I had information that the most irreligious[2] Constantius had sent Letters to the Bishops remaining in Ariminum; and I have taken pains to get copies of them from true brethren and to send them to you, and also what the Bishops answered; that you may know the irreligious craft of the Emperor, and the firm and unswerving purpose of the Bishops towards the truth.

Interpretation of the Letter[k].

Constantius, Victorious and Triumphant, Augustus, to all Bishops who are assembled at Ariminum.

That the divine and adorable Law is our chief care, your excellencies are not ignorant; but as yet we have been unable to receive the twenty Bishops sent by your wisdom, and charged with the legation from you, for we are pressed by a necessary expedition against the Barbarians; and as ye know, it beseems to have the soul clear from every care, when one handles the matters of the Divine Law. Therefore we have ordered the Bishops to await our return at Adrianople; that, when all public affairs are well-arranged, then at length we may hear and weigh their suggestions. Let it not then be grievous to your constancy to await their return, that, when they come back with our answer to you, ye may be able to bring matters to a close which so deeply affect the well-being of the Catholic Church.

29. This was what the Bishops received at the hands of three messengers.

Reply of the Bishops.

The letter of your humanity we have received, most religious Lord Emperor, which reports that, on account of stress of public affairs, as yet you have been unable to attend to our legates; and in which you command us to await their return, until your godliness shall be advised by them of what we have defined conformably to our ancestors. However, we now profess and aver at once by these presents, that we shall not recede from our purpose, as we also instructed our legates. We ask then that you will with serene countenance command these letters of our mediocrity to be read before you; as well as will graciously receive those, with which we charged our legates. This however your gentleness comprehends as well as we, that great grief and sadness at present

---

[k] These two Letters are both in Socr. ii. 15. p. 878. in a different version ii. 37. And the latter is in Theod. Hist. from the Latin original.

prevail, because that, in these your most happy days, so many Churches are without Bishops. And on this account we again request your humanity, most religious Lord Emperor, that, if it please your religiousness, you would command us, before the severe winter weather sets in, to return to our Churches, that so we may be able, unto God Almighty and our Lord and Saviour Christ, His Only-begotten Son, to fulfil together with our flocks our wonted prayers in behalf of your imperial sway, as indeed we have ever performed them, and at this time make them.

NOTE on Chapter II.

Concerning the Confessions at Sirmium.

NOTE ON COUNC. ARIM. AND SELEU.

IT has been thought advisable to draw up, as carefully as may be, a statement of the various Arian Confessions which issued at Sirmium, with the hope of presenting to the reader in a compendious form an intricate passage of history.

1. A.D. 351. *Confession against Photinus,*
(*First Sirmian.* supr. p. 118.)

This Confession was published at a Council of Eastern Bishops, (Coustant in Hil. p. 1174, note 1,) and was drawn up by the whole body, Hil. de Syn. 37. (according to Sirmond. Diatr. 1. Sirm. p. 366. Petavius de Trin. 1. 9. §. 8. Animadv. in Epiph. p 318 init. and Coustant. in Hil 1. c.) or by Basil of Ancyra (as Valesius conjectures in Soz. iv. 22. and Larroquanus, de Liberio, p. 147.) or by Mark of Arethusa, Socr. ii. 30. but he confuses together the dates of the different Confessions, and this is part of his mistake, (vid. Vales. in loc. Coustant. in Hil. de Syn. l. c. Petav. Animad. in Epiph. l. c.) It was written in Greek.

Till Petavius[a], Socrates was generally followed in ascribing all three Sirmian Confessions to this one Council, though at the same time he was generally considered mistaken as to the year E. g. Baronius places them all in 357. Sirmond defended Baronius against Petavius; (though in Facund. x. 6. note c, he agrees with Petavius,) and assigning the third Confession to 359, adopted the improbable conjecture of two Councils, the one Catholic and the other Arian, held at Sirmium at the same time, putting forth respectively the first and second Creeds somewhat after the manner of the contemporary rival Councils of Sardica. Pagi, Natalis Alexander, Valesius, de Marca, Tillemont, S. Basnage, Montfaucon, Coustant, Larroquanus (de la Roque,) agree with Petavius in placing the Council at which Photinus was deposed, and the Confession published by it, in A. D. 351. Mansi dates it at 358.

[a] Dicam non jactantiæ causâ, sed ut eruditi lectoris studium excitem, fortassis audacius, ab hinc mille ac ducentis propemodum annis liquidam ac sinceram illorum rationem ignoratam fuisse. Quod nisi certissimis argumentis indiciisque monstravero, nihil ego deprecabor, quin id vanissimè à me dictum omnes arbitrentur. Petav Animadv. in Epiph. p. 306. Nos ex antiquis patribus primum illud odorati sumus, tres omnino conventus Episcoporum eodem in Sirmiensi oppido, non iisdem temporibus celebratos fuisse. ibid. p. 113.

Sirmian Confessions.

This was the Confession which Pope Liberius signed according to Baronius, N. Alexander, and Coustant in Hil. note n. p. 1335-7, and as Tillemont thinks probable

In p. 114, note b. supr. the successive condemnations of Photinus are enumerated; but as this is an intricate point on which there is considerable difference of opinion among critics, it may be advisable to state them here, as they are determined by various writers.

NOTE I. ON COUNC ARIM AND SELEU.

Petavius, (de Photino Hæretico, 1.) enumerates in all five Councils:—1. at Constantinople, A.D. 336, when Marcellus was deposed, vid. supr. p. 109, note m. (where for " same" year, read " next" year.) 2. At Sardica, A.D. 347. 3. At Milan, A.D. 347. 4. At Sirmium, 349. 5. At Sirmium, when he was deposed, A.D. 351. Of these the 4th and 5th were first brought to light by Petavius, who omits mention of the Macrostich in 345.

Petavius is followed by Natalis Alexander, Montfaucon, (vit Athan.) and Tillemont; and by De Marca, (Diss. de temp Syn. Sirm.) and S. Basnage, (Annales,) and Valesius, (in Theod. Hist. ii. 16. p. 23. Socr. ii. 20.) as regards the Council of Milan, except that Valesius places it with Sirmond in 346; but for the Council of Sirmium in 349, they substitute a Council of Rome of the same date, while de Marca considers Photinus condemned again in the Eusebian Council of Milan in 355. De la Roque, on the other hand, (Larroquan. Dissert. de Photino Hær.) considers that Photinus was condemned, 1. in the Macrostich, 344 [345]. 2. at Sardica, 347. 3. at Milan, 348. 4. at Sirmium, 350. 5. at Sirmium, 351.

Petavius seems to stand alone in assigning to the Council of Constantinople, 336, his first condemnation.

2. A.D 357. *The Blasphemy of Potamius and Hosius,*
(*Second Sirmian.* supr. p. 122.)

Hilary calls it by the above title, de Syn. 11. vid. also Soz. iv. 12. p. 554. He seems also to mean it by the blasphemia Ursacii et Valentis, contr. Const. 26.

This Confession was the first overt act of disunion between Arians and Semi-Arians.

Sirmond, de Marca and Valesius, (in Socr. ii 30,) after Phæbadius, think it put forth by a Council; rather, at a Conference of a few leading Arians about Constantius, who seems to have been present; e. g. Ursacius, Valens, and Germinius. Soz. iv. 12. Vid. also Hil. Fragm. vi. 7.

It was written in Latin, Socr. ii. 30. Potamius wrote very barbarous Latin, judging from the Tract ascribed to him in Dacher. Spicileg. t. 3. p. 299, unless it be a translation from the Greek. vid. also Galland Bibl. t. v. p. 96. Petavius thinks the Creed not written, but merely subscribed by Potamius de Trin. i. 9. §. 8. and Coustant. in Hil. p. 1155, note f, that it was written by Ursacius, Valens, and Potamius. It is remarkable that the Greek in Athanasius is clearer than the original.

This at first sight is the Creed which Liberius signed, because

NOTE I. ON COUNC. ARIM. AND SELEU.

S. Hilary speaks of the latter as " perfidia Ariana," Fragm. 6. Blondel, (Prim. dans l'Eglise, p 484) Larroquanus, &c. are of this opinion. And the Roman Breviary, Ed. Ven. 1482, and Ed. Par. 1543, in the Service for S. Eusebius of Rome, August. 14. says that " Pope Liberius consented to the Arian misbelief," Launnoi. Ep. v. 9. c. 13 Auxilius says the same, ibid. vi. 14. Animadv. 5. n 18. Petavius grants that it must be this, *if* any of the three Sirmian, (Animadv. in Epiph. p. 316,) but we shall see his own opinion presently.

3 A.D. 367. *The foregoing interpolated.*

A creed was sent into the East in Hosius's name, Epiph. Hær. 73. 14. Soz. iv. 15. p 558, of an Anomœan character, which the " blasphemia" was not And S. Hilary may allude to this when he speaks of the " deliramenta Osii, et *incrementa* Ursacii et Valentis," contr. Const. 23. An Anomœan Council of Antioch under Eudoxius of this date, makes acknowledgments to Ursacius, Valens, and Germinius Soz iv. 12 fin. as being agents in the Arianising of the West.

Petavius and Tillemont considers this Confession to be the " blasphemia' interpolated. Petavius throws out a further conjecture, which seems gratuitous, that the whole of the latter part of the Creed is a later addition, and that Liberius only signed the former part. Animadv. in Epiph. p. 316.

4. A.D. 358. *The Ancyrene Anathemas.*

The Semi-Arian party had met in Council at Ancyra in the early spring of 358 to protest against the " blasphemia," and that with some kind of correspondence with the Gallic Bishops who had just condemned it, Phæbadius of Agen writing a Tract against it, which is still extant They had drawn up and signed, besides, a Synodal Letter, eighteen anathemas, the last against the " One in substance." These, except the last, or the last six, they submitted at the end of May to the Emperor who was again at Sirmium. Basil, Eustathius, Eleusius, and another formed the deputation; and their influence persuaded Constantius to accept the Anathemas, and even to oblige the party of Valens, at whose " blasphemia" they were levelled, to recant and subscribe them.

5. A.D. 358. *Semi-Arian Digest of Three Confessions.*

The Semi-Arian Bishops, pursuing their advantage, composed a Creed out of three, that of the Dedication, the first Sirmian, and the Creed of Antioch against Paul 264—270, in which the " One in substance" is said to have been omitted or forbidden. Soz. iv. 15. This Confession was imposed by Imperial authority on the Arian party, who signed it So did Liberius, Soz. ibid. Hil. Fragm. vi 6. 7; and Petavius considers that this is the subscription by which he lapsed. de Trin. i. 9. §. 5. Animadv. in Epiph. p. 316. and S. Basnage, in Ann. 358. 13.

It is a point of controversy whether or not the Arians at this time suppressed the " blasphemia." Socrates and Sozomen say

that they made an attempt to recall the copies they had issued, and even obtained an edict from the Emperor for this purpose, but without avail. Socr. ii. 30 fin Soz iv. 6. p. 543. NOTE I. ON COUNC. ARIM. AND SELEU.
Athanasius, on the other hand, as we have seen, supr. p 123, relates this in substance of the third Confession of Sirmium, not of the " blasphemia" or second.

Tillemont follows Socrates and Sozomen; considering that Basil's influence with the Emperor enabled him now to insist on a retractation of the " blasphemia." And he argues that Germinius in 366, being suspected of orthodoxy, and obliged to make profession of heresy, was referred by his party to the formulary of Ariminum, no notice being taken of the " blasphemia," which looks as if it were suppressed, whereas Germinius himself appeals to the third Sirmian, which is a proof that it was not suppressed. Hil. Fragm. 15. Coustant. in Hil. contr. Const. 26, though he does not adopt the opinion himself, observes, that the charge brought against Basil, Soz. iv. 132. Hil. l. c by the Acacians of persuading the Africans against the second Sirmian is an evidence of a great effort on his part at a time when he had the Court with him to suppress it. We have just seen Basil uniting with the Gallic Bishops against it.

6. A.D. 359. *The Confession with a date,*
(*third Sirmian,* supr. p. 83)

The Semi-Arians, with the hope of striking a further blow at their opponents by a judgment against the Anomœans, Soz. iv. 16 init. seem to have suggested a general Council, which ultimately became the Councils of Seleucia and Ariminum If this was their measure, they were singularly out-manœuvred by the party of Acacius and Valens, as we have seen in Athanasius's work. A preparatory Conference was held at Sirmium at the end of May in this year; in which the Creed was determined which should be laid before the great Councils which were assembling. Basil and Mark were the chief Semi-Arians present, and in the event became committed to an almost Arian Confession. Soz iv 16. p. 562. It was finally settled on the Eve of Pentecost, and the dispute lasted till morning. Epiph. Hær. 73. 22. Mark at length was chosen to draw it up, Soz. iv. 22. p. 573. yet Valens so managed that Basil could not sign it without an explanation. It was written in Latin, Socr. ii. 30. Soz iv. 17. p. 563. Coustant, however, in Hil. p. 1152, note i, seems to consider this dispute and Mark's confession to belong to the same date (May 22,) in the foregoing year; but p. 1363, note b, to change his opinion.

Petavius, who, Animadv. in Epiph. p. 318, follows Socrates in considering that the second Sirmian is the Confession which the Arians tried to suppress, nevertheless, de Trin. i. 9. § 8. yields to the testimony of Athanasius in behalf of the third, attributing the measure to their dissatisfaction with the phrase " Like in all things," which Constantius had inserted, and with Basil's explanation on subscribing it, and to the hopes of publishing a bolder creed which their increasing influence with Constantius inspired. He does

NOTE 1 ON COUNC. ARIM. AND SELEU. not think it impossible, however, that an attempt was made to suppress both. Coustant, again, in Hil. p. 1363, note b, asks *when* it could be that the Eusebians attempted to suppress the second Confession; and conjectures that the ridicule which followed their dating of the third and their wish to get rid of the " Like in all things," were the causes of their anxiety about it. He observes too with considerable speciousness that Acacius's second formulary at Seleucia (Confession ixth, supr. p. 123.) and the Confession of Nice (xth, supr. p. 125) resemble second editions of the third Sirmian. Valesius in Socr. ii. 30. and Montfaucon in Athan. Syn. §. 29. take the same side.

Pagi in Ann 357. n. 13. supposes that the third Sirmian was the Creed signed by Liberius. Yet Coustant. in Hil. p. 1335, note n, speaking of Liberius's, " perfidia Ariana," as S. Hilary calls it, says, " Solus Valesius existimat tertiam [confessionem] hic memorari." whereas Valesius, making four, not to say five, Sirmian Creeds, understands Liberius to have signed, not the third, but an intermediate one, between the second and third, as Petavius does, in Soz. iv. 15 and 16. Moreover, Pagi fixes the date as A. D. 358. ibid.

This Creed, thus drawn up by a Semi-Arian, with an Acacian or Arian appendix, then a Semi-Arian insertion, and after all a Semi-Arian protest on subscription, was proposed at Seleucia by Acacius, Soz. iv. 22. and at Ariminum by Valens, Socr. ii. 37. p. 132.

7 A. D. 359. *Nicene Edition of the third Sirmian,*
(*Tenth Confession*, supr. p. 125)

The third Sirmian was rejected both at Seleucia and Ariminum; but the Eusebians, dissolving the Council of Seleucia, kept the Fathers at Ariminum together through the summer and autumn. Meanwhile at Nice in Thrace they confirmed the third Sirmian, Socr. ii. 37. p. 141. Theod. Hist. ii. 16. with the additional proscription of the word hypostasis, apparently lest the Latins should by means of it evade the condemnation of the " One in substance." This Creed, thus altered, was ultimately accepted at Ariminum; and was confirmed in January 360 at Constantinople; Socr. ii. 41. p 153. Soz. iv. 24 init.

Liberius retrieved his fault on this occasion; for, whatever was the confession he had signed, he now refused his assent to the Ariminian, and, if Socrates is to be trusted, was banished in consequence, Socr. ii. 37. p. 140.

NOTE on Page 147.

On the alleged Confession of Antioch against Paul of Samosata.

A number of learned writers have questioned the fact, testified by three Fathers, S. Athanasius, S. Basil, and S. Hilary, of the rejection of the word ὁμοούσιον in the Antiochene Council against Paul between A.D. 264—270. It must be confessed that both S. Athanasius and S. Hilary speak from the statements of the Semi-arians, without having seen the document which the latter had alleged, while S. Basil who speaks for certain lived later. It must also be confessed, that S. Hilary differs from the two other Fathers in the reason he gives for the rejection of the word. There is, however, a further argument urged against the testimony of the three Fathers of a different kind. A Creed, containing the word, is found in the acts of the Council of Ephesus 431, purporting to be a Definition of faith "of the Nicene Council, touching the Incarnation, and an Exposition against Paul of Samosata" This Creed, which, (it is supposed,) is by mistake referred to the Nicene Council, is admitted as genuine by Baronius, J. Forbes, Instr. Hist. Theol. i. 4 §. 1. Le Moyne, Var. Sacr. t. 2 p. 255. Wormius, Hist. Sabell. p. 116—119. (vid. Routh Rell. t. 2. p. 523) Simon de Magistris, Præf. ad Dionys. Alex p xl. Feverlin. Diss. de P. Samos §. 9. Molkenbuhr, Dissert. Crit 4. Kern, Disqu. Hist. Crit. on the subject; Dr. Burton in Faber's Apostolicity of Trinitarianism, vol ii. p. 302 and Mr. Faber himself. As, however, I cannot but agree with the President of Magdalen l c. that the Creed is of a later date, (in his opinion, post lites exortas Nestorianas,) or at least long after the time of Paul of Samosata, I will here set down one or two peculiarities in it which make me think so.

The Creed is found in Harduin Concil. t 1. p 1640 Routh, Rell. t. 2 p. 524. Dionys. Alex. Oper. Rom. 1696 [1796]. p. 289. Burton, Testimonies, p. 397—399. Faber, Trinitarianism, vol. 2. p. 287.

1. Now first, the Creed in question has these words: ὅλον ὁμοούσιον θεῷ καὶ μετὰ τοῦ σώματος, ἀλλ᾽ οὐχὶ κατὰ τὸ σῶμα ὁμοούσιον τῷ θεῷ. Now to enter upon the use of the word ὁμοούσιον, as applied to the Holy Trinity, would be foreign to my subject; and to refer to the testimony of the three Fathers, would be assuming the point at issue; but still there are other external considerations besides, which may well be taken into account.

(1) And first the Fathers speak of it as a new term, i. e. in Creeds, " To meet the irreligion of the Arian heretics, the Fathers framed the new name Homousion." August. in Joann. 97. n. 4. He says that it was misunderstood at Ariminum " propter novitatem verbi." contr. Maxim. ii. 3. though it was the legitimate " off-spring of the ancient faith." Vigilius also says, " an ancient

subject received the new name Homousion." Disp. Ath. et Ar. t. v. p. 695. (the paging wrong.) Bibl. P. Col. 1618. vid Le Moyne. Var. Sacr. l. c.

(2) Next Sozomen informs us, Hist. iv. 15 (as we have seen above, p 162.) that the Creed against Paul was used by the Semi-arians at Sirmium, A.D. 358, in order to the composition of the Confession which Liberius signed. Certainly then, if this be so, we cannot suspect it of containing the ὁμοούσιον.

(3) Again, we have the evidence of the Semi-arians themselves to the same point in the documents which Epiphanius has preserved, Hær. 73. They there appeal to the Council against Paul as an authority for the use of the word οὐσία, and thereby to justify their own ὁμοιούσιον, which they would hardly have done, if that Council had sanctioned the ὁμοούσιον as well as οὐσία. But moreover, as we have seen, supr. p. 162. the last Canon of their Council of Ancyra actually pronounced anathema upon the ὁμοούσιον, but if so, with what face could they appeal to a Council which made profession of it?

(4) And there is nothing improbable in the Antiochene Council having suppressed or disowned it; on the contrary, under their circumstances it was almost to be expected. The Fathers concerned in the first proceedings against Paul, Dionysius, Gregory of Neocæsarea, Athenodorus, and perhaps Firmilian, were immediate disciples of Origen, who is known to have been very jealous of the corporeal ideas concerning the Divine Nature which Paul (according to Athanasius and Basil) imputed to the word ὁμοούσιον. There were others of the Fathers who are known to have used language of a material cast, and from them he pointedly differs. Tertullian speaks of the Divine Substance as a corpus, in Prax. 7. and he adopts the Valentinian word προβολὴ, as Justin had used προβληθὲν γέννημα, (vid. supr. p. 97, note h) whereas Origen in his controversy with Candidus, who was of that heresy, condemns it; and he speaks in strong language against the work of Melito of Sardis, περὶ ἐνσωμάτου θεοῦ, in Genes Fragm t 2 p. 25. whom he accuses of teaching it. vid. also de Orat. 23 His love of Platonism would tend the same way, for the Platonists, in order to mark their idea of the perfection and simplicity of the Divine Nature, were accustomed to consider It "above substance."

Thus Plotinus calls the Divine Being the "origin of being and more excellent than substance." 5 Ennead v. 11. and says that He "transcends all, and is the cause of them, but is not they." ibid. c. ult. The views of physical necessity too, which the material system involved, led him to speak of His energy and will being His substance. 6 Enn. viii. 13. And hence Origen, " Nor doth God partake of substance, rather He is partaken, than partakes." contr. Cels. vi. 64. And thus the word ὑπερούσιον is used by Pseudo-Dion. de div. nom. i. n. 2. whose Platonic tone of thought is well known; as by S. Maximus, " Properly substance is not predicated of God, for He is ὑπερούσιος." in Pseudo-Dion. de div nom. v. init. Vid. also Dam. F. O. i. 4. and 8. pp 137. 147. while S. Greg. Naz. also speaks of Him as ὑπὲρ τὴν οὐσίαν. Orat. 6. 12

Nay further, in Joann. t. 20. 16. Origen goes so far as to object to the phrase ἐκ τῆς οὐσίας τοῦ πατρὸς γεγεννῆσθαι τὸν υἱὸν, but still assigning the reason that such a phrase introduced the notion of a μείωσις, or the like corporeal notions, into our idea of God.

It is scarcely necessary to add, that there was no more frequent charge against the ὁμοούσιον in the mouths of the Arians, than that it involved the Gnostic and Manichæan doctrine of materiality in the Divine Nature. vid. supr. p. 17, note l. p. 63, note h.

NOTE II.
ON COUNC. ARIM. AND SELEU.

Again we know also that S. Dionysius did at first decline or at least shrink from the word ὁμοούσιον, accepting it only when the Bishop of Rome urged it upon him. But an additional reason for such reluctance is found in the rise of Manicheism just in the time of these Councils against Paul, a heresy which adopted the word ὁμοούσιον in its view of the doctrine of the Holy Trinity, and that in a material sense; so that the very circumstances of the case exactly fall in with and bear out the account of their rejection of the word given by the two Fathers.

(5) Nor is there any thing in S. Hilary s reason for it inconsistent with the testimony of S. Athanasius and S. Basil. Both accounts may be true at once. The philosophical sense of οὐσία, as we have seen, supr. p 152, note a, was that of an individual or unit. When then the word ὁμοούσιος was applied to the Second Person in the Blessed Trinity, or He was said to be *of one substance* with the Father, such a doctrine, to those who admitted of no mystery in the subject, involved one of two errors, according as the οὐσία was considered a spiritual substance or a material. Either it implied that the Son of God was a part of God, or μέρος ὁμοούσιον, which was the Manichæan doctrine; or if the οὐσία were immaterial, then, since it denoted an individual being, the phrase " one in substance" involved Sabellianism Paul then might very naturally have urged this dilemma upon the Council, and said, " Your doctrine implies the ὁμοούσιον, which is Manichæan, unless it be taken, as I am willing to take it, in a Sabellian sense " And thus it might be at once true as Athanasius says, that Paul objected, " Unless Christ has of man become God, it follows that He is One in substance with the Father; and if so, of necessity there are three substances, &c." supr. § 45. and also, according to Hilary's testimony, " Homoüsion Samosatenus confessus est; sed nunquid melius Ariani negaverunt?" de Syn. 86.

2. The Creed also says, μετὰ τῆς θεότητος ὢν κατὰ σάρκα ὁμοούσιος ἡμῖν.

There are strong reasons for saying that the phrase ὁμοούσιος ἡμῖν is of a date far later than the Council of Antioch.

(1) Waterland considers the omission of the phrase in the Athanasian Creed as an argument that it was written not lower than Eutychian times," A.D. 451. " A tenet," he observes of it, " expressly held by *some* of the ecclesiastical writers before Eutyches's time, but seldom or never omitted in the Creeds or Confessions about that time, or after. To be convinced," he proceeds, " of the truth of this . . . . article, one need but look into the Creeds and Formularies of those times, viz. into that of

NOTE II. ON COUNC. ARIM. AND SELEU. Turribius of Spain in 447, of Flavian of Constantinople, as also of Pope Leo in 449, of the Chalcedon Council in 451, of Pope Felix III in 485, and Anastasius II in 496, and of the Church of Alexandria in the same year; as also into those of Pope Hormisdas, and the Churches of Syria, and Fulgentius, and the Emperor Justinian, and Pope John II, and Pope Pelagius I, within the 6th century. In all which we shall find either express denial of one nature, or express affirmation of two natures, or *the doctrine of Christ's consubstantiality with us*, or all three together, though *they are all omitted in the Athanasian Creed.*" vol. iv p. 247.

(2) The very fact of Eutyches denying it seems to shew that the phrase was not familiar, or at least generally received, in the Church before. " Up to this day," he says in the Council of Constantinople, A.D. 448, " I have never said that the Body of our Lord and God was consubstantial with us, but I confess that the Holy Virgin was consubstantial with us, and that our God was incarnate of her." Conc. t. 2. p 164, 5. The point at issue, as in other controversies, seems to have been the reception or rejection of a phrase, which on the one hand was as yet but in local or private use, and on the other was well adapted to exclude the nascent heresy. The Eutychians denied in like manner the word φύσις, which, it must be confessed, was seldom used till their date, when the doctrine it expressed came into dispute. And so of the phrase ὁμοούσιον τῷ πατρί, and of ὑπόστασις; vid Note, supr. p. 71.

Now the phrase " consubstantial with us" seems to have been introduced at the time of the Apollinarian controversy, and was naturally the Catholic counter-statement to the doctiine of Apollinaris that Christ's body was " consubstantial to the Godhead," a doctrine which, as Athanasius tells us, ad Epict. 2. was new to the world when the Apollinarians brought it forward, and, according to Epiphanius, was soon abandoned by them, Hær. 77, 25. It is natural then to suppose that the antagonist phrase, which is here in question, came into use at that date, and continued or was dropped accoiding to the prevalence of the heretical tenet. Moreover both sections into which the Apollinarians soon split, seemed to have agreed to receive the phrase " consubstantial with us," and only disputed whether it *continued* to be predicable of our Lord's body on and after its union with the divine Nature. vid. Leont. de fraud. Apollin. and this of course would be an additional reason against the general Catholic adoption of the phrase. It occurs however in the Creed of John of Antioch, A.D. about 431, on which S. Cyril was reconciled to him. Rustic. contr. Aceph p. 799. but this is only twenty-one years before the Council of Chalcedon, in which the phrase was formally received, as the ὁμοούσιον τῷ πατρί was received at Nicæa. ibid. p. 805.

The counter-statement more commonly used by the orthodox to that of the flesh being ὁμοούσιον θεότητι, was not " consubstantial with us," but "consubstantial with Mary." S. Amphilochius speaks thus generally, " It is plain that the holy Fathers said that the Son was consubstantial with His Father according to the Godhead and *consubstantial with His Mother* according to the manhood." apud. Phot. Bibl p. 789. Proclus, A.D. 434, uses the word ὁμόφυλον, and still with "the Virgin." τῷ πατρὶ κατὰ τὴν θεότητα ὁμοούσιος, οὕτως ὁ αὐτὸς καὶ τῇ παρθένῳ κατὰ τὴν σάρκα ὁμόφυλος. ad Arm. p. 618. circ. init. vid. also p. 613 fin. p. 618. He uses the word ὁμοούσιον frequently of the Divine Nature as above, yet this does not suggest the other use of it. Another term is used by Athanasius, τὸν ἠνώμενον πατρὶ κατὰ πνεῦμα, ἡμῖν δὲ κατὰ σάρκα. apud Theod. Eranist. ii. p. 139 Or again that He took flesh of Mary, e.g. οὐκ ἐκ Μαρίας ἀλλ᾽ ἐκ τῆς ἑαυτοῦ οὐσίας σῶμα. ad Epict. 2. Or τέλειος ἄνθρωπος, e g. Procl. ad Arm. p. 613. which, though Apollinaris denied, Eutyches allowed, Concil. t. 2. p. 157. Leon. Ep. 21.

NOTE II. ON COUNC. ARIM. AND SELEU.

However, S. Eustathius (A.D 325) says that our Lord's soul was ταῖς ψυχαῖς τῶν ἀνθρώπων ὁμοούσιος, ὥσπερ καὶ ἡ σὰρξ ὁμοούσιος τῇ τῶν ἀνθρώπων σαρκί. ap Theod. Eranist. i. p. 56. vid. also Leon. contr. Nestor. et Eutych. p. 977. and S. Ambrose, ibid. Dial. ii. p 139. ὁμοούσιον τῷ πατρὶ κατὰ τὴν θεότητα, καὶ ὁμοούσιον ἡμῖν κατὰ τὴν ἀνθρωπότητα, but the genuineness of the whole extract is extremely doubtful, as indeed the Benedictines almost grant. t 2. p. 729. Waterland, Athan. Creed, ch. 7. p. 254. seems to thmk the internal evidence strong against its genuineness, but yields to the external; and Coustant. App. Epist. Pont. Rom. p. 79. considers Leontius a different author from the Leontius de Sectis, on account of his *mistakes*. Another instance is found in Theophilus ap. Theod. Eranist ii. p. 154.

This contrast becomes stronger still when we turn to documents of the alleged date of the Confession. A letter of one of the Councils 263—270, or of some of its Bishops, is still extant, and exhibits a very different phraseology. Instead of ὁμοούσιος ἡμῖν we find the vaguer expressions, not unlike Athanasius, &c of the Son " being made flesh and made man," and " the Body from the Virgin," and " man of the seed of David," and "partaking of flesh and blood." Routh Rell t 2. p 473. And the use of the word οὐσία is different; and its derivatives are taken to convey the idea, neither of the divine nature of our Lord nor the human, but of the divine nature substantiated or become a substance, in the material world; almost as if under the feeling that God in Himself is *above* substance, as I had just now occasion to mention. E. g. Pseudo-Dionysius asks πῶς ὁ ὑπερούσιος Ἰησοῦς ἀνθρωποφυιαῖς ἀληθείαις οὐσίωται. Myst. Theol. iii. vid. also de Div Nom. 1. 2. and Epist. 4. Hence Africanus says, οὐσίαν ὅλην οὐσιωθείς, ἄνθρωπος λέγεται. African. Chron. ap. Routh t. 2. p. 125. In like manner the Antiochene Fathers insist, καθὸ Χριστὸς, ἓν καὶ τὸ αὐτὸ ὢν τῇ οὐσίᾳ. Routh Rel. t. 2. p. 474. and Malchion at the same Council accuses Paul of not admitting οὐσιῶσθαι ἐν τῷ ὅλῳ σωτῆρι τὸν υἱὸν τὸν μονογενῆ. ibid p. 476. or that the Son was " substantially present in the whole Saviour." vid. also p. 485. In all these passages οὐσία is used for nothing else than substance, whereas in the phrase ὁμοούσιον ἡμῖν it rather stands for φύσις or γένος. And so much was the former its meaning in the earlier times that Hippolytus plainly denies that men are one substance one with another; for he asks, μὴ πάντες ἓν σῶμά ἐσμεν κατὰ τὴν οὐσίαν; contr. Noet. 7. And this moreover altogether agrees with what was said above, that in Paul's argument against the ὁμοούσιον πατρὶ the

NOTE II. ON COUNC ARIM. AND SELEU

word ουσία was taken (and rightly) in what Aristotle as Anastasius, Hodeg. 6. p. 96 and Theorian Leg. p 441. after him, assigns as the proper sense of the word, viz. an individual, and not a common nature.

3. The Creed also speaks of our Lord as ἓν πρόσωπον σύνθετον ἐκ θεότητος οὐρανίου καὶ ἀνθρωπείας σαρκός.

Now the word σύνθετον, in the Latin *compositum*, is found in the fragment of Malchion's disputation in the Council. Routh Rell. t. 2. p 476. But πρόσωπον and σύνθετον πρόσωπον seem to me of a later date.

The word persona, applied to our Lord in His two natures and in contrast with them, is to be found in Tertull. contr. Prax. 27. Though, however, it was not absolutely unknown to ecclesiastical authors, this is a very rare instance of its early occurrence.

We also find Novatian de Trin. 21. speaking of the "regula circa Personam Christi;" and considering his great resemblance to Tertullian, it may be supposed that persona here denotes, not merely our Lord's subsistence in the Holy Trinity, but in His two natures. But on the other hand, he uses Christus absolutely for the Second Person all through his Treatise, e g 9 init. " Regula veritatis docet nos credere *post patrem* etiam in Filium Dei Christum Jesum, *Dominum Deum nostrum,* sed Dei filium, &c." Again, " Christus habet gloriam ante mundi institutionem. 16. vid. also 13. where he speaks of Christ being *made* flesh, as if the name were synonymous with " Word" in the text, John 1, 14. And, moreover, subsequently to " persona Christi," he goes on to speak of " *secundam* personam *post Patrem*." 26 and 31. vid. also 27.

However, in spite of these instances, one might seem to say confidently, if a negative can be proved, that it was not in common use at soonest before the middle of the fourth century, and perhaps not till much later.

(1.) I have not discovered it in S. Athanasius's treatises against Apollinarianism, which were written about 370, except in two places, which shall be spoken of presently. Nor in S. Gregory Naz.'s Ep 202. ad Nectar. and Ep 101. 102. ad Cledon. Nor in S. Gregory Nyssen. Fragm. in Apollinarem. Nor in Theodoret's Eranistes, except in one place, in a Testimony, given to S. Ambrose, and which has already been mentioned as probably spurious. Nor is it found in the Creed of Damasus, by whom Apollinaris was condemned, vid. Epp 2 and 3; nor among the testimonies of the Fathers cited at the Council of Ephesus; nor in Epiphanius's Creed, Ancor 121. vid. also 75.

(2.) It is not used in passages where it might have been expected, but other modes of speech are usual instead ; and that by a sort of rule, so as to make them almost technical, or with such variety of expression as pointedly to mark the omission ; e. g. for " two natures and one Person" we always find οὐκ ἄλλο, ἄλλο,— τίς,—ἕν,—ὁ αὐτός. &c. &c.

S Irenæus:—*Non* ergo *alterum* filium hominis novit Evangelium, nisi hunc qui ex Mariâ, &c. et *eundem* hunc passum resurrexisse ... Etsi linguâ quidem confitetur *unum* Jesum Christum,

... *alterum* quidem passum, et natum, &c. et esse *alterum* eorum, &c. Hær. iii. 16 n. 5 6. *unus* quidem *et idem* existens, n 7. per multa dividens Filium Dei. n 8. *unum et eundem*, ibid. Si *alter*, ... *alter*, ... quoniam *unum* eum novit Apostolus, &c. n. 9. The passage upon the subject is extended to c. xxiv

NOTE II. ON COUNC. ARIM. AND SELEU.

S. Ambrose:—*Unus* in utrâque [divinitate et carne] loquitur Dei Filius; quia in *eodem* utraque natura est; et si *idem* loquitur, non uno semper loquitur modo. de fid. ii. 9. vid. 58. Non divisus sed *unus;* quia utrumque *unus*, et *unus* in utroque ... *non* enim *alter* ex Patre, *alter* ex Virgine, sed *idem* aliter ex Pater, aliter ex Virgine, de Incarn. 35 vid. 47. 75. and Non enim quod ejusdem substantiæ est, *unus*, sed *unum* est, 77. where persona follows of the Holy Trinity

S. Hilary:—*Non alius* filius hominis quam qui filius Dei est neque alius in forma Dei quam qui in forma servi perfectus homo natus est, ... habens in se et totum verumque quod homo est, et totum verumque quod Deus est de Trin. x. 19. Cum *ipse ille* filius hominis *ipse* sit *qui et* filius Dei, quia totus hominis filius totus Dei filius sit, &c. ... Natus autem est, *non* ut esset *alius atque alius*, sed ut ante hominem Deus, sucipiens hominem, homo et Deus possit intelligi. ibid. 22. Non potest ... ita *ab se dividuus* esse, ne Christus sit; cum *non alius* Christus, *quam* qui in forma Dei, &c. *neque alius* quam qui natus est, &c. ... *neque alius* quam qui est mortuus, &c in cœlis autem *non alius* sit quam qui &c. ibid. ut non *idem* fuerit *qui et.* &c ibid. 50. Totum ei Deus Verbum est, totum ei homo Christus est, ... *nec* Christum *aliud* credere quam Jesum, nec Jesum aliud prædicare quam Christum. 52.

And in like manner S. Athanasius:—ἄλλος, ἄλλος ἕτερος, ἕτερος· εἷς καὶ αὐτός· ταυτόν· ἀδιαίρετος, Orat. iv. §. 15 and 29. ἄλλος, ἄλλος. §. 30 ἕνα καὶ τὸν αὐτόν §. 31 οὐχ ὡς τοῦ λόγου κεχωρισμένου. ibid. τὸν πρὸς αὐτοῦ ληφθέντα, ᾧ καὶ ἡνῶσθαι πιστεύεται, ἄνθρωπον ἀπ' αὐτοῦ χωρίζουσι. ibid τὴν ἀνέκφραπτὸν ἕνωσιν §. 32. τὸ θεῖον ἓν καὶ ἁπλοῦν μυστήριον. ibid. τὴν ἑνότητα. ibid ὅλον αὐτὸν ἄνθρωπόν τε καὶ θεὸν ὁμοῦ. §. 35. vid. especially the long discussion in Orat. iii. §. 30—58. where there is hardly a technical term.

Other instances of ecclesiastical language are as follows:— *Medium* inter Deum et hominum *substantiam* gerens Lactant. Instit. iv. 13. θεὸς καὶ ἄνθρωπος τέλειος ὁ αὐτός. Meliton. apud Routh, Rell. i. p. 115. ex eo quod Deus est, et ex illo quod homo .. permixtus et sociatus .. alterum vident, alterum non vident. Novat. de Trin. 25. vid. also 11, 14, 21, and 24. duos Christos ... unum, alium. Pamphil Apol. ap. Routh, Rell. t. 4. p. 320. ὁ αὐτός ἐστιν ἀεὶ πρὸς ἑαυτὸν ὡσαύτως ἔχων Greg. Nyss t. 2. p. 696 ἕνα καὶ τὸν αὐτόν. Greg. Naz. Ep 101. p 85 ἄλλο μὲν καὶ ἄλλο τὰ ἐξ ὧν ὁ Σωτήρ. οὐκ ἄλλος δὲ καὶ ἄλλος p 86.

Vid. also Athan. contr Apollin. i. 10 fin 11. fin. 13, e. 16. b. ii. 1 init. 5. e. 12 e. 18. circ. fin. Theoph. apud Theod. Eranist. ii. p 154. Hilar. ibid. p. 162. Attic. ibid. p. 167. Jerom. in Joan. Ieros. 35.

A corresponding phraseology and omission of the term "person" is found in the undoubted Epistle of the Antiochene Fathers;

NOTE II. ON COUNC. ARIM AND SELEU. τὸ ἐκ τῆς παρθένου σῶμα χωρῆσαν πᾶν τὸ πλήρωμα τῆς θεότητος σωματικῶς, τῇ θεότητι ἀτρέπτως ἥνωται καὶ τεθεοποίηται οὐ χάριν ὁ αὐτὸς θεὸς καὶ ἄνθρωπος κ.τ.λ. Routh, Rell t. 2. p 473. οὕτω καὶ ὁ Χριστὸς πρὸ τῆς σαρκώσεως ὡς εἷς ὠνόμασται. καθὸ Χριστὸς ἓν καὶ τὸ αὐτὸ ὢν τῇ οὐσίᾳ. ibid. p. 474. εἰ ἄλλο μὲν .. ἄλλο δὲ ... δύο υἱούς. ibid. p. 485. And so Malchion, Unus factus est ... unitate subsistens, &c. ibid. p 476.

(3) It is indisputable too that the word πρόσωπον is from time to time used of our Lord by the early writers in its ordinary vague sense, which is inconceivable if it were already received in creeds as an ecclesiastical symbol.

E. g. S. Clement calls the Son the " person" or countenance, πρόσωπον, " of the Father." Strom. v. 6. p. 665. and Pædag. i. 7. p. 132. vid. also Strom. vii. 10. p. 886. And so ἐν προσώπῳ πατρὸς, Theoph. ad Autol ii. 22 (vid. supr. p. 114, note d.) and even Cyril Alex. Dial. v. p. 554 Vid also Cyril. Catech. xii. 14 fin. ὁμοιοπρόσωπον. Chrysostom speaks of δύο πρόσωπα, i.e human and divine, διῃρημένα κατὰ τὴν ὑπόστασιν, in Hebr Hom iii. 1 fin. where too he has just been speaking against Paul of Samosata, against whom the Creed which we are examining is alleged to have been written. vid. also Amphiloch. ap. Theod. Eranist. i p. 67. who speaks of Christ as saying, " My Father is greater than I," " from the flesh and not ἐκ προσώπου τῆς θεότητος." In these passages πρόσωπον seems to stand for *character*, as is not unusual in Athanasius, vid supr. p. 22, note z, where instances are given. And thus I would explain those passages referred to just above, in which he seems to use πρόσωπον for *person*, in Apoll. ii. 2 and 10. viz ἐν διαιρέσει προσώπων, which Le Quien (in Damasc dialect. 43.) most unnecessarily calls an instance, and as he thinks solitary, of πρόσωπον being used for nature, though Athan. in one of the two passages explains the word himself, speaking of προσώπων ἢ ὀνομάτων. And this seems a truer explanation, though perhaps less natural, than to render it (supr. p. 22.) " not as if there were division of persons " These passages of Athan might make us less decisive than Montfaucon as to the internal evidence against the fragment given in t. i. p. 1294. He says, after Sirmond in Facund. xi. 2. that it contains a doctrine " ab Athanasianâ penitus abhorrentem ;" and this, because the Latin version, (another reason, but of a different kind, why it is difficult to judge of it,) speaks broadly of " duas personas, unam circa hominem, alteram circa Verbum." But besides the above instances, we find the same use in an extract from a work of Hippolytus preserved by Leontius, Hippol. t. 2. p. 45. where he speaks of Christ as δύο προσώπων μεσίτης, God and men.

Again S. Hilary speaks of utriusque naturæ personam. de Trin. ix. 14. ejus hominis quam assumpsit persona. in Psalm 63. n. 3. vid also in Psalm 138. n 5. and S. Ambrose, in personâ hominis de Fid. ii. n. 61. v. n. 108 124. Ep. 48. n. 4 From a passage quoted from Paschasius Diaconus, de Spir. §. ii. 4. p. 194. by Petavius (de Trin iv. 4. §. 3.) it seems that the use of the word *persona* in the sense of quality or state had not ceased even in the 6th century.

Further, it would seem as if the vague use of the word " person," as used in speaking of the Holy Trinity, which S. Theophilus and S. Clement above exemplify, on the whole ceased with the rise of the Sabellian controversy and the adoption of the word, (as in Hippol. contr. Noet. 14.) as a symbol against the heresy. It is natural in like manner that till the great controversy concerning the Incarnation which Apollinaris began, a similar indistinctness should prevail in its use relatively to that doctrine.

NOTE II ON COUNC. ARIM. AND SELEU.

And hence S. Cyril in his 4th anathema is obliged to explain the word by the more accurately defined term *hypostasis*: εἴ τις προσώποις δυσί, ἡγοῦν ὑποστάσεσι, κ. τ λ. Vid. also the caution or protest of Vincentius Lirens. Comm. 14.

(4) Moreover, a contrast is observable between the later accounts or interpretations of early writings and those writings themselves as far as we have them; words and phrases being imputed, which in the originals exist only in the ideas themselves intended by them

E. g. Ephrem of Antioch reports that S. Peter of Alexandria, S. Chrysostom, S. Basil, S. Gregory Nazianzen, &c. acknowledge the doctrine of " the union of two natures and one Subsistence and one Person." ap. Phot. cod. 229 p. 805—7. but Chrysostom, &c. uses the words and phrases, ἕνωσις, συνάφεια, ἓν ὁ θεὸς λόγος καὶ ἡ σάρξ; Nazianzen is silent about persona in his Ep. ad Cledon. to which Ephrem there refers, and Peter in all that remains of him uses such words as σάρξ γενόμενος οὐκ ἀπελείφθη τῆς θεότητος· γέγονεν ἐν μητρᾷ τῆς παρθένου σάρξ θεὸς ἦν φύσει καὶ γέγονεν ἄνθρωπος φύσει. Routh Rell. t. 3. p. 344—346.

Again, let it be observed how S. Maximus comments upon S. Gregory Nazianzen's words in the following passage: " The great Gregory Theologus seems to me thus to teach in his great Apologetic, ' One, ἕν, out of both, and both through One,' *as if he would say*, for as there is one out of both, *that is*, of two natures, One as a whole from parts according to the definition of *hypostasis*, so," &c. t 2 p. 282.

Instances of this kind, which are not unfrequent, make one suspicious of such passages of the Fathers as come to us in translation, as Theodoret's and Leontius's extract from S. Ambrose, of which notice has been taken above; especially as the common Latin versions in the current editions of the Greek Fathers offer parallel instances of the insertion of the words persona, &c. not in the original, merely for the sake of perspicuity.

(5) It might be shewn too that according as alleged works of the Fathers are spurious or suspected, so does persona appear as one of their theological terms. The passage of S. Ambrose above cited is in point; but it would carry us too far from the subject to illustrate this as fully as might be done; nor is it necessary. Another specimen, however, may be taken from S Athanasius. The absence of πρόσωπον from his acknowledged works has already been noticed; but let us turn to the fragments at the end of vol. 1. of the Benedictine edition E. g. p. 1279 is a fragment which Montfaucon says olet quidpiam peregrinum, et videtur maxime sub finem Eutychianorum hæresin impugnare; it contains the word πρόσωπον. And a third is the letter to Dionysius falsely

174 *Alleged Confession of Antioch*

NOTE ON COUNC. ARIM AND SELEU

ascribed to Pope Julius, in which as before πρόσωπον occurs, n. 2. Coust. Ep. Pont Rom. Append. p. 62. And for a fourth we may refer to the ἔκθεσις τῆς κατὰ μέρος πίστεως ascribed to S. Gregory Thaumaturgus, one of the Antiochene Fathers, but which according to Eulogius ap Phot. ccd. 230. p. 846. is an Apollinarian forgery; it too uses the word "persona" of the union of natures in our Lord. And for a fifth to the Serm. in S. Thomam, which is quoted by the 6th General Council as S. Chrysostom's, but which Montfaucon and his other Editors consider spurious, and Tillemont considers preached at Edessa, A.D. 402. It contains the word πρόσωπον. Ed. Ben. tom. 8. part 2. p. 14.

(6.) Too many words would have been spent on this point, were it not for the eminent writers who have maintained the genuineness of the Creed in question; and in particular, were it not for the circumstance, which is at first sight of great cogency, that Tertullian, whose acquaintance with Greek theology is well known, not only contains in his contr. Prax. a fully developed statement of the ecclesiastical doctrine of the Incarnation, but uses the very word *persona* or πρόσωπον which has here been urged in disproof of the genuineness of the Creed under consideration.

Such passages shall here be subjoined as contain the word in its ecclesiastical sense, as far as I have met with them

In the extracts of the letters of Apollinaris and his disciples who wrote against each other (A.D. 380) the word occurs ap. Leont. p. 1033. b. p. 1037 b. p 1039. b. as well as the ὁμοούσιον ἡμῖν as noticed above.

Also in an extract of Apollinaris, ap Theod. Eranist. ii p. 173.

By an auctor against the Arians whom Sirmond called antiquissimus. Opp. t. i. p. 223.

By S. Athanasius, that is, as quoted by Euthymius ap Petav. Incarn. iii 15, note 19.

By S Gregory Nyss ap. Damasc. contr. Jacob. t. i. p. 424.

By S. Amphilochius, ap. Damasc. ibid. et ap. Anast. Hod. 10. p. 162 and ap. Ephrem ap. Phot. p. 828

In a Greek Version of S. Ambrose, ap. Phot. p. 805.

By S. Chrysostom, Ep. ad Cæsar. fin.

By Isidore Pelus, p. 94. Epist. i. 360.

In Pelagius's Creed, A.D. 418. in S. August. Opp. t. 12. p. 210.

By S. Augustine, contr Serm. Arian. 8. Ep. ad Volusian. 137. n. 11. de Corr. et Grat. 30.

By Proclus ad Armen. p. 613.

After the third General Council, A.D. 431, of course the word becomes common.

(7.) It may be objected, that Paul of Samosata himself maintained a Nestorian doctrine, and that this would naturally lead to the adoption of the word πρόσωπον to represent our Lord's unity in His two natures, as it had already been adopted 60 years before by Hippolytus to denote His Divine subsistence against Noetus. But there is no good evidence of Paul's doctrine being of this nature, though it seems to have tended to Nestorianism in his followers. I allude to a passage in Athan. Orat iv. §. 30.

where he says, that some of the Samosatenes so interpreted Acts x. as if the Word was sent to "preach peace through Jesus Christ" As far as the fragments of the Antiochene Acts state or imply, he taught more or less, as follows.—that the Son's pre-existence was only in the divine foreknowledge, Routh Rell. t 2. p. 466. that to hold His substantial pre-existence was to hold two Gods, ibid. p 467. that He was, if not an instrument, an impersonal attribute, p. 469. that His manhood was not " unalterably made one with the Godhead," p 473. " that the Word and Christ were not one and the same," p. 474. that Wisdom was in Christ as in the prophets, only more abundantly, as in a temple; that He who appeared was not Wisdom, p. 475. in a word as it is summed up, p. 484. that " Wisdom was born with the manhood, not substantially, but according to quality." vid. also p. 476. 485. All this plainly shews that he held that our Lord's personality was in His Manhood, but does not shew that he held a second personality in His godhead; rather he considered the Word impersonal, though the Fathers in Council urge upon him that he ought to hold two Sons, one from eternity, and one in time, p. 485.

NOTE II. ON COUNC. ARIM. AND SELEU.

Accordingly the Synodal Letter after his deposition speaks of him as holding that Christ came not from Heaven, but from beneath. Euseb. Hist. vii. 30. S. Athanasius's account of his doctrine is altogether in accordance, (vid. supr. p 16, note i.) that Paul taught that our Lord was a mere man, and that He was advanced to His divine power, ἐκ προκοπῆς.

However, since there was a great correspondence between Paul and Nestorius, (except in the doctrine of the personality and eternity of the Word, which the Arian controversy determined and the latter held,) it was not unnatural that reference should be made to the previous heresy of Paul and its condemnation when that of Nestorius was on trial. Yet the Contestatio against Nestorius which commences the Acts of the Council of Ephesus, Harduin. Conc. t. i. p. 1272. and which draws out distinctly the parallel between them, says nothing to shew that Paul held a double personality. And though Anastasius tells us, Hodeg. c. 7. p. 108. that the "holy Ephesian Council shewed that the tenets of Nestorius agreed with the doctrine of Paul of Samosata," yet in c. 20. p. 323, 4 he shews us what he means by saying that Artemon also before Paul " divided Christ in two." Ephrem of Antioch too says that Paul held that " the Son before ages was one, and the Son in the last time another." ap. Phot. p. 814. but he seems only referring to the words of the Antiochene Acts, quoted above. Again, it is plain from what Vigilius says in Eutych. t. v. p. 731. Ed. Col. 1618. (the passage is omitted in Ed. Par. 1624.) that the Eutychians considered that Paul and Nestorius differed; the former holding that our Lord was a mere man, the latter a mere man only till He was united to the Word. And Marius Mercator says, " Nestorius circa Verbum Dei, *non* ut Paulus sentit, qui non substantivum, sed prolatitium potentiæ Dei efficax Verbum esse definit." p. 50. Ibas, and Theodore of Mopsuestia, though more suspicious witnesses, say the same, vid. Facund. vi. 3. iii. 2. and Leontius de Sectis, iii. p. 504

176 *Alleged Confession of Antioch against Paul of Samosata.*

NOTE II. ON COUNC. ARIM. AND SELEU.

The principal evidence in favour of Paul's Nestorianism consists in the Letter of Dionysius to Paul and his answer to Paul's Ten Questions, which are certainly spurious, as on other grounds, so on some of those here urged against the professed Creed of Antioch, but which Dr. Burton in his excellent remarks on Paul's opinions, Bampton Lectures, No. 102, admits as genuine. And so does the accurate and cautious Tillemont, who in consequence is obliged to believe that Paul held Nestorian doctrines; also Bull, Fabricius, Natalis Alexander, &c. In holding these compositions to be certainly spurious, I am following Valesius, Harduin, Montfaucon, Pagi, Mosheim, Cave, Routh, and others.

It might be inquired in conclusion, whether after all the Creed does not contain marks of Apollinarianism in it, which, if answered in the affirmative, would tend to fix its date. As, however, this would carry us further still from our immediate subject in this Volume, it has been judged best not to enter upon the question. Some indulgence may fairly be asked for what has been already said, from its bearing upon the history of the word ὁμοούσιον.

FOUR DISCOURSES OF S. ATHANASIUS,

ARCHBISHOP OF ALEXANDRIA,

AGAINST THE ARIANS.

DISCOURSE I.

CHAP. I.

INTRODUCTION.

Reason for writing; certain persons indifferent about Arianism; Arians not Christians, because sectaries always take the name of their founder.

1. OF all other heresies which have departed from the truth it is acknowledged, that they have but devised[a] a madness[1], and their irreligiousness[2] has long since become notorious to all men. For, that[b] their authors went out from us, it plainly follows, as the blessed John has written, that they neither thought nor now think with us. Wherefore, as saith[2] the Saviour, in that they gather not with us, they scatter with the devil, and keep an eye on those who slumber, that, by this second sowing[3] of their own mortal poison, they may have companions in death. But, whereas one heresy and that the

CHAP.
I.
§. 1.
¹ p. 2,
note e.
p. 91,
note q.
² p 1,
note a.
³ p 5,
note k.

---

[1] ἐπινοῆσαι. This is almost a technical word, and has occurred again and again already, as descriptive of heretical teaching in opposition to the received traditionary doctrine. It is also found *passim* in other writers Thus Socrates. speaking of the decree of the Council of Alexandria, 362, against Apollinaris, " for not originating, ἐπινοήσαντες, any *novel* devotion, did they introduce it into the Church, but what from the beginning the *Ecclesiastical Tradition* declared." Hist. iii 7. The sense of the word ἐπίνοια which will come into consideration below, is akin to this, being the view taken by the mind of an object independent of (whether or not correspondent to) the object itself.

[b] τὸ γὰρ ἐξελθεῖν ... δῆλον ἂν εἴη, 1 e τῷ and so intr. § 43. τὸ δὲ καὶ προσκυνεῖσθαι .... δῆλον ἂν εἴη

N

178 *Arians, unlike former heretics, appeal to Scripture.*

Disc. I.
¹ p. 79, note q.

last, which has now risen as harbinger¹ of Antichrist, the Arian, as it is called, considering that other heresies, her elder sisters, have been openly proscribed, in her cunning and profligacy, affects to array herself in Scripture language[c], like her father the devil, and is forcing her way back into the Church's paradise,—that with the pretence of Christianity, her smooth sophistry (for reason she has none) may deceive men into wrong thoughts of Christ,—nay, since she hath already seduced certain of the foolish, not only to corrupt their ears, but even to take and eat with Eve, till in their ignorance which ensues they think bitter sweet, and admire this loathsome heresy, on this account I have thought

Job 41, 4. Sept.

it necessary, at your request, to unrip *the folds of its breastplate*, and to shew the ill-savour of its folly. So while those who are far from it, may continue to shun it, those whom it has deceived may repent; and, opening the eyes of their heart, may understand that darkness is not light, nor falsehood truth, nor Arianism good; nay, that those[d] who call

---

[c] vid. infr §. 4 fin. That heresies before the Arian appealed to Scripture we learn from Tertullian, de Præscr. 42. who warns Catholics against indulging themselves in their own view of isolated texts against the voice of the Catholic Church. vid. also Vincentius, who specifies *obiter* Sabellius and Novatian Commonit 2. Still Arianism was contrasted with other heresies on this point, as in these two respects; (1.) they appealed to a *secret tradition*, unknown n. even to most of the Apostles, as the Gnostics, Iren. Hær. iii. 1. or they professed a gift of prophecy introducing fresh *revelations*, as Montanists, supr. p. 78. and Manichees, Aug contr. Faust. xxxii 6. (2) The Arians availed themselves of certain texts as objections, argued keenly and plausibly from them, and would not be driven from them. Orat. ii. §. 18. c. Epiph Hær. 69. 15. Or rather they took some words of Scripture, and made their own deductions from them; viz. " Son," " made," " exalted," &c. " Making their private irreligiousness as if a rule, they misinterpret all the divine oracles by it." Orat 1. §. 52. vid. also Epiph. Hær. 76 5 fin. Hence we hear so much of their θρυλληταὶ φωναί, λέξεις, ἴση, ῥητὰ, sayings in general circulation, which were commonly founded on some particular text e. g. infr. §. 22. " amply providing themselves with words of craft, they used to go about,&c περιήρχοντο "vid supr p 22. note y. Also ἄνω καὶ κάτω περιφέροντες, de decr. §. 13. τῷ ῥητῷ τεθρυλλήκασι τὰ πανταχοῦ Orat. ii. §. 18. τὸ πολυθρύλλητον σόφισμα, Basil. contr. Eunom ii. 14 τὴν πολυθρύλλητον διαλεκτικὴν, Nyssen contr Eun iii p 125. τὴν θρυλουμένην ἀπορροήν Cyril. Dial iv p.505. τὴν πολυθρυλλητὸν φωνήν. Socr ii. 43.

[d] These Orations or Discourses seem written to shew the vital importance of the point in controversy, and the unchristian character of the heresy, without reference to the word ὁμοούσιον. He has insisted in the works above translated, p. 130, ref. 2. that the enforcement of the symbol was but the rejection of the heresy, and accordingly he is here content to bring out the Catholic sense, as feeling that, if persons understood and embraced it, they would not scruple at the word. He seems to allude to what may be called the liberal or indifferent feeling as swaying the person for whom he writes, also infr. §. 7 fin. §. 9. §. 10 init. § 15 fin. §. 17. §. 21. § 23. He mentions in Apollin. 1. 6 one Rhetorius, who was an Egyptian, whose opinion, he says, it was " fearful to mention." S. Augustine

Arians for Christ follow Arius.

these men Christians, are in great and grievous error, as neither having studied Scripture, nor understanding Christianity at all, and the faith which it contains.

2. For what have they discovered in this heresy like to the religious Faith, that they vainly talk as if its supporters said no evil? This in truth is to call even Caiaphas[1] a Christian, and to reckon the traitor Judas still among the Apostles, and to say that they who asked Barabbas instead of the Saviour did no evil, and to recommend Hymenæus and Alexander as right-minded men, and as if the Apostle slandered them. But neither can a Christian bear to hear this, nor can he consider the man who dared to say it sane in his understanding. For with them for Christ is Arius, as with the Manichees Manichæus; and for Moses and the other saints they have made the discovery of one Sotades[2], a man whom even Gentiles laugh at, and of the daughter of Herodias. For of the one has Arius imitated the dissolute and effeminate tone, in the Thalias which he has written after him; and the other he has rivalled in her dance, reeling and frolicking in his blasphemies against the Saviour; till the victims of his heresy lose their wits and go foolish, and change the Name of the Lord of glory into the likeness of the *image of corruptible man*[3], and for Christians[4] come to be called Arians, bearing this badge of their irreligion.

3. For let them not excuse themselves; nor retort their disgrace on those who are not as they, calling Christians after the names of their teachers[e], that themselves may appear

Marginal references: CHAP. I. §. 2. [1] deDecr. § 2, p. 4. §. 24, p. 41. §. 27, p. 48. [2] p. 94, note a. [3] vid. Hil. de Trin. viii. 28. Rom. 1, 25. [4] p. 27, note h.

---

tells us that this man taught that " all heresies were in the right path, and spoke truth," " which," he adds, " is so absurd as to seem to me incredible." Hær. 72. vid. also Philastr. Hær 91.

[e] He seems to allude to Catholics being called Athanasians, vid. however p. 181, ref. 1. Two distinctions are drawn between such a title as applied to Catholics, and again to heretics, when they are taken by Catholics as a *note against them.* S. Augustine says, "*Arians* call Catholics Athanasians or Homousians, *not other heretics too.* But ye not only by Catholics *but also by heretics,* those who agree with you and those who disagree, are called

Pelagians, as *even by heresies* are Arians called Arians. But ye, and ye only, call us Traducianists, as Arians call us Homousians, as Donatists Macarians, as Manichees Pharisees, and as the other heretics use various titles." Op. imp. i. 75. It may be added that the heretical name *adheres,* the Catholic dies away. S Chrysostom draws a second distinction, " Are we divided from the Church? have we heresiarchs? are we called from man? is there any leader to us, as to one there is Marcion, to another Manichæus, to another Arius, to another some other author of heresy? for if we too have the name of any, still it is not those who began the heresy, *but our superiors*

180 *Self-condemned in that they are called after Arius*

Disc. I.

to have that Name in the same way. Nor let them make a jest of it, when they feel shame at their disgraceful appellation; rather, if they be ashamed, let them hide their faces, or let them recoil from their own irreligion. For never at any time did Christian people take their title from the Bishops[1] among them, but from the Lord, on whom we rest our faith. Thus, though the blessed Apostles have become our teachers, and have ministered the Saviour's Gospel, yet not from them have we our title, but from Christ we are and are named Christians. But for those who derive the faith which they profess from others, good reason is it they should §. 3. bear their name, whose property they have become[f]. Yes

[1] vid. however p. 179, note e, fin

and governors of the Church. We have not ' teachers upon earth,' " &c in Act. Ap. Hom 33 fin.

[f] vid. foregoing note. Also " Let us become His disciples and learn to live according to Christianity; for whoso is called by other name beside this, is not of God."Ignat. ad Magn.10 Hegisippus speaks of " Menandrians, and Marcionites, and Carpocratians, and Valentinians, and Basilidians, and Saturnilians," who " each in his own way and that a different one brought in his own doctrine." Euseb. Hist iv. 22. "There are, and there have been, my friends, many who have taught atheistic and blasphemous words and deeds, coming in the Name of Jesus; and they are called by us from the appellation of the men, whence each doctrine and opinion began.... Some are called Marcians, others Valentinians, others Basilidians, others Saturnilians," &c. Justin. Tryph. 35 " They have a name from the author of that most impious opinion Simon, being called Simonians." Iren. Hær 1. 23. " When men are called Phrygians, or Novatians, or Valentinians, or Marcionites, or Anthropians, or by any other name, they cease to be Christians; for they have lost Christ's Name, and clothe themselves in human and foreign titles." Lact Inst iv. 30. " A. How are you a Christian, to whom it is not even granted to bear the name of Christian? for you are not called Christian but Marcionite. M. And you are called of the Catholic Church, therefore ye are not Christians either. A Did we profess man's name, you would have spoken to the point, but if we are called from being all over the world, what is there bad in this?" Adamant. Dial. §. 1. p. 809. " We never heard of Petrines, or Paulines, or Bartholomeans, or Thaddeans, but from the first there was one preaching of all the Apostles, not preaching them, but Christ Jesus the Lord. Wherefore also they all gave one name to the Church, not their own, but that of their Lord Jesus Christ, since they began to be called Christians first at Antioch; which is the sole Catholic Church, having nought else but Christ's, being a Church of Christians, not of Christs, but of Christians; He being one, they from that one being called Christians. After this Church and her preachers, all others are no longer of the same character, making show by their own epithets, Manichæans, and Simonians, and Valentinians, and Ebionites." Epiph. Hær. 42. p. 366. " This is the fearful thing, that they change the name of Christians of the Holy Church, which hath no epithet but the name of Christ alone, and of Christians, to be called by the name of Audius, ' &c. ibid. 70. 15. vid. also Hær. 75. 6 fin. " Since one might properly and truly say that there is a ' Church of evil doers,' I mean the meetings of the heretics, the Marcionists, and Manichees, and the rest, the faith hath delivered to thee by way of security the Article ' And in One Holy Catholic Church,' that thou mayest avoid their wretched meetings; and ever abide with the Holy Church Catholic, in which thou wast regenerated. And if ever thou art sojourning in any city, inquire not simply where the Lord's House is, (for the sects of the profane also make an attempt to call their own dens, houses of the Lord,) nor merely where the

as other heretics after their leaders. 181

surely; while all of us are and are called Christians after Christ, Marcion broached a heresy time since and was cast out; and those who continued with the Bishop who ejected him remained Christians; but those who followed Marcion, were called Christians no more, but henceforth Marcionites. Thus Valentinus also, and Basilides, and Manichæus, and Simon Magus, have imparted their own name to their followers; and are accosted as Valentinians, or as Basilidians, or as Manichees, or as Simonians; and others, Cataphrygians from Phrygia, and from Novatus Novatians. So too Meletius, when ejected by Peter the Bishop and Martyr, called his party, no longer Christians, but Meletians [g]; and so in consequence when Alexander of blessed memory had cast out Arius, those who remained with Alexander, remained Christians; but those who went out with Arius, left the Saviour's Name to us who were with Alexander, and as to them they were henceforward denominated Arians. Behold then, after Alexander's death too, those who communicate with his successor Athanasius, and those with whom the said Athanasius communicates, are instances of the same rule; none of them bear his name [i], nor is he named from them, but all in like manner, and as is usual, are called Christians. For though we have a succession of teachers and become

CHAP. I.

i vid. however p. 179, note e.

Church is, but where is the Catholic Church. For this is the peculiar name of this Holy Body," &c. Cyril. Cat. xviii. 26. "Were I by chance to enter a populous city, I should in this day find Marcionites, Apollinarians, Cataphrygians, Novatians, and other such, who called themselves Christian; by what surname should I recognise the congregation of my own people, were it not called Catholic?.... Certainly that word 'Catholic' is not borrowed from man, which has survived through so many ages, nor has the sound of Marcion or Apelles or Montanus, nor takes heretics for its authors ..Christian is my name, Catholic my surname." Pacian. Ep. 1. "If you ever hear those who are called Christians, named, not from the Lord Jesus Christ, but from some one else, say Marcionites, Valentinians, Mountaineers, Campestrians, know that it is not Christ's Church, but the syna-

gogue of Antichrist." Jerom. adv. Lucif. fin.
g vid. supr. p. 89, note m. Meletius was Bishop of Lycopolis in the Thebais, in the first years of the fourth century. He was convicted of sacrificing to idols in the persecution, and deposed by a Council under Peter, Bishop of Alexandria, and subsequently martyr. Meletius separated from his communion, and commenced a schism; at the time of the Nicene Council it included as many as twenty-eight or thirty Bishops; in the time of Theodoret, a century and quarter later, it included a number of Monks. Though not heterodox, they supported the Arians on their first appearance, in their contest with the Catholics. The Council of Nicæa, instead of deposing them, allowed their Bishops a titular rank in their sees, but forbade them to exercise their functions.

Disc.
I.
their disciples, yet, because we are taught by them the things of Christ, we both are, and are called, Christians all the same. But those who follow the heretics, though they have innumerable successors in their heresy, yet for certain bear the name of him who devised it. Thus, though Arius be dead, and many of his party have succeeded him, yet those who think with him, as being known from Arius, are called Arians. And, what is a remarkable evidence of this, those of the Greeks who even at this time come into the Church, on giving up the superstition of idols, take the name, not of their catechists, but of the Saviour, and are henceforth for Greeks called Christians; while those of them who go off to the heretics, and again all who from the Church change to this heresy, abandon Christ's name, and at once are called Arians, as no longer holding Christ's faith, but having inherited Arius's madness.

§. 4. 4. How then can they be Christians, who for Christians are Ario-maniacs [h]? or how are they of the Catholic Church, who have shaken off the Apostolical faith, and become authors of what is new and evil? who, after abandoning the oracles of divine Scripture, call Arius's Thalias *a new wisdom?* and with reason too, for they are announcing a new heresy. And hence a man may marvel, that, whereas many have written many treatises and abundant homilies upon the Old Testament and the New, yet in none of them is a Thalia found; nay nor among the more respectable of the Gentiles, but among those only who sing such strains over their cups, amid cheers and jokes, when men are merry, that the rest may laugh; till this marvellous Arius, taking no grave pattern, and ignorant even of what is respectable, while he stole largely from other heresies, would be original in the ludicrous, with none but Sotades for his rival. For what beseemed him more, when he would dance forth against the Saviour, then to throw his wretched words of irreligion into dissolute and abandoned metres? that, while *a man,* as Wisdom says, *is known from*

vid.
Ecclus.
4, 24.

[h] vid. p. 91, note q Manes also was called mad; "Thou must hate all heretics, but especially him who even in name is a maniac." Cyril. Catech. vi. 20. vid. also ibid. 24 fin. —a play upon the name. vid. p. 114, note b.

In vain to appeal to Scripture, when doctrine is heretical. 183

the utterance of his word, so from those numbers should be seen the writer's effeminate soul and corruption of thought[1]. In truth, that crafty one did not escape detection; but, for all his many writhings to and fro, like the serpent, he did but fall into the error of the Pharisees. They, that they might transgress the Law, pretended to be anxious for the words of the Law, and that they might deny the expected and then present Lord, were hypocritical with God's name, and were convicted of blaspheming when they said, *Why dost Thou, being a man, make Thyself God*[k], *and sayest, I and the Father are one?* And so too, this counterfeit and Sotadean Arius, feigns to speak of God, introducing Scripture language[1],

CHAP. I.

John 10, 33.

[1] p. 178, note c.

---

[1] It is very difficult to gain a clear idea of the character of Arius. Athanasius speaks as if his Thalia was but a token of his personal laxity, and certainly the mere fact of his having written it seems incompatible with any remarkable seriousness and strictness. Yet Constantine and Epiphanius speak of him in very different terms, yet each in his own way, in the following extracts. It is possible that Constantine is only declaiming, for his whole invective is like a school exercise or fancy composition. Constantine too had not seen Arius at the time of this invective which was prior to the Nicene Council, and his account of him is inconsistent with itself, for he also uses the very strong and broad language about Arius quoted supr. p. 94, note a. " Look then, look all men, what words of lament he is now professing, being held with the bite of the serpent, how his veins and flesh are possessed with poison, and are in a ferment of severe pain; how his whole body is wasted, and is all withered and sad and pale and shaking, and all that is miserable, and fearfully emaciated. How hateful to see, and filthy is his mass of hair, how he is half dead all over, with failing eyes, and bloodless countenance, and woe-begone! so that all these things combining in him at once, frenzy, madness, and folly, for the continuance of the complaint, have made thee wild and savage. But not having any sense, what bad plight he is in, he cries out, ' I am transported with delight, and I leap and skip for joy, and I fly' and again, with boyish impetuosity, 'Be it so,' he says, 'we are lost.'" Harduin. Conc. t. i. p. 457. Perhaps this strange account may be taken to illustrate the words "mania" and "Ario-maniacs." S. Alexander too speaks of Arius's melancholic temperament, μελαγχολικοῖς ἡρμοσμένης δόξης κενῆς. Theod Hist 1. 3 p 741 S. Basil also speaks of the Eunomians as εἰς λαμπρὰν μελαγχολίαν παρενεχθέντας. contr. Eun. ii. 24. Elsewhere he speaks of the Pneumatomachists as worse than μελαγχολῶντες de Sp. S. 41. Epiphanius's account of Arius is as follows — " From elation of mind the old man swerved from the mark. He was in stature very tall, downcast in visage, with manners like wily serpent, captivating to every guileless heart by that same crafty bearing. For ever habited in cloke and vest he was pleasant of address, ever persuading souls and flattering, wherefore what was his very first work but to withdraw from the Church in one body as many as seven hundred women who professed virginity?" Hær. 69. 3. Arius is here said to have been tall, Athanasius, on the other hand, would appear to have been short, if we may so interpret Julian's indignant description of him, μηδὶ ἀνὴρ, ἀλλ' ἀνθρωπίσκος εὐτελὴς, "not even a man, but a common little fellow." Ep. 51. Yet S. Gregory Nazianzen speaks of him as "high in prowess, and humble in spirit, mild, meek, full of sympathy, pleasant in speech, more pleasant in manners, *angelical in person*, more angelical in mind, serene in his rebukes, instructive in his praises," &c. &c. Orat. 21. 9.

Disc. I. but is on all sides recognised as godless [k] Arius, denying the Son, and reckoning Him among the creatures.

[k] And so godless or atheist Aetius, supr. p. 81. vid. p. 3, note f. for an explanation of the word. In like manner Athan. says, ad Serap. iii. 2. that if a man says " that the Son is a creature, who is Word and Wisdom, and the Expression, and the Radiance, whom whoso seeth seeth the Father," he falls under the text, " Whoso denieth the Son, the same hath not the Father." " Such a one," he continues, " will in no long time say, *as the fool, There is no God*." In like manner he speaks of those who think the Son to be the Spirit as " without (ἔξω) the Holy Trinity, and *atheists*." Serap. iv. 6. because they really do not believe in the God *that is*, and there is none other but He. And so again, " As the faith delivered [in the Holy Trinity] is one, and this unites us to God, and he who takes aught from the Trinity, and is baptized in the sole Name of the Father or of the Son, or in Father and Son without the Spirit, gains nothing, but remains empty and incomplete, both he and the professed administrator, (for in the Trinity is the completion, [imitation,]) so whoso divides the Son from the Father, or degrades the Spirit to the creatures, hath neither the Son nor the Father, but is *an atheist* and worse than an infidel and any thing but a Christian." Serap. 1. 30. Eustathius speaks of the Arians as ἀνθρώπους ἀθέους, who were attempting κρατῆσαι τοῦ θείου ap. Theod. Hist. i. 7. p 760. Naz. speaks of the heathen πολύθεος ἀθεΐα. Orat. 25. 15. and he calls faith and regeneration " a denial of atheism, ἀθεΐας, and a confession of godhead, θεότητος, Orat. 23. 12. He calls Lucius, the Alexandrian Antipope, on account of his *cruelties*, " this second Arius, the more copious river of the atheistic spring, τῆς ἀθέου πηγῆς." Orat. 25. 11. Palladius, the Imperial officer, is ἀνὴρ ἄθεος ibid. 12.

CHAP. II.

EXTRACTS FROM THE THALIA OF ARIUS.

Arius maintains that God became a Father, and the Son was not always; the Son out of nothing; once He was not; He was not before His generation, He was created, named Wisdom and Word after God's attributes; made that He might make us; one out of many powers of God; alterable; exalted on God's foreknowledge what He was to be; not very God; but called so as others by participation; foreign in substance from the Father; does not know or see the Father, does not know Himself.

1. Now the commencement of Arius's Thalia and flippancy, effeminate in tone and nature, runs thus:—

" According to faith of God's elect, God's prudent ones,
Holy children, rightly dividing, God's Holy Spirit receiving,
Have I learned this from the partakers of wisdom,
Accomplished, divinely taught, and wise in all things.
Along their track, have I been walking, with like opinions,
I the very famous, the much suffering for God's glory;
And taught of God, I have acquired wisdom and knowledge."

And the mockeries which he utters in it, repulsive and most irreligious, are such as these [1]:—" God was not always a Father;" but " once God was alone and not yet a Father, but afterwards He became a Father." " The Son was not always;" for, whereas all things were made out of nothing, and all existing creatures and works were made, so the Word of God Himself was " made out of nothing," and " once He was not," and " He was not before His generation," but He as others " had an origin of creation." " For God," he says, " was alone, and the Word as yet was not, nor the Wisdom. Then, wishing to frame us, thereupon He made a certain one, and named Him Word and Wisdom and Son, that He might form us by means of Him." Accordingly, he says

[1] de Syn. §. 15. p. 94

that there are two wisdoms, first, the attribute coexistent with God, and next, that in this Wisdom the Son was generated, and was only named Wisdom and Word as partaking of it. " For Wisdom," saith he, " by the will of the wise God, had its existence in Wisdom." In like manner, he says, that there is another Word in God besides the Son, and that the Son again as partaking of it, is named Word and Son according to grace. And this too is an idea proper to their heresy, as shewn in other works of theirs, that there are many powers; one of which is God's own by nature and eternal; but that Christ, on the other hand, is not the true power of God; but, as others, one of the so-called powers; one of which, namely, the locust and the caterpillar[1], is called in Scripture, not merely the power, but the *great power*. The others are many and are like the Son, and of them David speaks in the Psalms, when he says, *The Lord of hosts* or *powers*. And by nature, as all others, so the Word Himself is alterable, and remains good by His own free will, while He chooseth; when, however, He wills, He can alter as we can, as being of an alterable nature. For " therefore," saith he, " as foreknowing that He would be good, did God by anticipation bestow on Him this glory, which afterwards, as man, He attained from virtue. Thus in consequence of His works fore-known[2], did God bring it to pass that He, being such, should come to be."

§. 6. 2. Moreover he has dared to say, that "the Word is not the very God;" "though He is called God, yet He is not very God," but "by participation of grace, He, as others, is God only in name." And, whereas all beings are foreign and different from God in substance, so too is " the Word alien and unlike in all things to the Father's substance and propriety," but belongs to things generated and created, and is one of these. Afterwards, as though he had succeeded to the devil's recklessness, he has stated in his Thalia, that " even to the Son the Father is invisible," and " the Word cannot perfectly and exactly either see or know His own Father;" but even what He knows and what He sees, He knows and sees "in proportion to His own measure," as we also know according to our own power. For the Son too, he says, not only knows not the Father exactly, for He fails in compre-

[1] de Syn. §. 18, p. 101. Joel 2, 25. Ps. 24, 10.

[2] p. 11, ref. 1. p. 114, note c.

hension ^a, but " He knows not even His own substance ;"— and that " the substances of the Father and the Son and the Holy Ghost, are separate in nature, and estranged, and disconnected, and alien¹, and without participation of each other²;" and, in his own words, " utterly unlike from each other in substance and glory, unto infinity." Thus as to "likeness of glory and substance," he says that the Word is entirely diverse from both the Father and the Holy Ghost. With such words hath the irreligious spoken; maintaining that the Son is distinct by Himself, and in no respect partaker of the Father. These are portions of Arius's fables as they occur in that jocose composition.

3. Who is there that hears all this, nay, the metre of the Thalia, but must hate, and justly hate, this Arius jesting on such matters as on a stage³? who but must regard him, when he pretends to name God and speak of God, but as the serpent counselling the woman? who, on reading what follows in his work, but must discern in his irreligious doctrine that error, into which by his sophistries the serpent in the sequel seduced the woman? who at such blasphemies is not transported? *The heaven*, as the Prophet says, *was astonished, and the earth shuddered* at the transgression of the Law. But the sun, with greater horror once, impatient of the bodily contumelies, which the common Lord of all voluntarily endured for us, turned away, and recalling his rays made that day sunless. And shall not all human kind

CHAP. II.

¹ p. 43, note b.
² p. 95, note d.

§. 7.

³ Ep. Encycl. 6.
Epiph. Hær.73. 1.

Jer. 2, 12. Sept.

---

^a Vid. supr p 96, note f. καταληψις was originally a Stoical word, and even when considered perfect, was, properly speaking, attributable only to an imperfect being. For it is used in contrast to the Platonic doctrine of ἰδεαι, to express the hold of things obtained by the mind through the senses; it being a Stoical maxim, nihil esse in intellectu quod non fuerit prius in sensu. In this sense it is also used by the Fathers, to mean real and certain knowledge after inquiry, though it is also ascribed to Almighty God. As to the position of Arius, since we are told in Scripture that none " knoweth the things of a man save the spirit of man which is in him," if καταληψις be an exact and complete knowledge of the object of contemplation, to deny that the Son comprehended the Father, was to deny that He was in the Father, i. e. the doctrine of the περιχωρησις. p 95, note d. or to maintain that He was a distinct, and therefore a created, being. On the other hand Scripture asserts that, as the Holy Spirit which is in God, " searcheth all things, yea, the deep things" of God, so the Son, as being " in the bosom of the Father," alone " hath declared Him." vid Clement. Strom. v 12. And thus Athan. speaking of Mark 13, 32. " If the Son is in the Father, and the Father in the Son, and the Father knows the day and the hour, it is plain that the Son too, being in the Father, and knowing the things in the Father, Himself also knows the day and the hour." Orat. iii 44.

at Arius's blasphemies be struck speechless, and stop their ears, and shut their eyes, to escape hearing them or seeing their author? Rather, will not the Lord Himself have reason to denounce men so irreligious, nay, so unthankful, in the words which He hath already uttered by the prophet Hosea, *Woe unto them, for they have fled from Me; destruction upon them, for they have transgressed against Me; though I have redeemed them, yet they have spoken lies against Me.* And soon after, *They imagine mischief against Me; they turn away to nothing.* For to turn away from the Word of God, which is, and to fashion to themselves one that is not, is to fall to what is nothing. For this was why the Ecumenical[1] Council, when Arius thus spoke, cast him from the Church, and anathematized him, as impatient of such irreligion. And ever since has Arius's error been reckoned for a heresy more than ordinary, being known as Christ's foe[2], and harbinger[3] of Antichrist. Though then so great a condemnation be itself of special weight to make men flee from that irreligious heresy[b], as I said above, yet since certain persons called Christian, either in ignorance or pretence, think it as I then said, little different from the Truth, and call its professors Christians[4]; proceed we to put some questions to them, according to our powers, thereby to expose the unscrupulousness of the heresy. Perhaps, when thus encountered, they will be silenced, and flee from it, as from the sight of a serpent.

---

[b] And so Vigilius of the heresies about the Incarnation, Etiamsi in erroris eorum destructionem nulli conderentur libri, hoc ipsum solum, quod hæretici sunt pronunciati, orthodoxorum securitati sufficeret. contr. Eutych. 1. p. 494.

CHAP. III.

THE IMPORTANCE OF THE SUBJECT.

The Arians affect Scripture language, but their doctrine new, as well as unscriptural. Statement of the Catholic doctrine, that the Son is proper to the Father's substance, and eternal. Restatement of Arianism in contrast, that He is a creature with a beginning: the controversy comes to this issue, whether one whom we are to believe in as God, can be so in name only, and is merely a creature. What pretence then for being indifferent in the controversy? The Arians rely on state patronage, and dare not avow their tenets.

1. IF then the use of certain phrases of divine Scripture changes, in their opinion, the blasphemy of the Thalia into blessing, of course they ought also to deny Christ with the present Jews, when they see how they study the Law and the Prophets; perhaps too they will deny the Law[1] and the Prophets like Manichees[a], because the latter read some portions of the Gospels. If such bewilderment and empty speaking be from ignorance, Scripture will teach them, that the devil, the author of heresies, because of the ill-savour which attaches to evil, borrows Scripture language, as a cloak wherewith to sow the ground with his own poison, and to seduce the simple. Thus he deceived Eve; thus he framed former heresies; thus he has persuaded Arius at this time to make a show of speaking against those former ones, that he may introduce his own without observation. And yet, after all, the man of craft hath not escaped. For being irreligious towards the Word of God, he lost his all at once[2], and betrayed to all men his ignorance of other heresies too[b]; and having not a particle of

CHAP. III. §. 8.

[1] p. 130, ref. 1.

[2] p. 2, note e.

---

[a] Faustus, in August. contr Faust. 11. 1. admits the Gospels, (vid. Beausobre Manich. t. 1. p. 291, &c) but denies that they were written by the reputed authors ibid xxxii. 2. but nescio quibus Semi-judæis. ibid.xxxiii.3. Accordingly they thought themselves at liberty to reject or correct parts of them. They rejected many of the facts, e. g. our Lord's nativity, circumcision, baptism, temptation, &c. ibid xxxii. 6.

[b] All heresies seem connected together and to run into each other. When the mind has embraced one, it is almost certain to run into others, apparently the most opposite, it is

truth in his belief, does but pretend to it. For how can he speak truth concerning the Father, who denies the Son, that reveals concerning Him? or how can he be orthodox concerning the Spirit, while he speaks profanely of the Word that supplies the Spirit? and who will trust him concerning the Resurrection, denying, as he does, Christ for us the first-begotten from the dead? and how shall he not err in respect to His incarnate presence[1], who is simply ignorant of the Son's genuine and true generation from the Father? For thus, the former Jews also, denying the Word, and saying, *We have no king but Cæsar*, were forthwith stripped of all they had, and forfeited the light of the Lamp, the odour of ointment, knowledge of prophecy, and the Truth itself, till now they understand nothing, but are walking as in darkness. For who was ever yet a hearer of such a doctrine[2]? or whence or from whom did the abettors and hirelings[c] of the heresy

[1] ἐνσάρκου παρουσίας.

[2] p. 12, note y.

---

quite uncertain which. Thus Arians were a reaction from Sabellians, yet did not the less consider than they that God was but one Person, and that Christ was a creature, supr. p. 41, note e. Apollinaris was betrayed into his heresy by opposing the Arians, yet his heresy started with the tenet in which the Arians ended, that Christ had no human soul. His disciples became, and even naturally, some of them Sabellians, some Arians. Again, beginning with denying our Lord a soul, he came to deny Him a body, like the Manichees and Docetæ The same passages from Athanasius will be found to refute both Eutychians and Nestorians, though diametrically opposed to each other and these agreed together, not only in considering nature and person identical, but, strange to say, in holding, and the Apollinarians too, that our Lord's manhood existed before its union with Him, which is the special heresy of Nestorius. Again, the Nestorians were closely connected with the Sabellians and Samosatenes, and the latter with the Photinians and modern Socinians And the Nestorians were connected with the Pelagians, and Aerius, who denied Episcopacy and prayers for the dead with the Arians; and his opponent the Semi-arian Eustathius with the Encratites. One reason of course of this peculiarity of heresy is, that when the mind is once unsettled, it may fall into any error. Another is that it *is* heresy; all heresies being secretly connected, as in temper, so in certain primary principles. And, lastly, the Truth only is a *real* doctrine, and therefore stable, every thing false is of a transitory nature and has no stay, like reflections in a stream, one opinion continually passing into another, and creations being but the first stages of dissolution. Hence so much is said in the Fathers of orthodoxy being a narrow way. Thus S. Gregory speaks of the middle and "royal" way. Orat. 32. 6. also Damasc. contr. Jacob. t 1. p. 398. vid. also Leon. Ep. 85. 1 p. 1051. Ep. 129. p 1254 "levissimâ adjectione corrumpitur." also Serm. 25. 1. p. 83. also Vigil. in Eutych. i. init Quasi inter duos latrones crucifigitur Dominus, &c. Novat. Trin. 30. vid. the promise, "Their ears shall hear a word behind thee, saying, This is the way, walk ye in it, *when ye turn to the right hand, and when ye turn to the left*." Is 30, 21.

[c] δωροδόκοι and so κέρδος τῆς φιλοχρηματίας, infr. §. 53. He mentions προστασίας φίλων, §. 10. And so S. Hilary speaks of the exemptions from taxes which Constantius granted the Clergy as a bribe to Arianize; "You concede taxes as Cæsar, thereby to invite Christians to a denial, you remit what is your own, that we may lose what is God's" contr. Const. 10. And again, of resisting Constantius as hostem blandientem, qui non dorsa cædit, sed ventrem palpat, non

gain it? who thus expounded to them when they were at school[1]? who told them, "Abandon the worship of the creation, and then draw near and worship a creature and a work[d]?" But if they themselves own that they have heard it now for the first time, how can they deny that this heresy is foreign, and not from our fathers[2]? But what is not from our fathers, but has come to light in this day, how can it be but that of which the blessed Paul has foretold, that *in the latter times some shall depart from the sound[3] faith, giving heed to seducing spirits and doctrines of devils, in the hypocrisy of liars; cauterized in their own conscience, and turning from the truth*[e]?

2. For, behold, we take divine Scripture, and thence discourse with freedom of the religious Faith, and set it up as a light upon its candlestick, saying:—Very Son of the Father, natural and genuine, proper to His substance, Wisdom Only-begotten, and Very and Only Word of God is He; not a creature or work, but an offspring proper to the Father's substance. Wherefore He is very God, existing one in substance[4] with the very Father; while other beings, to whom He said, *I said ye are Gods*, had this grace from the Father, only by

CHAP. III.
[1] p. 76, note 1.
de Syn. §. 9
p. 84.
[2] p. 73, note o.
1 Tim.
[4] 1. 2.
[3] ὑγιαινούσης. Socrat.
1. 6. Tit. 1, 14.
§. 9.
[4] ὁμοούσιος.

proscribit ad vitam, sed ditat in mortem, non caput gladio desecat, sed animam auro occidit ibid. 5. vid Coustant in loc. Liberius says the same, Theod. Hist. ii 13 And S Gregory Naz speaks of φιλοχρύσους μᾶλλον ἢ φιλοχρίστους Orat. 21. 21. On the other hand, Ep. Æg 22 Athan contrasts the Arians with the Meletians, as not influenced by secular views. But it is obvious that there were, as was natural, two classes of men in the heretical party,—the fanatical class who began the heresy and were its real life, such as Arius, and afterwards the Anomœans, in whom misbelief was a "mania," and the Eusebians, who cared little for a theory of doctrine or consistency of profession, compared with their own aggrandizement. With these must be counted numbers, who conformed to Arianism lest they should suffer temporal loss.

[d] vid. p. 3, note f. fin. This consideration, as might be expected, is insisted on by the Fathers, vid. Cyril. Dial. iv. p. 511, &c. v. p 566. Greg. Naz. 40. 42. Hil. Trin. viii. 28. Ambros. de fid. i. n. 69 and 104.

[e] This passage is commonly taken by the Fathers to refer to the Oriental sects of the early centuries, who fulfilled one or other of those conditions which it specifies It is quoted against the Marcionists by Clement Strom iii. 6. Of the Carpocratians apparently, Iren Hær i 25. Epiph. Hær. 27. 5. Of the Valentinians, Epiph. Hær. 31. 34 Of the Montanists and others, ibid. 48. 8 Of the Saturnilians (according to Huet) Origen in Matt. xiv. 16. Of apostolic heretics, Cyril. Cat iv. 27 Of Marcionites, Valentinians, and Manichees, Chrysost. de Virg. 5. Of Gnostics and Manichees, Theod. Hær. ii præf. Of Encratites, ibid. v. fin Of Eutyches, Ep. Anon. 190. (apud Garner Diss. v. Theod. p 901) Pseudo-Justin seems to consider it fulfilled in the Catholics of the fifth century, as being Anti-pelagians. Quæst. 22. vid. Bened note in loc. Besides Athanasius, no early author occurs to the writer of this, by whom it is referred to the Arians, except S. Alexander's Letter ap. Socr. 1 6. and, if he may hazard the conjecture, there is much in that letter like Athan.'s own writing.

participation[1] of the Word, through the Spirit. For He is the *expression* of the Father's *Person*, and *Light* from *Light*, and *Power*, and very *Image* of the Father's substance. For this too the Lord has said, *He that hath seen Me, hath seen the Father*. And He ever was and is, and never was not. For the Father being everlasting, His Word and His Wisdom must be everlasting[2].

3. On the other hand, what have these persons to shew us from the infamous Thalia? Or, first of all, let them study it themselves, and copy the tone of the writer; at least the mockery which they will encounter from others may instruct them how low they have fallen; and then let them proceed to explain themselves. For what can they say from it, but that "God was not always a Father, but became so afterwards; the Son was not always, for He was not before His generation; He is not from the Father, but He, as others, has come into subsistence out of nothing; He is not proper to the Father's substance, for He is a creature and work?" And "Christ is not very God, but He, as others, was made God by participation; the Son has not exact knowledge of the Father, nor does the Word see the Father perfectly; and neither exactly understands nor knows the Father. He is not the very and only Word of the Father, but is in name only called Word and Wisdom, and is called by grace Son and Power. He is not unalterable, as the Father is, but alterable in nature, as the creatures, and He comes short of perfect knowledge of the Father for comprehension." Wonderful this heresy, not plausible even, but making speculations against Him that is, that He be not, and every where putting forward blasphemy for blessing! Were any one, after inquiring into both sides, to be asked, whether of the two he would follow in faith, or whether of the two spoke fitly of God,—or rather let them say themselves, these abetters of irreligion, what, if a man be asked concerning God, (for *the Word was God*,) it were fit to answer[f]. For from this one question the whole case on both sides may be determined, what is fitting to say,—He was, or He was not; always, or before His birth;

---

[f] That is, " Let them tell us, is it right to predicate this or to predicate that of God, (of One who is God,) for such is the Word, viz that He was from eternity or was created," &c. &c.

eternal, or from this and from then; true, or by adoption, and from participation and in idea¹; to call Him one of things generated, or to unite Him to the Father, to consider Him unlike the Father in substance, or like and proper to Him; a creature, or Him through whom the creatures were generated; that He is the Father's Word, or that there is another Word beside Him, and that by this other He was generated, and by another Wisdom; and that He is only named Wisdom and Word, and is become a partaker of this Wisdom, and second to it?

CHAP. III.
¹ κατ' ἐπίνοιαν, vid. Orat. ii. §. 38.

4. Which of the two theologies sets forth our Lord Jesus Christ as God and Son of the Father, this with which ye have burst forth, or that which we have spoken and maintain from the Scriptures? If the Saviour be not God, nor Word, nor Son, you shall have leave to say what you will, and so shall the Gentiles, and the present Jews. But if He be Word of the Father and true Son, and God from God, and *over all blessed for ever*, is it not becoming to obliterate and blot out those other phrases and that Arian Thalia, as but a pattern of evil, a store of all irreligion, into which, whoso falls, *knoweth not that the dead are there, and that her guests are in the depths of hell.* This they know themselves, and in their craft they conceal it, not having the courage to speak out, but uttering something else². For should they speak, a condemnation would follow; and should they be suspected, proofs from Scripture will be cast³ at them from every side. Wherefore, in their craft, as children of this world, after feeding their so-called lamp from the wild olive, and fearing lest it should soon be quenched, (for it is said, *the light of the wicked shall be put out,*) they hide it under the bushel⁴ of their hypocrisy, and make a different profession, and boast of patronage of friends and authority of Constantius⁵, that what with their hypocrisy and their boasts, those who come to them may be kept from seeing how foul their heresy is. Is it not detestable even in this, that it dares not speak out, but is kept hid by its own friends, and fostered as serpents are? for from what sources have they got together⁶ these words? or from whom have they received what they venture to say⁷? Not any one man can they specify who has supplied it. For who is there in all mankind, Greek or Barbarian,

§. 10.

Rom. 9, 5.

Prov. 9, 18.

² p. 10, note u. p. 127, note g. ³ p. 53, note f.

Job 18, 5. ⁴ Ep. Æg. 18.

⁵ p. 5, note h. p. 190, note c.

⁶ συμφί-ενσαν, infra, §. 22. ⁷ p 12, note y.

O

who ventures to rank among creatures One who he confesses the while to be God, and says, that He was not till He was made? or who is there, who to the God in whom he has put faith, refuses to give credit, when He says, *This is My Beloved Son*, on the pretence that He is not a Son, but a creature? rather, such madness would rouse an universal indignation. Nor does Scripture afford them any pretext; for it has been often shewn, and it shall be shewn now, that their doctrine is alien to the divine oracles. Therefore, since all that remains is to say that from the devil came their mania, (for of such opinions he alone is sower[1],) proceed we to resist him;—for with him is our real conflict, and they are but instruments;—that, the Lord aiding us, and the enemy, as he is wont, being overcome with arguments, they may be put to shame, when they see him without resource who sowed this heresy in them, and may learn though late, that, as being Arians, they are not Christians[2].

CHAP. IV.

THAT THE SON IS ETERNAL AND INCREATE.

These attributes, being the points in dispute, are first proved by direct texts of Scripture. Concerning the " eternal power" of God in Rom. i. 20. which is shewn to mean the Son. Remarks on the Arian formula, " Once the Son was not," its supporters not daring to speak of " a time when the Son was not."

1. AT his suggestion then ye have maintained and ye think, that " there was once when the Son was not;" this is the first cloke of your views of doctrine which has to be stripped off. Say then what was once when the Son was not, O slanderous and irreligious men[a]? If ye say the Father, your blasphemy is but greater, for it is impious to say that He was " once," or to signify Him by the word " once." For He is ever, and is now, and as the Son is, so is He, and is Himself He that is, and Father of the Son. But if ye say that the Son was once, when He Himself was not, the answer is foolish and unmeaning. For how could He both be and not be? In this difficulty, you can but answer, that there was a time, when the Word was not; for your very adverb " once" naturally signifies this. And your other, " The Son was not before His generation," is equivalent to saying, " There was once when He was not," for both the one and the other signify that there is a time before the Word.

CHAP. IV. §. 11.

2. Whence then this your discovery? Why do ye, as *the heathen, rage, and imagine vain words against the Lord and*

Ps. 2, 1.

---

[a] Athan. observes that this formula of the Arians is a mere evasion to escape using the word " time " vid. also Cyril. Thesaur. iv. pp. 19, 20. Else let them explain,—" There was," *what* " when the Son was not?" or *what* was before the Son? since He Himself was before all times and ages, which He created (supr. p. 30, note n.) Thus, if " when" be a word of time, He it is who *was* " when" He *was not*, which is absurd. Did they mean, however, that it was the Father who " was" before the Son? This was true, if " before" was taken, not to imply time, but origination or beginning. And in this sense the first verse of St. John's Gospel may be interpreted " In the Beginning," or Origin, i. e. in the Father " was the Word." Thus Athan. himself understands that text, Orat iv. §. 1. vid also Orat. iii. §. 9. Nyssen. contr. Eunom. iii. p 106. Cyril. Thesaur 32. p. 312.

196   *Texts for the eternity of the Son.*

Disc. *against His Christ?* for no holy Scripture has used such
 I.   language of the Saviour, but rather "always" and "eternal"
John 1, and "co-existent always with the Father." For, *In the begin-*
 1.   *ning was the Word, and the Word was with God, and the*
      Word was God. And in the Apocalypse he[b] thus speaks;
Apoc.1, *Who is and who was and who is to come.* Now who can
 4.   rob "*who is*" and "*who was*" of eternity?" This too in
      confutation of the Jews hath Paul written in his Epistle to
Rom. 9, the Romans, *Of whom as concerning the flesh Christ, who is*
 5   *over all, God blessed for ever;* while silencing the Greeks,
Rom. 1, he has said, *The invisible things of Him from the creation of*
 20   *the world are clearly seen, being understood by the things that*
      are made, even His eternal Power and Godhead; and what
1 Cor. the Power of God is[c], he teaches us elsewhere himself, *Christ*
1, 24. *the Power of God and the Wisdom of God.* Surely in these
      words he does not designate the Father, as ye often whisper
      one to another, affirming that the Father is *His eternal*
      power. This is not so; for he says not, "God Himself is
      the power," but "His is the power." Very plain is it to
      all that "His" is not "He;" yet not something alien but
      rather proper to Him.

2 Cor. 3. Study too the context and *turn to the Lord; now the*
3,16 17. *Lord is that Spirit*[d]; and ye will see that it is the Son who

---

[b] τάδι λέγει. Our translation of the New Testament renders such phrases similarly, "he." διὸ λέγει "wherefore he saith," but in the margin "it." Eph. v. 14. εἴρηκε περὶ τῆς ἑβδόμης οὕτω. "he spake." Heb. iv. 4. And we may take in explanation "As the Holy Ghost saith, To-day," &c Heb iii 7. Or understand with Athan. διαλέγεται λέγων ὁ Παῦλος.infr. §. 57. ὡς εἶπεν ὁ 'Ιωάννης. Orat. iii. §. 30. vid. also iv. §. 31. On the other hand, "as the *Scripture* hath said," John vii. 42. "what saith the *Scripture?*" Rom. iv. 3. "that the *Scripture* saith is vain," James iv. 5 And so Athan. οἶδεν ἡ θεία γραφὴ λέγουσα. infr. §. 56. ἔθος τῇ θείᾳ γραφῇ . φησί Orat. iv. §. 27. λέγει ἡ γραφή. de decr. §. 22. φησὶν ἡ γραφή. de Syn. §. 52.

[c] Athan. has so interpreted this text, supr. p. 149. vid. Justinian's Comment for its various interpretations. It was either a received interpretation, or had been adduced at Nicæa, for Asterius had some years before these Discourses re-

plied to it, vid. supr. p. 101, and Orat. ii. §. 37.

[d] S Athanasius observes, Serap. i. 4—7. that the Holy Ghost is never in Scripture called simply "Spirit" without the addition "of God" or "of the Father" or "from Me" or of the article, or of "Holy," or "Comforter," or "of truth," or unless He has been spoken of just before. Accordingly this text is understood of the third Person in the Holy Trinity by Origen, contr. Cels. vi. 70. Basil de Sp. S. n. 52 Pseudo-Athan. de comm. ess. 6. On the other hand, the word πνεῦμα, "Spirit," is used more or less distinctly for our Lord's Divine Nature, whether in itself or as incarnate, in Rom. i. 4. 1 Cor. xv. 45. 1 Tim. iii. 16. Hebr. ix. 14. 1 Pet. iii. 18. John vi. 63, &c. Indeed the early Fathers speak as if the "Holy Spirit" which came down upon S. Mary might be considered the Word. E. g. Tertullian against the Valentinians, "If the Spirit of God

The Son is the Father's Eternal Power and Godhead. 197

is signified. For after making mention of the creation, he naturally speaks of the Framer's Power as seen in it, which Power, I say, is the Word of God, by whom all things were made. If indeed the creation is sufficient of itself alone, without the Son, to make God known, see that you fall not into the further opinion that without the Son it came to be. But if through the Son it came to be, and *in Him all things consist*, it must follow that he who contemplates the creation rightly, is contemplating also the Word who framed it, and through Him begins to apprehend the Father[1]. And if, as the Saviour also says, *No one[1] knoweth the Father, save the Son, and he to whom the Son shall reveal Him*, and if on Philip's asking, *Shew us the Father*, He said not, "Behold the creation," but, *He that hath seen Me, hath seen the Father*, reasonably doth Paul, while accusing the Greeks of contemplating the harmony and order of the creation without reflecting on the Framing Word within it; (for the creatures witness to their own Framer;) and wishing that through the creation they might apprehend the true God, and abandon their worship of it, reasonably hath He said, *His eternal Power and Godhead*, thereby signifying the Son.

CHAP. IV. §. 12.

Col. 1, 17.

vid. contr. Gent.

45—47. Mat.11, 27.

John 14, 9.

Rom 1, 20.

4. And whereas the sacred writers say, "Who exists before the ages," and *By whom He made the ages*, they thereby as clearly preach the eternal and everlasting being of the Son, even while they are designating God Himself. Thus, if Esaias says, *The Everlasting God, the Creator of the ends of the earth;* and Susanna said, *O Everlasting God;* and

Heb 1, 2.

Is. 40, 28. Sus. 42.

---

did not descend into the womb *to partake in flesh from the womb,* why did He descend at all?" de carn Chr. 19. vid. also ibid 5 and 14 contr. Prax. 26. Just. Apol. 1. 33. Iren. Hær. v. 1. Cypr. Idol. Van. 6. (p. 19. Oxf. Tr.) Lactant. Instit. iv. 12. vid. also Hilar. Trin. ii. 27. Athan. λόγος ἐν τῷ πνεύματι ἔπλαττε τὸ σῶμα. Serap. 1. 31 fin ἐν τῷ λόγῳ ἦν τὸ πνεῦμα ibid. iii. 6. And more distinctly even as late as S. Maximus, αὐτὸν ἀντὶ σπορᾶς συλλαβοῦσα τὸν λόγον, κεκύηκε. t 2. p. 309. The earliest ecclesiastical authorities are S. Ignatius ad Smyrn. init. and S Hermas (even though his date were A.D. 150.) who also says plainly, Filius autem

Spiritus Sanctus est. Past. iii 5 n. 5. The same use of "Spirit" for the Word or Godhead of the Word, is also found in Tatian. adv. Græc. 7. Athenag. Leg. 10. Theoph. ad Autol. ii 10. Iren. Hær. iv. 36. Tertull. Apol. 23. Lact. Inst. iv. 6. 8. Hilar. Trin. ix. 3. and 14. Eustath. apud Theod. Eran. iii. p 235. Athan. de Incarn. 22. (if it be Athan.'s) contr. Apoll. 1. 8. Apollinar. ap Theod. Eran. i.p. 71. and the Apollinarists passim. Greg. Naz. Ep 101. ad Cledon. p.85. Ambros. Incarn. 63. Severian. ap. Theod. Eran. ii p.167. Vid. Grot. ad Marc ii. 8. Bull. Def. F. N. 1. 2. §. 5 Constant. Præf. in Hilar. 57, &c. Montfaucon in Athan. Serap. iv. 19.

198   *Further texts for the eternity of the Son.*

Disc. I.
Bar. 4, 20. 22.
Baruch wrote, *I will cry unto the Everlasting in my days,* and shortly after, *My hope is in the Everlasting, that He will save you, and joy is come unto me from the Holy One;* yet forasmuch as the Apostle, writing to the Hebrews, says,

Hebr. 1, 3.
Who being the radiance of His glory and the Expression of His Person; and David too in the eighty-ninth Psalm, *And*

Ps. 90, 17.
Ps. 36, 9.
the brightness of the Lord be upon us, and, *In Thy Light shall we see Light,* who has so little sense as to doubt of the

[1] supr. pp. 20, 48.
eternity of the Son[1]? for when did man see light without the brightness of its radiance, that he may say of the Son, "There was once, when He was not," or "Before His generation He was not."

Ps. 145, 13.
5. And the words addressed to the Son in the hundred and forty-fourth Psalm, *Thy kingdom is a kingdom of all ages,* forbid any one to imagine any interval at all in which the Word did not exist. For if every interval is measured

[2] αἰώνων
by ages, and of all the ages[2] the Word is King and Maker, therefore, whereas no interval at all exists prior to Him[e], it

[3] αἰώνιος
were madness to say, "There was once when the Everlasting[3] was not," and "From nothing is the Son."

John 14, 6.
John 10, 14.
John 8, 12.
John 13, 13.
6. And whereas the Lord Himself says, *I am the Truth,* not "I became the Truth;" but always, *I am,—I am the Shepherd,—I am the Light,—*and again, *Call ye Me not, Lord and Master? and ye call Me well, for so I am,* who, hearing such language from God, and Wisdom, and Word of the Father, speaking of Himself, will any longer hesitate about its truth, and not forthwith believe that in the phrase *I am,* is signified that the Son is eternal and unoriginate?

§. 13.
7. It is plain then from the above that the Scriptures declare the Son's eternity; it is equally plain from what follows that the Arian phrases "He was not," and "before" and "when," are in the same Scriptures predicated of creatures. Moses, for instance, in his account of the generation of our system,

Gen. 2, 5.
says, *And every plant of the field, before it was in the earth,*

---

[e] Vid p 30, note n. The subject is treated at length in Greg. Nyss contr. Eunom. 1. t 2. Append. p. 93—101. vid. also Ambros de Fid. 1. 8—11. As time measures the material creation, so "ages" were considered to measure the immaterial, as the duration of Angels. This had been a philosophical distinction, Timæus says, εἰκών ἐστι χρόνος τῶ ἀγεννάτω χρόνω, ὃν αἰῶνα ποταγορεύομες vid. also Philon Quod Deus Immut. 6. Euseb. Laud. C. p. 501. Naz. Or. 38, 8.

and every herb of the field before it grew; for the Lord God had not caused it to rain upon the earth, and there was not a man to till the ground. And in Deuteronomy, *When the Most High divided to the nations.* And the Lord said in His own Person[1], *If ye loved Me, ye would rejoice because I said, I go unto the Father, for My Father is greater than I. And now I have told you before it come to pass, that when it is come to pass, ye might believe.* And concerning the creation He says by Solomon, *Or ever the earth was, when there were no depths, I was brought forth; when there were no fountains abounding with water. Before the mountains were settled, before the hills, was I brought forth.* And *Before Abraham was, I am.* And concerning Jeremias He says, *Before I formed thee in the womb, I knew thee.* And David in the Psalm says, *Before the mountains were brought forth, or ever the earth and the world were made, Thou art God from everlasting and world without end.* And in Daniel, *Susanna cried out with a loud voice and said, O everlasting God, that knowest the secrets, and knowest all things before they be.* Thus it appears that the phrases "once was not," and "before it came to be," and "when," and the like, belong to things generate and creatures, which come out of nothing, but are alien to the Word. But if such terms are used in Scripture of things generate, but "ever" of the Word, it follows, O ye God's enemies, that the Son did not come out of nothing, nor is in the number of generated things at all, but is the Father's Image and Word eternal, never having not been, but being ever, as the eternal Radiance[2] of a Light which is eternal. Why imagine then times before the Son? or wherefore blaspheme the Word as after times, by whom even the ages were made[3]? for how did time or age at all subsist when the Word, as you say, had not appeared, *through* whom *all things were made and without* whom *not one thing was made?* Or why, when you mean time, do you not plainly say, "a time was when the Word was not?" but you drop the word "time" to deceive the simple, while you do not at all conceal your own feeling, nor, even if you did, could you escape discovery. For you still simply mean times, when you say, "There was when He was not," and "He was not before His generation."

CHAP. IV.

Deut. 32, 8.

¹ δι' ἑαυ- τοῦ John 14, 28.

Prov 8, 23.

John 8, 58. Jer. 1, 5

Ps. 90, 1

Sus. 42.

² p. 39, note b.

³ p 108, note h. John 1, 3.

CHAP. V.

SUBJECT CONTINUED.

Objection, that the Son's eternity makes Him co-ordinate with the Father, introduces the subject of His Divine Sonship, as a second proof of His eternity. The word Son is introduced in a secondary, but is to be understood in a real sense. Since all things partake of the Father in partaking of the Son, He is the whole participation of the Father, that is, He is the Son by nature, for to be wholly participated is to beget.

Disc. I. §. 14.

1. WHEN these points are thus proved, their profaneness goes further. "If there never was, when the Son was not," say they, "but He is eternal, and co-exists with the Father, call Him no more the Father's Son, but brother ᵃ." O insensate and contentious! For if we said only that He was eternally with the Father, and not His Son, their pretended scruple would have some plausibility; but if, while we say that He is eternal, we also confess Him to be Son from the Father, how can He that is begotten be considered brother of Him who begets? And if our faith is in Father and Son, what brotherhood is there between them? and how can the Word be called brother of Him whose Word He is? This is not an objection of men really ignorant, for they comprehend how the truth lies; but it is a Jewish pretence, and that from those who, in Solomon's words, *through desire separate themselves* from the truth. For the Father and the Son were not generated from some pre-existing origin¹, that we may account Them brothers, but

Prov. 18, 1.

¹ vid. de Syn. §. 51. p. 152

ᵃ That this was an objection urged by Eunomius, has already been mentioned from S. Cyril, supr. p. 151, note z. It is implied also in the Apology of the former, §. 24. and in Basil. contr. Eunom. II. 28. Aetius was in Alexandria with George of Cappadocia, A. D. 356—8. and Athan. wrote these Discourses in the latter year, as the de Syn. at the end of the next. It is probable then that he is alluding to the Anomœan arguments as he heard them reported. vid. de Syn. l. c. where he says, "they say, *as you have written.*" §. 51. Ἀνόμοιος κατ' οὐσίαν is mentioned infr. §. 17. As the Arians here object that the First and Second Persons of the Holy Trinity are ἀδελφοί, so did they say the same in the course of the controversy of the Second and Third. vid. Athan. Serap. I. 15. IV. 2.

Our Lord eternal, because the Son.

the Father is the Origin of the Son and begat Him; and the Father is Father, and not the Son of any; and the Son is Son, and not brother.

2. Further, if He is called the eternal offspring[b] of the Father, He is rightly so called. For never was the substance of the Father imperfect[1], that what is proper to it should be added afterwards[2]; nor, as man from man, has the Son been begotten, so as to be later than His Father's existence, but He is God's offspring, and as being proper Son of God, who is ever, He exists eternally. For, whereas it is proper to men to beget in time, from the imperfection of their nature[3], God's offspring is eternal, for His nature is ever perfect[c]. If then He is not a Son, but a work made out of nothing, they have but to prove it; and then they are at liberty, as if speculating about a creature, to cry out, "There was once when He was

[1] ἀτελής
[2] ἐπισυμβαίνῃ, vid. p.
[3] infr. §. 26 fin. supr. p. 19, note s.

---

[b] In other words, by the Divine γέννησις is not meant an act but an eternal and unchangeable fact, in the Divine Essence. Arius, not admitting this, objected at the outset of the controversy to the phrase "always Father, always Son," Theod. Hist. 1.4.p.749. and Eunomius argues that, "if the Son is co-eternal with the Father, the Father was never such in act, ἐνεργὸς, but was ἀργός." Cyril. Thesaur v. p. 41. S. Cyril answers that works, ἔργα, are made ἔξωθεν, from without, but that our Lord, as St. Athanasius here says, is neither a "work" nor "from without" And hence he says elsewhere that, while men are fathers first in posse then in act, God is δυνάμει τι καὶ ἐνεργείᾳ πατήρ. Dial. 2. p. 458. (vid. supr. p. 65. note m.) Victorinus in like manner says, that God is potentiâ et actione Deus sed in æternâ, Adv. Ar. 1. p. 202. and he quotes S. Alexander, speaking apparently in answer to Arius, of a semper generans generatio. And Arius scoffs at ἀειγεννὴς and ἀγεννητογενής. Theod. Hist. 1. 4. p. 749. And Origen had said, ὁ σωτὴρ ἀεὶ γεννᾶται ap. Routh. Reliq. t. 4. p. 304. and S Dionysius calls Him the Radiance, ἄναρχον καὶ ἀειγενές. Athan. S. D. 15 S. Augustine too says, Semper gignit Pater, et semper nascitur Filius. Ep. 238. n. 24. Petav. de Trin. 11. 5. n. 7 quotes the following passage from Theodorus Abucara, "Since the Son's generation does but signify His having His existence from the Father, which He has ever, therefore He is ever begotten. For it became Him, who is properly (κυρίως) the Son, ever to be deriving His existence from the Father, and not as we who derive its commencement only. In us generation is a way to existence; in the Son of God it denotes the existence itself, in Him it has not existence for its end, but it is itself an end, τέλος, and is perfect, τέλειον." Opusc. 26.

[c] vid. foregoing note A similar passage is found in Cyril. Thesaur. v. p. 42. Dial. 11. fin. This was retorting the objection; the Arians said, "How can God be ever perfect, who added to Himself a Son?" Athan. answers, "How can the Son not be eternal, since God is ever perfect?" vid Greg. Nyssen. contr. Eunom Append. p. 142. Cyril. Thesaur. x. p. 78. As to the Son's perfection, Aetius objects ap. Epiph. Hær. 76. p. 925, 6, that growth and consequent accession from without were essentially involved in the idea of Sonship, whereas S. Greg. Naz. speaks of the Son as not ἀτιλῆ πρότερον, ἵνα τέλειον, ὥσπερ νόμος τῆς ἡμετέρας γεννήσεως. Orat. 20. 9 fin. In like manner, S. Basil argues against Eunomius, that the Son is τέλειος, because He is the Image, not as if copied, which is a gradual work, but as a χαρακτὴρ, or impression of a seal, or as the knowledge communicated from master to scholar, which comes to the latter and exists in him perfect, without being lost to the former. contr. Eunom. 11. 16 fin.

not;" for things which are generate were not, and came to be. But if He is Son, as the Father says, and the Scriptures proclaim, and "Son" is nothing else than what is generated from the Father; and what is generated from the Father is His Word, and Wisdom, and Radiance; what is to be said but that, in maintaining "Once the Son was not," they rob God of His Word, like plunderers, and openly predicate of Him that He was once without His proper Word and Wisdom, and that the Light was once without radiance, and the Fountain was once barren[1] and dry[2]? For though they pretend alarm at the name of time, because of those who reproach them with it, and say, that He was before times, yet whereas they assign certain periods, in which they imagine He was not, they are most irreligious still, as equally suggesting times, and imputing to God's nature[3] an absence of His rational Word[4].

§. 15. 3. But if on the other hand, while they acknowledge with us the name of "Son," from an unwillingness to be publicly and generally condemned, they deny that the Son is the proper offspring of the Father's substance, on the ground that this must imply parts and divisions[5]; what is this but to deny that He is very Son, and only in name to call Him Son at all? And is it not a grievous error, to have material thoughts about what is immaterial, and because of the weakness of their proper nature to deny what is natural and proper to the Father? It does but remain[6], that they should deny Him also, because they understand not how God is[7], and what the Father is, now that, foolish men, they measure by themselves the Offspring of the Father. And persons in such a state of mind as to consider that there cannot be a Son of God, demand our pity; but they must be interrogated and exposed for the chance of bringing them to their senses.

4. If then, as you say, "the Son is from nothing," and "was not before His generation," He, of course, as well as others, must be called Son, and God, and Wisdom only by participation; for thus all other creatures consist, and by sanctification are glorified. You have to tell us then, of what He is partaker[8]. All other things partake the Spirit, but He, according to you, of what is He partaker? of the Spirit? Nay, rather the Spirit Himself takes from the Son, as He Himself

To be begotten is to participate wholly.   203

says; and it is not reasonable to say that the latter is sanc- CHAP.
tified by the former. Therefore it is the Father that He par- V.
takes; for this only remains to say. But this, which is participated, what is it or whence[1]? If it be something external [1] p. 15,
provided by the Father, He will not now be partaker of the note e.
Father, but of what is external to Him; and no longer will
He be even second after the Father, since He has before Him
this other; nor can He be called Son of the Father, but
of that, as partaking which, He has been called Son and God.
And if this be extravagant and irreligious, when the Father
says, *This is My Beloved Son*, and when the Son says that Matt.
God is His own Father, it follows that what is partaken is 3, 17.
not external, but from the substance of the Father. And as
to this again, if it be other than the substance of the Son, an
equal extravagance will meet us; there being in that case
something between this that is from the Father and the
substance of the Son, whatever that be [d].

5. Such thoughts then being evidently extravagant and un- §. 16.
true, we are driven to say that what is from the substance of
the Father, and proper to Him, is entirely the Son; for it
is all one to say that God is wholly participated, and that He
begets; and what does begetting signify but a Son? And
thus of the Son Himself, all things partake according to the
grace of the Spirit coming from Him[2]; and this shews that the [2] de Decr.
Son Himself partakes of nothing, but what is partaken from the §. 31.
p. 57.

[d] Here is taught us the strict unity of the Divine Substance. When it is said that the First Person of the Holy Trinity communicates divinity to the Second, it is meant that that one Essence which is the Father, also is the Son Hence the force of the word ὁμοούσιον, which was in consequence accused of Sabellianism, but was distinguished from it by the particle ὁμοῦ, " together," which implied a difference as well as unity;—whereas ταὐτοούσιον or συνούσιον implied, with the Sabellians, an identity or a confusion. The Arians, on the other hand, as in the instance of Eusebius, &c. supr. p 63, note g. p. 116, note h. considered the Father and the Son two οὐσίαι The Catholic doctrine is that, though the Divine Substance is both the Father Ingenerate and also the Only-begotten Son, it is not itself ἀγέννητος or γεννητή; which was the objection urged against the Catholics by Aetius, Epiph. Hær. 76. 10. Thus Athan. says, de Decr §. 30 " He has given the authority of all things to the Son, and, having given it, is *once more*, πάλιν, the Lord of all things through the Word." supr. p 55. Again, " the Father having given all things to the Son, has all things *once again*, πάλιν...for the Son's Godhead is the Godhead of the Father." Orat.iii.§ 36 fin. Hence ἡ ἐκ τοῦ πατρὸς εἰς τὸν υἱὸν θεότης ἀρρεύστως καὶ ἀδιαιρέτως τυγχάνει. Expos. F 2. vid supr. p 145, note r. " Vera et æterna substantia, in se tota permanens, totam se coæternæ veritati nativitatis indulsit." Fulgent. Resp. 7. And S. Hilary, " Filius in Patre est et in Filio Pater, non per transfusionem, refusionemque mutuam, sed per viventis naturæ perfectam nativitatem." Trin. vii. 31

Father, is the Son; for, as partaking of the Son Himself, we are said to partake of God; and this is what Peter said, *that ye may be partakers*[1] *in a divine nature;* as says too the Apostle, *Know ye not, that ye are a temple of God?* and *We are the temple of the Living God.* And beholding the Son, we see the Father; for the thought[2] and comprehension of the Son, is knowledge concerning the Father, because He is His proper offspring from His substance. And since to be partaken no one of us would ever call affection or division of God's substance, (for it has been shewn and acknowledged that God is participated, and to be participated is the same thing as to beget;) therefore that which is begotten is neither affection nor division of that blessed substance. Hence it is not incredible that God should have a Son, the Offspring of His own substance; nor do we imply affection or division of God's substance, when we speak of "Son" and "Offspring;" but rather, as acknowledging the genuine, and true, and Only-begotten of God, so we believe.

6. If then, as we have stated and are shewing, what is the Offspring of the Father's substance be the Son, we cannot hesitate, rather, we must be certain, that the same[3] is the Wisdom and Word of the Father, in and through whom He creates and makes all things; and His Brightness too, in whom He enlightens all things, and is revealed to whom He will; and His Expression and Image also, in whom He is contemplated and known, wherefore *He and His Father are one,* and whoso looketh on Him, looketh on the Father; and the Christ, in whom all things are redeemed, and the new creation wrought afresh. And on the other hand, the Son being such Offspring, it is not fitting, rather it is full of peril, to say, that He is a work out of nothing, or that He was not before His generation. For he who thus speaks of that which is proper to the Father's substance, already blasphemes the Father Himself[4]; since he really thinks of Him what He falsely imagines of His offspring.

CHAP. VI.

SUBJECT CONTINUED.

Third proof of the Son's eternity, viz. from other titles indicative of His consubstantiality, as the Creator; as One of the Blessed Trinity; as Wisdom; as Word; as Image. If the Son a perfect Image of the Father, why is He not a Father also? because God, being perfect, is not the origin of a race. Only the Father a Father because the Only Father, only the Son a Son because the Only Son. Men are not really fathers and really sons, but shadows of the True The Son does not become a Father, because He has received from the Father, to be immutable and ever the same

1. THIS thought is of itself a sufficient refutation of the Arian heresy; however, its heterodoxy will appear also from the following:—If God be Maker and Creator, and create His works through the Son, and we cannot regard things which come to be, except as being through the Word, is it not blasphemous, God being Maker, to say, that His Framing Word and His Wisdom once was not? it is the same as saying, that God is not Maker, if He had not His proper Framing Word which is from Him, but that That by which He frames, accrues to Him from without[1], and is alien from Him, and unlike[2] in substance.

CHAP. VI.
§. 17.

[1] p. 43, note b.
[2] ἀνόμοιος

2. Next, let them tell us this,—or rather learn from it how irreligious they are in saying "Once He was not," and, "He was not before His generation;"—for if the Word is not with the Father from everlasting, the Trinity[3] is not everlasting; but a One[4] was first, and afterwards by addition it became a Three[5]; and so as time went on, it seems, what we know concerning God grew and took shape[6]. And further, if the Son is not proper offspring of the Father's substance, but of nothing has come to be, then of nothing the Trinity consists, and once there was not a Three, but a One; and a Three once with deficiency, and then complete; deficient, before the Son was generated, complete when He had come

[3] τριάς
[4] μονάς
[5] τριάς
[6] vid. Orat. iv. §. 13.

206 *If the Son not eternal, the Holy Trinity not eternal.*

Disc. I.

¹ p. 191, note d.

to be; and henceforth a thing generated is reckoned with the Creator, and what once was not has divine worship and glory with Him who was ever¹. Nay, what is more serious still, the Three is discovered to be unlike Itself, consisting of strange and alien natures and substances. And this, in other words, is saying, that the Trinity has a generated consistence. What sort of a worship then is this, which is not even like itself, but is in process of completion as time goes on, and is now not thus, and then again thus? For probably it will receive some fresh accession, and so on without limit, since at first and at starting it took its consistence by way of accessions. And so undoubtedly it may decrease on the contrary, for what is added plainly admits of being subtracted.

§. 18.

²deDecr. §. 31. p. 56.

3. But this is not so: perish the thought; the Three is not generated; but there is an eternal and one Godhead in a Three, and there is one Glory of the Holy Three. And ye presume to divide it into different natures; the Father being eternal, yet ye say of the Word which is seated by Him, "Once He was not;" and, whereas the Son is seated by the Father, yet ye think to place Him far from Him. The Three is Creator and Framer, and ye fear not to degrade It to things which are from nothing; ye scruple not to equal servile beings to the nobility of the Three, and to rank the King, the Lord of Sabaoth, with subjects². Cease this confusion of things unassociable, or rather of things which are not with Him who is. Such statements do not glorify and honour the Lord, but the reverse; for he who dishonours the Son, dishonours also the Father. For if theological doctrine is now perfect in a Trinity, and this is the true and only worship of Him, and this is the good and the truth, it must have been always so, unless the good and the truth be something that came after, and theological doctrine is completed by additions. I say, it must have been eternally so; but if not eternally, not so at present either, but at present so, as you suppose it was from the beginning,—I mean, not a Trinity now. But such heretics no Christian would bear; it belongs to Greeks, to introduce a generated Trinity, and to level It with things generate; for these do admit of deficiencies and additions; but the faith of Christians acknowledges the blessed Trinity as unalterable and perfect and ever what It

was, neither adding to It what is more, nor imputing to It any loss, (for both ideas are irreligious,) and therefore it dissociates it from all things generated, and it guards as indivisible and worships the unity of the Godhead Itself; and shuns the Arian blasphemies, and confesses and acknowledges that the Son was ever; for He is eternal, as is the Father, of whom He is the Eternal Word,—to which subject let us now return again.

4. If God be, and be called, the Fountain of wisdom and life,—as He says by Jeremiah, *They have forsaken Me the Fountain of living waters;* and again, *A glorious high throne from the beginning, is the place of our sanctuary; O Lord, the Hope of Israel, all that forsake Thee shall be ashamed, and they that depart from Me shall be written in the earth, because they have forsaken the Lord, the Fountain of living waters;* and in the book of Baruch it is written, *Thou hast forsaken the Fountain of wisdom,*—this implies that life and wisdom are not foreign to the Substance of the Fountain, but are proper to It, nor were at any time without existence[1], but were always. Now the Son is all this, who says, *I am the Life,* and, *I Wisdom dwell with prudence.* Is it not then irreligious to say, "Once the Son was not?" for it is all one with saying, "Once the Fountain was dry, destitute of Life and Wisdom." But a fountain it would then cease to be; for what begetteth not from itself, is not a fountain[2]. What a load of extravagance! for God promises that those who do His will shall be as a fountain which the water fails not, saying by Isaiah the prophet, *And the Lord shall satisfy thy soul in drought, and make thy bones fat; and thou shalt be like a watered garden, and like a spring of water, whose waters fail not.* And yet these, whereas God is called and is a Fountain of wisdom, dare to insult Him as barren[3] and void of His proper Wisdom. But their doctrine is false; truth witnessing that God is the eternal Fountain of His proper Wisdom; and, if the Fountain be eternal, the Wisdom also must needs be eternal. For in It were all things made, as David says in the Psalm, *In Wisdom hast Thou made them all;* and Solomon says, *The Lord by Wisdom hath formed the earth, by understanding hath He established the heavens.*

5. And this Wisdom is the Word, and by Him, as John says,

§. 19.
Jer. 2,
13.
Jer. 17,
12.

Bar. 3,
12.

[1] ἀνύ-
[1] John
14, 6.
Prov. 3,
12.

[2] p 202,
ref. 2.

Isa. 58,
12.

[3] ἄγονν

Ps. 104,
24.
Prov. 3,
19.

all things were made, and without Him was made not one thing[a]. And this Word is Christ; for *there is One God, the Father, from whom are all things, and we for Him; and One Lord Jesus Christ, through whom are all things, and we through Him.* And if all things are through Him, He Himself is not to be reckoned with that " all." For he who dares[1] to call Him, through whom are all things, one of that " all," surely will have like speculations concerning God, from whom are all. But if he shrinks from this as extravagant, and excludes God from that all, it is but consistent that he should also exclude from that all the Only-Begotten Son, as being proper to the Father's substance. And, if He be not one of the all[2], it is sin to say concerning Him, " He was not," and " He was not before His generation." Such words may be used of the creatures; but as to the Son, He is such as the Father is, of whose substance He is proper Offspring, Word, and Wisdom[3]. For this is proper to the Son, as regards the Father, and this shews that the Father is proper to the Son; that we may neither say that God was ever without His Rational Word[b], nor that the Son was non-existing[4]. For wherefore a

DISC. I.
John 1, 3.
1 Cor. 8, 6.
[1] vid. Petav. de Trin. ii. 12. § 4.
[2] de Decr. §. 30. supr. p. 54.
[3] de Decr. §. 17. p. 28.
[4] ἀνύπαρκτον

[a] The words " that was made" which end this verse were omitted by the ancient citers of it, as Irenæus, Clement, Origen, Eusebius, Tertullian, nay, Augustine, but because it was abused by the Eunomians, Macedonians, &c. as if derogatory to the divinity of the Holy Spirit, it was quoted in full, as by Epiphanius, Ancor. 75. who goes so far as to speak severely of the ancient mode of citation. vid Fabric. and Routh, ad Hippol. contr. Noet. 12.

[b] ἄλογος vid. supr. p. 25, note c, where other instances are given from Athan. and Dionysius of Rome; also p. 2, note e. vid. also Orat. iv. 2. 4. Sent. D. 23. Origen, supr. p. 48. Athenag. Leg. 10. Tat. contr. Græc. 5. Theoph. ad Autol. ii 10. Hipp. contr. Noet. 10 Nyssen. contr. Eunom. vii. p. 215. viii. pp 230, 240. Orat Catech. 1. Naz. Orat. 29. 17 fin. Cyril. Thesaur. xiv. p. 145. (vid. Petav. de Trin. vi. 9.) It must not be supposed from these instances that the Fathers meant that our Lord was literally what is called the *attribute* of reason or wisdom in the Divine Essence, or in other words that He was God merely viewed as He is wise; which would be a kind of Sabellianism. But, whereas their opponents said that He was but *called* Word and Wisdom *after* the attribute, (vid supr. p 95, note c,) they said that such titles marked, not only a typical resemblance to the attribute, but so full a correspondence and (as it were) coincidence in *nature* with it, that whatever relation that attribute had to God, such in kind had the Son,—that the attribute was His symbol, and not His mere archetype; that our Lord was eternal and proper to God, because that attribute was, which was His title, vid. Athan. Ep Æg. 14 that our Lord was that Essential Reason and Wisdom,— not *by* which the Father *is* wise, but *without* which the Father was *not* wise;— not, that is, in the way of a formal cause, but in *fact*. Or, whereas the Father Himself is Reason and Wisdom, the Son is the necessary result of that Reason and Wisdom, so that, to say that there was no Word, would imply there was no Divine Reason; just as a radiance implies a light; or, as Petavius remarks, l. c. quoting the words which follow shortly after in the text, the eternity of the Original implies the

If our Lord the Image of the Father, He is from His substance.

Son, if not from Him? or wherefore Word and Wisdom, if not ever proper to Him? When then was God without Him who is proper to Him? or how can a man consider that which is proper, as foreign and alien[1] in substance? for other things, according to the nature of things generate, are without likeness in substance with the Maker; but are external to Him, made by the Word at His grace and will, and thus admit of ceasing to be, if it so pleases Him who made them[c]; for such is the nature of things generate[2]. But as to what is proper to the Father's substance, (for this we have already found to be the Son,) what daring is it and irreligion to say that "This comes from nothing," and that "It was not before generation," but was adventitious[3], and can at some time cease to be again?

6. Let a person only dwell upon this thought, and he will discern how the perfection and the plenitude of the Father's substance is impaired by this heresy, however, he will see its extravagance still more clearly, if he considers that the Son is the Image and Radiance of the Father, and Expression, and Truth. For if, when Light exists, there be withal its Image, viz. Radiance, and a Subsistence existing, there be of it the entire Expression, and a Father existing, there be His Truth, viz. the Son[4], let them consider what depths of irreligion they fall into, who make time the measure of the Image and Countenance of the Godhead. For if the Son was not before His generation, Truth was not always in God, which it were a sin to say; for, since the Father was, there was ever in Him the Truth, which is the Son, who says, *I am the Truth.* And the Subsistence existing, of course there was forthwith its Expression and Image, for God's Image is not delineated from without[d], but God Himself hath begotten

CHAP. VI
§. 20.

[1] ἀλλο-τρίου-σίου

supr p. 150, ref. 1

[2] infr. p. 223, note 1.

[3] ἐπισυμ-βεβηκὸς p. 37, note y

[4] "the Son" omitted by Montf.

John 14, 6.

---

eternity of the Image, τῆς ὑποστάσεως ὑπαρχούσης, πάντως εὐθὺς εἶναι δεῖ τὸν χαρακτῆρα καὶ τὴν εἰκόνα ταύτης, § 20. vid. also infr § 31 de Decr. § 13 p. 21. §. 20. 23 pp. 35 40. Theod. Hist. 1. 3 p 737.

[c] This was but the opposite aspect of the tenet of our Lord's consubstantiality or eternal generation. For if He came into being at the will of God, by the same will He might cease to be, but if His existence is unconditional and necessary, as God's attributes might be, then as He had no beginning, so can He have no end, for He is in, and one with, the Father, who has neither beginning nor end. On the question of the "will of God" as it affects the doctrine, vid Orat III. § 59, &c.

[d] Athan. argues from the very name Image for our Lord's eternity. An Image, to be really such, must be an expression from the Original, not an external and detached imitation vid. supr note b. infr §. 26. p 217. Hence S. Basil, "He is an Image not made with the hand, or a work of art, but a living Image," &c supr. p 106, note d. vid. also contr Eunom II 16,17. Epiph Hær

P

it; in which seeing Himself, He has delight, as the Son Himself says, *I was His delight.* When then did the Father not see Himself in His own Image? or when had He not delight, that a man should dare to say, "The Image is out of nothing," and "The Father had not delight before the Image was generated?" and how should the Maker and Creator see Himself in a created and generated substance? for such as is the Father, such must be the Image. Proceed we then to consider the attributes of the Father, and we shall come to know whether this Image is really His. The Father is eternal, immortal, powerful, light, King, Sovereign, God, Lord, Creator, and Maker. These attributes must be in the Image, to make it true that he *that hath seen* the Son *hath seen the Father.* If the Son be not all this, but, as the Arians consider, a thing generate, and not eternal, this is not a true Image of the Father, unless indeed they give up shame, and go on to say, that the title of Image, given to the Son, is not a token of a similar substance[e], but His name[1] only. But this, on the other hand, O ye Christ's enemies, is not an Image, nor is it an Expression. For what is the likeness of what is out of nothing to Him who brought what was nothing into being? or how can that which is not, be like Him that is, being short of Him in once not being, and in its having its place among things generate?

7. However, such the Arians wishing Him to be, have contrived arguments such as this;—"If the Son is the Father's offspring and image, and is like in all things[2] to the Father, then it necessarily holds that as He is begotten, so He begets, and He too becomes father of a son. And again, he who is begotten from Him, begets in his turn, and so on

---

Disc. I. Prov. 8, 30.

§. 21.

John 14, 9.

[1] de Decr. §. 16, pp. 25. 26.

[2] ὅμοιος κατὰ πάντα, p. 115, note e. infr. §. 40. p. 237.

76, 3. Hilar Trin. vii. 41 fin. Origen observes that man, on the contrary, is an example of an external or improper image of God. Periarch, 1 2.§.6. It might have been more direct to have argued from the name of Image to our Lord's consubstantiality rather than eternity, as, e. g. S. Gregory Naz. "He is Image as one in substance, ὁμοούσιον, . . . for this is the nature of an image, to be a copy of the archetype." Orat. 36. vid. also de Decr. §. 20, 23. supra, pp. 35, 40 but for whatever reason Athan. avoids the word ὁμοούσιον in these

[e] ὁμοίας οὐσίας. And so §. 20. init. ὅμοιον κατ᾽ οὐσίαν, and ὅμοιος τῆς οὐσίας, §. 26 ὅμοιος κατ᾽ οὐσίαν, iii. 26. and ὅμοιος κατὰ τὴν οὐσίαν τοῦ πατρός. Ep. Æg 17. Also Alex. Ep. Encycl. 2. Considering what he says in the de Syn. §. 38, &c. supr. p. 136, note g, in controversy with the Semi-arians a year or two later, this use of their formula, in preference to the ὁμοούσιον, (vid. foregoing note,) deserve our attention

Why the Father only a Father and the Son only a Son. 211

without limit; for this is to make the Begotten like Him that begat Him." Authors of blasphemy, verily, are these foes of God[1]! who, sooner than confess that the Son is the Father's Image[f], conceive material and earthly ideas concerning the Father Himself, ascribing to Him severings[2] and effluences[3] and influences. If then God be as man, let Him be also a parent as man, so that His Son should be father of another, and so in succession one from another, till the series they imagine grows into a multitude of gods[4]. But if God be not, as man, as He is not, we must not impute to Him the attributes of man. For brutes and men, after a Creator has begun them, are begotten by succession; and the son, having been begotten of a father who was a son, becomes accordingly in his turn a father to a son, in inheriting from his father that by which he himself has come to be. Hence in such instances there is not, properly speaking, either father or son, nor do the father and the son stay in their respective characters, for the son himself becomes a father, being son of his father, but father of his son. But it is not so in

---

[1] The objection is this, that, if our Lord be the Father's Image, He ought to resemble Him in being a Father. S. Athanasius answers that God is not as man; with us a son becomes a father because our nature is ῥυστὴ, transitive and without stay, even shifting and passing on into new forms and relations; but that God is perfect and ever the same, what He is once that He continues to be, God the Father remains Father, and God the Son remains Son. Moreover men become fathers by detachment and transmission, and what is received is handed on in a succession; whereas the Father, by imparting Himself wholly, begets the Son; and a perfect nativity finds its termination in itself. The Son has not a Son, because the Father has not a Father. Thus the Father is the only true Father, and the Son only true Son, the Father only a Father, the Son only a Son; being really in Their Persons what human fathers are but by office, character, accident, and name; vid. supr. p. 18, note o. And since the Father is unchangeable as Father, in nothing does the Son more fulfil the idea of a perfect Image than in being unchangeable too. Thus S. Cyril. also Thesaur. 10. p. 124. And this perhaps may illustrate a strong and almost startling statement of some of the Greek Fathers, that the First Person in the Holy Trinity, considered as Father, is not God. E. g. εἰ δὲ θεὸς ὁ υἱός, οὐκ ἐπεὶ υἱὸς ὁμοίως καὶ ὁ πατήρ, οὐκ ἐστὶ πατήρ, θεὸς ἀλλ' ἐπεὶ οὐσία τοιάδε, ἥς ἐστι πατὴρ καὶ ὁ υἱὸς θεός Nyssen. t. 1 p. 915. vid. Petav. de Deo i 9 §. 13. Should it be asked, "What is the Father if not God?" it is enough to answer, "the Father." Men differ from each other as being individuals, but the characteristic difference between Father and Son is, not that they are individuals, but that they are Father and Son. In these extreme statements it must be ever borne in mind that we are contemplating divine things according to our notions, not in fact i. e. speaking of the Almighty Father, as such; there being no real separation between His Person and His Substance. It may be added, that, though theologians differ in their decisions, it would appear that our Lord is not the Image of the Father's person, but of the Father's substance, in other words, not of the Father considered as Father, but considered as God. That is, God the Son is like and equal to God the Father, because they are both the same God; vid. p. 149, note x. also next note.

the Godhead; for not as man is God; for the Father is not from father; therefore doth He not beget one who shall beget; nor is the Son from effluence¹ of the Father, nor is He begotten from a father that was begotten; therefore neither is He begotten so as to beget. Thus it belongs to the Godhead alone, that the Father is properly ^g father, and the Son properly son, and in Them, and Them only, does it hold that the Father is ever Father and the Son ever Son. Therefore he who asks why the Son has not a son, must inquire why the Father had not a father. But both suppositions are indecent and irreligious exceedingly. For as the Father is ever Father and never could be Son, so the Son is ever Son and never could be Father. For in this rather is He shewn to be the Father's Expression and Image, remaining what He is and not changing, but thus receiving from the Father to be one and the same. If then the Father change, let the Image change; for so is the Image and Radiance in its relation towards Him who begat It. But if the Father is unalterable, and what He is that He continues, necessarily does the Image also continue what He is, and will not alter. Now He is Son from the Father; therefore He will not become other than is proper to the Father's substance. Idly then have the foolish ones devised this objection also, wishing to separate the Image from the Father, that they might level the Son with things generated.

Disc. I.

¹ ἀποῤ-ῥοίας

§. 22.

² ἕστηκιν

---

^g κυρίως, vid. p 18, note o. Elsewhere Athan. says, "The Father being one and only is Father of a Son one and only; and in the instance of Godhead only have the names Father and Son stay, and are ever; for of men if any one be called father, yet he has been son of another, and if he be called son, yet is he called father of another; so that in the case of men the names father and son do not properly, κυρίως, hold " ad Serap. 1. 16. also ibid. iv. 4 fin. and 6. vid. also κυρίως, Greg Naz. Orat. 29. 5. ἀληθῶς, Orat. 25, 16. ὄντως, Basil. contr. Eunom. 1 5. p. 215

CHAP. VII.

OBJECTIONS TO THE FOREGOING PROOF.

Whether, in the generation of the Son, God made One that was already, or One that was not

1. RANKING Him among these, according to the teaching of Eusebius, and accounting Him such as the things which come into being through Him, the Arians revolted from the truth, and used, when they commenced this heresy, to go about with dishonest phrases which they had got together[1]; nay, up to this time some of them[a], when they fall in with boys in the market-place, question them, not out of divine Scripture, but thus, as if bursting with *the abundance of their heart;*—" He who is, did He make him who was not, from Him who is, or him who was? therefore did He make the Son, whereas He was, or

[1] p. 193, ref. 6.

Mat. 12, 34.

---

[a] This miserable procedure, of making sacred and mysterious subjects a matter of popular talk and debate, which is a sure mark of heresy, had received a great stimulus about this time by the rise of the Anomœans. Eusebius's testimony to the profaneness which attended Arianism upon its rise, has been given above, p. 75, note h. The Thalia is another instance of it. S. Alexander speaks of the interference, even judicial, in its behalf against himself, of disobedient women, δι' ἐντυχίας γυναικαρίων ἀτάκτων ἃ ἠπάτησαν, and of the busy and indecent gadding about of the younger, ἐκ τοῦ περιτροχάζειν πᾶσαν ἀγυιὰν ἀσέμνως. ap. Theod. Hist. 1. 3. p. 730. also p. 747. also of the men's buffoon conversation, p 731. Socrates says that "in the Imperial Court, the officers of the bedchamber held disputes with the women, and in the city in every house there was a war of dialectics" Hist. ii. 2. This mania raged especially in Constantinople, and S. Gregory Naz. speaks of " Jezebels in as thick a crop as hemlock in a field." Orat. 35. 3. vid. supr. p. 91, note q. He speaks of the heretics as " aiming at one thing only, how to make good or refute points of argument," making " every market-place resound with their words, and spoiling every entertainment with their trifling and offensive talk." Orat. 27. 2 The most remarkable testimony of the kind though not concerning Constantinople, is given by S. Gregory Nyssen, and often quoted, " Men of yesterday and the day before, mere mechanics, off-hand dogmatists in theology, servants too and slaves that have been flogged, runaways from servile work, are solemn with us and philosophical about things incomprehensible.... With such the whole city is full; its smaller gates, forums, squares, thoroughfares, the clothes-venders, the money-lenders, the victuallers Ask about pence, and he will discuss the Generate and Ingenerate ; inquire the price of bread, he answers, Greater is the Father, and the Son is subject , say that a bath would suit you, and he defines that the Son is out of nothing." t 2 p. 898.

214 As God exists without place, and creates without materials,

Disc. I.

whereas He was not[b]?" And again, " Is the Ingenerate one or two ?" and " Has He free will, and yet does not alter at His own choice, as being of an alterable nature? for He is not as a stone to remain by Himself unmoveable." Next they turn to women, and address them in turn in this womanish language; " Hadst thou a son before bearing? now, as thou hadst not, so neither was the Son of God before His generation." In such language do the disgraceful men sport and revel, and liken God to men, pretending to be Christians, but changing God's glory *into an image made like to corruptible man*[1].

Rom. 1, 23.
[1] p 179, ref. 3.

§. 23.

2. Words so senseless and dull deserve no answer at all; however, lest their heresy appear to have any foundation, it may be right, though we go out of the way for it, to refute them even here, especially on account of the women who are so readily deceived by them. When they thus speak, they should inquire of an architect, whether he can build without materials; and if he cannot, whether it follows that God could not make the universe without materials[2]. Or they should ask every man, whether he can be without place; and if he cannot, whether it follows that God is in place[3]; that so they may be brought to shame even by their audience. Or why is it that, on hearing that God has a Son, they deny Him by the parallel of themselves; whereas, if they hear that He creates and makes, no longer do they object their human ideas? they ought in creation also to entertain the same, and to supply God with materials, and so deny Him to be Creator, till they end in herding with Manichees. But if the bare idea of God transcends such thoughts, and, on very first hearing, a man believes and knows that He is in being, not as we are, and yet in being as God, and creates not as man creates, but yet creates as God, it is plain that He begets also not as men beget, but begets as God. For God does not make man His

[2] supr. p. 18. note o.
[3] de Decr. §. 11. p. 17, 18.

---

[b] This objection is found in Alex. Ep. Encycl. 2. ἐ ὢν ἐιὸς τὸν μὴ ὄντα ἐκ τοῦ μὴ ὄντος. Again, ὄντα γιγίννηκι ἢ οὐκ ὄντα Greg. Orat. 29. 9. who answers it Pseudo-Basil. contr. Eunom. iv. p. 281. 2. Basil calls the question πολυθρύλλητον, contr. Eunom. 11 14. It will be seen to be but the Arian formula of " He was not before His generation," in another shape ; being but this, that the very fact of His being begotten or a Son, implies a beginning, that is, a time when He was not; it being by the very force of the words absurd to say that " God begat Him that *was*," or to deny that " God begat Him that was *not*." For the symbol, οὐκ ἦν πρὶν γιννηθῇ, vid. note at the end of this Discourse.

pattern; but rather we men, for that God is properly, and CHAP. alone truly [1], Father of His Son, are also called fathers of our VII own children; for of Him *is every fatherhood in heaven and* [1 p 56, note k.] *earth named.* And their positions, while unscrutinized, Eph. 3, 15. have a shew of sense; but if any one scrutinize them by reason, they will but bring on them derision and mockery.

3. For first of all, as to their first question, which is such as §. 24. this, how dull and vague it is! they do not explain who it is they ask about, so as to allow of an answer, but they say abstractedly, "He who is," "him who is not." Who then "is," and what "are not," O Arians? or who "is," and who "is not?" what are said "to be," what "not to be?" for He that is, can make things which are not, and which are, and which were before. For instance, carpenter, and goldsmith, and potter, each, according to his own art, works upon materials previously existing, making what vessels he pleases; and the God of all Himself, having taken the dust of the earth existing and already brought to be, fashions man; that very earth, however, whereas it was not once, He has at one time made by His own Word. If then this is the meaning of their question, the creature on the one hand plainly was not before its generation, and men, on the other, work the existing material; and thus their reasoning is inconsequent, since both "what is" becomes, and "what is not" becomes, as these instances shew. But if they speak concerning God and His Word, let them complete their question and then ask, Was the God "who is" ever without rational Word[2]? and, whereas He [2 ἄλογος p. 208, note b.] is Light, was He ray-less? or was He always Father of the Word? Or again in this manner, Has the Father "who is" made the Word "who is not," or has He ever with Him His Word, as the proper offspring of His substance? This will shew them that they do but presume and venture on sophisms about God and Him who is from Him. Who indeed can bear to hear them say that God was ever without rational Word? this is what they fall into a second time, though endeavouring in vain to escape it and to hide it with their sophisms. Nay, one would fain not hear them disputing at all, that God was not always Father, but became so afterwards, (which is necessary for their fantasy, that His Word once was not,) considering the number of the

proofs already adduced against them, while John besides says, *The Word was*, and Paul again writes, *Who being the brightness of His glory*, and *Who is over all, God blessed for ever Amen.*

4. They had best have been silent, but since it is otherwise, it remains to meet their shameless question with a bold retort¹. Perhaps on seeing the counter absurdities which beset themselves, they may cease to fight against the truth. After many prayers ᶜ then that God would be gracious to us, thus we might ask them in turn, God who is, has He so become², whereas He was not? or is He also before His generation³? whereas He is, did He make Himself, or is He of nothing, and being nothing before, did He suddenly appear Himself? Indecent is such an inquiry, yea, indecent and very blasphemous, yet parallel with theirs; for the answer they make, abounds in irreligion. But if it be blasphemous and utterly irreligious thus to inquire about God, it will be blasphemous too to make the like inquiries about His Word.

5. However, by way of exposing a question so senseless and so dull, it is necessary to answer thus:—whereas God is, He was eternally; since then the Father is ever, His Radiance ever is, which is His Word. And again, God who is, hath from Himself His Word who also is; and neither hath the Word been added⁴, whereas He was not before, nor was the Father once without a Word. For this assault upon the Son makes the blasphemy recoil upon the Father; as if He devised for Himself a Wisdom, and Word, and Son from without⁵, for whichever of these titles you use, you denote the offspring from the Father, as has been said. So that this their objection does not hold; and naturally, for denying the Word they in consequence ask questions which are irrational⁶. As then if a person saw the sun, and then inquired concerning its radiance, and said, "Did that which is make

---

ᶜ This cautious and reverent way of speaking is a characteristic of S Athanasius "I had come to the resolution to be silent at this time, but on the exhortation of your holiness, &c. I have in few words written this Epistle, and even this hardly, of which do you supply the defects," &c ad Serap i 1 vid ii init. ad Epict. 13 fin. ad Max. init.   Præf ad Monach. "The unwearied habit of the religious man is to worship the All (τὸ πᾶν) in silence, and to hymn God his Benefactor with thankful cries,.... but since," &c. contr. Apoll. 1. init. "I must ask another question, bolder, yet with a religious intention, be propitious, O Lord, &c" Orat iii. 63 vid p 20, ref 1 p 25, note c. p. 153, note d.

that which was, or that which was not," he would be held not to reason sensibly, but to be utterly mazed, because he fancied what is from the Light to be external to it, and was raising questions, when and where and whether it were made; in like manner, thus to speculate concerning the Son and the Father and thus to inquire, is far greater madness, for it is to conceive of the Word of the Father as external to Him, and to image the natural offspring as a work, with the avowal, "He was not before His generation."

6. Nay, let them over and above take this answer to their question;—The Father who was, made the Son who was, for *the Word was made flesh;* and, whereas He was Son of God, He made Him in consummation of the ages also Son of Man, unless forsooth, after Samosatene, they affirm that He did not even exist at all, till He became man.

John 1, 14.

7. This is sufficient from us in answer to their first question; and now on your part, O Arians, remembering your own words, tell us whether He who was needed Him who was not for the framing of the universe, or Him who was? Ye said that He made for Himself His Son out of nothing, as an instrument whereby to make the universe. Which then is superior, that which needs or that which supplies the need? or does not each supply the deficiency of the other? Ye rather prove the weakness of the Maker, if He had not power of Himself to make the universe, but provided for Himself an instrument from without[d], as carpenter might do or shipwright, unable to work any thing, without axe and saw? Can any thing be more irreligious! yet why should one dwell on its heinousness, when enough has gone before to shew that their doctrine is a mere fantasy?

§. 26.

---

[d] ὄργανον, vid. p. 12, note g. p. 118, note n. p. 62, note f This was alleged by Arius, Socr. 1. 6. and by Eusebius, Eccles. Theol. 1 8. supr p. 62, note f. and by the Anomœans, supr p 12, note x

CHAP. VIII.

OBJECTIONS CONTINUED.

Whether we may decide the question by the parallel of human sons, which are born later than their parents. No, for the force of the analogy lies in the idea of connaturality. Time is not involved in the idea of Son, but is adventitious to it, and does not attach to God, because He is without parts and passions. The titles Word and Wisdom guard our thoughts of Him and His Son from this misconception. God not a Father, as a Creator, in posse from eternity, because creation does not relate to the substance of God, as generation does.

Disc. I.

1. Nor is answer needful to their other very simple and foolish inquiry, which they put to women; or none besides that which has been already given, namely, that it is not suitable to measure divine generation by the nature of men. However, that as before they may pass judgment on themselves, it is well to meet them on the same ground, thus:— Plainly, if they inquire of parents concerning their son, let them consider whence is the child which is begotten. For, granting the parent had not a son before his begetting, still, after having him, he had him, not as external or as foreign, but as from himself, and proper to his substance and his unvarying image, so that the former is beheld in the latter, and the latter is contemplated in the former. If then they assume from human examples that generation implies time, why not from the same infer that it implies the Natural and the Proper[a], instead of extracting serpent-like from the earth only what turns to poison? Those who ask of parents, and

---

[a] supr. p. 13, note u. The question was, *What* was that sense of Son which would apply to the Divine Nature? The Catholics said that its essential meaning *could* apply, viz. consubstantiality, whereas the point of posteriority to the Father depended on a condition, *time*, which could not exist in the instance of God. p. 16, note k. The Arians on the other hand, said that to suppose a true Son, was to think of God irreverently, as implying division, change, &c. The Catholics replied that the notion of materiality was quite as foreign from the Divine Essence as time, and as the Divine Sonship was eternal, so was it also clear both of imperfection or extension.

God's Son like man's, in connaturality, not in point of time. 219

say, " Hadst thou a Son before thou didst beget him ?" CHAP. VIII.
should add, " And if thou hadst a son, didst thou purchase
him from without as a house or any other possession¹ ?" And ¹ p. 21.
then thou wouldest be answered, " He is not from without, but
from myself." For things which are from without are possessions,
and pass from one to another; but my son is from me, proper
and similar to my substance², not become mine from another, ³ p. 210,
but begotten of me; wherefore I too am wholly in him, while note e.
I remain myself what I am ᵇ." For so it is; though the parent
be distinct in time, as being man, who himself has come to
be in time, yet he too would have had his child ever co-
existent with him, but that his nature was a restraint and
made it impossible. For Levi too was already in the loins of
his great-grandfather, before his own generation, and his
grandfather begot him. When then the man comes to that age
at which nature supplies the power, immediately, with nature
unrestrained, he becomes father of the son from himself. There- §. 27.
fore, if on asking parents about children, they get for answer, that
children which are by nature are not from without, but from
their parents, let them confess in like manner concerning the
Word of God, that He is simply from the Father. And if
they make a question of the time, let them say what is to
restrain God (for it is necessary to prove their irreligion

ᵇ It is from expressions such as this that the Greek Fathers have been accused of tritheism The truth is, every illustration, as being incomplete on one or other side of it, taken by itself, tends to heresy. The title Son by itself suggests a second God, as the title Word a mere attribute, and the title Instrument a creature. All heresies are partial views of the truth, and are wrong, not so much in what they say, as in what they deny. The truth, on the other hand, is a positive and comprehensive doctrine, and in consequence necessarily mysterious and open to misconception. vid. p. 43, note d. p. 140, note n. When Athan. implies that the Eternal Father is in the Son, though remaining what He is, as a man in his child, he is intent only upon the point of the Son's connaturality and equality, which the Arians denied. In like manner he says in a later Discourse, " In the Son the Father's godhead is beheld. The Emperor's countenance and form are in His Image, and the countenance of His Image is in the Emperor. For the Emperor's likeness in His Image is an unvarying likeness, $ἀπαράλλακτος$, so that he who looks upon the Image, in it sees the Emperor, and again he who sees the Emperor, recognises that He is in the Image. The Image then might say, ' I and the Emperor are one.' " Orat III. § 5. And thus the Auctor de Trin. refers to " Peter, Paul, and Timothy having three subsistencies and one humanity." 1. p. 918. S. Cyril even seems to deny that each individual man may be considered a separate substance except as the Three Persons are such. Dial. 1. p. 409. and S. Gregory Nyssen is led to say that, strictly speaking, the abstract *man*, which is predicated of separate individuals, is still one, and this with a view of illustrating the Divine Unity. ad Ablab. t. 2. p. 449. vid. Petav. de Trin. iv. 9.

220 *As Son images connaturality, so Radiance co-existence,*

Disc. I.

on the very ground on which their scoff is made), let them tell us, what is there to hinder God from being always Father of the Son; for that what is begotten must be from its father is undeniable.

2. Moreover, they will pass judgment on themselves as to all such speculations concerning God, if, as they questioned women on the subject of time, so they inquire of the sun concerning its radiance, and of the fountain concerning its issue[1]. They will find that these, though an offspring, always exist with those things from which they are[c]. And if parents, such as these, have in common with their children nature and duration, why, if they suppose God inferior to things that come to be[d], do they not openly say out their own irreligion? But if they do not dare to say this openly, and the Son is confessed to be, not from without, but a natural offspring from the Father, and that there is nothing which is a hindrance to God, (for not as man is He, but more than the sun, or rather the God of the sun,) it follows that the Word co-exists with the Father both as from Him and as ever, through whom the Father caused that all things which were not should be. That then the Son comes not of nothing but is eternal and from the Father, is certain even from the nature of the case; and the question of the heretics to parents exposes their perverseness; for they confess the point of nature, and now have been put to shame on the point of time.

[1] p. 20.

§. 28.

3. As we said above, so now we repeat, that the divine generation must not be compared to the nature of men, nor the Son considered to be part of God, nor generation to imply any passion whatever; God is not as man; for men beget passibly, having a transitive nature, which waits for periods by reason of its weakness. But with God this cannot be; for He is not composed of parts, but being impassible and simple, He is impassibly and

---

[c] The question is not, whether in matter of fact, in the particular case, the rays would issue after, and not with the first existence of the luminous body, for the illustration is not used to shew *how* such a thing may be, or to give an *instance* of it, but to convey to the mind a correct *idea* of what it is proposed to teach in the Catholic doctrine.

[d] S. Athanasius's doctrine is, that, God containing in Himself all perfection, whatever is excellent in one created thing above another, is found in its perfection in Him. If then such generation as radiance from light is more perfect than that of children from parents, that belongs, and transcendently, to the All-perfect God.

indivisibly Father of the Son[1]. This again is strongly evidenced and proved by divine Scripture. For the Word of God is His Son, and the Son is the Father's Word and Wisdom; and Word and Wisdom is neither creature nor part of Him whose Word He is, nor an offspring passibly begotten. Uniting then the two titles[2], Scripture speaks of "Son," in order to herald the offspring of His substance natural and true; and, on the other hand, that none may think of the Offspring humanly, while signifying His substance, it also calls Him Word, Wisdom, and Radiance; to teach us that the generation was impassible, and eternal, and worthy of God[e]. What affection then, or what part of the Father is the Word and the Wisdom and the Radiance? So much may be impressed even on these men of folly; for as they asked women concerning God's Son, so[3] let them inquire of men concerning the Word, and they will find that the Word which they put forth is neither an affection of them nor a part of their mind. But if such be the word of men, who are passible and partitive, why speculate they about passions and parts in the instance of the immaterial and indivisible God, that under pretence of reverence[f] they may deny the true and natural generation of the Son?

CHAP VIII.
[1] p. 19.
[2] p. 140, note n.
[3] Orat. iii. 67.

[e] This is a view familiar to the Fathers, viz. that in this consists our Lord's Sonship, that He is the Word or as S. Augustine says, Christum ideo Filium quia Verbum. Aug. Ep. 102. 11 "If God is the Father of a Word, why is not He which is begotten a Son?" de Decr §. 17. supr. p 27. "If I speak of Wisdom, I speak of His offspring." Theoph ad Autolyc. i 3. "The Word, the genuine Son of Mind" Clem Protrept. p. 58. Petavius discusses this subject accurately with reference to the distinction between Divine generation and Divine Procession. de Trin. vii. 14.

[f] Heretics have frequently assigned reverence as the cause of their opposition to the Church; and if, even Arius affected it, the plea may be expected in any other. "O stultos et impios metus," says S. Hilary, "et irreligionem de Deo sollicitudinem." de Trin. iv. 6. It was still more commonly professed in regard to the Catholic doctrine of the Incarnation. Thus Manes, About ut Dominum nostrum Jesum Christum per naturalia mulieris descendisse confitear, ipse enim testimonium dat, quia desinibus Patris descendit. Archel Disp. p. 185. "We, as saying that the Word of God is incapable of defilement, even by the assumption of mortal and vulnerable flesh, fear not to believe that He is born of a Virgin, ye" Manichees, "because with impious perverseness ye believe the Son of God to be capable of it, dread to commit him to the flesh." August. contr. Secund. 9. Faustus "is neither willing to receive Jesus of the seed of David, nor made of a woman....nor the death of Christ itself, and burial, and resurrection, &c " August. contr Faust xi. 3. As the Manichees denied our Lord a body, so the Apollinarians denied Him a rational soul, still under pretence of reverence, because, as they said, the soul was necessarily sinful. Leontius makes this their main argument, ὁ νοῦς ἁμαρτητικός ἐστι. de Sect. iv p 507 vid. also Greg. Naz. Ep. 101. ad Cledon p. 89. Athan. in Apoll. i 2. 14. Epiph. Ancor. 79. 80.

222   The Eternal Son is not of will, but of nature.

Disc. I.

4. Enough was said above to shew that the offspring from God is not an affection; and now it has been shewn in particular that the Word is not begotten according to affection. The same may be said of Wisdom; God is not as man; nor must they here think humanly of Him. For, whereas men are capable of wisdom, God partakes in nothing, but is Himself the Father of His own Wisdom, of which whoso partakes is given the name of wise. And this Wisdom is not a passion, nor a part, but an Offspring proper to the Father. Wherefore He is ever Father, nor is the character of Father adventitious[1] to God, lest He seem alterable; for if it is good that He be Father, yet He has not ever been Father, then good has not ever been in Him.

[1] ἐπιγί-γνη

§. 29.

5. But, observe, say they, God was always a Maker, nor is the power of framing adventitious to Him; does it follow then, that, because He is the Framer of all, therefore His works also are eternal, and is it wicked to say of them too, that they were not before generation? Senseless are these Arians; for what likeness is there between Son and Work, that they should parallel a father's with a maker's function? How is it that, with that difference between offspring and work, which has been shewn, they remain so ill-instructed? Let it be repeated then, that a work is external to the nature, but a Son is the proper offspring of the substance; it follows that a work need not have been always, for the workman frames it when He will; but an offspring is not subject to will, but is proper to the substance[2]. And a man may be and may be

[2] vid. Orat. iii. §. 59, &c.

Athan. &c. call the Apollinarian doctrine Manichean in consequence. vid. in Apoll. ii. 8. 9. &c. Again, the Eranistes in Theodoret, who advocates a similar doctrine, will not call our Lord man. "I consider it important to acknowledge an assumed *nature*, but to call the Saviour of the world *man* is to impair our Lord's glory." Eranist. ii. p. 83. Eutyches, on the other hand, would call our Lord *man*, but refused to admit His human *nature*, and still with the same profession. "Ego," he says, "sciens sanctos et beatos patres nostros refutantes *duarum naturarum* vocabulum, et non *audens* de natura tractare Dei Verbi, qui in carnem venit, in veritate non in phantasmate *homo* fac- tus," &c. Leon. Ep. 21. 1 fin. "Forbid it," he says at Constantinople, "that I should say that the Christ was of two natures, or should discuss the nature, φυσιολογεῖν, of my God." Concil t. 2. p. 157. And so in this day popular Tracts have been published, ridiculing St. Luke's account of our Lord's nativity under pretence of reverence towards the God of all, and interpreting Scripture allegorically on Pantheistic principles. A modern argument for Universal Restitution takes the same form; "Do not *we* shrink from the notion of another's being sentenced to eternal punishment; and *are we more merciful than God?*" vid. Matt. xvi. 22, 23.

called Maker, though the works are not as yet; but father he cannot be called, nor can he be, unless a son exist. And if they curiously inquire why God, though always with the power to make, does not always make, (though this also be the presumption of madmen, for *who hath known the mind of the Lord, or who hath been His Counsellor?* or *how shall the thing formed say* to the potter, *why hast thou made me thus?* however, not to leave even a weak argument unnoticed,) they must be told, that although God always had the power to execute, yet the things generated had not the power of being eternal [g]. For they are out of nothing, and therefore were not before their generation; but things which were not before their generation, how could these co-exist with the ever-existing God? Wherefore God, looking to what was good for them, then made them all when He saw that, when produced, they were able to abide. And as, though He was able, even from the beginning in the time of Adam, or Noe, or Moses, to send His own Word, yet He sent Him not until the consummation of the ages; for this He saw to be good for the whole creation, so also things generated did He make when He would, and as was good for them. But the Son, not being a work, but proper to the Father's offspring, always is; for, whereas the Father always is, so what is proper to His substance must always be; and this is His Word and His Wisdom. And that creatures should not be in existence, does not disparage the Maker; for He hath the power of framing them, when He wills; but for the offspring not to be ever with the Father, is a disparagement of the perfection of His substance. Wherefore His works were framed, when He would, through His Word; but the Son is ever the proper offspring of the Father's substance.

Rom. 11, 24.
Rom. 9, 20.

---

[g] Athan.'s argument is as follows: that, as it is of the *essence* of a son to be *connatural* with the father, so is it of the *essence* of a creature to be of *nothing*, ἐξ οὐκ ὄντων; therefore, while it was *not* impossible *from the nature of the case*, for Almighty God is to be always Father, it *was* impossible for the same reason that He should be always a Creator. vid. infr. §. 58. where he takes, "They shall perish," in the Psalm, not as a fact but as the definition of the *nature* of a creature. Also ii. §. 1. where he says, "It is proper to creatures and works to have said of them, ἐξ οὐκ ὄντων and οὐκ ἦν πρὶν γεννηθῇ." vid. Cyril. Thesaur. 9. p. 67. Dial. ii. p. 460. on the question of being a Creator *in posse*, vid. supra, p. 65, note m.

CHAP. IX.

OBJECTIONS CONTINUED.

Whether is the Ingenerate one or two? Inconsistent in Arians to use an unscriptural word; necessary to define its meaning. Different senses of the word If it means "without Father," there is but One Ingenerate; if "without beginning or creation," there are two Inconsistency of Asterius. "Ingenerate" a title of God, not in contrast with the Son, but with creatures, as is "Almighty," or "Lord of powers." "Father" is the truer title, as not only Scriptural, but implying a Son, and our adoption as sons.

Disc. I. §. 30.

1. THESE considerations encourage the faithful, and distress the heretical, perceiving, as they do, their heresy overthrown thereby. Moreover, their further question " whether the Ingenerate be one or two^a," shews how false are their views, how treacherous and full of guile. Not for the Father's honour ask they this, but for the dishonour of the Word. Accordingly, should any one, not aware of their craft, answer, " the Ingenerate is one," forthwith they spirt out their own venom, saying, " Therefore the Son is among things generate, and well have we said, He was not before His generation." Thus they make any kind of disturbance and confusion, pro-

---

^a The word ἀγέννητον was in the philosophical schools synonymous with "God," hence by asking whether there were two Ingenerates, the Anomœans implied that there were two Gods, if Christ was God in the sense in which the Father was. Hence Athan. retorts, φάσκοντες, οὐ λέγομεν δύο ἀγέννητα, λέγουσι δύο θεούς Orat. III. 16 also II. 38. Plato used ἀγέννητον of the Supreme God, (supr. p. 51, note b) the Valentinians, Tertull. contr. Val. 7. and Basilides, Epiph. Hær. 31 10 S. Clement uses it, supr. p. 147, note t. and S. Ignatius applies it to the Son, p 147. S. Dionysius Alex. puts as an hypothesis in controversy the very position of the Anomœans, on which their whole argument turned. ap. Euseb Præp. VII. 19. viz. that ἡ ἀγεννησία is the very οὐσία of God, not an attribute

Their view is drawn out at length in Epiph. Hær. 76 S. Athanasius does not go into this question, but rather confines himself to the more popular form of it, viz. the Son is by His very name not ἀγέννητος, but γεννητός, but all γεννητὰ are creatures, which he answers, as de Decr. §. 28. supr. p 53 by saying that Christianity had brought in a new idea into theology, viz the sacred doctrine of a true Son, ἐκ τῆς οὐσίας This was what the Arians had originally denied, ἓν τὸ ἀγέννητον ἓν δὲ τὸ ὑπ' αὐτοῦ ἀληθῶς, καὶ οὐκ ἐκ τῆς οὐσίας αὐτοῦ Euseb. Nic. ap. Theod. Hist. 1 5. When they were urged *what* according to them was the middle idea to which the Son answered, if they would not accept the Catholic, they would not define but merely said, γέννημα, ἀλλ' οὐκ ὡς ἓν τῶν γεννημάτων, vid. p. 10, note n.

vided they can but separate the Son from the Father, and reckon the Framer of all among His works. Now first they may be convicted on this score, that, while blaming the Nicene Bishops for their use of phrases not in Scripture, though these not injurious, but subversive of their irreligion, they themselves went off upon the same fault, that is, using words not in Scripture [1], and those in contumely of the Lord, knowing *neither what they say nor whereof they affirm*. For instance, let them ask the Greeks, who have been their instructors, (for it is a word of their invention, not Scripture,) and when they have been instructed in its various significations, then they will discover that they cannot even question properly, on the subject which they have undertaken. For they have led me to ascertain [2] that by " ingenerate" is meant what has not yet come to be, but is possible to be, as wood which is not yet become, but is capable of becoming, a vessel; and again what neither has nor ever can come to be, as a triangle quadrangular, and an even number odd. For neither has nor ever can a triangle become quadrangular; nor has ever, nor can ever, even become odd. Moreover, by " ingenerate" is meant, what exists, but not generated from any, nor having a father at all. Further, Asterius, that unprincipled sophist, the patron too of this heresy, has added in his own treatise, that what is not made, but is ever, is " ingenerate[b]." They ought then, when they ask the question, to add in what sense they take the word " ingenerate," and then the parties questioned would be able to answer to the point.

[1] p 31, note p. 1 Tim
[2] p. 52, note d.

2. But if they still are satisfied with merely asking, " Is the Ingenerate one or two?" they must be told first of all, as ill-educated men, that many are such and nothing is such, many which are capable of generation, and nothing is not

§ 31.

---

[b] The two first senses here given answer to the two first mentioned, de Decr. §. 28. and, as he there says, are plainly irrelevant. The third in the de Decr. which, as he there observes, is ambiguous and used for a sophistical purpose, is here divided into third and fourth, answering to the two senses which alone are assigned in the de Syn. §. 46. and on them the question turns. This is an instance, of which many occur, how Athan. used his former writings and worked over again his former ground, and simplified or cleared what he had said In the de Decr. A D. 350, we have three senses of ἀγέννητον, two irrelevant and the third ambiguous; here in Orat. 1. (358,) he divides the third into three; in the de Syn (359,) he rejects and omits the two first, leaving the two last, which are the critical senses

capable, as has been said. But if they ask according as Asterius ruled it, as if "what is not a work but was always" were ingenerate, then they must constantly be told that the Son as well as the Father must in this sense be called ingenerate. For He is neither in the number of things generated, nor a work, but has ever been with the Father, as has already been shewn, in spite of their many variations for the sole sake of testifying against the Lord, " He is of nothing" and " He was not before His generation." When then, after failing at every turn, they betake themselves to the other sense of the question, " existing but not generated of any nor having a father," we shall tell them that the Ingenerate in this sense is only one, namely the Father ; and they will take nothing by their question^c. For to say that God is in this sense Ingenerate, does not shew that the Son is a thing generate, it being evident from the above proofs that the Word is such as He is who begat Him. Therefore if God be ingenerate, His Image is not generate, but an Offspring[1], which is His Word and His Wisdom. For what likeness has the generate to the Ingenerate? (one must not weary to use repetition;) for if they will have it that the one is like the other, so that he who sees the one beholds the other, they are like to say that the Ingenerate is the image of creatures; the end of which is a confusion of the whole subject, an equalling of things generated with the Ingenerate, and a denial of the Ingenerate by measuring Him with the works; and all to reduce the Son into their number.

[1] p. 209, note d.

§. 32. 3. However, I suppose even they will be unwilling to proceed to such lengths, if they follow Asterius the sophist. For he, earnest as he is in his advocacy of the Arian heresy, and maintaining that the Ingenerate is one, runs counter to them in saying, that the Wisdom of God is ingenerate and unoriginate also; the following is a passage out of his work[a]: " The Blessed Paul said not that he preached Christ the power of God or the wisdom of God, but, without the article, *God's power and God's wisdom;* thus preaching that the proper power of God Himself, which is natural to Him and

[2] de Syn. §. 18. p. 101. infr. ii. 37.
1 Cor. 1, 24.

---

^c These two senses of ἀγένητον unbegotten and unmade were afterwards expressed by the distinction of η and ν, ἀγέννητον and ἀγένητον vid. Damasc. F. O. 1. 8. p. 135. and Le Quien's not.

co-existent with Him ingenerately, is something besides." And again, soon after: "However, His eternal power and wisdom, which truth argues to be unoriginate and ingenerate; this must surely be one." For though misunderstanding the Apostle's words, he considered that there were two wisdoms; yet, by speaking still of a wisdom co-existent with Him, he declares that the Ingenerate is not simply one, but that there is another ingenerate with Him. For what is co-existent, co-exists not with itself, but with another. If then they agree with Asterius, let them never ask again, "Is the Ingenerate one or two," or they will have to contest the point with him; if, on the other hand, they differ even from him, let them not take up their defence upon his treatise, lest, *biting one another, they be consumed one of another.*

Gal. 5, 15.

4. So much on the point of their ignorance; but who can say enough on their want of principle? who but would justly hate them while possessed by such a madness? for when they were no longer allowed to say "out of nothing" and "He was not before His generation," they hit upon this word "ingenerate," that, by saying among the simple that the Son was generate, they might imply the very same phrases "out of nothing," and "He once was not;" for in such phrases things generate and creatures are implied. If they have confidence in their own positions, they should stand to them, and not change about so variously[1]; but this they will not, from an idea that success is easy, if they do but shelter their heresy under colour of the word "ingenerate." Yet after all, this term is not used in contrast with the Son, clamour as they may, but with things generate; and the like may be found in the words "Almighty" and "Lord of the Powers[d]." For if we say that the Father has power and mastery over all things by the Word, and the Son rules the Father's kingdom, and has the power of all, as His Word, and as the Image of the Father, it is quite plain that neither here is the Son

§. 33

[1] p 84, note b.

---

[d] The passage which follows is written with his de Decr. before him. At first he but uses the same topics, but presently he incorporates into this Discourse an actual portion of his former work, with only such alterations as an author commonly makes in transcribing. This, which is not unfrequent with Athan. shews us the care with which he made his doctrinal statements, though they seem at first sight written off. It also accounts for the diffuseness and repetition which might be imputed to his composition, what seems superfluous being often only the insertion of an extract from a former work.

Disc. reckoned among that all, nor is God called Almighty and
I. Lord with reference to Him, but to those things which through the Son come to be, and over which He exercises power and mastery through the Word. And therefore the Ingenerate is specified not by contrast to the Son, but to the things which through the Son come to be. And excellently: since God is not as things generate, but is their Creator and Framer through the Son. And as the word "Ingenerate" is specified relatively to things generate, so the word "Father" is indicative of the Son. And he who names God Maker and Framer and Ingenerate, regards and apprehends things created and generated; and he who calls God Father, thereby conceives and contemplates the Son. And hence one might marvel at the obstinacy which is added to their irreligion, that, whereas the term "ingenerate" has the aforesaid good sense, and admits of being used religiously [1], they, in their own heresy, bring it forth for the dishonour of the Son, not having read that he who honoureth the Son honoureth the Father, and he who dishonoureth the Son, dishonoureth the Father. If they had any concern at all [e] for reverent speaking and the honour due to the Father, it became them rather, and this were better and higher, to acknowledge and call God Father, than to give Him this name. For, in calling God ingenerate, they are, as I said before, calling Him from His works, and as Maker only and Framer, supposing that hence they may imply that the Word is a work after their own pleasure. But that He who calls God Father, names Him from the Son, being well aware that if there be a Son, of necessity through that Son all things generate were created. And they, when they call Him Ingenerate, name Him only from His works, and know not the Son any more than the Greeks; but He who calls God Father, names Him from the Word, and knowing the Word, He acknowledges Him to be Framer of all, and understands that through Him all things were made.

[1] de Syn § 47 p 147. vid. John 5, 23.

§. 34. 5. Therefore it is more pious and more accurate to denote God from the Son and call Him Father, than to name Him from His works only and call Him Ingenerate [f]. For the

[e] Here he begins a close transcript of the de Decr §. 30. supr. p. 55. the last sentence, however, of the paragraph being an addition

[f] The arguments against the word Ingenerate here brought together are also found in Basil, contr. Eunom 1. 5. p 215. Greg. Naz Orat. 31. 23. Epiph.

Ingenerate not a word of Scripture. 229

latter title, as I have said, does nothing more than refer to all the works, individually and collectively, which have come to be at the will of God through the Word; but the title Father, has its significance and its bearing¹ only from the Son. ¹ἵσταται And, whereas the Word surpasses things generate, by so much and more doth calling God Father surpass the calling Him Ingenerate. For the latter is unscriptural and suspicious, because it has various senses; so that, when a man is asked concerning it, his mind is carried about to many ideas; but the word Father is simple and scriptural, and more accurate, and only implies the Son. And "Ingenerate" is a word of the Greeks, who know not the Son; but "Father," has been acknowledged and vouchsafed by our Lord. For He, knowing Himself whose Son He was, said, *I am in the Father, and the Father is in Me, and He that hath seen Me, hath seen the Father,* and *I and the Father are One*ᵍ; but no where is He found to call the Father Ingenerate. Moreover, when He teaches us to pray, He says not, "When ye pray, say, O God Ingenerate," but rather, *When ye pray, say, Our Father, which art in heaven.* And it was ²· His will that the Summary² of our faith should have the same bearing, in bidding us be baptized, not into the name of Ingenerate and generate, nor into the name of Creator and creature, but into the Name of Father, Son, and Holy Ghost. For with such an initiation we too, being of the works, are made sons, and using the name of the Father, acknowledge from that name the Word in the Father Himself also ʰ. A vain thing then is their argument about the term "Ingenerate," as is now proved, and nothing more than a fantasy.

CHAP. IX.

John 14, 10 9. 10, 30.

Luke 11, 2.
² p 123, ref. 1.

Hær. 76. p. 941. Greg. Nyss. contr. Eunom. vi. p. 192. &c Cyril. Dial. ii. Pseudo-Basil. contr. Eunom. iv. p. 283.

ᵍ These three texts are found together frequently in Athan. particularly in Orat. iii. where he considers the doctrines of the "Image" and the περιχώρησις. vid. de Decr. §. 21. §. 31. de Syn. §. 45. Orat iii. 3. 5. 6. 10. 16 fin. 17. Ep. Æg. 13. Sent. D.

26 ad Afr. 7 8. 9. vid. also Epiph. Hær. 64. 9 Basil Hexaem. ix. fin. Cyr. Thes. xii. p. 111. Potam. Ep. ap. Dacher. t 3 p 299. Hil. Trin. vii. 41. et supr Vid. also Animadv in Eustath. Ep. ad Apoll Rom. 1796. p. 58.

ʰ Here ends the extract from the de Decretis. The sentence following is added as a close.

CHAP. X.

OBJECTIONS CONTINUED.

How the Word has free-will, yet without being alterable. He is unalterable because the Image of the Father, proved from texts.

Disc. I. §. 35.

¹ἀυτεξού-σιος
² προαί-ρεσιν

1. As to their question whether the Word is alterable[a], it is superfluous to examine it; it is enough simply to write down what they say, and so to shew its daring irreligion. How they trifle, appears from the following questions:—" Has He free will¹, or has He not? is He good from choice² according to free will, and can He, if He will, alter, being of an alterable nature? or, as wood or stone, has He not His choice free to be moved and incline hither and thither?" It is but agreeable to their heresy thus to speak and think; for, when once they have framed to themselves a God out of nothing and a created Son, of course they also adopt such terms as are suitable to a creature. However, when in their controversies with Churchmen they hear from them of the real and only Word of the Father, and yet venture thus to speak of Him, does not their doctrine then become the most loathsome that can be found? Is it not enough to distract a man on mere hearing, though unable to reply, and to make him stop his ears, from astonishment at the novelty of what he hears them say, which even to mention is to blaspheme? For if the Word be alterable and changing, where will He stay, and what will be the end of His progress? how shall the alterable possibly be like the Unalterable? How should he who has seen the alterable, be considered to have seen the Unalterable? in which of His states shall we be able to behold in Him the Father? for it is plain that not at all times shall

---

[a] τρεπτός, i. e. not, changeable, but of a moral nature capable of improvement. Arius maintained this in the strongest terms at starting "On being asked whether the Word of God is capable of altering as the devil altered, they scrupled not to say, " Yea, He is capable." Alex. ap. Socr. 1. 6. p. 11

The Son unalterable, because the Father's Image.

we see the Father in the Son, because the Son is ever altering, and is of changing nature. For the Father is unalterable and unchangeable, and is always in the same state and the same; but if, as they hold, the Son is alterable, and not always the same, but ever of a changing nature, how can such a one be the Father's Image, not having the likeness of His unalterableness[1]? how can He be really in the Father, if His moral choice is indeterminate? Nay, perhaps, as being alterable, and advancing daily, He is not perfect yet. But away with such madness of the Arians, and let the truth shine out, and shew that they are beside themselves. For must not He be perfect who is equal to God? and must not He be unalterable, who is one with the Father, and His Son proper to His substance? and the Father's substance being unalterable, unalterable must be also the proper Offspring from it. And if they slanderously impute alteration to the Word, let them learn how much their own reason is in peril[2]; for from the fruit is the tree known. For this is why he who hath seen the Son, hath seen the Father, and why the knowledge of the Son is knowledge of the Father.

[1] supr. §. 22. init.
p. 212.
[2] p. 2, note e.

2. Therefore the Image of the unalterable God must be unchangeable; for *Jesus Christ is the same yesterday, to-day, and for ever.* And David in the Psalm says of Him, *Thou, Lord, in the beginning hast laid the foundation of the earth, and the heavens are the work of Thine hands. They shall perish, but Thou remainest; and they all shall wax old as doth a garment. And as a vesture shalt Thou fold them up, and they shall be changed, but Thou art the same, and Thy years shall not fail.* And the Lord Himself says of Himself through the Prophet, *See now that I, even I am He,* and *I change not.* It may be said indeed that what is here expressed relates to the Father; yet it suits the Son also to speak it, specially because, when made man, He manifests His own identity and unalterableness to such as suppose that by reason of the flesh He is changed and become other than He was. More trustworthy are the sacred writers, or rather the Lord, than the perversity of the irreligious. For Scripture, as in the above-cited passage of the Psalter, signifying under the name of heaven and earth, that the nature of all things generate and created is alterable and changeable, yet excepting the

§. 36.
Heb. 13, 8.
Heb. 1, 10–12.
Deut. 32, 39.
Mal. 3, 6.

Son from these, shews us thereby that He is in no wise a thing generate, nay teaches that He changes every thing else, and is Himself not changed, in saying, *Thou art the same, and Thy years shall not fail.* And with reason; for things generate, being from nothing[1], and not being before their generation, because, in truth, they come to be after not being, have a nature which is changeable; but the Son, being from the Father, and proper to His substance, is unchangeable and unalterable as the Father Himself. For it were sin to say that from that substance which is unalterable was begotten an alterable word and a changeable wisdom. For how is He longer the Word, if He be alterable? or can that be Wisdom which is changeable? unless perhaps, as accident in substance[2], so they would have it, viz. as in any particular substance, a certain grace and habit of virtue exists accidentally, which is called Word and Son and Wisdom, and admits of being taken from it and added to it. For they have often expressed this sentiment, but it is not the faith of Christians; as not declaring that He is truly Word and Son of God, or that the wisdom intended is the true Wisdom. For what alters and changes, and has no stay in one and the same condition, how can that be true? whereas the Lord says, *I am the Truth.* If then the Lord Himself speaks thus concerning Himself, and declares His unalterableness, and the sacred writers have learned and testify this, nay and our notions of God acknowledge it as religious, whence did these men of irreligion draw this novelty? from their heart as from a seat of corruption did they vomit it forth[3].

CHAP. XI.

TEXTS EXPLAINED; AND FIRST, PHIL. ii. 9, 10.

Various texts which are alleged against the Catholic doctrine; e. g. Phil. ii. 9, 10. Whether the words "Wherefore God hath highly exalted" prove moral probation and advancement. Argued against, first, from the force of the word "Son;" which is inconsistent with such an interpretation. Next, the passage examined Ecclesiastical sense of "highly exalted," and "gave," and "wherefore;" viz as being spoken with reference to our Lord's manhood. Secondary sense; viz as implying the Word's "exaltation" through the resurrection in the same sense in which Scripture speaks of His descent in the Incarnation, how the phrase does not derogate from the nature of the Word.

1. BUT since they allege the divine oracles and force on them a misinterpretation, according to their private sense[a], it becomes necessary to meet them just so far as to lay claim to these passages, and to shew that they bear an orthodox sense, and that our opponents are in error. They say then, that the Apostle writes, *Wherefore God also hath highly exalted Him, and given Him a Name which is above every name; that at the Name of Jesus every knee should bow, of things in heaven and things in earth and things under the earth;* and David, *Wherefore God, even Thy God, hath anointed Thee with the oil of gladness above Thy fellows.* Then they

CHAP. XI. §. 37.

Phil. 2, 9. 10.

Ps.45,9.

---

[a] vid. supr. p. 78, note n. "We must not make an appeal to the Scriptures, nor take up a position for the fight, in which victory is not, or is doubtful, or next to doubtful. For though this conflict of Scripture with Scripture did not end in a drawn battle, yet the true order of the subject required that that should be laid down first, which now becomes but a point of debate, viz. *who have a claim to the faith itself, whose* are the Scriptures." Tertull. de Præscr. 19. " Ruffinus says of S. Basil and S Gregory, "Putting aside all Greek literature, they are said to have passed thirteen years together in studying the Scriptures alone, and followed out their sense not *from their private opinion,* but by the writings and authority of the Fathers, &c." Hist. 11. 9. "Seeing the Canon of Scripture is perfect, &c. what need we join unto it the authority of the Church's understanding and interpretation? because the Scripture being of itself so deep and profound, all men do not understand it in one and the same sense, but *so many men, so many opinions* almost may be gathered out of it; for Novatian expounds it one way, Photinus another, Sabellius, &c." Vincent. Comm. 2. Hippolytus has a passage very much to the same purpose. contr. Noet. 9 fin.

urge, as something acute: "If He was exalted and received grace, on a wherefore, and on a wherefore He was anointed, He received the reward of His good choice; but having acted from choice, He is altogether of an alterable nature." This is what Eusebius[1] and Arius have dared to say, nay to write; while their partizans do not shrink from conversing about it in full market-place[2], not seeing how mad an argument they use. For if He received what He had as a reward of His good choice, and would not have had it, unless He had needed it and had His work to shew for it, then having gained it from virtue and promotion[3], with reason had He "therefore" been called Son and God, without being very Son. For what is from another by nature, is a real offspring, as Isaac was to Abraham, and Joseph to Jacob and the Radiance to the Sun; but the so-called sons from virtue and grace, have but in place of nature a grace by acquisition, and are something else besides[4] the gift itself; as the men who have received the Spirit by participation, concerning whom Scripture saith, *I have begotten and exalted children, and they have rebelled against Me*[5]. And of course, since they were not sons by nature, therefore, when they altered, the Spirit was taken away and they were disinherited; and again on their repentance that God who thus at the beginning gave them grace, will receive them, and give light, and call them sons again. But if they say this of the Saviour also, it follows that He is neither very God nor very Son, nor like the Father, nor in any wise has God for a Father of His being according to substance, but of the mere grace given to Him, and for a Creator of His being according to substance, after the similitude of all others. And being such, as they maintain, it will be manifest further that He had not the name "Son" from the first, if so be it was the prize of works done and of that very same advance which He made when He became man, and took the form of a servant; but then, when, after becoming *obedient unto death*, He was, as the text says, *highly exalted*, and received that *Name* as a grace, *that at the Name of Jesus every knee should bow*.

2. What then was before this, if then He was exalted, and then began to be worshipped, and then was called Son, when

Disc. I.

[1] of Nicomedia, vid. Theod. Hist.i.5.
[2] p. 213, note a.
[3] βιλτιώ- σεως
[4] p. 237, ref. 1.
Is. 1, 2. Sept.
[5] vid. Euseb. Nic. supr.
§. 38.
Phil. 2, 8.

The text brought by the Arians tells against themselves. 235

He became man? For He seems Himself not to have promoted[1] the flesh at all, but rather to have been Himself promoted through it, if, according to their perverseness, He was then exalted and called Son, when He became man. What then was before this? One must urge the question on them again, to make it understood what their irreligious doctrine results in[b]. For if the Lord be God, Son, Word, yet was not all these before He became man, either He was something else beside these, and afterwards became partaker of them for His virtue's sake, as we have said; or they must adopt the alternative, (may it fall upon their heads!) that He was not before that time, but is wholly man by nature, and nothing more. But this is no sentiment of the Church, but of Samosatene and of the present Jews. Why then, if they think as Jews, are they not circumcised with them too, instead of pretending Christianity, while they are its foes? For if He was not, or was indeed, but afterwards was promoted, how were all things made by Him, or how in Him, were He not perfect, did the Father delight[2]? And He, on the other hand, if now promoted, how did He before rejoice in the presence of the Father? And, if He received His worship after dying, how is Abraham seen to worship Him in the tent[3], and Moses in the bush? and, as Daniel saw, myriads of myriads, and thousands of thousands were ministering unto Him? And if, as they say, He had His promotion now, how did the Son Himself make mention of that His glory before and above the world, when He said, *Glorify Thou Me, O Father, with the glory which I had with Thee before the world was.* If, as they say, He was then exalted, how did He before that *bow the heavens and come down;* and again, *the Highest gave His thunder?* Therefore, if, even before the world was made, the

CHAP. XI
¹ βιλτίω.
ras

² vid. Prov. 8, 30.

ᴊ p. 120, note g.

John 17, 5.

Ps. 18, 9. 13.

---

[b] The Arians perhaps more than other heretics were remarkable for bringing objections against the received view, rather than forming a consistent theory of their own. Indeed the very vigour and success of their assault upon the truth lay in its being a mere assault, not a positive and substantive teaching. They therefore, even more than others, might fairly be urged on to the consequences of their positions. Now the text in question, as it must be interpreted if it is to serve as an objection, was an objection also to the received doctrine of the Arians. They considered that our Lord was above and before all creatures from the first, and then Creator, how then could He be exalted above all? They surely, as much as Catholics, were obliged to explain it of our Lord's manhood. They could not then use it as a weapon against the Church, until they took the ground of Paul of Samosata.

236 *Our Lord not exalted, but a cause and standard for us.*

Disc
1.
Son had that glory, and was Lord of glory and the Highest, and descended from heaven, and is ever to be worshipped, it follows that He had no promotion from His descent, but rather Himself promoted the things which needed promotion; and if He descended to effect their promotion, therefore He did not receive in reward the name of the Son and God, but rather He Himself has made us sons of the Father, and made men gods, by becoming Himself man.

§. 39.

¹ θιοποι-
ήση

3. Therefore He was not man, and then become God, but He was God, and then became man, and that to make us gods¹. Since, if when He became man, only then He was called Son and God, but before He became man, God called the ancient people sons, and made Moses a god of Pharaoh, (and Scripture says of many, *God standeth in the congregation of gods*,) it is plain that He is called Son and God later than they. How then are all things through Him, and He before all? or how is He *first-born of the whole creation*², if He has others before Him who are called sons and gods? And how is it that those first partakers ᶜ do not partake of the Word? This opinion is not true, it is an evasion of our present Judaizers. For how in that case can any at all know God as their Father? for adoption there cannot be apart from the real Son, who says, *No one knoweth the Father, save the Son, and he to whomsoever the Son will reveal Him.* And how can there be deifying apart from the Word and before Him? yet, saith He to their brethren the Jews, *If He called them gods, unto whom the Word of God came.* And if all that are called sons and gods, whether in earth or in heaven, were adopted and deified through the Word, and the Son Himself is the Word, it is plain that through Him are they all, and He Himself before all, or rather He Himself only is very Son³, and He alone is very God from the very God, not receiving these prerogatives as a reward for His virtue, nor being

Ps. 81, (82,) 1, Sept.

Col. 1, 15
² vid.
infr. 11.
§. 62.

Mat.11, 27.

John10, 35

³ p. 18, note o.

ᶜ In this passage Athan. considers that the participation of the Word is deification, as communion with the Son is adoption; also that the old Saints, inasmuch as they are called "gods" and "sons," did partake of the Divine Word and Son, or in other words were gifted with the Spirit. He asserts the same doctrine very strongly in Orat. iv. §. 22. On the other hand, infr. 47. he says expressly that Christ received the Spirit in Baptism *that He might give it to man.* There is no real contradiction in such statements, what was given in one way under the Law, was given in another and fuller under the Gospel.

something else beside[1] them, but being all these by nature and according to substance. For He is Offspring of the Father's substance, so that one cannot doubt that after the resemblance of the unalterable Father, the Word also is unalterable.

4. Hitherto we have met their irrational conceits with the true conceptions[d] implied in the Word "Son," as the Lord Himself has given us. But it will be well next to expound the divine oracles, that the unalterableness of the Son and His unchangeable nature, which is the Father's[2], as well as their perverseness, may be still more fully proved. The Apostle then, writing to the Philippians, says, *Let this mind be in you, which was also in Christ Jesus; who, being in the form of God, thought it not robbery to be equal with God; but made Himself of no reputation, and took upon Him the form of a servant, and was made in the likeness of men. And, being found in fashion as a man, He humbled Himself, and became obedient to death, even the death of the cross Wherefore God also hath highly exalted Him, and given Him a Name which is above every name; that at the Name of Jesus every knee should bow, of things in heaven, and things in earth, and things under the earth, and that every tongue should confess that Jesus Christ is Lord, to the glory of God the Father.* Can any thing be plainer and more express than this? He was not from a lower state promoted; but rather, existing as God, He took the form of a servant, and in taking it, did not promote but humbled Himself. Where then is there here any reward of virtue, or what advancement and promotion in such humiliation? For if, being God, He became man, and descending from on high He is still said to be exalted, where is He exalted, being God? this withal being plain, that, since God is highest of all, His Word must necessarily be highest also. Where then could He be exalted higher, who is in the Father and like the Father in all things[3]?

5. Therefore He is beyond the need of any addition; nor is such as the Arians think Him. For though the Word did descend in order to be exalted, and so it is written, yet what need was there that He should humble Himself,

CHAP. XI.
[1] p. 234, ref. 4

§. 40.

[2] πατρικὴ
φύσις
Phil. 2, 5—11.

[3] ὅμοιος κατὰ πάντα,
p. 115,
note e
p. 210,
ref. 3.

---

[d] ταῖς ἐννοίαις χρώμενοι, πρὸς τὰς ἐπι- νοίας ἀπηντήσαμεν. cf. οὐχὶ ἐπίνοια, παρά- νοια δὲ μᾶλλον, &c. Basil. contr. Eunom. 1. 6. init

as if to seek that which He had already? And what grace did He receive who is the Giver of grace[1]? or how did He receive that Name for worship, who is always worshipped by His Name? Nay, certainly before He became man, the sacred writers invoke Him, *Save me, O God, for Thy Name's sake;* and again, *Some put their trust in chariots, and some in horses, but we will remember the Name of the Lord our God* And while He was worshipped by the Patriarchs, concerning the Angels it is written, *Let all the Angels of God worship Him.* And if, as David says in the 71st Psalm, *His Name remaineth before the sun, and before the moon from one generation to another,* how did He receive what He had always, even before He now received it? or how is He exalted, being before His exaltation, the Most High? or how did He receive the right of being worshipped, who before He now received it, was ever worshipped?

6. It is not a dark saying but a divine mystery[e]. *In the beginning was the Word, and the Word was with God, and the Word was God;* but for our sakes afterwards the *Word was made flesh.* And the term in question, *highly exalted,* does not signify that the substance of the Word was exalted, for He was ever and is *equal to God,* but the exaltation is of the manhood. Accordingly this is not said before the Word became flesh; that it might be plain that *humbled* and *exalted* are spoken of His human nature; for where there is humble estate, there too may be exaltation; and if because of His taking flesh *humbled* is written, it is clear that *highly exalted* is also said because of it. For of this was man's[2] nature in want, because of the humble estate of the flesh and of death. Since then the Word, being the Image of the Father and immortal, took the form of a servant, and as man underwent for us death in His flesh, that thereby He might offer Himself for us through death to the Father; therefore also, as man, He is said because of us and for us to be highly exalted, that as by His death

---

[e] Scripture is full of mysteries, but they are mysteries of *fact*, not of words. Its dark sayings or ænigmata are such, because in the nature of things they cannot be expressed clearly. Hence contrariwise, Orat. ii. §. 77 fin. he calls Prov. 8, 22. an enigma, with an allusion to Prov. 1, 6. Sept. In like manner S. Ambrose says, Mare est scriptura divina, habens in se sensus profundos, et altitudinem propheticorum *ænigmatum*, &c. Ep. ii. 3 What is commonly called "explaining away" Scripture, is this transference of the obscurity from the subject to the words used.

He is exalted, that is, in respect of His manhood.

we all died in Christ, so again in the Christ Himself we might be highly exalted, being raised from the dead, and ascending into heaven, *whither the forerunner is for us entered, not into the figures of the true, but into heaven itself, now to appear in the presence of God for us.* But if now for us the Christ is entered into heaven itself, though He was even before and always Lord and Framer of the heavens, for us therefore is that present exaltation also written. And as He Himself, who sanctifies all, says also that He sanctifies Himself to the Father for our sakes, not that the Word may become holy, but that He Himself may in Himself sanctify all of us, in like manner we must take the present phrase, *He highly exalted Him,* not that He Himself should be exalted, for He is the highest, but that He may become righteousness for us ᶠ; and we may be exalted in Him, and that we may enter the gates of heaven, which He has also opened for us, the forerunners saying, *Lift up your heads, O ye gates, and be ye lift up, ye everlasting doors, and the King of Glory shall come in.* For here also not on Him were shut the gates, who is Lord and Maker of all, but because of us is this too written, to whom the door of paradise was shut. And therefore in a human relation, because of the flesh which He bore, it is said of Him, *Lift up, O ye gates, and shall come in,* as if a man were entering; but in a divine relation on the other hand it is said of Him, since *the Word was God,* that He is the *Lord* and the *King of glory.* Such our exaltation the Spirit foreannounced in the eighty-ninth Psalm, saying, *And in Thy righteousness shall they be exalted, for Thou art the glory of their strength.* And if the Son be Righteousness, then He is not exalted as being Himself in need, but it is we who are exalted in that Righteousness, which is He.

7. And so too the words *gave Him,* are not written for the Word Himself; for even before He became man, He was

---

ᶠ When Scripture says that our Lord was exalted, it means in that sense in which He could be exalted; just as, in saying that a man walks or eats, we speak of him not as a spirit, but as in that system of things to which the idea of walking and eating belong. Exaltation is not a word which can belong to God; it is unmeaning, and *therefore is not* applied to Him in the text in question. Thus, e. g. S. Ambrose: "Ubi humiliabus, ibi obediens. Ex eo enim nascitur obedientia, ex quo humilitas, *et in eo desinit,* &c." ap. Dav. alt. n. 39.

worshipped, as we have said, by the Angels and the whole creation in what is proper¹ to the Father; but because of us and for us this too is written of Him. For as Christ died and was exalted as man, so, as man, is He said to take what, as God, He ever had, that even this so high a grant of grace might reach to us. For the Word was not impaired in receiving a body, that He should seek to receive a grace, but rather He deified² that which He put on, nay, *gave* it graciously to the race of man. For as He was ever worshipped as being the Word and existing in the form of God, so being what He ever was, though become man and called Jesus, He still has, as before, the whole creation under foot, and bending their knees to Him in this Name, and confessing that the Word's becoming flesh, and undergoing death in flesh, hath not happened against the glory of His Godhead, but *to the glory of God the Father*. For it is the Father's glory that man, made and then lost, should be found again; and, when the prey of death, that He should be made alive, and should become God's temple. For whereas the powers in heaven, both Angels and Archangels, were ever worshipping the Lord, as they are now worshipping Him in the Name of Jesus, this is our grace and high exaltation, that even when He became man, the Son of God is worshipped, and the heavenly powers are not startled at seeing all of us, who are of one body with Him³, introduced into their realms. And this had not been, unless He who existed in the form of God had taken on Him a servant's form, and had humbled Himself, permitting His body to reach unto death.

§. 43. 8. Behold then what men considered the foolishness of God because of the Cross, has become of all things most honoured. For our resurrection is stored up in it; and no longer Israel alone, but henceforth all the nations, as the Prophet foretold, leave their idols and acknowledge the true God, the Father of the Christ. And the delusion of demons is come to nought, and He only who is really God is worshipped in the Name of our Lord Jesus Christ. For in that the Lord, even when come in human body and called Jesus, was worshipped and believed to be God's Son, and that through Him the Father was known, it is plain, as has been said, that not the Word, considered as the Word⁴,

The Person of the Word humbled and man's nature exalted. 241

received this so great grace, but we. For because of our relationship to His Body we too have become God's temple, and in consequence are made God's sons, so that even in us the Lord is now worshipped, and beholders report, as the Apostle says, that God is in them of a truth [g]. As also John saith in the Gospel, *As many as received Him, to them gave He power to become children of God;* and in his Epistle he writes, *By this we know that He abideth in us by His Spirit which He hath given us.* And this too is an evidence of His goodness towards us that, while we were exalted because that the Highest Lord is in us, and on our behalf grace was given to Him, because that the Lord who supplies the grace has become a man like us, He on the other hand, the Saviour, humbled Himself in taking *our body of humiliation,* and took a servant's form, putting on that flesh which was enslaved to sin [h]. And He indeed gained nothing from us for

John 1, 12.

1 John 3, 24.

---

[g] ὄντως ἐν ὑμῖν ὁ θεός. 1 Cor. 14, 25. Athan. interprets ἐν in not *among*; as also in 1 John 3, 24. just afterwards. Vid. ἐν ἐμοί Gal. 1, 24. ἐντὸς ὑμῖν. Luke 17, 21. ἐσκήνωσεν ἐν ἡμῖν. John 1, 14. on which text Hooker says, "It pleased not the Word or Wisdom of God to take to itself some one person among men, for then should that one have been advanced which was assumed and no more, but Wisdom, to the end she might save many, built her house of that Nature which is common unto all; she made not this or that man her habitation, but dwelt in us." Eccl. Pol. v. 52. §. 3. S. Basil in his proof of the divinity of the Holy Spirit has a somewhat similar passage to the text, "Man in common is crowned with glory and honour, and glory and honour and peace is reserved in the promises for every one who doeth good. And there is a certain glory of Israel peculiar, and the Psalmist speaks of a glory of his own, 'Awake up my glory;' and there is a glory of the sun, and according to the Apostle even a ministration of condemnation with glory. So many then being glorified, choose you that the Spirit alone of all should be without glory?" de Sp. S. c. 24.

[h] It was usual to say against the Apollinarians, that, unless our Lord took on Him our nature, *as it is,* He had not purified and changed it, as it is, but another nature; "The Lord came not to save Adam as free from sin, that He should become like unto him, but as, in the net of sin and now fallen, that God's mercy might raise him up with Christ." Leont.contr.Nestor.&c. ii. p. 996 Accordingly Athan. says elsewhere, "Had not sinlessness appeared *in the nature which had sinned,* how was sin condemned in the flesh?" in Apoll. ii. 6 "It was necessary for our salvation," says S. Cyril, "that the Word of God should become man, that human flesh *subject to corruption* and *sick with the lust of pleasures,* He might make His own; and, *whereas He is life and lifegiving,* He might *destroy the corruption,* &c..... For by this means, might sin in our flesh become dead." Ep. ad Success. i. p. 138. And S. Leo, "Non alterius naturæ erat ejus caro quam nostra, nec alio illi quam cæteris hominibus anima est inspirata principio, quæ excelleret, non diversitate generis, sed sublimitate virtutis." Ep. 35 fin. vid. also Ep. 28. 3. Ep. 31. 2. Ep. 165. 9. Serm. 22. 2. and 25. 5. It may be asked whether this doctrine does not interfere with that of the immaculate conception; but that miracle was wrought in order that our Lord might not be born in original sin, and does not affect, or rather includes, His taking flesh of the substance of the Virgin, i. e. of a fallen nature. If indeed sin were *of the substance* of our fallen nature, as some heretics have said, then He could not have taken our nature without

R

DISC. I.

His own promotion¹: for the Word of God is without want and full; but rather we were promoted from Him; for He is the *Light, which lighteneth every man that cometh into the world.*

¹ βελτίωσιν, external advance

9. And in vain do the Arians lay stress upon the conjunction *wherefore,* because Paul has said, *Wherefore hath God highly exalted Him.* For in saying this he did not imply any prize of virtue, nor the promotion from advance², but the cause why the exaltation was bestowed upon us. And what is this but that He who existed in form of God, the Son of a divine³ Father, humbled Himself and became a servant instead of us and in our behalf? For if the Lord had not become man, we had not been redeemed from sins: not raised from the dead, but remaining dead under the earth; not exalted into heaven, but lying in Hades. Because of us then and in our behalf are the words, *highly exalted* and *given.*

² προκοπῆς, internal advance, Luke 2, 52.

³ εὐγενοῦς

§. 44.

⁴ ἐκκλησιαστικός, vid. Serap. iv. 15. contr. Gent. 6. 7. 33.

⁵Orat.ii. §. 8.

10. This then I consider the sense of this passage, and that, a very ecclesiastical sense⁴. However, there is another way in which one might remark upon it, giving the same sense in a parallel way; viz. that, though it does not speak of the exaltation of the Word Himself, so far as He is Word⁵, (for He is, as was just now said, most high and like His Father,) yet by reason of His incarnation it alludes to His resurrection from the dead. For after saying, *He hath humbled Himself even unto death,* He immediately added, *Wherefore He*

partaking our sinfulness; but if sin be, as it is, a fault of the *will,* then the Divine Power of the Word could sanctify the human will, and keep it from swerving in the direction of evil. Hence S. Austin says, " We say not that Christ by the *felicity of a flesh* separated from sense *could not* feel the desire of sin, but that *by perfection of virtue,* and by a flesh not begotten through concupiscence of the flesh, He *had not* the desire of sin " Op Imperf. iv. 48. On the other hand, S. Athanasius expressly calls it Manichean doctrine to consider, τὴν φύσιν of the flesh ἁμαρτίαν, καὶ οὐ τὴν τράξιν. contr. Apoll. 1. 12 fin. or φυσικὴν εἶναι τὴν ἁμαρτίαν ibid. i. 14 fin. His argument in the next ch. is on the ground that all *natures* are from God, but God made man upright nor is the author of evil; (vid. also Vit

Anton. 20.) " not as if," he says, " the devil wrought in man a nature, (God forbid !) for of a nature the devil cannot be maker (δημιουργὸς) as is the impiety of the Manichees, but he wrought a bias of nature by transgression, and ' so death reigned over all men.' Wherefore, saith He, ' the Son of God came to destroy the works of the devil;' what works? that nature, which God made sinless, and the devil biassed to the transgression of God's command and the finding out of sin which is death, did God the Word raise again, so as to be secure from the devil's bias and the finding out of sin And therefore the Lord said, ' The prince of this world cometh and findeth nothing in Me ' " vid. also § 19. Ibid. ii. 6. he speaks of the devil having introduced the *law* of sin." vid. also §. 9.

viz. in the body, on the Resurrection, because He was God. 243

hath highly exalted Him; wishing to shew, that, although as man He is said to have died, yet, as being Life, He was exalted on the resurrection; for *He who descended, is the same also who rose again.* He descended in body, and He rose again because He was God Himself in the body. And this again is the reason why according to this meaning He brought in the conjunction *Wherefore;* not as a reward of virtue nor of advancement, but to signify the cause why the resurrection took place; and why, while all other men from Adam down to this time have died and remained dead, He only rose in integrity from the dead. The cause is this, which He Himself has already taught us, that, being God, He has become man. For all other men, being merely born of Adam, died, and death reigned over them; but He, the Second Man, is from heaven, for *the Word was made flesh,* and this Man is said to be from heaven and heavenly[1], because the Word descended from heaven; wherefore He was not held under death. For though He humbled Himself, suffering His own Body to reach unto death, in that it was capable[2] of death[1], yet it was highly exalted from earth, because He was God's Son in a body. Accordingly what is here said, *Wherefore God also hath highly exalted Him,* answers to St. Peter's words in the Acts, *Whom God raised up, having loosed the bonds of death, because it was not possible that He should be holden of it.* For as Paul has written, " Since being in form of God He became man, and humbled Himself unto death, therefore God also hath highly exalted Him," so also Peter says, " Since, being God, He became man, and signs and wonders proved

CHAP. XI

Eph. 4, 10 ἀναστάς, but ἀνα-βάς: ect t.

John 1, 14.

[1] in Apoll. 1 2.

[2] δεκτικόν

Acts 2, 24.

---

[1] It was a point in controversy with the extreme Monophysites, that is, the Eutychians, whether our Lord's body was naturally subject to death, the Catholics maintaining the affirmative, as Athanasius here. Eutyches asserted that our Lord had not a human nature, by which he meant among other things that His manhood was not subject to the *laws* of a body, but so far as He submitted to them, did so by an act of will in each particular case, and this, lest it should seem that He was moved by the πάθη against His will ἀκουσίως; and consequently that His manhood was not subject to death. But the Catholics maintained that He had voluntarily placed Himself *under* those laws, and died *naturally,* vid. Athan. contr. Apoll. 1. 17. and that after the resurrection His body became incorruptible, not according to nature, but by grace. vid. Leont. de Sect. x. p. 530. Anast. Hodeg c. 23. To express their doctrine of the ὑπερφυές of our Lord's manhood the Eutychians made use of the Catholic expression " ut voluit." vid. Athan. 1 c. Eutyches ap. Leon. Ep. 21. " quomodo voluit et scit," twice. vid. also Eranist. 1. p. 11. 11. p. 105. Leont. contr Nest. 1. p. 967. Pseudo-Athan. Serm. adv. Div. Hær. §. 8. (t. 2. p. 570.)

Disc. Him to beholders to be God, therefore it was not possible
I. that He should be holden of death." To man it was not
possible to prosper in this matter; for death belongs to man;
wherefore, the Word, being God, became flesh, that, being
put to death in the flesh, He might quicken all men by His
own power.

§. 45.   11. But since He Himself is said to be *exalted*, and God *gave*
¹ ἐλάτ- Him, and the heretics think this a defect¹ or affection in the
τωμα, ad
Adelph. substance ᵏ of the Word, it becomes necessary to explain how
4.   these words are used. He is said to be exalted from the
lower parts of the earth, because, on the other hand, death is
ascribed to Him. Both events are reckoned His, since it
was His Body¹, and none other's, that was exalted from the
dead and taken up into heaven. And again, the Body being
His, and the Word not being external to it, it is natural that
when the Body was exalted, He, as man, should, because of
the body, be spoken of as exalted. If then He did not become
man, let this not be said of Him; but if the Word became
flesh, of necessity the resurrection and exaltation, as in the
case of a man, must be ascribed to Him, that the death
which is ascribed to Him may be a redemption of the sins of

ᵏ At first sight it would seem as if St. Athanasius here used οὐσία substance for subsistence, or person; but this is not true except with an explanation. Its *direct* meaning is here, as usual, substance, though *indirectly* to come to imply subsistence. He is speaking of that Divine Essence which, though also the Almighty Father's, is as simply and entirely the Word's as if it were only His. Nay, even when the Substance of the Father is spoken of in a sort of contrast to that of the Son, as in the phrase οὐσία ἐξ οὐσίας, harsh as such expressions are, it is not accurate to say that οὐσία is used for subsistence or person, or that two οὐσίαι are spoken of. (vid. supr. p. 155, note f.) except, that is, by Arians, as Eusebius, supr. p. 63, note g. Just below we find φύσις τοῦ λόγου, §. 51 init.
¹ This was the question which came into discussion in the Nestorian controversy, when, as it was then expressed, all that took place in respect to the Eternal Word as man, belonged to His *Person*, and therefore might be predicated of Him; so that it was heretical not to confess the Word's body, (or the body of God in the Person of the Word,) the Word's death, (as Athan. in the text,) the Word's exaltation, and the Word's, or God's Mother, who was in consequence called θεότοκος, which was the expression on which the controversy mainly turned. "The Godhead," says Athan. elsewhere, "'dwelt in the flesh bodily; which is all one with saying, that, being God, He had a proper body, ἴδιον, and using this as an instrument, ἐργάνῳ, He became man, for our sakes; and because of this things *proper to the flesh are said to be His*, since He was in it, as hunger, thirst, suffering, fatigue, and the like, of which the flesh is capable, δεκτική; while *the works proper to the Word* Himself, as raising the dead, and restoring sight to the blind, and curing the issue of blood, He did Himself *through His body*, &c.'" Orat. III. 31. vid. the whole passage, which is as precise as if it had been written after the Nestorian and Eutychian controversies, though without the technical words then adopted.

men and an abolition of death, and that the resurrection and exaltation may for His sake remain secure for us. In both respects he hath said of Him, *God hath highly exalted Him*, and *God hath given to Him;* that herein moreover he may shew that it is not the Father that hath become flesh, but it is His Word, who has become man, and has received after the manner of men from the Father, and is exalted by Him, as has been said. And it is plain, nor would any one dispute it, that what the Father gives, He gives through the Son And it is marvellous and overwhelming verily, that the grace which the Son gives from the Father, that the Son Himself is said to receive; and the exaltation, which the Son effects from the Father, with that, the Son is Himself exalted. For He who is the Son of God, He Himself became the Son of Man; and, as Word, He gives from the Father, for all things which the Father does and gives, He does and supplies through Him; and as the Son of Man, He Himself is said after the manner of men to receive what proceeds from Him, because His Body is none other than His, and is a natural recipient of grace, as has been said. For He received it as far as man's nature[1] was exalted; which exaltation was its being deified. But such an exaltation the Word Himself always had according to the Father's Godhead[2] and perfection, which was His.

[1] τὸν ἄν-θρωπον

[2] τὴν πα-τρικὴν ἑαυτοῦ θεότητα, vid. p. 145, note r.

CHAP. XII.

TEXTS EXPLAINED; SECONDLY, PSALM xlv. 7, 8.

Whether the words "therefore," "anointed," &c. imply that the Word has been rewarded. Argued against first from the word "fellows" or "partakers." He is anointed with the Spirit in His manhood to sanctify human nature Therefore the Spirit descended on Him in Jordan, when in the flesh And He is said to sanctify Himself for us, and give us the glory He has received The word "wherefore" implies His divinity. "Thou hast loved righteousness," &c. do not imply trial or choice.

DISC.
I.
§. 46.

1. SUCH an explanation of the Apostle's words, confutes the irreligious men; and what the Psalmist says admits also the same orthodox sense, which they misinterpret, but which in the Psalmist is manifestly religious. He says then, *Thy throne, O God, is for ever and ever; a sceptre of righteousness is the sceptre of Thy Kingdom. Thou hast loved righteousness, and hated iniquity, therefore God, even Thy God, hath anointed Thee with the oil of gladness above Thy fellows.* Behold, O ye Arians, and acknowledge even hence the truth. The Psalmist speaks of all us as *fellows* or *partakers*[1] of the Lord; but were He one of things which come out of nothing and of things generate, He Himself had been one of those who partake. But, since He hymned Him as the eternal God, saying, *Thy throne, O God, is for ever and ever*, and has declared that all other things partake of Him, what conclusion must we draw, but that He is distinct from generated things, and He only the Father's veritable Word, Radiance, and Wisdom, which all things generate partake[2], being sanctified by Him in the Spirit[a]? And therefore He is here "anointed," not that He may become God, for He was

[1] μετόχους

[2] p. 15, note e.

[a] It is here said that all things *generate* partake the Son and are *sanctified* by the Spirit. How a γέννησις or adoption through the Son is necessary for every creature in order to its consistence, life, or preservation, has been explained, supr p. 32, note q Sometimes the Son was considered as the special Principle of reason, as by Origen, vid. ap. Athan. Serap iv. 9. vid. himself, de Incarn. 11. These offices of the Son and the Spirit are contrasted by S. Basil, in his de Sp S. τὸν προστάττοντα λόγον, τὸν δημιουργοῦντα λόγον, τὸ στεριοῦν πνεῦμα, &c. c. 16. n. 38.

Our Lord was anointed, as He was exalted, for us.

so even before; nor that He may become King, for He had the Kingdom eternally, existing as God's Image, as the sacred Oracle shews; but in our behalf is this written, as before. For the Israelitish kings, upon their being anointed, then became kings, not being so before, as David, as Ezekias, as Josias, and the rest; but the Saviour on the contrary, being God, and ever ruling in the Father's Kingdom, and being Himself the Dispenser of the Holy Ghost, nevertheless is here said to be anointed, that, as before, being said as man to be anointed with the Spirit, He might provide for us men, not only exaltation and resurrection, but the indwelling and intimacy[1] of the Spirit. And signifying this the Lord Himself hath said by His own mouth in the Gospel according to John, *I have sent them into the world, and for their sakes do I sanctify Myself, that they may be sanctified in the truth*[2]. In saying this He has shewn that He is not the sanctified, but the Sanctifier; for He is not sanctified by other, but Himself sanctifies Himself, that we may be sanctified in the truth. He who sanctifies Himself is Lord of sanctification. How then does this take place? What does He mean but this? "I, being the Father's Word, I give to Myself, when become man, the Spirit; and Myself, become man, do I sanctify in Him, that henceforth in Me, who am Truth, (for *Thy Word is Truth*,) all may be sanctified"

2. If then for our sake He sanctifies Himself, and does this when He becomes man, it is very plain that the Spirit's descent on Him in Jordan, was a descent upon us, because of His bearing our body. And it did not take place for promotion[3] to the Word, but again for our sanctification, that we might share His anointing, and of us it might be said, *Know ye not that ye are God's Temple, and the Spirit of God dwelleth in you?* For when the Lord, as man, was washed in Jordan, it was we who were washed in Him and by Him[4]. And when He received the Spirit, we it was who by Him were made recipients of It. And moreover for this reason, not as Aaron or David or the rest, was He anointed with oil, but in another way above all His fellows, *with the oil of gladness*; which He Himself interprets to be the Spirit, saying by the Prophet, *The Spirit of the Lord is upon Me,*

CHAP. XII.

[1] οἰκειό-τητα

John 17, 19.

[2] vid. Cyril. Thesaur. 20. p. 197.

§. 47.

[3] ἐπὶ βελτίωσιν

1 Cor. 3, 16.

[4] Pusey on Baptism, 2d Ed. pp. 275—293.

Isai. 61, 1.

Disc. *because the Lord hath anointed Me;* as also the Apostle
1. has said, *How God anointed Him with the Holy Ghost.*
Acts 10, When then were these things spoken of Him but when
38. He came in the flesh and was baptized in Jordan, and the
Spirit descended on Him? And indeed the Lord Himself
John 16, said, *The Spirit shall take of Mine;* and *I will send Him;*
14. 7. and to His disciples, *Receive ye the Holy Ghost.* And
20, 22. notwithstanding, He who, as the Word and Radiance of
the Father, gives to others, now is said to be sanctified,
because now He has become man, and the Body that is
sanctified is His. From Him then we have begun to receive
1 John the unction and the seal, John saying, *And ye have an*
2, 20. *unction from the Holy One;* and the Apostle, *And ye were*
Eph. 1, *sealed with the Holy Spirit of promise.* Therefore because
13. of us and for us are these words.

3. What advance then of promotion, and reward of virtue
or generally of conduct, is proved from this in our Lord's
instance? For if He was not God, and then had become
God, if not being King He was preferred to the Kingdom,
your reasoning would have had some faint plausibility.
But if He is God and the throne of His kingdom is everlasting, in what way could God advance? or what was there
wanting to Him who was sitting on His Father's throne?
And if, as the Lord Himself has said, the Spirit is His, and
takes of His, and He sends It, it is not the Word, considered
¹ p. 240, as the Word¹ and Wisdom, who is anointed with the Spirit
ref. 4. which He Himself gives, but the flesh assumed by Him
which is anointed in Him and by Him ᵇ; that the sanctifi-

ᵇ Elsewhere Athan. says that our Lord's Godhead was the immediate anointing or chrism of the manhood He assumed. "God needed not the anointing, nor was the anointing made without God; but God both applied it, and also received it in that body which was capable of it." in Apollin. ii. 3. and τὸ χρῖσμα ἐγὼ ὁ λόγος, τὸ δὲ χρισθὲν ὑπ' ἐμοῦ ὁ ἄνθρωπος. Orat. iv. § 36. vid Origen. Periarch. ii. 6. n, 4. And S. Greg Naz still more expressly, and from the same text as Athan. "The Father anointed Him ' with the oil of gladness above His fellows,' *anointing the manhood with the Godhead.*" Orat. x. fin. Again, "This [the Godhead] is the anointing of the manhood, not sanctifying by an energy as the other Christs [anointed] but by a presence of Him whole who anointed, ὅλου τοῦ χρίοντος, whence it came to pass that what anointed was called man and what was anointed was made God." Orat. 30. 20. "He Himself anointed Himself; anointing as God the body with His Godhead, and anointed as man " Damasc. F O. iii 3. Dei Filius, sicut pluvia in vellus, toto divinitatis unguento nostram se fudit in carnem. Chrysolog. Serm. 60. It is more common, however, to consider that the anointing was the descent of the Spirit, as Athan. says at the beginning of this section, according to Luke iv. 18. Acts x. 38.

cation coming to the Lord as man, may come to all men from Him. For not of Itself, saith He, doth the Spirit speak, but the Word is He who gives It to the worthy. For this is like the passage considered above; for as the Apostle has written, *Who existing in form of God thought it not robbery to be equal with God, but humbled Himself, and took a servant's form,* so David celebrates the Lord, as the everlasting God and King, but sent to us and assuming our body which is mortal. For this is his meaning in the Psalm, *All Thy garments*[c] *smell of myrrh, aloes, and cassia;* and it is represented by Nicodemus and by Mary's company, when he came bringing *a mixture of myrrh and aloes, about an hundred pounds weight;* and they *the spices which they had prepared* for the burial of the Lord's body.

[Ps. 45, 9.]
[John 19, 39.]
[Luke 24, 1.]

4. What advancement[1] then was it to the Immortal to have assumed the mortal? or what promotion is it to the Everlasting to have put on the temporal? what reward can be great to the Everlasting God and King in the bosom of the Father? See ye not, that this too was done and written because of us and for us, that us who are mortal and temporal, the Lord, become man, might make immortal, and bring into the everlasting kingdom of heaven? Blush ye not, speaking lies against the divine oracles? For when our Lord Jesus Christ had been among us, we indeed were promoted, as rescued from sin; but He is the same[2]: nor did He alter, when He became man, (to repeat what I have said,) but, as has been written, *The Word of God abideth for ever.* Surely as, before His becoming man, He, the Word, dispensed to the saints the Spirit as His own[3], so also when made man, He sanctifies all by the Spirit and says to His Disciples, *Receive ye the Holy Ghost.* And He gave to Moses and the other seventy; and through Him David prayed to the Father, saying, *Take not Thy Holy Spirit from me.* On the other hand, when made man, He said, *I will send to you the Paraclete, the Spirit of truth;* and He sent Him, He, the Word of God, as being faithful.

[§. 48. ¹προκοπή]
[² p. 23, note a. infra.]
[§. 51. Isai. 40, 8. λόγος but ῥῆμα ό.]
[³ p. 236, note c.]
[Ps. 51, 11.]
[John 15, 26.]

---

[c] Our Lord's manhood is spoken of as a garment; more distinctly afterwards, "As Aaron was himself, and did not change on putting round him the high priest's garment, but remaining the same, was but clothed &c. Orat. ii. 8. On the Apollinarian abuse of the idea, vid. note in loc.

5. Therefore *Jesus Christ is the same yesterday, to-day, and for ever*, remaining unalterable, and at once gives and receives, giving as God's Word, receiving as man. It is not the Word then, viewed as the Word, that is promoted; for He had all things and has them always; but men, who have in Him and through Him their origin [d] of receiving them. For, when He is now said to be anointed in a human respect, we it is who in Him are anointed; since also, when He is baptized, we it is who in Him are baptized. But on all these things the Saviour throws much light, when He says to the Father, *And the glory which Thou gavest Me, I have given to them, that they may be one, even as We are one*. Because of us then He asked for glory, and the words occur, *took* and *gave* and *highly exalted*, that we might take, and to us might be given, and we might be exalted, in Him; as also for us He sanctifies Himself, that we might be sanctified in Him[1].

[d] The word origin, ἀρχὴ, implies the doctrine, more fully brought out in other passages of the Fathers, that our Lord has deigned to become an instrumental cause, as it may be called, of the life of each individual Christian. For at first sight it may be objected to the whole course of Athan.'s argument thus,—What connection is there between the sanctification of Christ's manhood and ours? how does it prove that human nature is sanctified because a particular specimen of it was sanctified in Him? S. Chrysostom explains, "He is born of our substance you will say, 'This does not pertain to all,' yea, to all. He mingles (ἀναμίγνυσιν) Himself with the faithful individually, through the mysteries, and whom He has begotten those He nurses from Himself, not puts them out to other hands," &c. Hom. 82. in Matt. 5. And just before, "It sufficed not for Him to be made man, to be scourged, to be sacrificed; but He assimilates us to Him (ἀναφύρει ἑαυτὸν ἡμῖν) nor merely by faith, but really, has He made us His body." Again, "That we are commingled (ἀνακιρασθῶμεν) into that flesh, not merely through love, but really, is brought about by means of that food which He has bestowed upon us." Hom. 46. in Joann 3. And so S Cyril writes against Nestorius "Since we have proved that Christ is the Vine, and we branches as adhering to a communion with Him, not spiritual merely but bodily, why clamours he against us thus bootlessly, saying that, since we adhere to Him, not in a bodily way, but rather by faith and the affection of love according to the Law, therefore He has called, not His own flesh the vine, but rather the Godhead?" in Joann. 10. p 863, 4. And Nyssen· "As they who have taken poison, destroy its deadly power by some other preparation.... so when we have tasted what destroys our nature, we have need of that instead which restores what was destroyed.... But what is this? nothing else than that Body which has been proved to be mightier than death, and was the beginning, κατήρξατο, of our life. For a little leaven," &c Orat Catech. 37 Decoctâ quasi per ollam carnis nostræ cruditate, sanctificavit in æternum nobis cibum carnem suam Paulin Ep.23. Of course in such statements nothing *material* is implied, or, as Hooker says, "The mixture of His bodily substance with ours is a thing which the ancient Fathers disclaim Yet the mixture of His flesh with ours they speak of, to signify what our very bodies through mystical conjunction receive from that vital efficacy which we know to be in His, and from bodily mixtures they borrow divers similitudes rather to declare the truth than the manner of coherence between His sacred and the sanctified bodies of saints." Eccl Pol v. 56. §. 10. But without some explanation of this nature, language such as S. Athanasius's in the text seems a mere matter of words. vid infr. § 50 fin.

6. But if they take advantage of the word *wherefore*, as connected with the passage in the Psalm, *Wherefore God, even Thy God, hath anointed Thee,* for their own purposes, let these novices in Scripture and masters in irreligion know, that, as before, the word *wherefore* does not imply reward of virtue or conduct in the Word, but the reason why He came down to us, and of the Spirit's anointing which took place in Him for our sakes. For he says not, "Wherefore He anointed Thee in order to Thy being God or King or Son or Word;" for so He was before and is for ever, as has been shewn; but rather, "Since Thou art God and King, therefore Thou wast anointed, since none but Thou couldest unite man to the Holy Ghost, Thou the Image of the Father, in which[1] we were made in the beginning; for Thine is even the Spirit." For the nature of things generate could give no warranty for this, Angels having transgressed, and men disobeyed[e]. Wherefore there was need of God; and the Word is God; that those who had become under a curse, He Himself might set free. If then He was of nothing, He would not have been the Christ or Anointed, being one among others and having fellowship as the rest[2]. But, whereas He is God, as being Son of God, and is everlasting King, and exists as Radiance and Expression of the Father, wherefore fitly is He the expected Christ, whom the Father announces to mankind, by revelation to His holy Prophets, that as through Him we have come to be, so also in Him all men might be redeemed from their sins, and by Him all things might be ruled[f]. And this is the cause of

CHAP. XII.
§. 49.

[1] p. 254, note 1.

[2] p. 15, note e.

Heb. 1, 3.

---

[e] ἀγγίλων μὲν παραβάντων, ἀνθρώπων δὲ παρακούσαντων vid infr. § 51 init. And so ad Afr. 7 ἀγγίλων μὲν παραβάντων, τοῦ δὲ Ἀδὰμ παρακούσαντος, where the inference is added more distinctly, "and all creatures needing the grace of the Word," who is ἄτρεπτος, whereas τρεπτὰ τὰ γενητά. vid. supr p 32, note q. vid. infr. Orat. ii. iii. Cyril. in Joann. lib. v. 2. On the subject of the sins of Angels. vid. Huet Origen ii 5 § 16. Petav. Dogm t 3. p 87 Dissert Bened in Cyril. Hier. iii. 5. Natal. Alex. Hist. Æt. i Diss. 7.

[f] The word *wherefore* is here declared to denote the *fitness* why the Son of God should become the Son of man. His Throne, as God, is for ever, He has loved righteousness, *therefore* He is equal to the anointing of the Spirit, as man. And so S. Cyril on the same text, as in l. c. in the foregoing note. "In this ineffable unity of the Trinity, whose words and judgments are common in all, the Person of the Son has fitly undertaken to repair the race of man, that, since He it is by whom all things were made, and without whom nothing is made, and who breathed the truth of rational life into men fashioned of the dust of the earth, so He too should restore to its lost dignity our nature thus fallen from the citadel of eternity, and

252 *The Word gave His flesh the Spirit, and it did miracles.*

Disc. I. the anointing which took place in Him, and of the incarnate presence of the Word ^g; which the Psalmist foreseeing, celebrates, first His Godhead and kingdom, which is the Father's,

Ps.45,5. in these tones, *Thy throne, O God, is for ever and ever; a sceptre of righteousness is the sceptre of Thy Kingdom;* then,

v. 8. announces His descent to us thus, *Wherefore God, even thy God, hath anointed Thee with the oil of gladness above Thy fellows.*

§. 50. 7. What is there to wonder at, what to disbelieve, if the Lord who gives the Spirit, is here said Himself to be anointed with the Spirit, at a time when, necessity requiring it, He did not refuse in respect of His manhood to call Himself inferior to the Spirit? For the Jews saying that He cast out devils in Beelzebub, He answered and said to them, for the exposure

Mat.12,28. of their blasphemy, *But if I through the Spirit of God cast out devils.* Behold, the Giver of the Spirit here says that He casts out devils in the Spirit; but this is not said, except because of His flesh. For since man's nature is not equal of itself to casting out devils, but only in power of the Spirit, therefore as man He said, *But if I through the Spirit of God cast out devils.* Of course too He signified that the blasphemy offered to the Holy Ghost is greater than that against

ib. v.32. His humanity, when He said, *Whosoever shall speak a word against the Son of man, it shall be forgiven him;* such as

Mat.13,55. were those who said, *Is not this the carpenter's son?* but they who blaspheme against the Holy Ghost, and ascribe the deeds of the Word to the devil, shall have inevitable punishment ^h. This is what the Lord spoke to the Jews, as

---

should be the reformer of that of which He had been the maker." Leon. Ep. 64. 2. vid. Athan. de Incarn 7. fin. 10. In Illud omn. 2. Cyril. in Gen. i. p 13.

^g ἔνσαρκος παρουσία This phrase which has occurred above, §. 8. p. 190, is very frequent with Athan. vid. infr. §. 53, 59, 62 fin. n. 6, 10, 55, 66 twice, 72 fin. iii. 28, 35. Incarn. 20. Sent. D 9. Ep. Æg. 4. Serap 1. 3, 9. vid. also Cyril Catech. iii. 11. xii. 15. xiv. 27, 30. Epiph. Hær. 77. 17. The Eutychians avail themselves of it at the Council of Constantinople, vid. Hard Conc. t 2 pp. 164, 236.

^h He enters into the explanation of this text at some length in Serap iv.

8. &c. Origen, he says, and Theognostus understand the sin against the Holy Ghost to be apostasy from the grace of Baptism, referring to Heb. vi. 4. So far the two agree, but Origen went on to say, that the proper power or virtue of the Son extends over rational natures alone, e. g. heathens, but that of the Spirit only over Christians; those then who sin against the Son or their reason, have a remedy in Christianity and its baptism, but nothing remains for those who sin against the Spirit. But Theognostus, referring to the text, "I have many things to say but ye cannot bear them now; howbeit when He, the Spirit of Truth," &c. argued that to sin

man; but to the disciples shewing His Godhead and His majesty, and intimating that He was not inferior but equal to the Spirit, He gave the Spirit and said, *Receive ye the Holy Ghost,* and *I send Him,* and *He shall glorify Me,* and *Whatsoever He heareth, that He shall speak.* As then in this place the Lord Himself, the Giver of the Spirit, does not refuse to say that through the Spirit He casts out devils, as man; in like manner He the same, the Giver of the Spirit, refused not to say, *The Spirit of the Lord is upon Me, because He hath anointed Me,* in respect of His having become flesh, as John hath said; that it might be shewn in both these particulars, that we are they who need the Spirit's grace in our sanctification, and again who are unable to cast out devils without the Spirit's power. Through whom then and from whom behoved it that the Spirit should be given but through the Son, whose also the Spirit is? and when were we enabled to receive It, except when the Word became man? and, as the passage of the Apostle shews, that we had not been redeemed and highly exalted, had not He who exists in form of God taken a servant's form, so David also shews, that no otherwise should we have partaken the Spirit and been sanctified, but that the Giver of the Spirit, the Word Himself, had spoken of Himself as anointed with the Spirit for us. And therefore have we securely received it, He being said to be anointed in the flesh; for the flesh being first sanctified in Him[1], and He being said, as man, to have received for its sake, we have the sequel of the Spirit's grace, receiving *out of His fulness.*

8. Nor do the words, *Thou hast loved righteousness and hated iniquity,* which are added in the Psalm, shew, as again you suppose, that the Nature of the Word is alterable, but rather by their very force signify His unalterableness. For since of things generate the nature is alterable, and the one portion had transgressed and the other disobeyed, as has been said, and it is not certain how they will act, but it often happens that he who is now good afterwards alters and becomes different, so that one who was but now righteous,

CHAP. XII.

John 20, 22. 16, 13. 14.

Is. 61, 1.

[1] p. 250, note d

John 1, 16.

§. 51.

---

against the Son was to sin against inferior light, but against the Spirit was to reject the full truth of the Gospel. And then he goes on to give the same interpretation as here in the text, as a passage of great force and beauty.

254 *The flesh made superior to the Serpent in the Word.*

Disc. I.

soon is found unrighteous, wherefore there was here also need of one unalterable, that men might have the immutability of the righteousness of the Word as an image and type for virtue[1]. And this thought commends itself strongly to the right-minded. For since the first man Adam altered, and through sin death came into the world, therefore it became the second Adam to be unalterable; that, should the Serpent again assault, even the Serpent's deceit might be baffled, and, the Lord being unalterable and unchangeable, the Serpent might become powerless in his assaults against all. For as when Adam had transgressed, his sin reached unto all men, so, when the Lord had become man and had overthrown the Serpent, that so great strength of His is to extend through all men, so that each of us may say, *For we are not ignorant of his devices.* Good reason then that the Lord, who ever is in nature unalterable, loving righteousness and hating iniquity, should be anointed and Himself sent on mission, that, He, being and remaining the same[1], by taking this alterable flesh, *might condemn sin in it,* and might secure its freedom, and its ability[k] henceforth *to fulfil the righteousness of the law* in itself, so as to be able to say, *But we are not in the flesh but in the Spirit, if so be that the Spirit of God dwelleth in us.*

2 Cor. 2, 11.

[1] p. 249, ref. 2.
Rom. 8, 3.
v. 4.
v. 9.

§. 52.   9. Vainly then, here again, O Arians, have ye made this conjecture, and vainly alleged the words of Scripture, for God's Word is unalterable, and is ever in one state, not as it may happen[1], but as the Father is, since how is He like

---

[1] Vid. Athan. de Incarn 13. 14. vid. also Gent. 41 fin. and supr. p 29, note k. Cum justitia nulla esset in terrâ, doctorem misit, quasi vivam legem. Lactant. Instit. iv. 25. "The Only-begotten was made man like us,....as if lending us His own stedfastness." Cyril. in Joann. lib. v. 2. p. 473. vid. also Thesaur. 20. p. 198. August. de Corr et Grat. 10—12. Damasc. F. O. iv. 4 But the words of Athan. embrace too many subjects to illustrate distinctly in a note.

[k] "Without His sojourning here at all, God was able to speak the Word only and undo the curse....but then the power indeed of Him who gave command had been shewn, but man had been but such as Adam before the fall, receiving grace from without, not having it united to the body ...Then, had he been again seduced by the serpent, a second need had arisen of God's commanding and undoing the curse; and this had gone on without limit, and men had remained under guilt just as before, being in slavery to sin, and ever sinning, they had ever needed pardon, and never been made free, being in themselves carnal, and ever defeated by the Law by reason of the infirmity of the flesh " Orat. ii. 68. And so in Incarn. 7. he says that repentance might have been pertinent, had man merely offended, without *corruption* following; but that that *corruption* involved the necessity of the Word's vicarious sufferings and intercessory office.

[1] ἁπλῶς. οὐκ ἁπλῶς ὡρίσθη, ἀλλ' ἀκριβῶς ἐξητάσθη Socr 1. 9. p 31

the Father, unless He be thus? or how is all that is the Father's, the Son's also, if He has not the unalterableness and unchangeableness of the Father[1]? Not as being subject to laws[m], and as influenced this way and that, does He love this and hate that, lest, if from fear of forfeiture He chooses the opposite, we admit in another way that He is alterable; but, as being God and the Father's Word, He is a just judge and lover of virtue, or rather its dispenser. Therefore being just and holy by nature, on this account He is said to love righteousness and to hate iniquity; as much as to say, that He loves and takes to Him the virtuous, and rejects and hates the unrighteous. And divine Scripture says the same of the Father; *The Righteous Lord loveth righteousness. Thou hatest all them that work iniquity;* and, *The Lord loveth the gates of Sion, more than all the dwellings of Jacob;* and, *Jacob have I loved, but Esau have I hated;* and in Esaias, there is the voice of God again saying, *I the Lord love righteousness, and hate robbery of unrighteousness.* Let them then expound those former words as these latter; for the former also are written of the Image of God: else, misinterpreting these as those, they will conceive that the Father too as alterable. But, since the very hearing others say this is not without peril, we do well to think that God is said to love righteousness and to hate robbery of unrighteousness, not as if influenced this way and that, and capable of the contrary, selecting one thing and not choosing another, for this belongs to things generated, but that, as a judge, He loves and takes to Him the righteous and withdraws from the bad. It follows then to think the same concerning the Image of God also, that He loves and hates no otherwise than thus. For such must be the nature of the Image as is Its Father, though the Arians in their blindness fail to see either that Image or any other truth of the divine oracles. For being forced from the conceptions or rather misconceptions[n] of their own hearts, they fall back upon passages of divine Scripture, and here too from want of understanding, according to their

---

[m] Eunomius said that our Lord was utterly separate from the Father, " by natural law," νόμῳ φύσεως, S. Basil observes, " as if the God of all had not power over Himself, ἑαυτοῦ κύριος, but were in bondage under the decrees of necessity." contr. Eunom. ii. 30.

[n] ἐννοιῶν μᾶλλον δὲ παρανοιῶν. vid. p. 237, note d. And so κατ' ἐπίνοιαν, ἀλλὰ μᾶλλόν ἐστιν ἀπόνοια Orat ii. §. 38.

wont, they discern not their meaning; but laying down their own irreligion as a sort of canon of interpretation°, they wrest the whole of the divine oracles into accordance with it. And so on the bare mention of such doctrine, they deserve nothing but the reply, *Ye do err, not knowing the Scriptures nor the power of God;* and if they persist in it, they must be put to silence, by the words, *Render to* man *the things that are* man's, *and to God the things that are God's.*

° ἰδίαν vid. p. 233, note a. p. 257. ref. 4. ἰδίων κακονοιῶν, Orat. ii. §. 18. Instead of professing to examine Scripture or to acquiesce in what they had been taught, the Arians were remarkable for insisting on certain abstract positions or inferences on which they make the whole controversy turn. Vid. Socrates's account of Arius's commencement, " If God has a Son, he must have a beginning of existence," &c. &c. and so the word ἀγέννητόν.

CHAP. XIII.

TEXTS EXPLAINED; THIRDLY, HEBREWS 1. 4.

Additional texts brought as objections; e. g. Hebr. i. 4 vii. 22 Whether the word "better" implies likeness to the Angels; and "made" or "become" implies creation Necessary to consider the circumstances under which Scripture speaks. Difference between "better" and "greater," texts in proof. "Made" or "become" a general word. Contrast in Heb. 1. 4 between the Son and the Works in point of nature. The difference of the punishments under the two Covenants shews the difference of the natures of the Son and the Angels. "Become" relates not to the nature of the Word, but to His manhood and office and relation towards us. Parallel passages in which the term is applied to the Eternal Father.

1. BUT it is written, say they, in the Proverbs, *The Lord created Me the beginning of His ways, for His works*[1]; and in the Epistle to the Hebrews the Apostle says, *Being made so much better than the Angels, as He hath by inheritance obtained a more excellent Name than they.* And soon after, *Wherefore, holy brethren, partakers of the heavenly calling, consider the Apostle and High Priest of our profession, Christ Jesus, who was faithful to Him that appointed Him*[2]. And in the Acts, *Therefore let all the house of Israel know assuredly, that God hath made that same Jesus whom ye have crucified both Lord and Christ*[3]. These passages they brought forward at every turn, mistaking their sense, under the idea that they proved that the Word of God was a creature and work and one of things generate; and thus they deceive the thoughtless, making the language of Scripture their pretence, but instead of the true sense sowing[4] upon it the poison of their own[5] heresy. For had they known, they would not have been irreligious against *the*[5] *Lord of glory*, nor have wrested the good words of Scripture. If then henceforward openly adopting Caiaphas's way, they

CHAP. XIII.
§. 53.
Prov. 8, 22
¹ vid. Orat. ii. §. 19—72.
Heb. 1, 4.
Heb. 3, 1
² vid. Orat. ii. §. 2—11.
³ vid. Orat. ii. §. 11—18.
Acts 2, 36.
⁴ p. 5, note k.
⁵ ἴδιον
1 Cor. 2, 8.

s

Disc.
I.

vid.
1 Kings
8, 27.
Zech. 2,
10. Bar.
3, 37.
¹ p. 252,
note g.

² p. 190,
note c.

³ ἐνσώμα-
τον

have determined on judaizing, and are ignorant of the text, —that verily God shall dwell upon the earth, let them not inquire into the Apostolical sayings; for they were out of place with Jews. Or, if mixing themselves up with the godless Manichees ᵃ, they deny that *the Word was made flesh*, and His incarnate presence¹, then let them not bring forward the Proverbs, for this is out of place with the Manichees. But if for preferment-sake, and the lucre of avarice which follows², and the desire for good repute, they venture not on denying the text, *The Word was made flesh*, since so it is written, either let them rightly interpret the words of Scripture, of the embodied³ presence of the Saviour, or, if they deny their sense, let them deny too that the Lord became man. For it is unseemly, while confessing that *the Word became flesh*, yet to be ashamed at what is written of Him, and on that account to corrupt the sense.

§. 54.

⁴ p. 22,
note z

Acts 8,
34.

Matt.
24, 3.

vid.
1 Thes.
4, 13.
2 Thes.
2, 1. &c.

2 Tim.
2, 17.
1 Tim
1, 20

2. Thus, it is written, *So much better than the Angels;* let us then first examine this. Now it is right and necessary, as in all divine Scripture, so here, faithfully to expound the time of which the Apostle wrote, and the person⁴, and the point; lest the reader, from ignorance missing either these or any similar particular, may be wide of the true sense. This understood that inquiring eunuch, when he thus besought Philip, *I pray thee, of whom doth the Prophet speak this? of himself, or of some other man?* for he feared lest, expounding the lesson unsuitably to the person, he should wander from the right sense. And the disciples, wishing to learn the time of what was foretold, besought the Lord, *Tell us,* said they, *when shall these things be? and what is the sign of Thy coming?* And again, hearing from the Saviour the events of the end, they desired to learn the time of it, that they might be kept from error themselves, and might be able to teach others; as, for instance, when they have learned, they set right the Thessalonians, who were going wrong. When then one knows properly these points, his understanding of the faith is right and healthy; but if he mistakes any such points, forthwith he falls into heresy. Thus the party of Hymenæus and Alexander were beside the time, when they said that the resurrection had

---

ᵃ Vid. the same contrast, de Syn. § 33. p. 130 supr. §. 8. p 189. Orat. iv. § 23.

which the Arians neglect. 259

already been, and the Galatians were after the time, in making much of circumcision now. And to miss the person was the lot of the Jews, and is still, who think that of one of themselves is said, *Behold, a Virgin shall conceive,* and *bear a Son, and they shall call His Name Emmanuel, which is being interpreted, God with us;* and that, *A prophet shall the Lord your God raise up to you,* is spoken of one of the Prophets; and who, as to the words, *He was led as a sheep to the slaughter,* instead of learning from Philip, conjecture them spoken of Esaias or some other of the Prophets which have been [b]

CHAP. XIII
Is 7, 14.
Mat. 1, 23.
Deut 18, 15.
Is 53, 7.

3. Such has been the state of mind under which Christ's enemies has fallen into their execrable heresy[1]. For had they known the person, and the subject, and the season of the Apostle's words, they would not have expounded of Christ's divinity what belongs to His manhood, nor in their folly have committed so great an act of irreligion. Now this will be readily seen, if one expounds properly the beginning of this passage. For the Apostle says, *God who at sundry times and diverse manners spake in times past unto the fathers by the prophets, hath in these last days spoken unto us by His Son;* then again shortly after he says, *when He had by Himself purged our sins, He sat down on the right hand of the Majesty on high, having become*[2] *so much better than the Angels, as He hath by inheritance obtained a more excellent Name than they.* It appears then that the Apostle's words make mention of that time, when God spoke unto us by His Son, and when a purging of sins took place Now when did He speak unto us by His Son, and when did purging of sins take place? and when did He become man? when, but subsequently to the Prophets in the last days? Next, proceeding with his account of the economy in which we were concerned, and speaking of the last times, he is naturally led to observe that not even in the former times was God silent with men, but spoke to them by the Prophets. And, whereas the Prophets ministered, and the

§. 55
¹ μυσαράν
Heb. 1, 1.
² γενόμε-
νος
being
made.
E V.

---

[b] The more common evasion on the part of the Jews was to interpret the prophecy of their own sufferings in captivity. It was an idea of Grotius that the prophecy received a first fulfilment in Jeremiah. vid. Justin Tryph. 72 et al. Iren. Hær. iv 33. Tertull. in Jud. 9. Cyprian. Testim. in Jud ii 13. Euseb. Dem. iii 2. &c.

Disc. I. Law was spoken by Angels, while the Son too came on earth, and that in order to minister, he was forced to add, *Become so much better than the Angels*, wishing to shew that, as much as the son excels a servant, so much also the ministry of the Son is better than the ministry of servants. Contrasting then the old ministry and the new, the Apostle deals freely with the Jews, writing and saying, *Become so much better than the Angels*. This is why throughout he uses no comparison, such as " become greater," or " more honourable," lest we should think of Him and them as one in kind[1], but *better* is his word, by way of marking the difference of the Son's nature from things generated. And of this we have proof from divine Scripture; David, for instance, saying in the Psalm, *One day in Thy courts is better than a thousand:* and Solomon crying out, *Receive my instruction and not silver, and knowledge rather than choice gold. For wisdom is better than rubies; and all the things that may be desired are not to be compared to it.* Are not wisdom and stones of the earth different in substance[3] and separate[4] in nature? Are heavenly courts at all akin to earthly houses? Or is there any similarity between things eternal and spiritual, and things temporal and mortal? And this is what Esaias says, *Thus saith the Lord unto the eunuchs that keep My sabbaths, and choose the things that please Me, and take hold of My Covenant; even unto them will I give in Mine house, and within My walls, a place and a name better than of sons and of daughters. I will give them an everlasting name that shall not be cut off.* In like manner there is nought akin between the Son and the Angels; so that the word *better* is not used to compare but to contrast, because of the difference[5] of His nature from them. And therefore the Apostle also Himself, when he interprets the word *better*, places its force in nothing short of the Son's excellence[6] over things generated, calling the one Son, the other servants; the one, as a Son with the Father, sitting on the right; and the others, as servants, standing before Him, and being sent, and fulfilling offices. Scripture, in speaking thus, implies, O Arians, not that the Son is generate, but rather other than things generate, and proper to the Father, being in His bosom.

[1] ὁμογενῶν, vid p. 169.
[2] κρείττων, superior or above. Ps. 84, 10 Prov 8, 10. 11.
[3] ἑτεροούσια
[4] ἄλλα
Is. 56, 4. 5.
[5] τὸ ἄλλαττον
[6] διαφορᾷ
§. 56.

He became better, that is, came to be through generation.

4. Nor does even the expression *become*, which here occurs, shew that the Son is generate, as ye suppose. If indeed it were simply *become* and no more, a case might stand for the Arians, but, whereas they are forestalled with the word *Son* throughout the passage, shewing that He is other than things generate, so again not even the word *become* occurs absolutely [d], but *better* is immediately subjoined. For the writer thought the expression immaterial, knowing that in the case of one who was confessedly a genuine Son, to say *become* is the same with saying that He was generated, and that He is *better*. For it matters not though we speak of what is generate, as " become" or " made;" but on the contrary, things generate cannot be called generate, God's handiwork as they are, except so far as after their making they partake of the Son who is the true Generate, and are therefore said to have been generated also, not at all in their own nature, but because of their participation of the Son in the Spirit[e]. And this again divine Scripture recognises; for it

[c] There is apparently much confusion in the arrangement of the paragraphs that follow, though the appearance may perhaps arise from Athan.'s incorporating some passage from a former work into his text. vid p 227, note d. It is easy to suggest alterations, but not any thing satisfactory. The same ideas are scattered about. Thus συγκριτικῶς occurs in n. 3 and n. 5. The Son's seat on the right, and Angels in ministry, n 3. fin n. 10. n. 11. " Become" interpreted as " is generated and is," n. 4. and n. 11. The explanation of " become," n. 4. n. 9. n 11.—n. 14. The Word's ἐπιδημία is introduced in n. 7. and 8. παρουσία being the more common word; ἐπιδημία occurs Orat. ii. §. 67 init. Serap. 1. 9. Vid. however p 268, notes n and o. If a change must be suggested, it would be to transfer n. 4. after n. 8. and n. 10 after n. 3.

[d] ἀπολελυμένως vid also Orat. ii. 54. 62 in. 22. Basil. contr Eunom. i. p. 244. Cyril. Thesaur. 25. p. 236. διαλελυμένως Orat. iv. 1.

[e] In this translation, γεννητόν and γενητόν have been considered as synonymous, in spite of such distinction in the reading, as Montfaucon adopts, and this under the impression that that distinction is of a later date, Athan. as Basil after him, apparently not recognising it. The Platonists certainly spoke of the Almighty as ἀγένητος, and the world as γενητός, and the Arians took advantage of this phraseology. If then Athan. did not admit it, he would naturally have said so; whereas his argument is, " True, the world or creation is γενητός, but only by μετουσία, as partaking of Him who is the one and only real γεννητός, or Son." vid. p. 32, note q. That is, he does not discriminate between two *distinct* ideas, " Son" and " creature" confused by a common name, but he admits their connection, only explains it, or, to speak logically, instead of considering γεννητόν and γενητόν as *equivocal* words, he uses them as synonymous and one, with a primary and secondary meaning. Afterwards they were distinguished, p. 226, note c. In like manner, our Lord is called μονογενής. Athan. speaks of the γένεσις of human sons, and of the Divine, de Decr. §. 11. and in de Syn. §. 47. he observes that S Ignatius calls the Son γεννητὸς καὶ ἀγέννητος, without a hint about the distinction of roots. Again, one of the original Arian positions was that our Lord was a γέννημα ἀλλ' οὐκ ὡς ἓν τῶν γεννημάτων, which Athan. frequently notices and combats, vid. Orat. ii. 19. But instead of answering it by substituting γενητῶν, as if ποιημάτων, for γεννημάτων, he allows that γέννημα may be taken as synonymous with κτίσμα,

262 *The Son not compared to, but contrasted with, Angels.*

Disc. I. John 1, 3
Ps 104, 24
Job 1, 3.
Gen. 21, 5

not only says in the case of things generate, *All things came to be through Him, and, without Him there was not any thing made,* and, *In wisdom hast Thou made them all;* but in the case of sons also which are generate, *To Job there came seven sons and three daughters,* and, *Abraham was an hundred years old when there came to him Isaac his son;* and Moses said, *If to any one there come sons.* Therefore since the Son is other than things generate, alone the proper offspring of the Father's substance, this plea of the Arians about the word *become* is worth nothing.

5. If moreover, baffled so far, they should still violently insist that the language is that of comparison, and that comparison in consequence implies oneness of kind[1], so that the Son is of the nature of Angels, they will in the first place incur the disgrace of rivalling and repeating what Valentinus held, and Carpocrates, and those other heretics, of whom the former said that the Angels were one in kind with the Christ, and Carpocrates that Angels are framers of the world[f]. Perchance it is under the instruction of these masters that they compare the Word of God with the Angels; though surely amid such speculations, they will be moved by the Psalmist, saying, *Who is he among the gods that shall be like unto the Lord?* and, *Among the gods there is none like unto Thee, O Lord.* However, they must be answered, with the chance of their profiting by it, that comparison confessedly does belong to subjects one in kind, not to those which differ. No one, for instance, would compare God with man, or again man with brutes, nor wood with stone, because their natures are unlike; but God is beyond comparison, and man is com-

¹ ὁμογενῆ, p 200, ref. 1.

§. 57.

Ps 89,7.
Ps 86,8.

---

and only argues that there is a *special sense* of it in which it applies to the Word, not *as one of a number,* as the Arians said, but solely, incommunicably, as being the μονογενής. In the passage before us, which at first seems to require the distinction, he does but say, 1. that the Son is not γενητὸς or γεννητός, "generate," i. e. in the general sense, 2 that He is generated, γιγνῆσθαι or γεγεννῆσθαι, as the μονογενής; 3. that the γενητὰ or γεννητὰ (creatures) are called γενητὰ, or said γιγίννησθαι, as partaking of the γεννητὸς υἱός 4 that (in themselves) they are properly said γεγονέναι or πεποιῆσθαι. It may be admitted, as evident even from this pas-

sage, that though Athan. does not distinguish between γενητὸν and γεννητὸν, yet he considers γιγεννῆσθαι or γέννημα as especially appropriate to the Son, γεγονέναι and γινόμενος to the creation.

f These tenets and similar ones were common to many branches of the Gnostics, who paid worship to the Angels, or ascribed to them the creation; the doctrine of their consubstantiality with our Lord arose from their belief in emanation. S Athanasius here uses the word ὁμογενής, not ὁμοούσιος which was usual with them, vid Bull D. F. N. II. 1. §. 2 as with the Manichees after them, Beausobre, Manich. III. 8.

pared to man, and wood to wood, and stone to stone. Now in such cases we should not speak of *better*, but of " rather " and " more;" thus Joseph was comely rather than his brethren, and Rachel than Leah; star[1] is not better than star, but is the rather excellent in glory; whereas in bringing together things which differ in kind, then *better* is used to mark the difference, as has been said in the case of wisdom and jewels. Had then the Apostle said, " by so much has the Son precedence of the Angels," or " by so much greater," you would have had a plea, as if the Son were compared with the Angels; but, as it is, in saying that He is *better*, and differs as far as Son from servants, the Apostle shews that He is other than the Angels in nature.

6. Moreover by saying that He it is who has *laid the foundation of all things*, he shews that He is other than all things generate. But if He be other and different in substance[2] from their nature, what comparison of His substance[3] can there be, or what likeness to them? though, even if they have any such thoughts, Paul shall refute them, who speaks to the very point, *For unto which of the Angels said He at any time, Thou art My Son, this day have I begotten Thee? And of the Angels He saith, Who maketh His Angels spirits, and His ministers a flame of fire.* Observe here, §. 58. the word *made* belongs to things generate, and he calls them things made; but to the Son he speaks not of making, nor of becoming, but of eternity and kingship, and a Framer's office, exclaiming, *Thy Throne, O God, is for ever and ever;* and, *Thou, Lord, in the beginning hast laid the foundation of the earth, and the heavens are the works of Thine hands; they shall perish, but Thou remainest.* From which words even they, were they but willing, might perceive that the Framer is other than things framed, the former God, the latter things generate, made out of nothing. For what has been said, *They shall perish,* is said, not as if the creation were destined for destruction, but to express the nature of things generate by the issue to which they tend[4]. For things which admit of perishing, though through the grace[5] of their Maker they perish not, yet have come out of nothing, and themselves witness that they once were not. And on this account, since their nature is such, it is said of the Son,

CHAP. XIII.

[1] Orat. ii. §. 20.

[2] ἑτερο-
[3] οὐσίου p 144, note k.

Heb. 1, 10.

Heb. 1, 5. 7.

v. 8. 10.

[4] p. 223,
[5] note g. p. 32, note q.

Disc. I.

Thou remainest, to shew His eternity; for not having the capacity of perishing, as things generate have, but having eternal duration, it is foreign to Him to have it said, "He was not before His generation," but proper to Him to be always, and to endure together with the Father. And though the Apostle had not thus written in his Epistle to the Hebrews, still his other Epistles, and the whole of Scripture, would certainly forbid their entertaining such notions concerning the Word. But since he has here expressly written it, and, as has been above shewn, the Son is Offspring of the Father's substance, and He is Framer, and other things are framed by Him, and He is the Radiance and Word and Image and Wisdom of the Father, and things generate stand and serve in their place below the Trinity, therefore the Son is different in kind and different in substance from things generate, and on the contrary is proper to the Father's substance and one in nature to it[g]. And hence it is that the Son too says not, *My Father is better than I*, lest we should conceive Him to be foreign to His Nature, but *greater*, not indeed in greatness, nor in time, but because of His generation from the Father Himself[h]; nay, in saying *greater* He again shews that He is proper to His substance.

John 14, 28.

§. 59. 7. And the Apostle's own reason for saying, *so much better than the Angels*, was not any wish in the first instance to compare the substance[1] of the Word to things generate, (for He cannot be compared, rather they are incommeasurable,) but regarding the Word's visitation[2] in the flesh, and the economy which He then sustained, He wished to shew that He was not like those who had gone before Him; so that, as much as He excelled in nature those who were sent afore by Him, by so much also the grace which came from and through Him was better than the ministry through Angels[i]. For it is the function of servants, to demand the fruits and no more; but of the Son and Master to forgive the debts and to transfer the vineyard.

[1] p 263, ref. 3 §. 60. 62 64. 11. §. 18.
[2] ἐπιδημίαν

[g] Here again is a remarkable avoidance of the word ὁμοούσιον He says that the Son is ἑτερογενὴς καὶ ἑτεροούσιος τῶν γεννητῶν, καὶ τῆς τοῦ πατρὸς οὐσίας ἴδιος καὶ ὁμοφυής. vid. pp. 209, 210, notes d. e
[h] Athan. otherwise explains this text, Incarn. contr. Arian. 4. if it be his. This text is thus taken by Basil. contr. Eun. iv. p. 289. Naz Orat. 30. 7. &c. &c
[i] He also applies this text to our Lord's economy and ministry, de Sent. D. 11. in Apoll. ii. 15.

8. Certainly what the Apostle proceeds to say shews the excellence of the Son over things generate; *Therefore we ought to give the more earnest heed to the things which we have heard, lest at any time we should let them slip. For if the word spoken by Angels was stedfast, and every transgression and disobedience received a just recompence of reward; how shall we escape, if we neglect so great salvation; which at the first began to be spoken by the Lord, and was confirmed unto us by them that heard Him.* But if the Son were in the number of things generate, He was not better than they, nor did disobedience involve increase of punishment because of Him; any more than in the Ministry of Angels there was not, according to each Angel, greater or less guilt in the transgressors, but the Law was one, and one was its vengeance on transgressors. But, whereas the Word is not in the number of generate things, but is Son of the Father, therefore, as He Himself is better and His acts better and transcendent, so also the punishment is worse. Let them contemplate then the grace which is through the Son, and let them acknowledge the witness which He gives even from His works, that He is other than things generated, and alone the very Son in the Father and the Father in Him. And the Law [k] was spoken by Angels, and perfected no one, needing the visitation of the Word, as Paul hath said; but that visitation has perfected the work of the Father. And then, from Adam unto Moses death reigned; but the presence of the Word abolished death. And no longer in Adam are we all dying; but in Christ we are all reviving. And then, from Dan to Bersabe was the Law proclaimed, and in Judæa only was God known, but now, unto all the earth has gone forth their voice, and all the earth has been filled with the knowledge of God, and the disciples have made disciples of all the nations, and now is fulfilled what is

CHAP. XIII.
Heb. 2, 1—3.

Heb. 7, 19.
John 17, 4.
Rom. 5, 14.
2 Tim. 1, 10.
1 Cor. 15, 22.
vid. Ps. 76, 1. and 19, 4.
Is. 11, 9.
Mat. 28, 19.

---

[k] Part of this chapter, as for instance n. 7, 8. is much more finished in point of style than the general course of his Orations. It may be indeed only the natural consequence of his warming with his subject, but this beautiful passage looks very much like an insertion. Some words of it are found in Sent. D. 11. written a few years sooner. He certainly transcribed himself in other places, as S. Leo, e g. repeats himself in another controversy. Athan is so very eloquent and rich a writer whenever he is led into comments upon Scripture, that one almost regrets he had ever to adopt a controversial tone; except indeed that Arianism has given occasion to those comments, and that that tone is of course a lesson of doctrine to us, and therefore instructive.

written, *They shall be all taught of God.* And then what was revealed, was but a type; but now the truth has been manifested. And this again the Apostle himself describes afterwards more clearly, saying, *By so much was Jesus made a surety of a better testament;* and again, *But now hath He obtained a more excellent ministry, by how much also He is the Mediator of a better covenant, which was established upon better promises.* And, *For the Law made nothing perfect, but the bringing in of a better hope did.* And again he says, *It was therefore necessary that the patterns of things in the heavens should be purified with these; but the heavenly things themselves with better sacrifices than these.* Both in the verse before us then, and throughout, does he ascribe the word *better* to the Lord, who is better and other than generated things. For better is the sacrifice through Him, better the hope in Him; and also the promises through Him, not merely as great compared with small, but the one differing from the other in nature, because He who conducts this economy, is *better* than things generated.

§. 60. 9. Moreover the words *He is become surety*[1] denotes the pledge in our behalf which He has provided. For as, being the *Word,* He *became flesh,* and *become* we ascribe to the flesh, for it is generated and created, so do we here the expression *He is become,* expounding it according to a second sense, viz. because He has become man. And let these contentious men know, that they fail in this their perverse purpose; let them know that Paul does not signify that His substance[2] has become, knowing, as He did, that He is Son and Wisdom and Radiance and Image of the Father; but here too he refers the word *become* to the ministry of that covenant, in which death which once ruled is abolished. Since here also the ministry through Him has become better, in that *what the Law could not do in that it was weak through the flesh, God sending His own Son in the likeness of sinful flesh, and for sin condemned sin in the flesh,* ridding it of the trespass, in which, being continually held captive, it admitted not the Divine mind. And having rendered the flesh capable[3] of the Word, He made us walk, no longer according to the flesh, but according to the Spirit, and say again and again, "But we are not in the flesh but in the Spirit," and, "For the Son of God came into the world, not to judge the world, but to redeem all men, and that the world might be saved through Him." Formerly the world, as guilty, was under judgment from the Law; but now the Word has taken on Himself the judgment, and having suffered in the body for all, has bestowed salvation to all[1]. With a view to this, hath John exclaimed, *The law was given by Moses, but grace and truth came by Jesus Christ.* Better is grace than the Law, and truth than the shadow.

10. *Better* then, as has been said, could not have been brought to pass by any other than the Son, who sits on the right hand of the Father. And what does this denote but the Son's genuineness[1], and that the Godhead of the Father is the same as the Son's[2]? For in that the Son reigns in His Father's kingdom, is seated upon the same throne as the Father, and is contemplated in the Father's Godhead, therefore is the Word God, and whoso beholds the Son, beholds the Father; and thus there is one God. Sitting then on the right, yet hath He not His Father on the left[m], but, whatever is right[3] and precious in the Father, that also the Son has, and says, *All things that the Father hath are Mine.* Wherefore also the Son, though sitting on the right, also sees the Father on the right, though it be as become man that He says, *I saw the Lord always before My face, for He is on My right hand, therefore I shall not fall.* This shews moreover that the Son is in the Father and the Father in the Son; for the Father being on the right, the Son is on the right; and while the Son sits on the right of the Father, the Father is in the Son. And the Angels indeed minister ascending and descending; but concerning the Son he saith, *And let all the*

CHAP. XIII.
v. John 3, 17.

John 1, 17.

§. 61.

1 τὸ γνή-
2 σιον p. 145, note r.

3 δεξιόν

John 16, 15.

Ps. 16, 9.

Heb. 1, 6.

---

[1] vid Incarn. passim. Theod Eranist. iii. pp. 196—198, &c. &c. It was the tendency of all the heresies concerning the Person of Christ to explain away or deny the Atonement. The Arians, after the Platonists, insisted on the pre-existing Priesthood, as if the incarnation and crucifixion were not of its essence. The Apollinarians resolved the Incarnation into a manifestation, Theod. Eran. i. The Nestorians denied the Atonement, Procl. ad Armen. p. 615. And the Eutychians, Leont. Ep. 28, 5.

[m] Nec ideo tamen quasi humanâ formâ circumscriptum esse Deum Patrem arbitrandum est, ut de illo cogitantibus dextrum aut sinistrum latus animo occurrat, aut id ipsum quod sedens Pater dicitur, flexis poplitibus fieri putandum est, ne in illud incidamus sacrilegium, &c. August. de Fid. et Symb. 14. Does this passage of Athan.'s shew that the Anthropomorphites were stirring in Egypt already?

268 *The word "become" marks the incarnation and ministry.*

Disc. I.

vid. John 17, 4.

Mark 10, 45. John 14, 10. 9. [1] p. 229, note g.

Angels of God worship Him. And when Angels minister, they say, " I am sent unto thee," and, " The Lord has commanded," but the Son, though He say in human fashion, " I am sent," and comes to finish the work and to minister, nevertheless says, as being Word and Image, *I am in the Father, and the Father in Me;* and, *He that hath seen Me, hath seen the Father*[1]; and, *The Father that abideth in Me, He doeth the works;* for what we behold in that Image, are the Father's works.

11. What has been already said ought to prevail with those persons who are fighting against the very truth; however, if, because it is written, *become better,* they refuse to explain *become*, as used of the Son, to be " has been generated and is[n]," or again as referring to the better covenant having come to be[o], as we have said, but consider from this expression that the Word is called generate, let them hear the same again in a concise form, since they have forgotten §. 62. what has been said. If the Son be in the number of the Angels, then let the word *become* apply to Him as to them, and let Him not differ at all from them in nature; but be they either sons with Him, or be He an Angel with them; sit they one and all together on the right hand of the Father, or be the Son standing with them all as a ministering Spirit, sent forth to minister Himself as they are. But if on the other hand Paul distinguishes the Son from things generate, saying, *To which of the Angels said He at any time, Thou art My Son?* and the one frames heaven and earth, but they are made by Him; and He sitteth with the Father, but they stand by ministering, who does not see that he has not used the word *become* of the substance[2] of the Word, but of the ministration come through Him? For, as, being the *Word*, He *became flesh,* so when become man, He became by so much better in His ministry than the ministry which came by the Angels, as Son excels servants and Framer things framed. Let them cease therefore to take the word *become* of the substance of the Son, for He is not one of generated things; and let them acknowledge that it is indicative of His ministry and the economy which came to pass.

[2] p 59, ref. 1.

12. But how He became better in His ministry, being

[n] Of His divine nature, n. 4 —n 8.   [o] Of His human nature, n. 9. and 10.

better in nature than things generate, appears from what has been said before, which, I consider, is sufficient in itself to put them to shame. But if they carry on the contest, it will be proper upon their rash daring to close with them, and to oppose to them those similar expressions which are used concerning the Father Himself. This may serve to prevail with them to refrain their tongue from evil, or may teach them the depth of their folly. Now it is written, *Become my strong rock and house of defence, that Thou mayest save me.* And again, *The Lord became a defence for the oppressed,* and the like which are found in divine Scripture. If then they apply these passages to the Son, which perhaps is nearest to the truth, then let them acknowledge that the sacred writers ask Him, as not being generate, to become to them *a strong rock and house of defence;* and for the future let them understand *become,* and *He made,* and *He created,* of His incarnate presence. For then did He become *a strong rock and house of defence,* when He bore our sins in His own body upon the tree, and said, *Come unto Me, all ye that labour and are heavy laden, and I will give you rest.*

13. But if they refer these passages to the Father, will they, when it is here also written, "Become" and "He became," venture so far as to affirm that God is generate? Yea, they will dare, as they thus argue concerning His Word; for the course of their argument carries them on to conjecture the same things concerning the Father, as they devise concerning His Word. But far be such a notion ever from the thoughts of all the faithful! for neither is the Son in the number of things generated, nor do the words of Scripture in question, *Become,* and *He became,* denote beginning of being, but that succour which was given to the needy. For God is always, and one and the same, but men came to be afterwards through the Word, when the Father Himself willed it; and God is invisible and inaccessible to generated things, and especially to men upon earth. When then men in infirmity invoke Him, when in persecution they ask help, when under injuries they pray, then the Invisible, being a lover of man, shines forth upon them with His beneficence, which He exercises through and in His proper Word. And forthwith

Chap XIII.

Ps 31,3.

Ps. 9, 9.

Mat. 11, 28.

§. 63.

the divine manifestation is made to every one according to his need, and is made to the weak health, and to the persecuted a *refuge* and *house of defence;* and to the injured He says, *While thou speakest I will say, Here I am.* What defence then comes to each through the Son, that each says that God has come to be to himself, since succour comes from God Himself through the Word. Moreover the usage of men recognises this, and every one will confess its propriety. Often succour comes from man to man; one has undertaken toil for the injured, as Abraham for Lot; and another has opened his home to the persecuted, as Abdias to the sons of the prophets; and another has entertained a stranger, as Lot the Angels; and another has supplied the needy, as Job those who begged of him. As then, should one and the other of these benefitted persons say, " Such a one became an assistance to me," and another " and to me a refuge," and " to another a supply," yet in so saying would not be speaking of the original becoming or the substance of their benefactors, but of the beneficence coming to themselves from them, so also when the sacred writers say concerning God, *He became* and *become Thou,* they do not denote any original becoming, for God is unoriginate and not generate, but the salvation which is made to be unto men from Him.

§ 64. 14. This being so understood, it is parallel also respecting the Son, that whatever, and however often, is said, such as, *He became* and *become,* should ever have the same sense: so that as, when we hear the words in question *become better than the Angels* and *He became,* we should not conceive any original becoming of the Word, nor in any way fancy from such terms that He is generate; but should understand Paul's words of His ministry and economy when He became man. For when *the Word became flesh and dwelt among us* and came to minister and to grant salvation to all, then He became to us salvation, and became life, and became propitiation; then His economy in our behalf became much better than the Angels, and He became the Way and became the Resurrection And as the words *Become my strong rock* do not denote that the substance of God Himself became, but His lovingkindness, as has been said, so also here the *having become better than the Angels*, and, *He became*, and, *by so much is Jesus become a better surety*, do not signify that the substance [1] of the Word is generate, (perish the thought!) but the beneficence which towards us came to be through His incarnation; unthankful though the heretics be, and obstinate in behalf of their irreligion.

[1] p 268, ref 2.

NOTE on page 214.

On the meaning of the formula πρὶν γεννηθῆναι οὐκ ἦν, in the Nicene Anathema.

NOTE ON DISC. I.

It was observed p. 61, note d, that there were two clauses in the Nicene Anathema which required explanation. One of them, ἐξ ἑτέρας ὑποστάσεως ἢ οὐσίας, has been discussed in the Note, pp. 66—72; the other, πρὶν γεννηθῆναι οὐκ ἦν, shall be considered now.

Bishop Bull has suggested a very ingenious interpietation of it, which is not obvious, but which, when stated, has much plausibility, as going to explain, or rather to sanction, certain modes of speech in some early Fathers of venerable authority, which have been urged by heterodox writers, and given up by Catholics of the Roman School, as savouring of Arianism. The foregoing pages have made it abundantly evident that the point of controversy between Catholics and the Arians was, not whether our Lord was God, but whether He was Son of God; the solution of the former question being involved in that of the latter. The Arians maintained that the very word "Son" implied a *beginning*, or that our Lord was not Very God; the Catholics said that it implied *connaturality*, or that He was Very God as one with God. Now five early writers, Athenagoras, Tatian, Theophilus, Hippolytus, and Novatian, of whom the authority of Hippolytus is very great, not to speak of Theophilus and Athenagoras, whatever be thought of Tatian and of Novatian, seem to speak of the divine generation as taking place immediately before the creation of the world, that is, as if not eternal, though at the same time they teach that our Lord existed before that generation. In other words they seem to teach that He was the Word from eternity, and became the Son at the beginning of all things; some of them expressly considering Him, first as the λόγος ἐνδιάθετος, or Reason, in the Father, or (as may be speciously represented,) a mere attribute; next, as the λόγος προφορικὸς, or Word, terms which have been already explained, p. 113, note z. This doctrine, when divested of figure and put into literal statement, might appear nothing more or less than this,—that at the beginning of the world the Son was created after the likeness of the Divine attribute of Reason, as its image or expiession, and thereby became the Divine Word; was made the instrument of creation, called the Son from that ineffable favour and adoption which God had bestowed on him, and in due time sent into the world to manifest God's perfections to mankind;—which, it is scarcely necessary to say, is the doctiine of Arianism.

Note on "before His generation" in the Nicene Anathema. 273

Thus S. Hippolytus says,
Τῶν δὲ γινομένων ἀρχηγὸν καὶ σύμβουλον καὶ ἐργάτην ἐγέννα λόγον, ὃν λόγον ἔχων ἐν ἑαυτῷ ἀόρατόν τε ὄντα τῷ κτιζομένῳ κόσμῳ, ὁρατὸν ποιεῖ· προτέραν φωνὴν φθεγγόμενος, καὶ φῶς ἐκ φωτὸς γεννῶν, προῆκεν τῇ κτίσει κύριον. contr. Noet. 10.

And S. Theophilus:
Ἔχων οὖν ὁ θεὸς τὸν ἑαυτοῦ λόγον ἐνδιάθετον ἐν τοῖς ἰδίοις σπλάγχνοις, ἐγέννησεν αὐτὸν μετὰ τῆς ἑαυτοῦ σοφίας ἐξερευξάμενος πρὸ τῶν ὅλων.... ὁπότε δὲ ἠθέλησεν ὁ θεὸς ποιῆσαι ὅσα ἐβουλεύσατο, τοῦτον τὸν λόγον ἐγέννησε προφορικὸν, πρωτότοκον πάσης κτίσεως. ad Autol. ii. 10—22.

Bishop Bull, Defens. F. N. iii. 5—8. meets this representation by maintaining that the γέννησις which S. Hippolytus and other writers spoke of, was but a metaphorical generation, the real and eternal truth being shadowed out by a succession of events in the Economy of time, such as is the Resurrection, (Acts xiii. 33.) nay, the Nativity; and that of these His going forth to create the worlds was one. And he maintains, ibid. iii. 9. that such is the mode of speaking adopted by the Fathers after the Nicene Council as well as before. And then he adds, (which is our present point,) that it is even alluded to and recognised in the Creed of the Council, which anathematizes those who say that "the Son was not before His generation," i. e. who deny that "the Son *was* before His *generation*," which statement accordingly becomes indirectly a Catholic truth.

I am not aware whether any writer has preceded or followed this great authority in this view[a]. The more obvious mode of understanding the Arian formula is this, that it is an argument *ex absurdo*, drawn from the force of the word Son, in behalf of the Arian doctrine; it being, as they would say, a truism, that, "whereas He was begotten, He was not *before* He was begotten," and the denial of it a contradiction in terms. This certainly does seem to myself the true force of the formula; so much so, that if Bishop Bull's explanation be admissible, it must, in order to its being so, first be shewn to be reducible to this sense, and to be included under it.

The point at issue between the two interpretations is this; whether the clause πρὶν γεννηθῆναι οὐκ ἦν is intended for a *denial* of the *contrary* proposition, "He was before His generation," as Bishop Bull says; or whether it is what Aristotle calls an enthymematic sentence, *assuming* the falsity, as confessed on all hands, of that

---

[a] Waterland expresses the view here taken, and not Bishop Bull's; vol. 1. p. 114 Bull's language, on the other hand, is very strong, "Sæpe olim, ut verum ingenuè fatear, animum meum subiit *admiratio, quid* effato isto, ' Filius priusquam nasceretur, non erat,' *sibi voluerint* Ariani. De nativitate Christi ex beatissima Virgine dictum non esse exponendum constat.... Itaque de nativitate Filii loquuntur, quæ hujus universi creationem antecessit. *Quis* vero, inquam, *sensus* dicti hujus, ' Filius non erat, sive non existebat, priusquam nasceretur ex Patre ante conditum mundum?' Ego sane nullus dubito, quin hoc pronunciatum Arianorum oppositum fuerit Catholicorum istorum sententiæ, qui docerent, Filium quidem paulo ante conditum mundum inexplicabili quodam modo ex Patre progressum fuisse ad constituendum universa," &c. D. F. N. iii. 9. §. 2.

T

NOTE ON DISC. I

contrary proposition, as self-contradictory, and directly denying, not it, but "He was from everlasting." Or, in other words, whether it opposes the position of the five writers, or the great Catholic doctrine itself, and whether in consequence the Nicene Fathers are in their anathema indirectly sanctioning that position, or stating that doctrine. Bull considers that both sides *contemplated* the proposition, "He was before His generation,"— and that the Catholics asserted or defended it; some reasons shall here be given for the contrary view.

1. Now first, let me repeat, what was just now observed by the way, that the formula in question, when taken as an enthymematic sentence, or *reductio ad absurdum*, exactly expresses the main argument of the Arians, which they brought forward in so many shapes, as feeling that their cause turned upon it, "He is a Son, *therefore* He had a beginning." Thus Socrates records Arius's words in the beginning of the controversy, (1) "If the Father begat the Son, He who is begotten has a beginning of existence, (2) therefore once the Son was not, ἦν ὅτε οὐκ ἦν; (3) therefore He has His subsistence from nothing, ἐξ οὐκ ὄντων ἔχει τὴν ὑπόστασιν." Socr. i. 5. The first of these propositions exactly answers to the οὐκ ἦν πρὶν γεννηθῆναι taken enthymematically, and it may be added that when so taken, the three propositions will just answer to the three first formulæ anathematized at Nicæa, two of which are indisputably the same as two of them; viz. ὅτι ἦν ποτὲ ὅτε οὐκ ἦν, ὅτι πρὶν γεννηθῆναι οὐκ ἦν, ὅτι ἐξ οὐκ ὄντων ἐγένετο. On the other hand, we hear nothing in the controversy of the position which Bull conceives to be opposed by Arius, ("He *was* before His generation,") that is, supposing the formula in question does not allude to it, unless indeed it is worth while to except the statement reprobated in the Letter of the Arians to Alexander, ὄντα πρότερον, γεννηθέντα εἰς υἱὸν, which has been explained, p. 97, note m.

2. Next, it should be observed that the other formulæ here, as elsewhere, mentioned, are enthymematic also, or carry their argument with them, and that, an argument resolvable often into the original argument derived from the word "Son." Such are ὁ ὢν τὸν μὴ ὄντα ἐκ τοῦ ὄντος ἢ τὸν ὄντα, and ἓν τὸ ἀγένητον ἢ δύο. And in like manner as regards the question of the τρεπτὸν; "Has He free will," thus Athanasius states the Arian objection, "or has He not? is He good from choice according to free will, and can He, if He will, alter, being of an alterable nature? as wood or stone, has He not His choice free to be moved, and incline hither and thither?" supr §. 35. p. 230. That is, they wished the word τρεπτὸς to carry with it its own self-evident application to our Lord, with the alternative of an absurdity, and so to prove His created nature.

3. In §. 32 supr. p. 227. S. Athanasius observes that the formula of the ἀγένητον was the later substitute for the original formulæ of Arius; "when they were no longer allowed to say, 'out of nothing,' and 'He was not before His generation,' they hit upon this word Ingenerate, that, by saying among the simple that the Son was generate, *they might imply the very same phrases* ' out of nothing' and ' He once was not '" Here he does not in so many

words say that the argument from the ἀγέννητον was a *substitute* for the οὐκ ἦν πρὶν γεννηθῆναι, yet surely it is not unfair so to understand him. But it is plain that the ἀγέννητον was brought forward merely to express by an appeal to philosophy and earlier Fathers, that to be a Son was to have a beginning and a creation, and not to be God. This therefore will be the sense of the οὐκ ἦν πρὶν γεννηθῆναι. Nay, when the Arians asked, " Is the ἀγέννητον one or two," they actually did assume that it was granted by their opponents that the Father only was ἀγέννητος ; which it was not, if the latter held, nay, if they had sanctioned at Nicæa, as Bull says, that our Lord ἦν πρὶν γεννηθῇ ; and moreover which they knew and confessed was not granted, if their own formula οὐκ ἦν πρὶν γεννηθῆναι was directed against this statement.

4. Again, it is plain that the οὐκ ἦν πρὶν γεννηθῆναι, is used by S. Athanasius as the *same* objection with ὁ ὢν τὸν μὴ ὄντα ἐκ τοῦ ὄντος, &c. E. g. he says, " We might ask them in turn, God who is, has He so become, whereas He was not? *or* is He also before His generation? whereas He is, did He make Himself, or is He of nothing, &c. §. 25. p. 216. Now the ὁ ὢν τὸν μὴ ὄντα, &c. is evidently an *argument*, and that, grounded on the absurdity of saying ὁ ὢν τὸν ὄντα. S. Alexander's Encyclical Letter, (vid Socr 1. 6.) compared with Arius's original positions and the Nicene Anathemas as referred to above, is a strong confirmation In these three documents the formulæ agree together, except one ; and that one, which in Arius's language is " he who is begotten has a beginning of existence," is in the Nicene Anathema, οὐκ ἦν πρὶν γεννηθῆναι, but in S. Alexander's circular, ὁ ὢν θεὸς τὸν μὴ ὄντα ἐκ τοῦ μὴ ὄντος πεποίηκεν. The absence of the οὐκ ἦν πρὶν, &c. in S. Alexander is certainly remarkable. Moreover the two formulæ are treated as synonymous by Greg. Naz. Orat 29. 9. Cyril. Thesaur. 4. p. 29 fin. and by Basil as quoted below. But indeed there is an internal correspondence between them, shewing that they have but one meaning. They are really but the same sentence in the active and in the passive voice

5. A number of scattered passages in Athanasius lead us to the same conclusion. For instance, if the Arian formula had the sense which is here maintained, of being an argument against our Lord's eternity, the Catholic answer would be, " He could not be *before* His generation because His generation is *eternal*, as being from the Father." Now this is precisely the language Athanasius uses, when it occurs to him to introduce the words in question. Thus in Orat. ii. §. 57. he says, " The creatures began to come to be (γίνεσθαι); but the Word of God, not having beginning (ἀρχὴν) of being, surely did not begin to be, nor begin to come to be, but was always. And the works have a beginning (ἀρχὴν) in the making, and the beginning precedes things which come to be ; but the Word not being of such, rather Himself becomes the Framer of those things which have a beginning And the being of things generate is measured by their becoming (ἐν τῷ γίνεσθαι), and at some beginning (origin) doth God begin to make them through the Word, that it may be known that they were not before their generation (πρὶν γενέσθαι), but the Word hath His being in no other

origin than the Father," (vid. supr. p. 195, note a.) "whom they themselves allow to be unoriginate, so that He too exists unoriginately in the Father, being His offspring not His creature." We shall find that other Fathers say just the same. Again, we have already come to a passage where for "His generation," he substitutes "making," a word which Bull would not say that either the Nicene Council or S. Hippolytus would use; clearly shewing that the Arians were not quoting and denying a Catholic statement in the οὐκ ἦν πρὶν, &c. but laying down one of their own. "Who is there in all mankind, Greek or Barbarian, who ventures to rank among creatures One whom he confesses the while to be God, and says that "He was not *before He was made, πρὶν ποιηθῇ.*" Orat.i. §. 10. p. 194. Arius, who is surely the best explainer of his own words, says the same; that is, he interprets "generation" by "making," or confesses that he is bringing forward an argument, not opposing a dogma; "Before His generation," he says, "*or* creation, *or* destination, (ὁρισθῇ, Rom. 1, 4.) *or* founding, (vid. Prov. 8, 23.) He was not; for He was not ingenerate." Theod. Hist. i. 4. Eusebius of Nicomedia also, in a passage which has already come before us, says distinctly, "*It is plain to any one*, that what has been made was not before its *generation;* but what came to be has an origin of being." de Syn. §. 17. supr. p. 99.

6. If there are passages in Athanasius which seem to favour the opposite interpretation, that is, to imply that the Catholics held or allowed, as Bp. Bull considers, that "before His generation, He was," they admit of an explanation. E g. " How is He not in the number of the creatures, if, as they say, He was not before His generation? for it is proper to the creatures and works, not to be before their generation. Orat. ii. §. 22. This might be taken to imply that the Arians said "He was not," and Catholics "He was." But the real meaning is this, "How is He not a creature, if the *formula be true*, which they use, 'He was not before His generation?' for it may indeed properly be *said* of creatures that 'they were not before their generation.'" And so again when he says, "if the Son was not before His generation, Truth was not always in God ," supr. §. 20. p. 209. he does not thereby imply that the Son *was* before His generation, but he means, "if it be *true* that, &c" "if the *formula holds*," "if it can be *said* of the Son, 'He was not, &c.'" Accordingly, shortly afterwards, in a passage already cited, he says the same of the Almighty Father in the way of parallel; "God who is, hath He so become, whereas He was not, or *is He too before His generation?*" §. 25. p. 216. not implying here any generation at all, but urging that the question is *idle* and *irrelevant*, that the formula is *unmeaning* and does not *apply to*, cannot be *said* of, Father or Son.

7. Such an explanation of these passages, as well as the view here taken of the formula itself, receive abundant confirmation from S. Gregory Nazianzen and S. Hilary. What has been maintained is, that when S. Athanasius says, "if the Son *is* not before His generation, then, &c." he does but mean, "if it can be *said*," "if the words can be *used or applied* in this case." Now the two Fathers just mentioned both decide that it is not true, *either*

that the Son *was* before His generation, *or* that He was not; in other words, that the question is unmeaning and irrelevant, which is just the interpretation which has been here given to Athanasius. But again, in thus speaking, they thereby assert also that they did *not* hold, that they do *not* allow, that formula which Bull considers the Nicene Fathers defended and sanctioned, as being Catholic and in use both before the Council and after, viz. " He *was* before His generation." Thus S. Gregory in the passage in which he speaks of "did He that is make Him that is not, &c." and "before His generation, &c " as one and the same, expressly says, " In His case, to be begotten *is concurrent* with existence and is from the beginning," and that *in contrast* to the instance of men; who, he says, do fulfil in a manner " He who is, &c." (Levi being in the loins of Abraham,) i. e. fulfil Bull's proposition, " He was before generation " He proceeds, " I say that *the question is irrelevant,* not the answer difficult." And presently, after mentioning some idle inquiries by way of parallel, he adds, " more ill-instructed, be sure, is it to decide whether what was generated *from the beginning* was or was not *before* generation, πρὸ τῆς γεννήσεως." Orat 29. 9.

8. S. Hilary, on the other hand, is so full on the subject in his de Trin. xii. and so entirely to the point for which I would adduce him, that but a few extracts of what might be made, are either necessary or practicable. He states and argues on the formula expressly as an *objection;* "Adjiciant hæc argutα satis atque auditu placentia; Si, inquit, natus est, cœpit; et cùm cœpit, non fuit; et cùm non fuit, non patitur ut fuerit. Atque *idcirco* piæ intelligentiæ sermonem esse contendant, Non fuit ante quàm nasceretur, *quia* ut esset, qui non erat, non qui erat, natus est." n. 18. He answers the objection in the same way, " Unigenitus Deus neque non fuit aliquando non filius, neque fuit aliquid ante quam filius, neque quidquam aliquid ipse nisi filius," n. 15. which is in express words to *deny,* "He was before His generation." Again, as Gregory, " Ubi pater auctor est, ibi et nativitas est; et verò ubi auctor æternus est, ibi et nativitatis æternitas est." n. 21. And he substitutes " being always born" for " being before birth;" " Numquid ante tempora æterna esse, id ipsum sit quod est, eum qui erat nasci? quia nasci quod erat, jam non nasci est, sed se ipsum demutare nascendo. . . Non est itaque id ipsum, natum ante tempora æterna semper esse, et esse antequam nasci." n. 30. And he concludes, in accordance with the above explanation of the passages of Athanasius which I brought as if objections, thus: Cum itaque natum semper esse, nihil aliud sit confitendum esse, quàm natum, id sensui, antequàm nascitur *vel fuisse vel non fuisse,* non subjacet. n. 31.

9. It may seem superfluous to proceed, but as Bishop Bull is an authority not lightly to be set aside, a passage from S. Basil shall be added Eunomius objects, " God begat the Son either being or not being, &c ... to him that is, there needs not generation." He replies that Eunomius, "*because* animals first are not, and then are generated, and he who is born to-day, yesterday did not exist, *transfers* this conception to the subsistence of the Only-begotten;

NOTE ON DISC. I.

and says, *since* He has been generated, He was not before His generation, πρὸ τῆς γεννήσεως." contr. Eunom. ii. 14. And he solves the objection as the other Fathers, by saying that our Lord is from everlasting, speaking of S. John, in the first words of his Gospel, as τῇ αἰδιότητι τοῦ πατρὸς τοῦ μονογενοῦς συνάπτων τὴν γέννησιν. §. 15.

These then being the explanations which the contemporary and next following Fathers give of the Arian formula which was anathematized at Nicæa, it must be observed that the line of argument which Bishop Bull is pursuing, does not lead him to assign any direct reasons for the substitution of a different interpretation in their place He is engaged, not in commenting on the Nicene Anathema, but in proving that the Post Nicene Fathers admitted that view or statement of doctrine which he conceives *also* implied in that anathema; and thus the sense of the anathema, instead of being the subject of proof, is, as he believes, one of the proofs of the point which he is establishing. However, since these other collateral evidences which he adduces, may be taken to be some sort of indirect comment upon the words of the Anathema, the principal of them in point of authority, and that which most concerns us, shall here be noticed: it is a passage from the second Oration of Athanasius.

While commenting on the words, ἀρχὴ ὁδῶν εἰς τὰ ἔργα in the text, " The Lord has created Me the beginning of His ways unto the works," S. Athanasius is led to consider the text "first born of every creature," πρωτότοκος πάσης κτίσεως; and he says that He who was μονογενὴς from eternity, became by a συγκατάβασις at the creation of the world πρωτότοκος This doctrine Bp. Bull considers declaratory of a going forth, πρόελευσις, or figurative *birth* from the Father, at the beginning of all things.

It will be observed that the very point to be proved is this, viz. not that there was a συγκατάβασις merely, but that according to Athanasius there was a γέννησις or proceeding from the Father, and that the word πρωτότοκος marks it. Bull's words are, that " Catholici quidam Doctores, qui post exortam controversiam Arianam vixerunt, ... illam τοῦ λόγου ... ex Patre *progressionem* (quam et συγκατάβασιν, hoc est, condescensionem eorum nonnulli appellârunt,) ad condendum hæc universa agnovere; and ejus etiam *progressionis respectu* ipsum τὸν λόγον à Deo Patre quasi *natum* fuisse et omnis creaturæ *primogenitum* in Scripturis dici confessi sunt. D. F. N. iii. 9. §. 1. Now I consider that S Athanasius does not, as this sentence says, understand by primogenitus that our Lord was "progressionis respectu à Deo Patre *quasi natus.*" He does not seem to me to speak of a generation or birth of the Son at all, though figurative, but of the birth of *all things,* and that *in* Him.

That Athanasius does not call the συγκατάβασις of the Word a birth, as denoted by the term πρωτότοκος, is plain from his own avowal in the passage to which Bull refers. " No where in the Scriptures,' he says, "is He called πρωτότοκος τοῦ Θεοῦ, first born *of God,* nor creature of God, but Only-begotten, Word, Wisdom, have their relation to the Father, and are proper to Him." ii 62. Here surely he expressly denies Bull's statement that "first born" means "à Deo natus," "born of God." Such additions as παρὰ τοῦ πατρὸς, he says, are reserved for μονογενὴς and λόγος.

NOTE ON DISC. I.

He goes on to say *what* the term πρωτότοκος does mean; viz instead of having any reference to a προέλευσις from the Father, it refers solely to the creatures, our Lord is not called πρωτότοκος, because His προέλευσις is *a type of His eternal generation*, but because by that προέλευσις He became the *Prototype of all creation*. He, as it were, stamped His image, His Sonship, upon creation, and became the first born in the sense of being the Archetypal Son. If this is borne out by the passage, Athanasius, it is plain, does not speak of any γέννησις whatever at the era of creation, though figurative, πρωτότοκος does but mean μονογενὴς πρωτεύων ἐν τῇ κτίσει, or ἀρχὴ τῆς κτίσεως, or πρωτότυπον γέννημα, or μόνος γεννητὸς ἐν τοῖς γενητοῖς; and no warrant is given, however indirect, to the idea that in the Nicene Anathema, the Fathers implied an allowance of the proposition, "He was before His generation."

As the whole passage occurs in the Discourse which immediately follows, it is not necessary to enter formally into the proof of this view of it, when the reader will soon be able to judge of it for himself. But it may be well to add two passages, one from Athenagoras, the other from St. Cyril, not in elucidation of the words of Athanasius, but of the meaning which I would put upon them.

The passage from Athenagoras is quoted by Bull himself, who of course is far from denying the doctrine of our Lord's Archetypal office; and does but wish in addition to find in Athanasius the doctrine of a γέννησις Athenagoras says that the Son is "the first offspring, πρῶτον γέννημα, of the Father, not as come to be, γενόμενον, (for God being Eternal Mind had from the beginning in Himself the Word, as having Reason eternally, λογικὸς ὤν,) but that, while as regards matter heavy and light were mixed together," (the passage is corrupt here,) "He went forth, προελθὼν, as an *idea* and *energy*," i e. as an Agent to create, and a Form and Rule to create by And then he goes on to quote the very text on which Athanasius is employed when he explains πρωτότοκος. "And the Prophetic Spirit confirms this doctrine, saying, "The Lord hath created Me a beginning (origin) of His ways, for His works." Leg. 10.

And so S. Cyril, "He is Only-begotten according to nature, as being alone from the Father, God from God, Light kindled from Light; and He is First-born for our sakes, that, *as if to some immortal root* the whole creation might be ingrafted and might bud forth from the Everlasting For all things were made by Him, and *consist* for ever and are *preserved in Him*." Thesaur. 25. p. 238.

In conclusion it may be suggested whether the same explanation which has here been given of Athanasius's use of πρωτότοκος does not avail more exactly to the defence of two of the five writers from the charge of inaccurate doctrine, than that which Bull has preferred.

NOTE ON DISC. I.

As to Athenagoras, we have already seen that he does not speak of a γέννησις at all in his account of creation, but simply calls the Son πρῶτον γέννημα, i. e. πρωτότυπον γέννημα.

Nor does Tatian approach nearer to the doctrine of a γέννησις. He says that at the creation the Word ἔργον πρωτότοκον τοῦ πατρὸς γίνεται· τοῦτον ἴσμεν τοῦ κόσμου τὴν ἀρχήν. ad Græc. 5. Here the word ἔργον, which at first sight promises a difficulty, does in fact explain both himself and Athenagoras. He says that at creation the Word became, γίνεται, not a *Son* (figuratively), as Bull would grant to the parties whom he is opposing, but a *work*. It was His great condescension, συγκατάβασις, to be accounted the first of the works, as being their *type;* that as they were to be raised to an adoption and *called* sons, so He for that purpose might stoop to creation, and be *called* a work. As Tatian uses the word ἀρχὴ in the concluding clause, there is great reason to think that he is alluding to the very text which Athanasius and Athenagoras expressly quote, in which Wisdom is said to be "created a beginning, ἀρχὴ, of ways, unto the *works,* εἰς τὰ ἔργα."

As to Novatian, Bishop Bull himself observes that it is a question whether he need be understood to speak of any generation but That which is eternal; nor does Pamelius otherwise explain him.

www.ingramcontent.com/pod-product-compliance
Lightning Source LLC
Chambersburg PA
CBHW070240230426
43664CB00014B/2360